THE INSIDER'S GUIDE TO FOREIGN STUDY

Everything You Need to Know About More Than 400 Academic Adventures Abroad

Benedict A. Leerburger

ADDISON-WESLEY PUBLISHING COMPANY, INC.

Reading, Massachusetts   Menlo Park, California   New York
Don Mills, Ontario   Wokingham, England   Amsterdam   Bonn
Sydney   Singapore   Tokyo   Madrid   Bogotá
Santiago   San Juan

Library of Congress Cataloging-in-Publication Data

Leerburger, Benedict A.
  The insider's guide to foreign study.

  Bibliography: p.
  Includes index.
  1. Foreign study. 2. American students—Foreign countries. I. Title.
LB2376.L32   1987   370.19'62   87-3493
ISBN 0-201-15745-4

Cover design by Copenhaver Cumpston
Text design by Anna Post
Set in 10-point Caslon by WordTech, Woburn, MA

ABCDEFGHIJ-DO-8987

First printing, October 1987

For Julie, Marian, Ellen, Christopher,
and all their friends, whose pleasures and pitfalls
abroad helped make this book possible

Contents

Preface

In 1978 our elder daughter, Marian, was one of a handful of high school sophomores selected to participate in an American Field Service short-term exchange program. She spent two weeks with a family in rural Vermont attending school with a girl her own age, experiencing a way of life totally foreign to her. Instead of her routine gym class, she, like her new AFS "sister," took part in the local high school's ski program on the slopes of Stratton Mountain. Driving a car to school gave way to a forty-minute ride in a school bus; the local basketball team, the focus of the school and town's interest, became also the focus of her own. Her Vermont "sister" accompanied our daughter home and joined our family for two weeks. Jorda gawked at the tall buildings, saw the lights of Broadway, and felt the excitement of a city she had only read about. She ate foods she had never eaten and participated in school activities totally unlike those in her own community. Although both girls traveled but a few hundred miles from their homes, the distance between their worlds was incalculable.

The Vermont exchange was but a beginning. Marian's curiosity was piqued. The following summer she participated in AFS's foreign exchange program, and for eight weeks was a member of a family in Bandung, Indonesia. She saw people, places, and sights of Java and Bali through the eyes of an insider. The Indonesians she met are still her friends; the boundaries of her world are no longer national. It is little wonder that her younger sister caught the wander bug. Ellen spent her AFS summer with a Danish family some fifty miles from Copenhagen.

When college decisions were made, both girls knew that wherever they went to school a part of their education would take place abroad. The Indonesian experience led Marian to spend a year studying in Sri Lanka, India, and Taiwan, while Ellen spent her Junior year in Madrid. The experiences of both girls have had a major influence on their lives and later career decisions.

Gathering information about the myriad foreign-study programs, then making intelligent choices among them, was surprisingly difficult. Our search for a college counselor totally familiar with the various options proved fruitless. It was maddening to discover that the book we most needed—an exhaustive reference that described each program and detailed costs, living conditions, credits offered, teaching methods, and travel options—did not exist. *The Insider's Guide to Foreign Study* was conceived to fill the void.

Comments from those just back from studying abroad can mean a great deal to the person thinking about which country to visit, which program to select, and most important, whether to actually leave a familiar environment to pursue an education in a foreign country. To obtain the insights, recommendations, do's and don'ts, and overall views of such experienced students, I sent questionnaires to participants in a wide variety of foreign study programs. Their response was most gratifying and, I trust, will be helpful to the reader. The names of these students were obtained through friends, as well as through the good offices of Geraldine Thompson, senior vice president of the American Institute of Foreign Study. Her help and that of her colleagues is deeply appreciated.

To obtain up-to-the-minute data on the many foreign-study opportunities currently open to students of all ages, I mailed detailed questionnaires to hundreds of colleges, universities, and foreign-study institutes. The many persons who contributed by filling out forms and answering a slew of phone questions also deserve my sincere thanks.

And, of course, the many students who shared their experiences deserve a special thank you. Their insights and discoveries make the road of next season's students a bit easier and much more fun.

Benedict A. Leerburger
August 1987

INTRODUCTION

The Hows and Whys of Foreign Study

In 1986, more than half a million Americans attended a school in a foreign country—more than any year in our history. The majority of these "students abroad" attended courses as part of their college program. The reasons Americans study abroad are varied. Perhaps John Barker, a senior majoring in philosophy at Louisiana State University and a 1985 exchange student at Katholieke Universiteit in Leuven, Belgium, expresses it best:

- *I had many objectives in wanting to study abroad: learning a foreign language; traveling; and learning to adjust to a new environment. But I had a set of priorities that made choosing a site rather difficult. First of all, because I had no knowledge of a foreign language, I needed to study in English. Yet, I didn't want to study in an English-speaking country. After all, I could do that in the U.S. Secondly, I wanted an academically rewarding year. My third priority concerned travel; I wanted to study in a country that was centrally located.*

Learning. Adventure. Travel. New experiences. A change of scene. Foreign study is a unique opportunity open to most students at some time during their academic career. Many follow John Barker's lead and head abroad to learn a language, explore, and travel. Others heed the words of Edwin O. Reischauer, professor of history at Harvard University and former U.S. ambassador to Japan:

- *While the world is becoming a single great global community, it retains attitudes and habits more appropriate to a different technological age.... Before long, humanity will face many grave difficulties that can only be solved on a global scale. Education, however, as it is presently conducted in this country, is not moving rapidly enough in the right direction to produce the knowledge about the outside world and the attitudes towards other peoples that may be essential for human survival within a generation or two.*

Advisors at the University of Wisconsin-Stevens Point counsel their students to think carefully about a foreign-study experience. They point out that:

3

- *if you are the inquisitive type you will be fascinated, puzzled, energized, frustrated, and exhilarated. If, on the other hand, all you want is a vacation, don't go. You can have a pleasant time in Miami Beach.*

There is no substitute for experience. The best way to understand a foreign culture is to live it. A student can study conversational Spanish fifty minutes a day, three days a week in an American classroom. Speaking Spanish in class, however, is no substitute for explaining to a waiter in Madrid that you want bottled water without, not with, carbonation. Viewing slides of Michelangelo's *The Last Judgment* can never have the impact of walking into the Sistine Chapel and drinking in both the painting and the building it was made for. One student expresses the sentiment of many:

- *I expected to find a world of difference. Sure, the friends I made in Holland were not like my American friends, but there were far more similarities than differences. As I was trying to understand my hosts, I discovered that they too were trying to understand Americans. By the time I left for home, I don't think anyone could tell the Americans from the Dutch. We simply merged into a single group.*

  - David Hockings, Atlanta, Georgia

Although it may not be a student's first consideration, the low cost of foreign study should not be ignored. Even with the unpredictably fluctuating value of the dollar, it is much less expensive to attend most foreign schools than it is to attend most private and some public colleges in the United States. Even taking into consideration the cost of round-trip transportation and local travel abroad, students and their parents are often amazed to discover that the bottom-line figure for a year of foreign study can range from a third to half that of attending a private school in the States. For example, compare the average annual U.S. private school tuition plus room and board of approximately $13,000 to $15,000 to the cost of attending one of the many SUNY London programs, which may cost less than $5,000 for tuition, board, and round-trip transportation, or a year studying at a major university in Madrid or Paris for less than $7,500.

Yet, studying abroad isn't for everyone. Leaving friends and family for even a few months can be rough. Adapting to unfamiliar foods, language, people, customs, and living conditions is a jolt even to experienced American wanderers. However, the rewards can be bountiful and unexpected. Students return home with a different perspective on their country, their world, and, most important, themselves. Some come home eager to return abroad at the next possible opportunity; some come home glad to have had the experience but anxious to resume their life in America. All come home changed.

- *Going abroad is a fantastic experience. You learn about yourself, your American culture. You learn a foreign culture and language. However, you have to deal with foreign expectations instead of making your own.*

  - Matthew S. Holland, Springfield College.

WHO SHOULD STUDY ABROAD?

Learning knows neither age nor national boundary. The options and opportunities for education outside the borders of America are practically limitless. Those interested in studying French, Italian, or Spanish cuisine can obtain lists of reputable, short-term foreign cooking schools from their local cooking schools, cooking magazines, or newspapers with cooking or food columns. Two- to six-week study-travel options are constantly advertised in travel magazines and also promoted by many college alumni associations. Students age 60 or older can take advantage of programs offered by Elderhostel (80 Boylston Street, Boston, MA 02116), which combine hosteling and foreign study. For the disabled traveler, the American branch of Mobility International (MIUSA, P.O. Box #3551, Eugene, OR 97403) provides information and publishes brochures and a newsletter. Their book *A World of Options* is an invaluable guide to foreign-study programs designed for the handicapped.

For the younger set, the largest group to enjoy the benefits of foreign study, there is a host of specific programs designed to satisfy the exacting requirements of the students:

- College undergraduates make up the largest group of foreign students. Many schools sponsor a Junior Year Abroad program directed at a specific program at a foreign school. Keep in mind, however, that most every American college and university honors any well-organized program and does not insist on a student's participating in its own program. It often pays to shop around for the program that best suits your own academic needs and purse. A program can run for a full academic year or a few weeks. Intensive six- to eight-week summer programs, particularly in language study, often provide a full semester credit. Some programs incorporate an internship experience in business, law, politics, publishing, or teaching along with a regular course load.

- Graduate students can find many programs that tie in directly to their chosen degree path. Although most foreign universities provide the opportunity to obtain a graduate degree by meeting their specific course requirements, many American universities accept credits from a foreign university toward their own requirements. Several foreign schools have special MBA programs aimed at American businesspeople interested in studying either European or Japanese business practices.

- High school students who are allowed to take a portion of their school year abroad often find the experience of attending a school away from home a challenging way to gain both academic and personal maturity. In addition, there are many summer programs designed for entering college freshmen that offer concentrated language study and travel opportunities. Colleges may accept these programs for full or partial credit toward a language requirement as well as for credit hours toward a degree.

CHOOSING A COURSE OF STUDY

Before considering the details of the many programs offered abroad, your first job, if you are a college or high school student, is to consult with your academic dean or advisor and ask two basic questions:

1. Does your school either have its own foreign-study program or accept credits from other programs?
2. Are you eligible to participate in a study-abroad program?

Often a school has its own overseas program and, to assure that its program is well attended, may be reluctant to allow their own students to participate in another school's program. Unless your school has a firm policy to accept only its own program's credits, don't be afraid to ask the direct question: Will you accept *X's* credits toward my degree requirements as well as your own?

It's also a must to obtain a statement in writing that your school will approve your satisfactory completion of a specific program. It is usually very easy to work out with your advisor a specific course of study given either by your home institution or another before you make a formal commitment to study abroad. However, since every college and university has its own standards and rules for accepting credits you *can never assume* that a program given by one reputable institution is acceptable to another. Thus:

PLAN YOUR PROGRAM WELL IN ADVANCE AND BE SURE YOU HAVE YOUR ADVISOR'S APPROVAL IN WRITING!

Types of Programs

There are many types of foreign study options available to you. All provide academic credit. Keep in mind, however, that these credits *may or may not* be accepted by your school. Four basic types are:

1. Programs sponsored by your own college or university.
2. Programs sponsored by another accredited American college or university, or by a consortium that may include your school. (While some consortia limit enrollment to students of member schools, many will accept any student meeting the entrance requirements. A list of the various consortia is in Appendix 2.)
3. Programs sponsored by professional organizations in the business of operating foreign-study programs. These organizations may be either commercial or nonprofit. Some operate their own schools abroad; others package programs often in direct competition with college programs. The major organizations sponsoring overseas study programs include:

American Field Service
International (AFS)
313 East 43rd Street
New York, NY 10017
(212) 949-4242

American Institute of
Foreign Study
102 Greenwich Avenue
Greenwich, CT 06830
(203) 869-9090

College Consortium for
International Studies
866 United Nations Plaza
New York, NY 10017
(212) 308-1556

Council on International
Educational Exchange
205 East 42nd Street
New York, NY 10017
(212) 661-1414

Experiment in International Living
School for International Training
Kipling Road
Brattleboro, VT 05301
(800) 451-4465 or (802) 257-7751

Institute of European Studies
223 West Ohio Street
Chicago, IL 60610
(312) 944-1750

International Student
Exchange Program
1242 35th Street, NW
Washington, DC 20057
(202) 625-4737

Semester at Sea
Institute of Shipboard Education
2E Forbes Plaza
University of Pittsburgh
Pittsburgh, PA 15260
(800) 854-0195 *or* (412) 624-6021

With the exception of special summer programs, most of the programs offered by these groups are included herein. I recommend, however, that you write or call these groups and request their latest brochures and costs. Compare similar programs for both cost and benefits.

4. Programs operated by a foreign college or university for its own students and a limited number of "foreign" students. Although most Americans enrolled in a given foreign school are graduate students interested in that school's specialized courses, many undergraduates are also allowed to enroll providing they meet eligibility requirements. The laws affecting direct enrollment vary from country to country. Because many countries provide either free or extremely low cost post-secondary school education, some universities have quotas or other restrictions for Americans and other "foreign" students. To find out if you can enroll directly in a specific foreign school, write the cultural attaché at the embassy of the country in which the school is located (see Appendix 1). For European community countries, a good description of programs, costs, and eligibility requirements can be found in *Higher Education in the European Community: A Student Handbook,* published by the Commission of the European Communities. It is available from the European Community Information Service, Suite 707, 2100 M Street, NW, Washington, DC 20037.

The first three types of programs listed above can be subdivided further into those programs:

- Held at a foreign institution but which employ the faculty from your own school, another U.S. college or university, or the host institution hired specifically to teach the American-designed program. These "island" programs usually band all American students together. Students all live in a leased dormitory or group of private residences. Courses are often conducted only in English. For some students there is a distinct advantage in the familiarity of courses taught in English by professors used to the "American" system. Students with difficulty learning languages may find these programs easier than a truly foreign learning experience. However, if you want the opportunity to live and study in a typical non-American setting, socializing with students from the host country, these programs are not for you.

- Fully integrated into a foreign college or university. Americans attend classes with students of the host country and other "foreign" students. Courses are taught in the language of the host country by regular university faculty members. Many American colleges and universities also supplement this type of arrangement with special courses limited to American participants. In most cases these special classes offer intensive language courses and cultural education and travel sessions.

- Held at a foreign institution with courses arranged for American students and taught by members of the host institution usually in the language of the host country. Programs usually provide Americans with the option to attend many regular college or university courses together with students from the host country. Americans are made to feel part of the school environment. They join school clubs, attend regular school social events, have the option to live in regular school dormitories, and have the same rights and privileges as the students from the host country. This is the most common foreign-study experience.

In addition to the basic types of overseas-study programs, there are a variety of special (and often unaccredited) programs offered by both U.S. and foreign schools and institutions. These include special summer programs, a few of which are included in this book. (For a more detailed listing, see *Vacation Study Abroad*, published by the Institute of International Education, 809 United Nations Plaza, New York, NY 10017.) Work/study programs, particularly in Israel, are also available, as are programs for those interested in learning but not necessarily in collecting academic credits. There are, for example, quite a few programs for those who want to study a particular foreign language, foreign business methods, architecture, or design.

A Word About Internships

There are a great many graduate and undergraduate foreign-study programs that provide internship opportunities. These programs, particularly in Western Europe, allow students to spend part of the academic year in the classroom and part teaching or working for the government of the host country, a local political party, or a local business, such as a publishing, banking, or law firm. Many of the internship programs provide a small stipend in addition to academic credit. Several programs in London, Bonn, and Dublin allow foreign students to work directly with elected members of the government, deal with constituents, and actually become involved in the legislative process. For the student interested in international relations and political science, these opportunities are an educational experience unavailable anywhere else.

Information about internships can be obtained from the International Association of Students in Economics and Business Management, 14 West 23rd Street, New York, NY 10010. The programs are available to students at more than sixty member U.S. colleges and universities. The association arranges job exchanges in fifty-six countries for students in economics and business management. Students interested in work/study/trainee programs in engineering, architecture, mathematics, and the natural and physical sciences should contact The Association for International Practical Training (AIPT), 320 Park View Building, 10480 Little Patuxent Parkway, Columbia, MD 21044. The *International Directory of Youth Internships,* a listing of about four hundred internships within the United Nations system, is available from Learning Resources in International Studies, 777 United Nations Plaza, New York, NY 10017.

Paying the Bills

Although any term of foreign study is, in general, considerably less expensive than a comparable period's tuition at a private American college or university, there are still school bills to be paid. Most U.S. colleges and universities allow you to apply federal, state, or local financial aid directly toward the cost of studying abroad. Student loans as well as school scholarships and fellowships also can be applied to foreign study. The Institute of International Education will provide you with scholarship and grant information if you pay a personal visit to their center at 809 United Nations Plaza, New York City. Published information is listed in the bibliography at the end of this book.

LIVING ABROAD

- *Avoid cliques with other U.S. students. Develop the courage to immerse yourself in the local culture. Don't try and create your American home away from home.*

  - Linda Murphy-Kelly, Columbia, Maryland

In choosing a foreign-study program there are many variables to consider in addition to the basic type of program. Most students first select the region or country that most appeals to them and then isolate and identify one or more study programs to investigate there. Choosing a country in which to live and study is a very personal decision. Some students want to spend time in the country of their heritage; others have had their curiosity piqued through their school's language or social studies program; and still others have been turned on to a particular country by a friend or relative.

Whatever your reason, be sure to consider all aspects of a foreign country — its people, way of life, standard of living, language, and political realities. Consider also where and with whom you want to live.

The various foreign study programs offer three basic housing arrangements: school dormitory; with a family; or, in a local rooming house, pensione, or apartment. (When traveling, most program participants stay in local hotels or hostels.) There are both advantages and disadvantages to all these arrangements.

Dormitory Life

This can be restricting. Rules are usually far more stringent than living on your own and there is less likelihood of learning the ways of the country than if you live with a native family or rough it in your own apartment. Living in a dormitory either with American students from your own group or fully integrated with local students in a foreign university is not unlike dormitory life in America. Lifestyles vary from school to school and from program to program. Dormitories range from a single room with a table and cot to glorified miniapartments complete with kitchen and laundry facilities. Most dorms are right on campus, a distinct advantage when it comes to being close to classes and not having to commute in an unfamiliar city. Many dormitories offer laundry facilities and most provide food in a common dining hall. Some however, offer only a room and do-it-yourself cooking arrangements. It pays to check out the complete facilities if you elect dorm life.

- *I lived in an international dorm with students from all over the world. Thirty or so countries were represented and our only common denominator was language. It's a great experience to speak a language other than English with someone from Japan or Spain and know that a foreign language made it possible.*

  - Linda Murphy-Kelly, Columbia, Maryland

- *I lived in a dorm but wouldn't do it again. Almost everyone spoke English and it was just too easy not to speak French or mingle with the French. I know living with a foreign family is not always easy but I would definitely do it the second time around.*

  - Cathy Bond, Misenheimer, North Carolina

- *My first semester I lived in a dorm. The rooms were small, the rules were rigid, and the food was awful. But I met great people and it was the cheapest and easiest form of living.*

  - Name withheld by request, Edina, Minnesota

Living with a Family

Usually you don't have much say in which family you get, it's often a coin toss. Often students who have a good relationship with their family — and most do — find they develop a lasting relationship that continues far beyond college days. Exchanges between a foreign family and a student's own family are quite common.

Most undergraduates elect family life, sometimes called a "homestay," as the best way to combine their academic life with their desire to learn both a foreign language and the lifestyle of people in a different country. Families open their homes either because they truly want to meet American students and share their family with them, because they want (or need) the extra money paid them for accepting you, or a combination of both. Some families are eager for American students to teach them English. This can present a minor problem since you have chosen family life to help you learn their language. Then, too, you may find yourself in a family with no command at all of English. Unless you have had more than an introductory language course you both will struggle for a while.

Families who accept you solely because they need the money can present more of a problem. You expect to blend into a typical foreign family and the last thing you want is to find yourself a paying boarder. Then, of course, you may find that the rules and regulations imposed on you as a family member are not to your liking. The kitchen may not always be available for that afternoon or late-evening snack, school friends may not be welcome, a curfew may be a new idea to you, or an evening meal of kidney pie or fresh eels may turn your stomach. Remember that one of the reasons you chose to study abroad is to learn and to live a foreign experience and that new social regulations and new foods are part of that experience. In many countries American dating customs are considered next to Satanism. Chaperones and a taboo on any public display of affection are still common in many parts of the world.

Then, of course, people are not always compatible. It's usually quite easy to switch families. But if you do elect to live with a foreign family and are unhappy at first, don't be too abrupt in deciding you want out. Give it a chance. Many programs have built a list of families who enjoy accepting Americans into their homes.

If you decide to live with a foreign family, there are a few things you can do before heading abroad:

- Ask the school or institute arranging your study program for a list of possible host families, as well as for the names of students who have previously lived with them.

- If you're going to live in a city, check with your local or school library and see if they have a map of that city. Find out if the family lives near your school or if you will have to take public transportation to and from classes.

- Write to both the family (in the language of the host country) and to previous "boarders." How many students live with the family? How many may live in a room with you? What will be expected of you? If you know for sure that you have been assigned a host family be sure to make the letter friendly and informal. Introduce yourself and assure your new family that you are not an ugly American but a student most anxious to learn about their culture and way of life. It is your first contact with people you will be close to for many months. Make it a positive first meeting.

- *My living arrangement was one of the program's fortés. My family lived in an apartment in downtown Vienna and did not hesitate to integrate me into their lives. They invited me to join them on weekend excursions, did all my laundry and cleaned my room weekly.*

  - Stephanie Abbajay, Toledo, Ohio

- *We lived with French families who were given a stipend to board us. Often, this created problems since many families seemed more eager to get the money than to make us really feel as if we were part of the family. However, we were all treated well as guests.*

  - Holly Lynch, Medford, Massachusetts

- *I loved the woman I lived with. She was older but very interested in the lives of young people. Three girls lived together and I had my own room in a great Parisian apartment. The cuisine was delicious and the apartment always clean.*

  - Carol Ann Blinken, New York, New York

- *I did not like where I lived in Italy. Five of us lived together in a rather small apartment. We were not allowed to use any of the rooms except our bedrooms. We all expected to use our Italian on a daily basis, but on our first day our landlady told us that she would rather speak English.*

  - Barbara del Rosario, Elmsford, New York

- *I lived with a wonderful Spanish family who had several children close to my own age. There were a few drawbacks in that I was only allowed to use the phone to receive calls and was not allowed to have friends visit.*

  - Karen M. Gately, Columbia, Maryland

- *I did not enjoy living with a Spanish family because of restrictions on the number of showers I was allowed. The cooking, however, was superb. I moved to my own apartment for the second semester.*

　　　　　　　　　　　　　　　　- Name withheld, Columbia, South Carolina

For those interested in arranging their own homestays there are several organizations in the United States that arrange families for international students:

International Christian Youth
Exchange
134 West 26th Street
New York, NY 10001
(212) 206-7307

Amigos de las Americas
5618 Star Lane
Houston, TX 77057
(713) 782-5290

Council of International Programs
1030 Euclid Avenue,
Cleveland, OH 44115
(216) 861-5478

Living on Your Own

Although many programs shy away from allowing students, particularly undergraduates, to rough it on their own, there are also quite a few that believe a true foreign experience covers more than life in the classroom. Boarding houses, furnished apartments, pensiones, and simple rooming houses are available in every large city. Housing officers associated with a program or individual school assist students in locating appropriate facilities, usually with a roommate or two to cut down on costs.

　　The benefits and potential problems of living on your own are the same in a foreign country as in America. Although facilities selected by a school or program housing official are usually checked out to assure that they meet the basic standards of the group, it's a good idea to ask direct questions when given a list to evaluate. Also, if you're going to live in a rented apartment or room, be sure you know what you must supply in the way of bedding, towels, and cooking equipment before heading abroad. Although many facilities do supply the basic necessities, a great many give you four walls, a roof, and some simple furniture. One thing you don't need when embarking on a four- or eight-month venture is the cost of setting up house in an unknown part of the world.

- *I rented a room from a spinster and enjoyed it. My rent was expensive, but I had total freedom.*

　　　　　　　　　　　　　　　　- Name withheld, Laurel, Maryland

- *My first semester I lived with a family. The second semester I lived in an apartment that the family owned. As a result, I didn't get to see my family as much as I wanted to. One can get involved in the culture and society much more easily living with a family.*

- Margaret Riley, Wayne, Pennsylvania

Cost of Living Abroad

Since money is always a consideration, it is a good idea to evaluate the basic costs of food, clothing, transportation, and entertainment in the country and city of your choice. There are many ways to do this, but the best way is by talking to students who have recently returned. Ask your school's overseas study director or an institute's program director for a list of these students. The embassies of foreign countries also will provide an indication of the basic cost of goods usually expressed in the country's own currency. Your local bank will provide the latest conversion rate from U.S. dollars to a foreign country's currency. These rates change daily, so don't expect the quote you get in January to mean too much in September. They are, however, an approximate guide. In general, you will find that living in any foreign city is more expensive than living in a country town. However, you will also discover that basic transportation on city buses, subways, and even in taxicabs is considerably less expensive than in America. The standard of living in a country is an indication of what you might expect when living with a family or visiting with newly made friends. You will discover that in many countries people live far better than you might have expected and, conversely, there are parts of the world where poverty overshadows all. Discovering how people live and cope with what they have and what they lack is a major part of any foreign experience.

To give you a rough guide to a country's standard of living, this book provides as part of the statistics given for each country a listing entitled "Households with Television." In comparing all the various countries' economic listings, it appears there is a relationship between a nation's standard of living and a family's ability to buy or rent a television. It's a rough guide but one not without merit. As a base for you to use as comparison, 85 percent of all American households have at least one TV (*Encyclopaedia Britannica*).

Speaking the Language

- *Do not use English. The more you use your foreign language the better you learn it. Living with a family or foreign roommate will further help you master the language.*

- Marian Leerburger, Millersville, Maryland

The two most common reasons for studying abroad are to learn about a foreign country and its people and to learn a foreign language. Without question, both these objectives are realized when you study abroad. When considering which program to attend, your current language proficiency is an extremely important factor. You will hear: "Don't worry, everyone speaks English." However, unless you're planning on studying in the Commonwealth, don't believe it. Yes, English is spoken by many people throughout the world, but don't count on a bus driver in Vienna or a waiter in Cannes for help unless you truly speak their language. Ah, but you've had a few years of high school French and received good grades your first year in college. Great! Now ask yourself: Can you really follow a professor's lecture in conversational—not stop- and -start classroom—French, or fully comprehend the front page of *Le Monde*?

Fortunately, most foreign-study program administrators are well aware of your abilities and have designed either special intensive language classes for you at the start of your overseas year or have programmed language classes or labs as part of your daily schedule. If you enroll directly in a foreign university, you probably will be required to take a language-proficiency examination prior to acceptance. You will also be encouraged to speak the language of your host country as much as possible. Stay with a family and it will come easy to you. Furthermore, you find that your foreign family and friends are extremely appreciative of your desire and growing ability to speak their language.

- *Don't be afraid to commit time in areas of unfamiliar languages; that is the only real way of learning. The whole process of learning a language is hyperaccelerated when you've no idea what the hell is going on.*

                              - Joseph Stergios, Minneapolis, Minnesota

TRAVELING ABROAD

- *Most of the learning experience comes in traveling, meeting people, visiting different places, etc. Take advantage of all your opportunities. If you miss a few classes — it's no great loss.*

                              - Barbara C. Caufman, Gambier, Ohio

Without question, every student returns from a foreign study adventure extolling the benefits of travel. The fact that travel is such an important part of the total overseas learning experience has not been ignored by those who plan foreign programs. The majority of the programs have a travel component built into them; many cover the cost of travel as part of the total package. One program, Semester at Sea, provides the opportunity for international travel through the mobility of a shipboard campus. Regardless of what program you elect or which country you choose as your base, you will find students teaming up with new-found friends exploring the cities and byways over weekends, during vacation periods, or between semesters. There are a great number of books and pamphlets designed to help you get more for your money or see the most important sights in a particular city or country. (Some of the more popular guides are listed in the bibliography.) You will have no difficulty locating people abroad willing and anxious to help you see their country. The following basics, however, should be kept in mind.

Passports and Visas

A U.S. passport is a legal document issued by the government guaranteeing that you are an American citizen. It conveys no special privileges but is required to travel abroad. A visa is a document, usually a fancy stamp impressed on a page in your passport, issued by a foreign government stating that you have that government's permission to visit its country for a specified period. Visa requirements vary from country to country and are fully outlined in the pamphlet "Visa Requirements of Foreign Governments" available at any Passport Agency. In the old days every country required you to apply well in advance for a visa. Every time you crossed a border your passport and visa were inspected by an official bureaucrat and stamped with great ceremony. Today, unless you are planning to stay on for several months, most European countries require only a valid passport for entry, not a visa. France, however, is one Western European country that requires a visa. If you're planning to spend a full academic year in a country, check with that country's consulate or embassy to determine whether you need a special student visa. Usually you can study as a tourist as long as you leave the country for a day or less sometime before the expiration of your tourist's duration. Then, when you re-enter the country your "tourist-time" begins anew.

Passport stamping is also a thing of the past; now a border immigration inspector checks your nationality, assures himself that your passport has not expired, and waves you through. However, a visa is still needed if you plan to visit Eastern Europe or many Asian countries. Some countries — Mexico, for example — require a tourist card, easily attainable from that country's embassy, consulate, or national airline.

A U.S. passport is valid for ten years (five if you're under eighteen) and costs $35 ($20 if you're under eighteen) plus a $7 processing fee (no fee if you apply by mail). The standard passport has forty-eight pages, most of which are blank and are for entry/exit stamps and visas. If you are planning to travel widely in countries that require visas you may want a ninety-six page passport, available at no extra charge. To obtain your passport, apply at:

- A U.S. Passport Agency in Boston, Chicago, Detroit, Honolulu, Houston, Los Angeles, Miami, New Orleans, New York, Philadelphia, San Francisco, Seattle, Stamford, Conn., or Washington, D.C.

- Most local county courthouses.

- Selected Post Offices.

You will need:

- Two identical photographs 2 inches square, color or black and white, on nonglossy paper, and taken within the last six months.

- Your birth certificate, naturalization certificate, or an expired passport that was issued you after age sixteen.

- Proof of identity, such as a driver's license (if you apply in person).

When you enter a foreign country you usually pass two separate check points: immigration or "passport control," and customs. An immigrations officer checks your nationality and visa (if one is required); the customs officer insures that you don't bring in or take out items forbidden by that country. Some countries limit the amount of their currency that can be brought in or out; some limit cigarettes and liquor. *All* ban the transport or possession of drugs. Anyone trying to sneak dope across *any* international border obviously hasn't seen the movie *Midnight Express*. The drug laws in the United States are nonexistent compared with those in most foreign countries. And the fact that you are a United States citizen bears no consequence. When you enter a foreign country, you come under the jurisdiction of their laws, administered by its police.

If your passport is lost or stolen while abroad, call the nearest American consulate. Be sure to record your passport's number and its place and date of issue. Keep this data along with your traveler's check numbers in a separate, secure place.

Money

- *Budget your money beforehand or it will be gone in no time.*
  - Cathy Bond, Misenheimer, North Carolina

One of the most difficult questions is the amount of spending money you will need during your overseas stay. The major problem, of course, is that you won't know how much traveling you will do until you're well into your program. Many of the programs listed here include estimated "personal" expenses based on students' past experience. However, tastes are as different as peoples' pocketbooks. A well-thought-out budget is an essential part of your planning.

Aside from the basic cost of tuition, round-trip transportation, room and board, program sponsored tours, and museum and site visits, consider the following in planning your personal expense budget:

- **LOCAL TRANSPORTATION**   In most cities outside the U.S., buses and subways are an inexpensive way to move about. The actual cost of local transportation can be determined before you leave by checking with a foreign government's consulate. Also ask for bus and subway maps; they're usually free from the consulate, but you may have to buy them abroad.

- **RECREATION**   This is another personal matter that varies from individual to individual. Consider what you currently spend for concerts, sporting events, movies, and the like. Also, you will find that cultural tastes vary. In many foreign countries people spend their free time congregating in pubs, beer gardens, or bistros rather than the American teen-agers' favorite pastime — "doing something" (which often costs nothing).

- **FOOD**   Aside from the meals you eat with your family or in the dormitory, consider weekend outings, snacks, and a few beers with some friends.

- **WEEKEND TRIPS**   Definitely plan to take time traveling. Budget the cost of transportation, a hostel or hotel, food, and visiting museums, then add the estimated cost of buying postcards, gifts, and souvenirs.

- **PERSONAL ITEMS**   Aside from the toiletries you will need, budget money to buy that bargain sweater in Portugal, Swatch watch in Switzerland, perfume in France, and the gifts you'll want to bring back to friends and relatives. You should also consider the cost of the gifts you will need abroad, when invited to someone's home it's often customary to bring flowers or some other inexpensive gift.

- **MISCELLANIES**   Other items to budget include postage, school supplies, film and picture processing (it's expensive overseas), laundry, and unexpected medical expenses.

Since the actual cost of living varies from country to country, you won't know how far your dollar will go until the last minute. As a general rule, however, the more expensive cities include Tokyo, Paris, Bonn, and London. Among the "bargain" cities are Lisbon, Madrid, Buenos Aires, and Warsaw. If possible carry both traveler's checks and a major credit card. Not only can you use a credit card instead of cash throughout the world but in an emergency money can be charged to a credit card or wired to you from home. For example, an American Express card holder may wire up to $1,000 to more than sixty foreign locations. It takes about twenty-four hours. Money is usually wired under an identification number (your passport), which you must know to pick up the funds.

Unless you're planning to spend at least six months in a single foreign city, don't consider trying to establish a foreign bank account. They are far more cumbersome than in America, more expensive, and really not necessary.

Getting About

Unless you own or rent a car, the most common form of foreign transportation is the train. In most countries train travel is efficient, economic, convenient, and fast. The Japanese Bullet Train moves in excess of 170 mph; the Train à Grande Vitesse (TGV) runs between Paris and Lyons at 168 mph. In Europe the average train speed is 80 mph. Intercity train travel is far more efficient in Europe than America. There are forty direct daily trains between Frankfurt and Cologne, for example. The "on-time" rate varies from 90 percent in Europe to less than 10 percent in India. Some Germans are known to set their clocks by a passing train. Try that in America! In addition, train travel affords an inexpensive way to enjoy the passing scenery or save the cost of a hostel by traveling at night. Trains are also a good way to meet new people. Expect compartment mates to engage you in conversation and willingly share their food and wine. It's part of the foreign experience.

If you're planning any extensive European travel, the various train passes, which can only be purchased outside of Europe, are most economical. The Eurail pass is the most common and is good for unlimited rail travel throughout sixteen European countries. It is available in: first class, unlimited mileage for from fifteen days to three months; and second class, unlimited mileage for those under twenty-six years of age (only one- or two-month cards are available). Group passes are also available if you and a group of three or more friends want to plan an excursion. In addition to the Eurail pass you can also buy a BritRail, France Vacances, Germanrail, Benelux Tourail, Scandinavian Rail, or a Spanish Cheque-tren pass. For additional information on train travel, contact your own tourist office or your host country's national tourist office. Most rail passes also cover free or reduced travel on ferries and buses. The Eurail pass, for example, allows you free Rhine River and lake steamer cruises. Enjoy a three-hour boat ride on the beautiful Lake of Lucerne at no cost. Remember, you must buy your rail pass before you leave America (or before you enter the country that issues the pass). The clock starts running when you take your first train trip, not when you buy the pass.

Air travel is far more expensive abroad than in the United States. Unless you are planning to travel between areas not served by trains or buses you can overspend your budget very quickly by flying.

If you are planning to drive while overseas it is a good idea to obtain an international driver's permit. Although many countries allow Americans eighteen years and over to drive with a valid U.S. driver's license, most countries require the international driver's permit. A list of those countries and a permit application are available from the American Automobile Association (AAA), 8111 Gatehouse Road, Falls Church, VA 22047, or from other local automobile clubs. You need two 2-inch photos and $5. The international permit is a supplement to your regular license, not a replacement. You will still need a valid driver's license.

Spending the Night

The most common place to stay while traveling is at a hostel. According to a foreign-study guide issued by the University of Wisconsin - Stephens Point, a hostel is:

- *...neither hotel, boarding house, dormitory, or home. It is, rather, a combination of them all. Hostels themselves come in all shapes and sizes. Some are luxurious, others are stark; some house hundreds, others only twenty; some are found in centuries old castles, others in modern buildings; some serve extravagant meals, others cold, simple suppers. British hostels often seem simply one step away from camping, while those in Switzerland, for example, are more plush. All are usually neat and orderly and most are in excellent locations.*

Although primarily designed for young travelers, you'll find users of all ages and from all countries. Each country sets its own rules and regulations. Generally, you will be expected to share in maintaining the facility, stay no more than three days and abstain from drinking and using drugs. Hostels in some countries, however, allow beer drinking in a ground-floor communal room and some permit limited smoking. You can also expect a curfew. Rules and regulations are posted in each hostel.

To use a hostel you must be a have a card issued by a member of the International Youth Hostel Federation, an organization of over sixty hostel associations worldwide. In the United States you can obtain a membership card from the American Youth Hostels (AYH), 1426 H Street NW, Suite 251, Washington, DC 20005. The cost of membership for those under eighteen and over fifty-nine is $10; If you fall between these ages the cost is $20. Membership runs from October 1 to December 31 of the following year.

The Ten Most Repeated Suggestions of Former Students Abroad

1. Keep a journal.
2. Buy books and ship them home. They're cheaper overseas.

3. Don't be an "ugly American." Listen, absorb the culture you're in; don't impose yours on them.
4. Just relax and have fun.
5. Take advantage of all your opportunities.
6. Go overseas without any hometown honey attachments.
7. Be outgoing and visit the local bars. They are the main social scene.
8. Make friends with the natives.
9. Travel, travel, travel.
10. Make it longer!

International Student Identity Card

Every student, regardless of age, should carry the international student ID card issued by the International Student Travel Conference (ISTC). The card, written in six languages, proves your student status and allows you discounts toward many student/youth flights, tours, museums and historic sites, accommodations, and guidebooks throughout the world, including the United States. Card holders also receive basic medical/accident insurance coverage for their travels outside the United States. The card can be obtained through the Council on International Educational Exchange (CIEE), 205 East 42nd Street, New York, NY 10017; or through any college or university issuing office appointed by CIEE. You will need: a 1 1/2-by-2-inch photo, proof of fulltime student status (signed statement from your school registrar or dean), and a $10 fee. You must be at least twelve years old; no upper age limit.

What About Terrorism?

- *Don't travel in large groups of Americans (except on tours). It makes the natives nervous, especially in bars.*

- Name withheld, Greenville, South Carolina

In 1986, soon after terrorist attacks in a Rome airport and a Berlin nightclub frequented by U.S. military personnel, followed by President Reagan's reprisals against Libya, Americans exhibited a general fear of foreign travel. Foreign-study programs were no exception to the universal withdrawal from overseas adventures. Sales of CIEE's student identification cards were off 30 percent, the Institute of European Studies saw its summer enrollment drop by 20 percent, and Louisiana State University and Villanova University both canceled their European summer-study programs.

Although William L. Gaines, president of the Institute of European Studies, has noted that "students have never been singled out as a target," a fear of a terrorist attacking a group of American students is always on the minds of students abroad and their parents. With the Libyan bombing, attacks against

Americans dropped off sharply. As one observer noted, "During the summer of '86, more Americans were killed by a terrorist on the Staten Island ferry than anywhere else in the world." The lack of any news of terrorism against Americans alleviated the general fear of foreign travel and by the fall of 1987 foreign-study enrollments rebounded. In 1988–89 the growing trend in study abroad is expected to continue.

A few basic rules that any foreign traveler should keep in mind:

- Avoid countries that are currently experiencing civil insurrection. Trips by Americans to Cuba, Lebanon, and Libya are prohibited by the U.S. government, and obtaining its permission to visit Iran, Iraq, Saudi Arabia, Syria, and most other Arab countries is virtually impossible. Countries such as Sri Lanka, Pakistan, the Philippines, and Northern Ireland, and areas such as the Basque region of Spain and military installations in Madrid, have experienced terrorist attacks against government installations. These attacks get major press attention, but as yet, tourists are not targets.

- Don't linger in airports. When you check in, go to the departing gate immediately and don't hang around the baggage areas. Upon landing, pick up your luggage and leave.

- Don't draw attention to yourself or the fact that you are an American. Flags and college stickers on your bags aren't necessary.

- Avoid typical styles of American dress. Sweatsuits are American; jeans are international.

- Stay away from places popular with American tourists and military personnel such as bars, nightclubs, English-language movie theaters, U.S. libraries, etc.

- Unless you have a reason to pay a personal visit to a U.S. embassy, do your business with it by phone.

The U.S. State Department maintains a hotline number (202) 647-5225 at their Citizens Emergency Center in Washington, D.C. to provide an up-to-the-minute source of information on international political hot spots.

COMING HOME

- *Leaving was harder than going. The friends I made abroad are from everywhere. Keeping in touch with them will be hard; many I know I'll never see again.*

  - Name withheld, Edina, Minnesota

■ *My last night in Amsterdam we all sat about talking about the problems of world
hunger, the EEC, and U.S.- Soviet relations. My first night home we sat in the frat
house discussing whether to buy a keg or a few cases. It's a different world.*

- Christopher D. Cynsan, Chester, Massachusetts

Just as there is culture shock while traveling abroad, so, too, many students
must make an adjustment when they return home. The longer your stay
abroad, the harder the adjustment. But every one reacts differently, and how
an individual is affected by a stay abroad will vary. Many students say that
some of their American friends have changed. In reality, the chances are that
studying, living, and coping in a foreign situation has had a maturing influence
on the returnee. The friend hasn't changed nearly as much as the homecoming
student. After all, values differ. What may have seemed important last year
somehow just doesn't seem to matter as much now.

Every returnee experiences the same problem of slipping back into the
routine of life at home. Some find it extremely easy; some study airline
schedules and travel books planning their next trip abroad. All survive and all
are the better for the experience.

PART ONE
THE WORLD

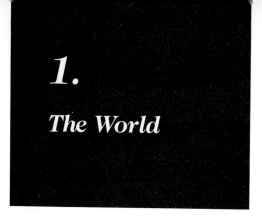

1.

The World

■ **INSTITUTE FOR SHIPBOARD EDUCATION**
2E Forbes Quadrangle
University of Pittsburgh
Pittsburgh, PA 15260 (412) 624-6021 or (800) 854-0195

PROGRAM: Semester at Sea is a unique foreign educational experience that provides an opportunity for international comparative study through the mobility of a shipboard campus. Students live, work, study, and travel on the *S.S. Universe*'s Around-the-World Voyage, visiting Japan, Korea, Taiwan, Hong Kong, Sri Lanka, India, Turkey, Greece, and Spain. Held in cooperation with the University of Pittsburgh, Semester at Sea offers courses in anthropology, business, communications, economics, fine arts, geography, history, literature, music and dance, oceanography, philosophy, political science, psychology, religion, and theater arts. Available to adult passengers "on a limited basis."

ADMITTANCE REQUIREMENTS: Students must be enrolled in an accredited degree program, have successfully completed a full semester (12 units or more), and have a GPA of 2.5 or better.

TEACHING METHODS: Students attend classes daily at sea between ports of call. Academic activities are organized in each country to complement the coursework. Faculty are from the U.S., with guest lecturers from various foreign countries. Field trips and onsite visits are part of the program.

EVALUATION: By faculty, based on periodic exams, papers, and performance.

CREDITS OFFERED: 12 to 15 semester hours.

HOUSING: Aboard ship in private cabins with complete facilities in each cabin.

DATES: Fall semester: September 11 through December 21; spring semester: January 27 through May 7.

COSTS: $8,845 includes tuition, room and board, and passage. (For an inside double room; outside triple, $8,845; outside double, $9,575.) Additional expenses, which average about $2,500, include travel to and from the ship plus personal expenses. Scholarships and work/study grants are available.

YEAR ESTABLISHED: 1965.

NUMBER OF STUDENTS IN 1985: 428.

APPLY: Prior to departure. Semester at Sea.

■ *Semester at Sea changed my life! I am so much more in tune to the world as a unified one. The exposure to Eastern Buddhism and Islam is just incredible. I honestly feel I learned so much more than I have during four years at Tufts. There is a lot of emphasis on self-discovery and creating your own reality. The students aboard were curious and the learning never ends.*

- Lisa Hirsch, Somerville, Massachusetts

■ **MICHIGAN STATE UNIVERSITY**
108 Center for International Programs
East Lansing, MI 48824 (517) 353-8920

PROGRAM: Social Science in Egypt, Israel, and England is a single-semester undergraduate program that emphasizes the social development in these three countries. Orientation in the U.S. and onsite.

ADMITTANCE REQUIREMENTS: Acceptable academic credentials, references, and recommendation from advisor. No language requirement.

TEACHING METHODS: Students take special courses in English arranged for the group and taught by both U.S. and local foreign faculty.

EVALUATION: By course faculty, based upon papers and examinations.

CREDITS OFFERED: 12 semester hours.

HOUSING: Students live in dormitories, hotels, and kibbutzim.

DATES: March 27 through June 4.

COSTS: Approximately $1,600, includes tuition, room and some meals, and program-related travel. Does not include round-trip transportation or personal expenses.

YEAR ESTABLISHED: 1981.

NUMBER OF STUDENTS IN 1985: Not available.

APPLY: By February 3. Dr. Charles A. Gliozzo, Office of Overseas Study

■ **OHIO UNIVERSITY**
1570 Granville Road
Lancaster, OH 43130 (614) 654-6711, ext. 260

PROGRAM: Undergraduate Study Tours visits "all parts of the world" and includes visits to museums and regional sites. Usually based on a program of independent study. Both pre- and post-orientation usually one day.

ADMITTANCE REQUIREMENTS: Open to both students and nonstudents.

TEACHING METHODS: In English. Courses are arranged and led by U.S. group leader.

EVALUATION: Final paper.

CREDITS OFFERED: 1 to 3 quarter hours.

HOUSING: In hotels.

DATES: December and March. Usually three weeks in duration.

COSTS: Tuition is $48 per quarter hour. Travel costs vary. For example, an 18-day trip to China in 1985 cost $2,299 per person round-trip from Columbus.

YEAR ESTABLISHED: 1970.

NUMBER OF STUDENTS IN 1985: 50.

APPLY: One month prior to departure. Professor Dee Mowry.

■ **UNIVERSITY OF MINNESOTA**
Minnesota Studies in International Development (MSID)
Extension Classes Offices of Study Abroad
202 Wesbrook Hall
77 Pleasant Street SE
Minneapolis, MN 55455
(612) 373-1855

PROGRAM: MSID "provides students an opportunity to obtain the field experience and the theoretical sophistication necessary to address effectively the problems development presents." Graduate and undergraduate students participate as interns in field-based, development-related research and action projects in Colombia, India, Jamaica, Kenya, and Senegal under the direction of host-country or international professionals.

ADMITTANCE REQUIREMENTS: One need not currently be a student to apply, but must have completed at least 90 quarter credits; have a 2.5 GPA; and attain, by time of departure, "a specified level of competence in the working language of the host country." Two required predeparture courses are offered at the University of Minnesota during the fall quarter to "provide interns with theoretical background and site-specific orientation."

TEACHING METHODS: Students work with mentors in the host country on such projects as small business and artisan programs, upgrade agro-forestry ventures, village planning, literacy programs, rural nutritional programs, etc. Working environments range "from simple mud and thatch houses to sophisticated offices."

EVALUATION: By mentors, based upon papers and written exams.

CREDITS OFFERED: Varies depending upon site and internship assignment.

HOUSING: MSID arranges for lodgings with assistance of local organizations. Homestays are encouraged. In Jamaica, students are responsible for their own housing.

DATES: Vary depending upon host country.

COSTS: Internships are full time and unpaid. Program costs vary from country to country, beginning at around $1,500.

YEAR ESTABLISHED: 1983.

NUMBER OF STUDENTS IN 1985: Not available.

APPLY: By June 1. Jody Jensen, ECOSA.

■ **UNIVERSITY OF THE PACIFIC**
McGeorge School of Law
3200 Fifth Avenue
Sacramento, CA 95817
(916) 739-7195

PROGRAM: The International Law Internship program is a fall semester post-juris doctor program consisting of six weeks of concentrated study in Salzburg, Austria, followed by a two-and-a-half a month internship experience with a private law firm or company legal department. Participants have a choice of 20 countries in which to intern including most European countries, Egypt, Hong Kong, and Taiwan. In addition to the semester program, McGeorge School of Law conducts four summer programs in London, Edinburgh, Salzburg, and Budapest.

ADMITTANCE REQUIREMENTS: Law school graduate and admission to the bar.

TEACHING METHODS: Students attend classes at local universities including Salzburg University and the Austro-American Institute of Education.

EVALUATION: By university professors, based upon written exams.

CREDITS OFFERED: 5 units of academic credit toward master of law.

HOUSING: Students are responsible for their own arrangements.

DATES: August 18 through December 19.

COSTS: Tuition: $3,180. Does not include room and board, transportation, or personal expenses.

YEAR ESTABLISHED: 1974.

NUMBER OF STUDENTS IN 1985:   Not available.

APPLY: January 15. Robert Taylor, Assistant to the Director.

PART TWO
CANADA

2.

Canada

Population: 25,638,000   **Capital:** Ottawa   **Languages:** English and French
Monetary Unit: Canadian dollar   **Government:** Federal multiparty, parliamentary
state (British monarch and Canadian prime minister)
Religion: 47% Roman Catholic; 41% Protestant   **Households with Television:** 97%

SELECTED COLLEGES AND UNIVERSITIES

Concordia University
1455 de Maisonneuve
Boulevard West
Montreal, Quebec H3G 1M8
(514) 848-2424

Dalhousie University
Halifax, Nova Scotia B3H 3J5
(902) 424-2211

McGill University
853 Sherbrooke Street West
Montreal, Quebec H3A 2T6
(514) 398-4455

McMaster University
Hamilton, Ontario L8S 4L8
(416) 525-9140

Simon Fraser University
Burnaby, British Columbia V5A 1S6
(604) 291-3111

University of British Columbia
2075 Wesbrook Mall
Vancouver, British Columbia V6T 1Z3
(604) 228-2211

University of Guelph
Guelph, Ontario N1G 2W1
(519) 824-4120

University of Toronto
Toronto, Ontario M5S 1A1
(416) 978-2011

FURTHER INFORMATION

Association of Universities and
Colleges in Canada
151 Slater Street
Ottawa, Ontario K1P 5N1
(613) 563-1236

Publishes Directory of Canadian
Universities *and* University Study
in Canada.

Canadian Bureau for
International Education
141 Laurier West, Suite 809
Ottawa, Ontario K1P 5J3
(613) 237-4820

Publishes Guide to Foreign Student
Authorizations for Canada.

Consulate General of Canada
1251 Avenue of the Americas
New York, NY 10020
(212) 586-2400

Distributes University Study in Canada.
*There are also Canadian consulates in
Atlanta, Boston, Buffalo, Chicago,
Cleveland, Dallas, Detroit, Los
Angeles, Minneapolis, Philadelphia,
San Francisco, Seattle, and
Washington, D.C.*

More Than One City

■ UNIVERSITY OF MAINE AT ORONO
Canadian-American Center
154 College Avenue
Orono, ME 04469
(207) 581-4222

PROGRAM: Canada Year is a broad program held in cooperation with the
Joint Operations Committee of the New England Land Grant universities and
a wide selection of Canadian universities. Students can enroll for a semester or
the full academic year in one of many Canadian universities. Courses cover
liberal arts, sciences, and Canadian studies. French immersion program at the
Université Laval, Quebec City. One- to 2-day orientation onsite.

ADMITTANCE REQUIREMENTS: Junior status recommended "but excep-
tions considered." 2.7 GPA, an interest in Canada, and recommendations.

TEACHING METHODS: Americans are fully integrated with Canadian students and attend regular classes taught by resident faculty. Courses may be in
English or French depending upon university selected. Many courses include
regional field trips.

EVALUATION: By Canadian faculty, based on class work, papers, and
examinations.

CREDITS OFFERED: Equivalent to the credit system at the selected Canadian university.

HOUSING: Students usually live in university dormitories but at some schools may elect to stay off-campus.

DATES: Vary depending on university selected.

COSTS: Vary depending on university selected.

YEAR ESTABLISHED: 1967.

NUMBER OF STUDENTS IN 1985:   15.

APPLY: Fall semester: March 1; spring semester: November 1. Lee-Ann Konrad, Canada Year Coordinator.

Ontario

London and Kitchener

■ **NEW HAMPSHIRE COLLEGE**
2500 North River Road
Manchester, NH 03104
(603) 668-2211 ext. 387

PROGRAM: The International Exchange Program is a full-year program held in cooperation with Fanshawe College, London, Ontario, and the University of Waterloo, Kitchener, Ontario. In this Canada/USA student-work-experience exchange program, students have internships at Canadian companies as well as classroom studies at the participating Canadian institutions.

ADMITTANCE REQUIREMENTS: For students of participating New England colleges. Must be U.S. citizen and have completed at least one year fulltime in a degree program. Good to excellent academic record. Interviews by home institution as well as prospective employer.

TEACHING METHODS: Classes are held at the cooperating college.

EVALUATION: By cooperating college faculty and employer.

CREDITS OFFERED: Up to 30 credits per year.

HOUSING: At participating Canadian university or local rooms and apartments.

DATES: Approximately, August 30 through May 20.

COSTS: Same tuition as home institution.

YEAR ESTABLISHED: Fanshawe College, 1980; University of Waterloo, 1983.

NUMBER OF STUDENTS IN 1985:   20 each school.

APPLY: By March 1. Dr. Francis Doucette, Learning Center.

Ottawa

■ **UNIVERSITY OF SOUTHERN CALIFORNIA**
Overseas Studies, CES 109
University Park
Los Angeles, CA 90089
(213) 746-2500

PROGRAM: USC's Canada Semester is an undergraduate program designed for American students interested in Canadian affairs. Courses concentrate on international relations and political science. Onsite orientation.

ADMITTANCE REQUIREMENTS: Sophomores and above in good academic standing.

TEACHING METHODS: Courses are taught by U.S. faculty members. Classes are not integrated with Canadian students.

EVALUATION: By course faculty member, based upon class work, papers, and periodic examinations.

CREDITS OFFERED: 16 semester hours.

HOUSING: Students live in private apartments.

DATES: Fall semester: early September through mid-December; spring semester: early January through mid-May.

COSTS: Approximately: $6,500 covers tuition, room and board, program-related travel. Does not include round-trip transportation or personal expenses. Some scholarships are available.

YEAR ESTABLISHED: 1985

NUMBER OF STUDENTS IN 1985: Not available.

APPLY: Fall semester by April 1; spring semester by October 1.

Quebec

■ **THE CALIFORNIA STATE UNIVERSITY**
400 Golden Shore
Long Beach, CA 90802
(213) 590-5655

PROGRAM: The CSU International Program in Canada is held in cooperation with all the public postsecondary institutions in the Province of Quebec, including the universities of McGill, Montreal, Quebec, and Sherbrooke. Students may apply as exchange students in any participating institution and take any course offered. One week onsite orientation.

ADMITTANCE REQUIREMENTS: Must be enrolled at a CSU campus. Juniors and above, including graduate students. 3.0 GPA.

TEACHING METHODS: Students take a combination of regular academic courses supplemented with program-sponsored courses, taught by foreign faculty. Language of course depends upon school. Some are in English; some in French.

EVALUATION: By foreign faculty and CSU resident director, based upon periodic and final examinations.

CREDITS OFFERED: 30 semester hours per year or 45 quarter units.

HOUSING: In dormitories and private apartments.

DATES: Approximately July 7 through May 2.

COSTS: Tuition: $0 (residents); $3,600 (nonresidents). Room and board: $2,950. Does not include round-trip transportation and living expenses estimated at approximately $2,660 per year.

YEAR ESTABLISHED: 1981.

NUMBER OF STUDENTS IN 1985: 11.

APPLY: By February 1. Dr. Kibbey M. Horne, Director of International Programs.

PART THREE

LATIN AMERICA AND THE CARIBBEAN

3.

Latin America

MORE THAN ONE COUNTRY

■ **HIGHER EDUCATION CONSORTIUM FOR URBAN AFFAIRS (HECUA)**
HECUA at Hamline University
St. Paul, MN 55104
(612) 646-8831

PROGRAM: Literature, Ideology, and Society in Latin America is an interdisciplinary program that studies Latin American development and social change. These issues are explored through literature and art and the study of ideology and how it shapes local perception of social realities. Immersion in language and culture is stressed through the use of Spanish in all coursework, field study, and homestays with Colombian families. The program is based in Bogotá, Colombia, with study-travel to Managua, Nicaragua, and San Juan, Puerto Rico. Courses cover: Latin American literature, Latin American art and society, social change in Latin America, history, economics, fine arts, sociology/social work, and advanced Spanish.

ADMITTANCE REQUIREMENTS: Sophomores and above in good academic standing, essay, recommendation from home institution, knowledge of Spanish.

TEACHING METHODS: Faculty are citizen-residents of the host country. Integration of regular classroom work (lectures, readings, discussions, etc.) with field study in communities and site visits.

EVALUATION: Varies according to program. Expect exams and periodic papers graded by local professors.

CREDITS OFFERED: HECUA programs are equivalent to a full semester load; typically four courses per semester (4-1-4 system) or 16 credit hours.

HOUSING: In Colombia, with local families; Puerto Rico — hotels; Nicaragua — first week in group home, second week with families.

DATES: February 2 through May 13.

COSTS: Tuition, room and board, and local field trips $4,300. Estimated living expenses $500 to $700. (Round-trip transportation — approximately $1,045 from Miami — not included.) Nonmember college students pay additional $150 administrative fee.

YEAR ESTABLISHED: 1984.

NUMBER OF STUDENTS IN 1985:   12.

APPLY: By November 30. Ms. Jean Leibman, Administrative Associate.

■ **HIGHER EDUCATION CONSORTIUM FOR URBAN AFFAIRS (HECUA)**
HECUA at Hamline University
St. Paul, MN 55104
(612) 646-8831

PROGRAM: South American Urban Semester is an interdisciplinary program that studies the relationship between third world development and the consequences of urbanization and the growth of cities in South America. Topics include theories and models of development, the impact of international trade and multinational corporations, the contrast between urban rich and poor, rural-urban migration, etc. Field study and family homestays immerse students in the language and culture. The program is based in Bogotá, Colombia for 12 1/2 weeks with study-travel throughout Colombia, Panama, Ecuador, and Peru. Also field study in Bucaramanga, Cartagena, Medellín, Cali, and Manizales. Courses cover: Wealth, poverty, and community development; community change in the Latin American city; history, economics, fine arts, sociology/social work, and advanced Spanish.

ADMITTANCE REQUIREMENTS: Sophomores and above in good academic standing, essay, recommendation from home institution, knowledge of Spanish.

TEACHING METHODS: Faculty are citizen-residents of the host country. Integration of regular classroom work (lectures, readings, discussions, etc.) with field study in communities and site visits.

EVALUATION: Varies according to program. Expect exams and periodic papers graded by local professors.

CREDITS OFFERED: HECUA programs are equivalent to a full semester load; typically four courses per semester (4-1-4 system) or 16 credit hours.

HOUSING: In Colombia, with local families; Ecuador and Peru — hotels.

DATES: August 24 through December 6.

COSTS: Tuition, room and board, and local field trips, $4,300. Estimated living expenses $500 to $700. (Round-trip transportation — approximately $1,045 from Miami — not included.) Nonmember college students pay additional $150 administrative fee.

YEAR ESTABLISHED: 1977.

NUMBER OF STUDENTS IN 1985: 25.

APPLY: By March 31. Ms. Jean Leibman, Administrative Associate.

■ **SCHOOL FOR FIELD STUDIES**
376 Hale Street
Beverly, MA 01915
(617) 927-7777

PROGRAM: The School for Field Studies, an independent, nonprofit organization, offers a variety of undergraduate study options to students interested in hands-on field research and courses on environmental issues. During the summer of 1985, more than 20 courses were offered. All courses are accredited through Northeastern University in Boston and cover: wildlife management, reintroduction of endangered species, coral reef ecology, deforestation, primate social behavior, etc. Students can perform field work in Kenya, Switzerland, Virgin Islands, Ecuador, Costa Rica, Panama, and the United States.

ADMISSIONS REQUIREMENTS: Open to students 16 years old and above. Acceptable academic record, essay, and references.

TEACHING METHODS: There are no formal classes. Students are integrated with other foreign nationals and are taught by both U.S. and foreign faculty members. Most learning is by doing.

EVALUATION: Program director is responsible for periodic and final exams based on field experiences.

CREDITS OFFERED: Summer courses: 8 quarter credits; semester program: 20 quarter credits; January program: 4 quarter credits per course.

HOUSING: Depends on course site. Students can live in cabins or tents.

DATES: Programs are held throughout the year; dates vary.

COSTS: Vary according to course and location. Financial aid is available in the form of grants and loans.

YEAR ESTABLISHED: 1980.

NUMBER OF STUDENTS IN 1985: 300 (summer).

APPLY: Rolling admissions. Admissions Department.

■ *Personally, my experience in Ecuador was the best thing I have ever done. Not only the travel-knowledge angle of the course, but the sense of personal satisfaction. I worked out the travel arrangements. I paid for it. I flew there alone. I did it myself. It's the type of independent experience I needed at this point in my life.*

- Laurie Saunders, Cheshire, Connecticut

4.

Mexico and Central America

MEXICO

Population: 80,472,000   **Capital:** Mexico City   **Language:** Spanish
Monetary Unit: Peso   **Government:** Federal Republic (President)
Religion: 93% Roman Catholic   **Households with Television:** 2%

SELECTED COLLEGES AND UNIVERSITIES

Cemanahuac
Apartado 21 C
Calle San Juan 4
Cuernavaca, Morelos

Private college offering courses in Mesoamerican culture, Spanish language and literature, anthropology, sociology, political science, weaving and pottery. Courses in Spanish and English range from a month to a semester in duration.

Universidad Iberoamericana
Cerro de las Torres 395
Campestre Churubusco
Mexico 21, D.F.

Offers a Junior Year in Mexico program for foreigners with courses in Spanish, history, sociology, philosophy, political science, and fine arts. Requires sophomores with "a basic knowledge of Spanish."

Universidad de las Américas
Apartado Postal 507, Dept D-3
San Andrés Cholula
Puebla

Private liberal arts school accredited by the Southern Association of Colleges and Universities. Offers special programs for American college students in both Spanish and English.

Universidad Autónoma
de Guadalajara
Paseo de las Águilas 7000
Guadalajara

Accepts a large number of foreign students (usually more than 1,000). Publishes a course directory in English.

Universidad Nacional Autónoma
de México
Ciudad Universitaria
Mexico 12, D.F.

*First classes were held in 1553. Today,
more than 300,000 students are enrolled. Offers a limited number of
scholarships to U.S. students. Course
directory in English and Spanish.
Publishes* Información para Estudiantes
del Extranjero.

FURTHER INFORMATION

Consulate General of Mexico
8 East 41st Street
New York, NY
(212) 689-0456

Embassy of Mexico
2829 16th Street, NW
Washington, DC 20009
(202) 234-6000

Mexican Government Tourist Office
405 Park Avenue
New York, NY 10022
(212) 838-2949

Secretaría de Relaciones Exteriores
Dirección General de Relaciones
Internacionales
Brasil 31
Mexico 1, D.F.

Publishes Guia del Estudiante Extranjero
en México *in Spanish and English.*

Cuernavaca

■ **AUGSBURG COLLEGE**
Center for Global Service & Education
731 21st Avenue South
Minneapolis, MN 55454
(612) 330-1159

PROGRAM: The Program in Global Community is a spring semester, undergraduate program that "focuses on issues related to global justice and human
liberation in light of the Christian gospel." Courses include: Spanish, history,
communications, political science, religion and economics. Travel to Honduras and Nicaragua complements the coursework. An integral part of the
program is "experimental education" in which students are encouraged to "be

out exploring on their own whenever possible." A three-day orientation in Edinburg, Texas, precedes the trip to Mexico.

ADMITTANCE REQUIREMENTS: Open to sophomores and above with acceptable academic standards. Freshmen are occasionally admitted. One college course in Spanish is requested.

TEACHING METHODS: Students are taught by both American and local faculty with lectures in English and Spanish. Classes are not integrated, but social integration is expected outside the classroom. Lectures, classwork, and local field trips.

EVALUATION: Periodic exams and papers evaluated by group leaders and fellow students in frequent reflection sessions.

CREDITS OFFERED: 4 semester credits (16 hours).

HOUSING: Students live in a large private house owned by the college. They also spend two weeks with a Mexican family and two weeks in a rural village, where students live and work alongside Mexican campesinoz.

DATES: Approximately February 5 through May 22.

COSTS: $3,865 includes tuition, room and board, round-trip transportation from Edinburg, Texas, plus all travel associated with the program. Estimated living expenses, $500.

YEAR ESTABLISHED: 1979.

NUMBER OF STUDENTS IN 1985:   16.

APPLY: By mid-October. Karen Martin-Schramm.

■ **THE EXPERIMENT IN INTERNATIONAL LIVING**
   Kipling Road
   Brattleboro, VT 05301
   (800) 451-4465

PROGRAM: The College Semester Abroad program is designed to allow undergraduate students to become immersed in a foreign culture by living with a local family and exploring individual personal and educational interests under professional guidance. Students on the Mexico program spend most of their stay in the Cuernavaca area, however, one week is spent at a location appropriate to a field study project. Courses cover: intensive language study, seminar on Mexican life and culture, history and politics, geography and economics, arts and humanities, social anthropology, methods and techniques of field work, and an independent study project. One-week orientation in Mexico City.

ADMITTANCE REQUIREMENTS: Sophomore standing or above and acceptable academic credentials. A year and a half of college Spanish or the equivalent.

TEACHING METHODS: Students work directly with their American instructors-advisors in planning and evaluating their individual program. Nonlanguage courses are in English. "The semester builds from the more structured language training and lectures and discussions on local life and culture to the independent study project."

EVALUATION: By individual students and their instructor/advisors, based on independent project, papers, reports, and examinations. Periodic meetings during the program and for several days at the conclusion.

CREDITS OFFERED: 16 semester hours.

HOUSING: Students live as family members with their host families.

DATES: Fall semester: September through December; spring semester: January through May.

COSTS: $4,900 includes tuition, room and board, all fees, and local travel. Does not include round-trip transportation.

YEAR ESTABLISHED: Not available.

NUMBER OF STUDENTS IN 1985:   Not available.

APPLY: For fall semester by May 15; spring semester by November 15. Admissions Office, College Semester Abroad.

■ **SANTA BARBARA CITY COLLEGE**
  721 Cliff Drive
  Santa Barbara, CA 93109
  (805) 965-0581

PROGRAM: The Intensive Spanish Language Program is a six-week undergraduate summer program held in cooperation with the Instituto de Estudios de America Latina (IDEAL). Courses concentrate on the Spanish language and Mexican culture. Two- to five-day period of orientation on the SBCC campus.

ADMITTANCE REQUIREMENTS: Acceptable academic credentials plus 12 units of college credit including freshman level Spanish.

TEACHING METHODS: Students attend regular classes at the Instituto de Estudios de America Latina. Courses are supplemented with field trips to local museums and cultural and historic sites. Some independent study.

EVALUATION: By class professors, based upon papers and periodic examinations. Students also complete evaluation forms upon completion of the program and comment on faculty, facilities, group leaders, and program in general.

CREDITS OFFERED: 6 semester hours.

HOUSING: Students live in apartments or with families.

DATES: Dates vary from year to year. Approximately from early July to mid-August.

COSTS: Approximately $690 to $810, including tuition and room and board. Does not include round-trip transportation and local travel.

YEAR ESTABLISHED: 1973.

NUMBER OF STUDENTS IN 1985:   55.

APPLY: By mid-May. Mr. John Romo, Dean of Instructional Services.

■ **STATE UNIVERSITY OF NEW YORK AT BROCKPORT**
Office of International Education
Brockport, NY 14420
(716) 395-2119

PROGRAM: Study in Mexico is a semester, summer, or academic year undergraduate experience that offers a concentration on Spanish language studies plus the history and culture of Mexico. Held in cooperation with the Center for Multicultural Studies. Local travel and trips to cultural and historic sites as well as archaeological field trips complement the program.

ADMITTANCE REQUIREMENTS: "Exceptional sophomores," juniors, and above with a 2.5 GPA and knowledge of Spanish.

TEACHING METHODS: Students attend regular courses taught in Spanish by the Spanish faculty. Americans are integrated with local students.

EVALUATION: By foreign faculty and group leaders, based on periodic papers, exams, and finals.

CREDITS OFFERED: 15 semester hours per semester.

HOUSING: Students live with local families.

DATES: Fall semester: early September through mid-December; spring semester: January 30 to May 5; summer program: July 7 through August 8.

COSTS: Approximately $3,000 per semester covers tuition, room and board, and program-related travel. Does not cover round-trip transportation, local travel, and personal expenses.

YEAR ESTABLISHED: 1980.

NUMBER OF STUDENTS IN 1985:   12.

APPLY: Fall semester by April 1; spring semester by November 1. Dr. John Perry, Director, Office of International Education.

■ **UNIVERSITY OF MINNESOTA**
   Extension Classes Offices of Study Abroad (ECOSA)
   202 Wesbrook Hall
   77 Pleasant Street SE
   Minneapolis, MN 55455
   (612) 373-1855

PROGRAM: Spanish and Anthropology in Mexico are a pair of winter quarter programs. The University of Minnesota offers two distinct programs. One concentrates on language study; the other on the anthropology, the Spanish language, and Mexican culture. Both are taught at Cemanahuac, an international language institute in Cuernavaca and both offer optional field trips.

ADMITTANCE REQUIREMENTS: Students in good academic standing. No established GPA required.

TEACHING METHODS: Students are taught by both U.S. and foreign faculty in groups consisting only of other Americans.

EVALUATION: By course instructors, based upon class work, papers, and final examination.

CREDITS OFFERED: 12 to 13 quarter credits.

HOUSING: Students live with Mexican families.

DATES: January 2 through March 9.

COSTS: $2,450 includes tuition for three courses, room and board, and program-related travel. Does not include round-trip transportation or personal expenses.

YEAR ESTABLISHED: 1980.

NUMBER OF STUDENTS IN 1985: 25.

APPLY: April 1. Jody Jensen, ECOSA.

Guadalajara

■ **NORTHWEST INTERINSTITUTIONAL COUNCIL ON STUDY ABROAD (NICSA)**
Oregon State University
International Education,
Corvallis, OR 97331
(503) 754-2394

PROGRAM: The NICSA program in Guadalajara is held in cooperation with the University of Washington, Washington State University, Western Washington University, Central Washington University, Eastern Washington University, Boise State University, University of Alaska-Fairbanks, University of Oregon, Oregon State University, and Portland State University. This is a one-term, undergraduate program, although students may elect to enroll for more than a single term. The courses are designed around a general liberal arts curriculum emphasizing history, economics, political science, language, art, literature, English, theater, geography, etc. Excursions play an important role, taking place on a weekly basis; one long (2- to 3-day) excursion each term. There is a 3-hour orientation on the individual campuses prior to departure and a 1-day onsite orientation.

ADMITTANCE REQUIREMENTS: A minimum 2.0 GPA plus good academic standing. One term of college Spanish or the equivalent.

TEACHING METHODS: Students attend a special center for Americans set up by NICSA. All classes are taught in English by either foreign or various northwest-school faculty members.

EVALUATION: By professors, based on class work, papers and periodic exams.

CREDITS OFFERED: 15 or 20 credits (quarter hours) per term.

HOUSING: Students live with local families arranged by an onsite homestay coordinator.

DATES: Fall term: September 15 through December 15; winter term: January 3 through March 20; spring term: April 1 through June 15.

COSTS: $1,595 including tuition, room and board, books, and local travel. Does not cover round-trip transportation or personal expenses. Nonresident students attending Oregon State University for one term pay resident tuition.

YEAR ESTABLISHED: 1963.

NUMBER OF STUDENTS IN 1985:   3.

APPLY: Fall term by June 1; winter term by October 15; spring term by January 3. American Heritage Association, P.O. Box #425, Lake Oswego, OR 97034, (503) 635-3703, or Judy Van Dyck or Ann Ferguson, International Education, OSU.

Mexico City

■ **ALMA COLLEGE**
   Alma, MI 48801
   (517) 463-7247

PROGRAM: Alma College Program of Studies in Mexico is held in cooperation with the Universidad Iberoamericana. This program is not in a structured academic setting such as most American schools. Rather, teachers and staff "leave enough freedom in the academic environment to allow students to meet their needs through consultation with the director." Courses specialize in Spanish language and Mexican culture. One-week onsite orientation with the director.

ADMITTANCE REQUIREMENTS: Sophomore and above with a minimum 2.0 GPA in good academic standing with letters of recommendation.

TEACHING METHODS: Small classes, usually six to nine students, in Spanish are complemented with visits to local sites and independent study. Direct involvement with Mexican staff and local residents is encouraged and expected.

EVALUATION: Foreign faculty in conjunction with the resident director plus papers and periodic exams.

CREDITS OFFERED: Up to 15 hours per semester.

HOUSING: All students reside in local homes.

DATES: Summer session: June 29 through August 9; fall semester: August 15 through December 13; spring semester: January 12 through May 15.

COSTS: Summer session: $1,700; fall semester: 3,825; spring semester: 3,925. Includes round-trip transportation from New York, room and board, plus basic texts and cultural activities.

YEAR ESTABLISHED: 1983.

NUMBER OF STUDENTS IN 1985:   3.

APPLY: Two months prior to departure to: Alda Dyal Chand, Director, International Education.

■ **BRIGHAM YOUNG UNIVERSITY**
  Study Abroad Programs
  204 HRCB
  Provo, UT 84602
  (801) 378-3308

PROGRAM: Spring Term in Mexico offers courses in Spanish Language, literature, and civilization. Local field trips to historic and cultural sites are part of the program.

ADMITTANCE REQUIREMENTS: Good academic standing with a 3.0 GPA requested. Adherence to BYU standards.

TEACHING METHODS: Classes are taught by BYU faculty in classrooms designated for the purpose. No foreign schools are involved, although American and Mexican students are integrated.

EVALUATION: Based on periodic exams. Evaluation determined by program director.

CREDITS OFFERED: From 6 to 9 credit hours.

HOUSING: Students live with a Mexican family.

DATES: Approximately April through June.

COSTS: Approximately $1,500 includes tuition, room and board, local travel. Does not cover round-trip transportation and additional travel.

YEAR ESTABLISHED: 1975.

NUMBER OF STUDENTS IN 1985: Not available.

APPLY: By February. Study Abroad Office.

■ **THE CALIFORNIA STATE UNIVERSITY**
400 Golden Shore
Long Beach, CA 90802
(213) 590-5655

PROGRAM: The CSU International Program in Mexico, held at the International Center at the Universidad Iberoamericana, is a full academic year undergraduate and graduate opportunity to study at the Mexican university. Students concentrate on courses relating to social sciences, business, language, linguistics, and the Mexican culture supplemented by special CSU programs. One-week orientation in Mexico City.

ADMITTANCE REQUIREMENTS: Must be enrolled at a CSU campus. Juniors and above, including graduate students. 2.75 GPA (3.0 for business), and two years of college Spanish or the equivalent.

TEACHING METHODS: Students take a combination of regular academic courses and supplemental program-sponsored courses taught by foreign faculty.

EVALUATION: By foreign faculty and CSU resident director, based upon periodic and final examinations.

CREDITS OFFERED: 30 semester hours per year or 45 quarter units.

HOUSING: In dormitories and private apartments.

DATES: Approximately July 26 through May 16.

COSTS: Tuition: $0 (residents); $3,600 (nonresidents); room and board: $1,800. Does not include round-trip transportation and living expenses (estimated at approximately $2,180 per year).

YEAR ESTABLISHED: 1973.

NUMBER OF STUDENTS IN 1985: 11.

APPLY: By February 1. Dr. Kibbey M. Horne, Director of International Programs.

■ **INSTITUTE OF EUROPEAN STUDY (IES)**
223 West Ohio Street
Chicago, IL 60610
(312) 944-1750

PROGRAM: IES is a nonprofit organization with formal relationships with more than forty American colleges and universities. The institute maintains ten undergraduate academic centers throughout the world which provide one-semester or full-academic-year programs. The IES Mexico City program is a one-semester or full-academic-year session held in cooperation with the Instituto Technológico Autónomo de México (ITAM). Courses cover art history, Spanish language and literature, anthropology, Latin American studies, business, history, economics, management, political science, and sociology. A major five-day trip each semester to Oaxaca, Morelia, or Yucatán. One-week orientation in Mexico City and Guanajuato.

ADMITTANCE REQUIREMENTS: Juniors and seniors only. Minimum of two years college Spanish or the equivalent. Faculty recommendations and an application essay. 85 percent of all students have a GPA between 2.80 and 3.75.

TEACHING METHODS: All courses are taught in Spanish by a Mexican faculty. Americans are fully integrated with local students. All students are required to take two courses in cultural studies, one of which must be Mexican history or civilization. Classes are supplemented by trips to local museums and historic sites.

EVALUATION: By faculty, based upon class work, periodic and final exams. Most courses require a research paper.

CREDITS OFFERED: 15 to 18 semester hours per semester.

HOUSING: Students live with local families.

DATES: Fall semester: July 29 through December 12; spring semester: January 6 through May 29.

COSTS: $2,900 per semester; $4,850 per year. Includes tuition, room and board, and program-related field trips. Does not include round-trip transportation, local travel or personal expenses (estimated at $2,100 per year). Some IES scholarship aid available; $1,500 for full-year students, $750 for one-semester students.

YEAR ESTABLISHED: 1983.

NUMBER OF STUDENTS IN 1985: 10.

APPLY: For fall semester by May 1; spring semester by November 15.

■ **RUTGERS, THE STATE UNIVERSITY OF NEW JERSEY**
Milledoler Hall, Rm. 205
New Brunswick, NJ 08903
(201) 932-7787

PROGRAM: Junior Year Abroad in Mexico is a full-year academic undergraduate program. Students attend regular classes at the Universidad National Autónoma de México (UNAM), which offers a broad selection of liberal arts courses with an emphasis on Spanish, Mexican and Latin American history, literature and culture, political science, anthropology, sociology, archaeology, art, etc. Group excursions to cultural and historic sites complement the program.

ADMITTANCE REQUIREMENTS: Good academic standing. No language prerequisite, however students will be interviewed to determine language ability for class placement. A thorough knowledge of Spanish "is essential. At a minimum, students should have completed coursework through first-year literature and preferably advanced grammar courses."

TEACHING METHODS: Students attend regular classes with Mexican students. All courses are in Spanish.

EVALUATION: By course instructors, based upon class work, papers, and examinations.

CREDITS OFFERED: 30 semester hours per year including presession.

HOUSING: Students live with local families.

DATES: Approximately, August 6 to mid-May.

COSTS: $5,442 New Jersey residents; $6,926 nonresidents. Includes tuition, room and board (except 23 days at holidays and between semesters), round-trip transportation from New York and group excursions. Does not cover personal expenses.

YEAR ESTABLISHED: 1972.

NUMBER OF STUDENTS IN 1985: limited to 30.

APPLY: By March 1. Director, Rutgers' Junior Year Abroad.

■ **UNIVERSITY OF NOTRE DAME**
420 Administration Building
Notre Dame, IN 46556
(219) 239-5882

PROGRAM: The University of Notre Dame Program in Mexico City is a full academic year (juniors may take a single-semester option) undergraduate program held in cooperation with Universidad Iberoamericana. Courses cover Spanish language, literature of Latin America, Mexican history, art and archaeology, political and economic development, and international relations. A special seminar is devoted to a social analysis on third world issues and problems. Some field trips and program-related travel.

ADMITTANCE REQUIREMENTS: At least sophomores standing with a 2.5 GPA and 3.0 in Spanish. Knowledge of Spanish. "A limited number of students from other institutions may be accepted if space permits."

TEACHING METHODS: All classes are in Spanish. Students can choose a variety of curricula offerings through the International Center or take regular courses at the Iberoamericana, linguistic ability permitting.

EVALUATION: By onsite directors appointed among Notre Dame faculty, based upon class work, papers, and examinations.

CREDITS OFFERED: At least 15 semester hours per semester.

HOUSING: Students live with Mexican families.

DATES: Fall semester: August 15 through December 14; spring semester: January 20 through May 16.

COSTS: $5,158 per semester includes tuition, room and board, program-related travel, and round-trip transportation from New York.

YEAR ESTABLISHED: 1970.

NUMBER OF STUDENTS IN 1985: 11.

APPLY: Fall semester by February 1; spring semester by September 15. Dr. Isabel Charles, Assistant Provost, Director, Foreign Studies Programs.

Puebla

■ UNIVERSITY OF WISCONSIN – PLATTEVILLE
Institute for Study Abroad Programs
1 University Plaza
Platteville, WI 53818
(608) 342-1726

PROGRAM: The Mexico program is a single-semester or full-academic-year undergraduate program held in cooperation with the College Consortium for International Studies (CCIS), Broome Community College (NY), and the Universidad de las Americas in Puebla. Courses are offered in Spanish (required), as well as art, business, archaeology, sociology, history, and the social sciences. A Mexican culture colloquium is also required. Orientation and program-related travel in Mexico.

ADMITTANCE REQUIREMENTS: Sophomore or above with a 2.5 GPA. Fluency in Spanish is not required, but the curriculum in English is very limited.

TEACHING METHODS: Students take courses at the University of the Americas. Most classes are in Spanish, but a few are in English.

EVALUATION: By UDLA faculty, based upon class work, papers, and examinations.

CREDITS OFFERED: 12 to 18 semester hours per semester.

HOUSING: Students live in dormitories on the UDLA campus.

DATES: Fall semester: August 6 through December 19; spring semester: January 5 through May 22.

COSTS: $1,400 per semester (Wisconsin and Minnesota residents); $2,400 (nonresidents). Includes tuition and housing. Does not cover meals (estimated at about $250 per semester), round-trip transportation, or personal expenses.

YEAR ESTABLISHED: 1978.

NUMBER OF STUDENTS IN 1985:   40.

APPLY: Fall semester by April 30; spring semester by December 1. Institute for Study Abroad Programs, 308 Warner Hall.

Yucatán

■ **CENTRAL COLLEGE**
Pella, IA 50219
(515) 628-5287

PROGRAM: Central College's Yucatán Program is a ten-week, undergraduate program that integrates Spanish language study with topics in Mexican civilization. The emphasis is on an intensive, field-centered approach.

ADMITTANCE REQUIREMENTS: Minimum 2.5 GPA, recommendations, and essay.

TEACHING METHODS: Special classes are taught by professors from the Iowa campus plus local instructors. Lectures and seminars are complemented by local field trips.

EVALUATION: By visiting and local professors. Resident director sends grades to home institution.

CREDITS OFFERED: 10 semester hours (15 quarter hours) per term.

HOUSING: Students live in the former governor's mansion.

DATES: Fall term: September 9 through November 20; winter term: December 2 through February 18; spring term: March 10 through May 21.

COSTS: $3,000 per ten-week term. Includes tuition, room, field trips, laundry, fees, and all meals. Does not cover round-trip transportation and personal expenses. Several work grants are available.

YEAR ESTABLISHED: 1966.

NUMBER OF STUDENTS IN 1985: 26.

APPLY: By April 15 for fall term; October 1 for winter term; December 15 for spring term. Mrs. Barbara Butler, Coordinator of International Studies.

BELIZE

Population: 171,100   **Capital:** Belmopan   **Language:** English
Monetary Unit: Belize dollar   **Government:** Constitutional monarchy
(British monarch and prime minister)   **Religion:** 62% Roman Catholic
Households With Television: Less than 1%.

UNIVERSITY

University College of Belize
P.O. Box 990
Belize City, Belize

FURTHER INFORMATION

Embassy of Belize
3400 International Drive, NW, Suite 2J
Washington, DC 20008
(202) 363-4500

Belmopan

■ **GOSHEN COLLEGE**
  Goshen, IN 46526
  (219) 533-3161

PROGRAM: Goshen's Study Service Trimester Abroad is a fourteen-week (one trimester), undergraduate program offering students the opportunity to concentrate on the region's language, history, and culture. Courses include history, geography, politics, crosscultural studies, and crosscultural sensitization, i.e., art, music, drama, etc. All students must be enrolled at Goshen the preceding trimester to attend orientation sessions.

ADMITTANCE REQUIREMENTS: For sophomores and above who meet acceptable academic standards.

TEACHING METHODS: Students attend special classes taught by a foreign faculty. Courses involve regular class work, field trips, research projects. Each student must also participate in a work assignment, such as hospital, school, community development project.

EVALUATION: By accompanying Goshen College faculty member(s), based upon class work and assessment of projects.

CREDITS OFFERED: 12 semester hours.

HOUSING: Students live with host families.

DATES: Fall trimester: September 11 through December 16; winter trimester: January 8 through April 14; spring trimester: April 24 through July 28.

COSTS: Tuition: $2,390; room and board: $1,040. Includes round-trip transportation and local field trips.

YEAR ESTABLISHED: Not available.

NUMBER OF STUDENTS IN 1985: Not available.

APPLY: One trimester prior to the program. Arlin Hunsberger, Director of International Education.

COSTA RICA

Population: 2,543,000   **Capital:** San José   **Language:** Spanish
Monetary Unit: Costa Rican colon   **Government:** Unitary multiparty republic (president)   **Religion:** 92% Roman Catholic
Households With Television: 5%

SELECTED COLLEGES AND UNIVERSITIES

Universidad de Costa Rica
San Pedro de Montes de Oca
San José

Universidad Nacional
Heredia
Publishes Oportunidades Académicas.

FURTHER INFORMATION

Consulate General of Costa Rica
211 East 43rd Street
New York, NY 10017
(212) 425-2620

Ministerio de Educación Pública
San José

Embassy of Costa Rica
1825 Connecticut Avenue, NW
Washington, DC 20009
(202) 234-2945

San José

■ **ASSOCIATED COLLEGES OF THE MIDWEST**
18 South Michigan Avenue; Suite 1010
Chicago, IL 60603
(312) 263-5000

PROGRAM: The ACM offers two one-semester programs in Costa Rica. The fall program, with some classes held at the University of Costa Rica, is orientated toward language study and an area of culture or society dealing with Costa Rica. The spring program focuses on field study in Costa Rica using field study methods and gathering information for a semester paper. Projects are undertaken in both the natural and social sciences. Both programs are held in cooperation with the member colleges: Beloit College, Carleton College, Coe College, Cornell College, Colorado College, Grinnell College, Knox College, Lake Forest College, Lawrence University, Macalester College, Monmouth College, Ripon College, and St. Olaf College.

ADMITTANCE REQUIREMENTS: Fall: Sophomores and above with at least one year of college Spanish. Spring: Sophomores and above with prior course work in proposed research discipline. One year of college Spanish. Familiarity with statistics and field work methodology highly recommended.

TEACHING METHODS: Fall: Courses are in Spanish; many held at the University of Costa Rica along with Costa Rican students; both U.S. and Costa Rican faculty. Spring: Mostly field work. Orientation in Spanish and English.

EVALUATION: Fall: Based upon papers and final exams in some courses. Spring: Based upon field project and presentation.

CREDITS OFFERED: 16 semester hours per semester.

HOUSING: Students live in private homes with local families and in the field.

DATES: Fall: Approximately September to December. Spring: Approximately February to May.

COSTS: Tuition is determined by home college. Room and board is approximately $850 for the fall semester and $925 for the spring semester. Plan on approximately $50 to $100 a month for local expenses.

YEAR ESTABLISHED: 1969.

NUMBER OF STUDENTS IN 1985: 30 per semester.

APPLY: Fall semester: early deadline is November 15; final deadline is March 30. Spring semester: early deadline is March 30; final deadline is November 15. Abby Schmelling, Program Associate.

■ **THE FLORIDA STATE UNIVERSITY**
College Programs Division
210 Williams Building
Tallahassee, FL 32306
(904) 644-2525

PROGRAM: The university offers an undergraduate summer study program in cooperation with Costarricense-Norteamericano. Students take courses in Spanish language and literature, history of Central America, governments of Central America, anthropology, and sociology. Two 2-hour periods of orientation at Florida State; one 2-hour period at San José.

ADMITTANCE REQUIREMENTS: For sophomore or higher with a minimum GPA of 2.5, some knowledge of Spanish and acceptable academic standing.

TEACHING METHODS: American students are integrated with foreign students. Lectures are in both English and Spanish. A working knowledge of Spanish is important. Classes, seminars, independent study, and field trips to local historic and archaeological sites and museums complement the courses.

EVALUATION: Determined by the Director of Courses at the Central Cultural and resident director, based upon periodic and final exams.

CREDITS OFFERED: Students must enroll in a minimum of 6 semester hours. A maximum of 9 semester hours can be awarded.

HOUSING: Students live with local host families arranged by Central Cultural.

DATES: First week in May through the first week in July.

COSTS: Tuition: Florida students: $30.78 per semester hour; non-Florida students: $109.78 per semester hour; room and board: $1,450.00. Round-trip transportation from Miami is included. Estimated living expenses for the program $200.

YEAR ESTABLISHED: 1968.

NUMBER OF STUDENTS IN 1985: 21.

APPLY: By February 14. Sherry Powell or Dr. Robert Coyne, College Programs Division.

■ **GOSHEN COLLEGE**
Goshen, IN 46526
(219) 533-3161

PROGRAM: Goshen's Study Service Trimester Abroad is a fourteen-week (one trimester), undergraduate program offering students the opportunity to concentrate on the region's language, history, and culture. Courses include history, geography, politics, crosscultural studies, and crosscultural sensitization, i.e., art, music, drama, etc. All students must be enrolled at Goshen the preceding trimester to attend orientation sessions.

ADMITTANCE REQUIREMENTS: For sophomores and above who meet acceptable academic standards.

TEACHING METHODS: Students attend special classes taught by a foreign faculty. Courses involve regular class work, field trips, research projects. Each student must also participate in a work assignment, such as hospital, school, community development project.

EVALUATION: By accompanying Goshen College faculty member(s), based upon class work and assessment of projects.

CREDITS OFFERED: 12 semester hours.

HOUSING: Students live with host families.

DATES: Fall trimester: September 11 through December 16; winter trimester: January 8 through April 14; spring trimester: April 24 through July 28.

COSTS: Tuition: $2,390; room and board: $1,040. Includes round-trip transportation and local field trips.

YEAR ESTABLISHED: 1968.

NUMBER OF STUDENTS IN 1985: 21.

APPLY: One trimester prior to the program. Arlin Hunsberger, Director of International Education.

■ **ORGANIZATION FOR TROPICAL STUDIES, INC. (OTS)**
P.O. Box DM Duke Station
Durham, NC 27706
(919) 684-5774

PROGRAM: The various eight-week graduate programs dealing with biological and ecological problems in tropical studies are held in cooperation with a consortium composed of thirty North American and four Costa Rican institutions of higher learning. OTS has offered more than ninety courses in such diverse subjects as terrestrial ecology, agriculture, biometeorology, earth science, forestry, limnology, and marine biology. Onsite preorientation session.

ADMITTANCE REQUIREMENTS: Applicants must be enrolled in, or accepted for, a graduate study program.

TEACHING METHODS: Most courses are intense, field-oriented research programs.

EVALUATION: By group leaders, fellow students, and course director.

CREDITS OFFERED: 8 semester hours (Graduate).

HOUSING: Students live at OTS field stations.

DATES: Winter and summer sessions.

COSTS: OTS member schools: $850; Non-OTS member schools: $1,450.

YEAR ESTABLISHED: 1964.

NUMBER OF STUDENTS IN 1985:   75.

APPLY: For winter session, October 1; summer session, March 1.

■ **UNIVERSITY OF DELAWARE**
  Newark, DE 19716
  (302) 451-2591

PROGRAM: The Semester in Costa Rica program is a spring undergraduate session that offers courses in history, agriculture, political science, art, music, English, Spanish, anthropology, literature, and Latin American studies.

ADMITTANCE REQUIREMENTS: Sophomore and above with a 3.0 GPA, recommendations of major advisor. Some knowledge of Spanish recommended.

TEACHING METHODS: Students do not take courses in a foreign school but are taught independently by both U.S. and local faculty. Some integration with local students. Lectures, field trips, and some independent study.

EVALUATION: By U.S. faculty, based upon class work, papers, and examinations.

CREDITS OFFERED: 15 semester hours.

HOUSING: With local families.

DATES: Approximately February 1 through mid-May.

COSTS: Approximately $3,900. Covers tuition, room and board, and course-related travel. Does not include round-trip transportation and personal expenses.

YEAR ESTABLISHED: 1983.

NUMBER OF STUDENTS IN 1985: 30.

APPLY: By October 15. Chairman, Department of Language and Literature.

■ **UNIVERSITY OF KANSAS**
  Lawrence, KA 66045
  (913) 864-3742

PROGRAM: Kansas's Costa Rican program, both graduate and undergraduate, is held in cooperation with the University of Costa Rica and the universities of Colorado, Minnesota, Nebraska, New Mexico State, and Colorado State. Participants may avail themselves of the full resources at the University of Costa Rica including an independent study program and the research facilities of the Office of Tropical Studies field stations, the Inter-American Agricultural Institute at Turrialba, the National Archives, and the Institute of Central American Studies. Four-week orientation program in San José (for academic credit) includes field trips to points of special interest.

ADMITTANCE REQUIREMENT: Sophomores and above with a minimum of 30 semester hours, 3.0 GPA, Spanish language proficiency, plus recommendations.

TEACHING METHODS: Students take regular classes at the University of Costa Rica taught in Spanish by local instructors. A U.S. faculty member is present for advising and consultation.

EVALUATION: By local professors, based upon class work, papers, and examinations.

CREDITS OFFERED: 30 to 36 semester hours per year.

HOUSING: During orientation and the first several months of study students live with local families. Beyond that period they may find their own living quarters in cooperation with the University of Costa Rica.

DATES: Approximately late January through November.

COSTS: Academic year: $3,100 includes tuition, room and board, orientation program, and group activities. Does not cover round-trip transportation, local travel, or personal expenses.

YEAR ESTABLISHED: 1960.

NUMBER OF STUDENTS IN 1985:   40.

APPLY: By November 1. Office of Study Abroad, 203 Lippincott.

PANAMA

Population: 2,181,000   **Capital:** Panama City   **Language:** Spanish
Monetary Unit: Balboa   **Government:** Multiparty republic (president)
Religion: 89% Roman Catholic   **Households With Television:** 4%

SELECTED COLLEGES AND UNIVERSITIES

Universidad de Panama
Estafeta Universitaria
Panama

Universidad Santa Maria La Antigua
Avenida 5-15 Catedral
Apartado 2143
Panama 1

Private Catholic school with approximately 1,500 students.

FURTHER INFORMATION

Consulate General of Panama
630 Fifth Avenue
New York, NY 10020
(212) 246-3771

Embassy of Panama
2862 McGill Terrace, NW
Washington, DC 20008
(202) 483-1407

Instituto para la Formacíon y
Aprovechamiento de Recursos
Humanos
Centro de Información y
Documentación (IFARHU/CIDI)
Avenida 7. España
Apartado 6337
Panama 7

Publishes Oportunidades de Estudio en
las Instituciones de Educación Superior
en Panama.

Panama City

■ **THE FLORIDA STATE UNIVERSITY**
College Programs Division
210 Williams Building
Tallahassee, FL 32306
(904) 644-2525

PROGRAM: The university has maintained a Panama Canal branch for the
past three decades. The school provides undergraduates the opportunity to
take a full spring semester course load in which the emphasis of study is on
Central American affairs. Approximately half the students are U.S. citizens,
the remainder are either Panamanian or other foreign nationals. Courses
cover: international affairs, inter-American studies, political science, history,
sociology, anthropology, business, and Spanish.

ADMITTANCE REQUIREMENTS: A minimum GPA of 2.5, plus acceptable
academic standing.

TEACHING METHODS: Courses are in English except when a subject dic-
tates Spanish. A working knowledge of German is also most important.
Classes, seminars, independent study and field trips to local historic and
archaeological sites and museums complement the courses.

EVALUATION: There is a final exam in most courses graded by either
American or foreign faculty member.

CREDITS OFFERED: Students must enroll in a minimum of 12 semester
hours. A maximum of 18 semester hours can be awarded.

HOUSING: Students live with host families.

DATES: First week in January through mid-May.

COSTS: Tuition: Florida students: $30.78 per semester hour; non-Florida students: $109.78 per semester hour; room and board: $2,100.00. Round-trip transportation from Miami is included. Estimated living expenses for the program: $400.

YEAR ESTABLISHED: 1958.

NUMBER OF STUDENTS IN 1985:   Not available.

APPLY: By November. Sherry Powell or Dr. Robert Coyne, College Programs Division.

5.

South America

ARGENTINA

Population: 31,030,000   **Capital:** Buenos Aires   **Language:** Spanish
Monetary Unit: Austral   **Government:** Federal republic (president)
Religion: 93% Roman Catholic   **Households With Television:** 7%

SELECTED COLLEGES AND UNIVERSITIES

Universidad de Buenos Aires
Ciudad Universitaria
1428 Buenos Aires

Universidad Nacional de Córdoba
Obispo Sanabria 242
5000 Córdoba

FURTHER INFORMATION

Consulate General of Argentina
12 West 56th Street
New York, NY 10019
(212) 397-1400

Embassy of Argentina
1600 New Hampshire Avenue, NW
Washington, DC 20009
(202) 387-0705

Secretaria de Planeamiento
de la Nación
25 de Mayo 459
1002 Buenos Aires

Publishes Catálogo de Cursos
Internacionales e Interamericanos.

Buenos Aires

■ **THE AMERICAN UNIVERSITY**
Washington, DC 20016
(202) 885-3800

PROGRAM: Semester in Argentina is a liberal arts/social science program held in cooperation with Catholic University. Courses include history, fine arts, languages, political science, etc. Field trips to Brazil are often scheduled. Preorientation at American University (usually over a weekend) and onsite.

ADMITTANCE REQUIREMENTS: Juniors and seniors with a "B" average or better.

TEACHING METHODS: Students are accompanied by a resident professor from American University who schedules seminars with public officials in addition to his or her own lectures. Foreign faculty members complement these lectures and teach specialized courses. Students also intern two days a week with one of the many local government or private organizations.

EVALUATION: Regular exams, midterms and finals, in addition to short seminar papers.

CREDITS OFFERED: 15 to 17 semester hours.

HOUSING: A combination of possibilities from local apartments to living with local families.

DATES: First semester: September to December; second semester: January to May.

COSTS: Tuition: $4,100 per semester; room and board: $2,000 per semester. Scholarships from American University available.

YEAR ESTABLISHED: Not available.

NUMBER OF STUDENTS IN 1985:   Not available.

APPLY: Rolling admissions. Apply 6 to 8 months prior to start of semester to: Dr. David C. Brown, Dean, Washington Semester and Study Program Abroad.

BRAZIL

Population: 138,403,000   **Capital:** Brasília   **Language:** Portuguese
Monetary Unit: Cruzeiro   **Government:** Multiparty federal republic (president)
Religion: 88% Roman Catholic   **Households With Television:** 55%

SELECTED COLLEGES AND UNIVERSITIES

Université de Brasília
Caixa Postal 15-2766
70000 Brasilia, D.F.

Université de Sao Paulo
Avenida Pádua Dias
13400 Piracicaba,
Sao Paulo

FURTHER INFORMATION

Consulate General of Brazil
630 Fifth Avenue
New York, NY 10020
(212) 757-3080

Embassy of Brazil
3006 Massachusetts Avenue, NW
Washington, DC 20008
(202) 745-2797

Rio de Janeiro

■ UNIVERSITY OF ARIZONA
Tucson, AZ 85721
(602) 621-4819

PROGRAM: The Semester in Brazil is an undergraduate program held in cooperation with the Pontificia Universidade Catolica do Rio de Janeiro, Arizona State University, and Northern Arizona University. Students take a general range of liberal arts courses with a concentration on Portuguese language studies. Onsite orientation.

ADMITTANCE REQUIREMENTS: For sophomores and above in good standing with their home institution plus four semesters of college Portuguese or the equivalent.

TEACHING METHODS: Students attend regular academic and special courses taught by both U.S. and foreign faculty. Classes are integrated with foreign students. Field trips complement course of study.

EVALUATION: Based upon student evaluations, reports from the director of each program, periodic and final examinations.

CREDITS OFFERED: 4 semester hours for summer session regular academic year varies.

HOUSING: Students live with families or in efficiency-type apartments.

DATES: Early July through December.

COSTS: Students pay regular tuition, if any, to U of A, plus approximately $1,500 for Brazil semester, room and board. Does not cover round-trip transportation, local travel, and personal expenses.

YEAR ESTABLISHED: 1977.

NUMBER OF STUDENTS IN 1985: 15.

APPLY: By June 1. Eugene von Teuber, Coordinator of International Studies, Rm.# 209, Robert L. Nugent Building.

Sao Paulo

■ **THE CALIFORNIA STATE UNIVERSITY**
400 Golden Shore
Long Beach, CA 90802
(213) 590-5655

PROGRAM: The CSU International Program in Brazil, held in cooperation with the University of Sao Paulo and Stanford University, is a full academic year undergraduate and graduate opportunity to study at the University of Sao Paulo. Students elect from the wide range of university course offerings supplemented by special CSU programs. One-week orientation in Brazil.

ADMITTANCE REQUIREMENTS: Must be enrolled at a CSU campus. Juniors and above including graduate students. 3.0 GPA and two years of college Portuguese.

TEACHING METHODS: Students take a combination of regular academic courses and supplemental program-sponsored courses taught by foreign faculty.

EVALUATION: By foreign faculty and CSU resident director based upon periodic and final examinations.

CREDITS OFFERED: 30 semester hours per year or 45 quarter units.

HOUSING: In dormitories and private apartments.

DATES: Full year, from June 28 to the following June 26.

COSTS: Tuition: $0 (residents); $3,600 (nonresidents); room and board: $2,000. Does not include round-trip transportation and living expenses (estimated at approximately $2,875 per year).

YEAR ESTABLISHED: 1979.

NUMBER OF STUDENTS IN 1985: 3.

APPLY: By February 1. Dr. Kibbey M. Horne, Director of International Programs.

■ **THE EXPERIMENT IN INTERNATIONAL LIVING**
Kipling Road
Brattleboro, VT 05301-0676
(800)451-4465

PROGRAM: The College Semester Abroad program is designed to allow students to become immersed in a foreign culture by living with a local family and exploring individual personal and educational interests under professional guidance. The Brazil program covers: intensive language study, seminar on Brazilian life and culture and rural development, history and politics, geography and economics, arts and humanities, social anthropology, and an independent study project. Orientation in Brattleboro and Sao Paulo. Three-week stay in Rio de Janeiro.

ADMITTANCE REQUIREMENT: Sophomore standing or above and acceptable academic credentials. No language prerequisite.

TEACHING METHODS: Students work directly with their American instructors in planning and evaluating their individual program. "The semester builds from the more structured language training and lectures and discussions on local life and culture to the independent study project."

EVALUATION: By individual students and their instructor/advisors based on independent project, papers, reports, and examinations. Periodic meetings during the program and for several days at the conclusion.

CREDITS OFFERED: Up to 16 semester hours.

HOUSING: Students live as family members with their host families.

DATES: Approximately, fall semester: September through December; spring semester: January through May.

COSTS: $6,300 includes tuition, room and board, all fees local travel, and round-trip transportation from Brattleboro, Vermont.

YEAR ESTABLISHED: 1976.

NUMBER OF STUDENTS IN 1985: 13.

APPLY: For fall semester by May 15; spring semester by November 15. Admissions Office, College Semester Abroad.

COLOMBIA

Population: 28,231,000   **Capital:** Bogotá: **Language:** Spanish
Monetary Unit: Peso   **Government:** Unitary multiparty republic (president)
Religion: 97% Roman Catholic   **Households With Television:** 2%

SELECTED COLLEGES AND UNIVERSITIES:

Universidad de Antioquia
Medellín, Antioquia

Universidad Nacional de Colombia
Cuidad Universitaria
Bogotá

FURTHER INFORMATION

Consulate General of Colombia
10 East 46th Street
New York, NY 10017
(212) 949-9898

Embassy of Colombia
2118 Leroy Place, NW
Washington, DC 20008
(202) 387-8338

Servicio Nacional de Aprendizaje
Carrera 14 n.
13-88, Bogotá

Publishes: Programas y Cursos
Internacionales.

Bogotá

■ **GREAT LAKES COLLEGES ASSOCIATION**
220 Collingwood, Suite 240
Ann Arbor, MI 48103
(312) 263-5000

PROGRAM: The GLCA Latin America Program offers a summer, a semester, or a full-year program primarily for undergraduates with some graduate opportunities. It is held in cooperation with the Universidad de los Andes, Pontificia Universidad de la Javeriana, Universidad Pedagógica Nacional, and Escuela Superior de Administración Pública, as well as with the member colleges of the GLCA: Albion College, Antioch College, Denison College, DePauw University, Earlham College, Hope College, Houghton College, Kalamazoo College, Kenyon College, Oberlin College, Ohio Wesleyan University, Wabash College, and The College of Wooster. All programs offer a wide range of courses at the GLCA's local Center including Latin American studies, Spanish language, history, art, political science, literature, sociology, anthropology. Students also have the option of taking a full range of university classes at the cooperating Colombian schools. There is a five-day onsite orientation.

ADMITTANCE REQUIREMENTS: Semester programs: Junior, senior, or graduate student with strong recommendations and approval of major advisor. Minimum through intermediate-level Spanish. In 1985 the average GPA was 3.2. Summer Program: Junior, senior, or graduate student with strong recommendations from major advisor.

TEACHING METHODS: All courses at the Center and the local universities are taught in Spanish by Colombian faculty. University students are fully integrated with local students. Courses are supplemented with local field trips, museums, etc. Students can also take advantage of internships and volunteer opportunities. Also, there are "special classes to fill gaps in students' knowledge of Latin American realities."

EVALUATION: Depends upon course; based on performance, papers, and examinations by local faculty.

CREDITS OFFERED: Summer: minimum of 6 semester hours; maximum of 12. Semester: minimum of 12 semester hours; maximum of 18.

HOUSING: All students live with host families.

DATES: Summer: June 9 through August 8. Teachers' Workshop: July 2 through August 1. Fall semester: August 25 through December 12. Spring semester: January 12 through May 8.

COSTS: Summer: $1,890; fall and spring semester: $4,090; includes tuition, and room and board. Round-trip transportation not included. Estimated living expenses, $900 for a fifteen-week semester.

YEAR ESTABLISHED: 1964.

NUMBER OF STUDENTS IN 1985: 32.

APPLY: Summer only: April 15; summer and fall: March 31; fall and full year: May 15; spring semester: October 15. Diane K. Snell, Director, GLCA Latin American Program, Kenyon College, Gambier, OH 43022 (614) 427-4733.

ECUADOR

Population: 9,647,000   **Capital:** Quito   **Language:** Spanish
Monetary Unit: Sucre   **Government:** Unitary multiparty republic (president)
Religion: 92% Roman Catholic   **Households with Television:** 2%

SELECTED COLLEGES AND UNIVERSITIES

Universidad Central del Ecuador
Quito

Universidad de Guayaquil
Guayaquil

FURTHER INFORMATION

Consulate General of Ecuador
1270 Avenue of the Americas
New York, NY 10020
(212) 683-7555

Embassy of Equador
2535 15th Street, NW
Washington, DC 20009
(202) 234-7200

Quito

■ **THE EXPERIMENT IN INTERNATIONAL LIVING**
Kipling Road
Brattleboro, VT 05301
(800) 451-4465

PROGRAM: The College Semester Abroad program is designed to allow undergraduate students to become immersed in a foreign culture by living with a local family and exploring individual personal and educational interests under professional guidance. Students on the Ecuador program spend most of their stay in Quito and Otavalo. Part of the semester is spent at a location appropriate to a field study project. Courses cover intensive language study, seminar on Ecuador life and culture, history and politics, geography and economics, arts and humanities, social anthropology, methods and techniques of field work, and an independent study project. One-week orientation in Brattleboro and Quito.

ADMITTANCE REQUIREMENTS: Sophomore standing or above and accept-able academic credentials. No language requirement.

TEACHING METHODS: Students work directly with their American in-structors-advisors in planning and evaluating their individual program. Nonlanguage courses are in English. "The semester builds from the more structured language training and lectures and discussions on local life and culture to the independent study project."

EVALUATION: By individual students and their instructor-advisors based on independent project, papers, reports, and examinations. Periodic meet-ings during the program and for several days at the conclusion.

CREDITS OFFERED: 16 semester hours.

HOUSING: Students live as family members with their host families.

DATES: Approximately, fall semester: September through December; spring semester: January through May.

COSTS: $5,900 includes tuition, room and board, all fees, local travel, and round-trip transportation from Brattleboro.

YEAR ESTABLISHED: Not available.

NUMBER OF STUDENTS in 1985:   Not available.

APPLY: For fall semester by May 15; spring semester by November 15. Admissions Office, College Semester Abroad.

PARAGUAY

Population: 3,381,000   **Capital:** Asunción   **Languages:** Spanish and Guarani
Monetary Unit: Paraguayan guarani   **Government:** Republic (president)
Religion: 96% Roman Catholic   **Households With Television:** 1%

SELECTED COLLEGES AND UNIVERSITIES

Universidad Católica "Nuestra Señora de la Asunción"
Independencia Nacional y Comuneros
Asunción

Private school with about 8,000 students.

Universidad Nacional de Asunción
España 1098
Asunción

FURTHER INFORMATION

Consulate General of Paraguay
1 World Trade Center, Suite 1609
New York, NY 10048
(212) 432-0733

Embassy of Paraguay
2400 Massachusetts Avenue, NW
Washington, DC 20008
(202) 483-6960

Asunción

■ **UNIVERSITY OF KANSAS**
Lawrence, KA 66045
(913) 864-3742

PROGRAM: The Kansas Paraguay Program, both graduate and undergraduate, is held in cooperation with the Universidad Nacional and Universidad Católica. Participants may avail themselves of the full resources at either of the universities or may enroll at the Institute of Languages or the Institute of Guarani to enhance their knowledge of the Guarani language.

ADMITTANCE REQUIREMENTS: Sophomores and above with a minimum of 30 semester hours, 3.0 GPA, Spanish language proficiency, plus recommendations.

TEACHING METHODS: Students take regular classes at the universities taught in Spanish by local instructors. A U.S. faculty member is present for advising and consultation.

EVALUATION: By local professors, based upon class work, papers, and examinations.

CREDITS OFFERED: 30 to 36 semester hours per year.

HOUSING: Students are encouraged to live with local families. They also have the option of arranging separate housing.

DATES: Approximately early March through November.

COSTS: Academic year: $3,100 includes tuition and room and board. Does not cover round-trip transportation, local travel, or personal expenses.

YEAR ESTABLISHED: 1982.

NUMBER OF STUDENTS IN 1985: 11.

APPLY: By November 1. Office of Study Abroad, 203 Lippincott.

PERÚ

Population: 20,207,000   **Capital:** Lima   **Languages:** Spanish and Quechua
Monetary Unit: Inti   **Government:** Unitary multiparty republic (president)
Religion: 92% Roman Catholic   **Households With Television:** 1%

SELECTED COLLEGES AND UNIVERSITIES

La Escuela de Administración de
Negocios Para Graduados (ESAN)
Apartado 1846
Lima 100

Universidad de Piura
Apartado Aereo 353
Piura

Pontificia Universidad Católica
del Perú
Apartado 1761
Lima

Universidad Nacional de la Ingeniería
Apartado 1301
Lima

FURTHER INFORMATION

Consulate General of Perú
805 Third Avenue
New York, NY 10022
(212) 644-2850

Ministerio de Educación Pública
Parque Universitario
Lima

Embassy of Perú
1700 Massachusetts Avenue, NW
Washington, DC 20036
(202) 833-9860

Lima

■ **THE CALIFORNIA STATE UNIVERSITY**
400 Golden Shore
Long Beach, CA 90802
(213) 590-5655

PROGRAM: The CSU International Program in Perú, held at the Pontifica Universidad Católica del Perú, is a full-academic-year undergraduate and graduate opportunity to study at the Perúvian university. The program is "best suited for students interested in Andean anthropology, Latin American studies, sociology, history, economics, and literature." One-week orientation in Lima.

ADMITTANCE REQUIREMENTS: Must be enrolled at a CSU campus. Juniors and above, including graduate students. 3.0 GPA with two years of college Spanish.

TEACHING METHODS: Students take a combination of regular academic courses in Spanish and supplemental program-sponsored (by the SOCCIS-Indiana consortium) classes taught by foreign faculty.

EVALUATION: By foreign faculty and CSU resident director based upon periodic and final examinations.

CREDITS OFFERED: 30 semester hours per year or 45 quarter units.

HOUSING: In dormitories and private apartments.

DATES: Approximately July 11 through the following July 5.

COSTS: Tuition: $0 (residents); $3,600 (nonresidents); room and board: $3,025. Does not include round-trip transportation and living expenses (estimated at $2,030 per year).

YEAR ESTABLISHED: 1978.

NUMBER OF STUDENTS IN 1985:   1.

APPLY: By February 1. Dr. Kibbey M. Horne, Director of International Programs.

■ **PENNSYLVANIA STATE UNIVERSITY**
Office of Education Abroad Programs
222 Boucke Building
University Park, PA 16802
(814) 865-7681

PROGRAM: The Business Administration Program at ESAN is a spring semester program held in cooperation with La Escuela de Administración de Negocios Para Graduados (ESAN). The program focuses on the problems of economic development and growth in Latin America. Courses cover Perúvian culture, international business, business administration and economics, and the Spanish language. Orientation at Penn State.

ADMITTANCE REQUIREMENTS: Juniors and seniors with a 2.5 GPA, good academic standing, and "must show evidence of maturity, stability, adaptability, self-discipline, and a strong academic motivation." Some specific course prerequisites.

TEACHING METHODS: The program is designed for American students and taught by the ESAN faculty. All lectures are in English. Americans are not integrated with local students.

EVALUATION: By course instructors, based upon class work, papers, and examinations.

CREDITS OFFERED: 15 semester hours.

HOUSING: Students live with Perúvian families, usually two or more students per family.

DATES: Mid-January through early May.

COSTS: Students pay the same as at the University Park Campus. 1986-87 tuition per semester was $2,250 for state residents; $5,150 for nonresidents; room and board: $2,750 per semester. Plus a $100 nonrefundable program fee.

YEAR ESTABLISHED: 1975.

NUMBER OF STUDENTS IN 1986:   6.

APPLY: By October 15.

6.

The Caribbean

DOMINICAN REPUBLIC

Population: 6,386,000   **Capital:** Santo Domingo   **Language:** Spanish
Monetary Unit: Dominican peso   **Government:** Multiparty republic (president)
Religion: 94% Roman Catholic   **Households With Television:** 2%

COLLEGES AND UNIVERSITIES

Instituto Cultural
Dominico Americano
Abraham Lincoln 21
Santo Domingo

Courses in both Spanish and English.

Universidad Autónoma de
Santo Domingo
Avenida Alma Mater
Cuidad Universitaria
Santo Domingo

This is the oldest university in the Americas, founded in 1538. More than 20,000 students now attend this public institution. Courses only in Spanish.

FURTHER INFORMATION

Consulate General of the
Dominican Republic
1270 Avenue of the Americas
New York, NY 10022
(212) 265-0630

Embassy of the Dominican Republic
1715 22nd Street, NW
Washington, DC 20008
(202) 332-6280

Santa Domingo

■ **GOSHEN COLLEGE**
Goshen, IN 46526
(219) 533-3161

PROGRAM: Goshen's Study Service Trimester Abroad is a fourteen-week (one trimester), undergraduate program offering students the opportunity to concentrate on the region's language, history, and culture. Courses include history, geography, politics, crosscultural studies, and crosscultural sensitization, i.e., art, music, drama, etc. All students must be enrolled at Goshen the preceding trimester to attend orientation sessions.

ADMITTANCE REQUIREMENTS: For sophomores and above who meet acceptable academic standards.

TEACHING METHODS: Students attend special classes taught by a foreign faculty. Courses involve regular class work, field trips, research projects. Each student must also participate in a work assignment, such as hospital, school, community development project.

EVALUATION: By accompanying Goshen College faculty member(s) based upon class work and assessment of projects.

CREDITS OFFERED: 12 semester hours.

HOUSING: Students live with host families.

DATES: Fall trimester: September 11 through December 16; winter trimester: January 8 through April 14; spring trimester: April 24 through July 28.

COSTS: Tuition: $2,390; room and board: $1,040. Includes round-trip transportation and local field trips.

YEAR ESTABLISHED: 1985.

NUMBER OF STUDENTS IN 1985: 21.

APPLY: One trimester prior to the program. Arlin Hunsberger, Director of International Education.

HAITI

Population: 5,427,000   **Capital:** Port-au-Prince   **Language:** French
Monetary Unit: Gourde   **Government:** Republic (president and national council)
Religion: 80% Roman Catholic   **Households With Television:** Less than 1%

UNIVERSITY

University d'État d'Haiti
Plâce des Heros de l'Indepéndance
Port-au-Prince

FURTHER INFORMATION

Consulate General of Haiti
60 East 42nd Street
New York, NY 10017
(212) 697-9767

Embassy of Haiti
2311 Massachusetts Avenue, NW
Washington, DC 20008
(202) 332-4090

Port-au-Prince

■ **GOSHEN COLLEGE**
Goshen, IN 46526
(219) 533-3161

PROGRAM: Goshen's Study Service Trimester Abroad is a fourteen-week (one trimester), undergraduate program offering students the opportunity to concentrate on the region's language, history, and culture. Courses include history, geography, politics, crosscultural studies, and crosscultural sensitization, i.e., art, music, drama, etc. All students must be enrolled at Goshen the preceding trimester to attend orientation sessions.

ADMITTANCE REQUIREMENTS: For sophomores and above who meet acceptable academic standards.

TEACHING METHODS: Students attend special classes taught by a foreign faculty. Courses involve regular class work, field trips, research projects. Each student must also participate in a work assignment, such as hospital, school, community development project.

EVALUATION: By accompanying Goshen College faculty member(s), based upon class work and assessment of projects.

CREDITS OFFERED: 12 semester hours.

HOUSING: Students live with host families.

DATES: Fall trimester: September 11 through December 16; winter trimester: January 8 through April 14; spring trimester: April 24 through July 28.

COSTS: Tuition: $2,390; room and board: $1,040. Includes round-trip transportation and local field trips.

YEAR ESTABLISHED: 1968.

NUMBER OF STUDENTS IN 1985:   Not available.

APPLY: One trimester prior to the program. Arlin Hunsberger, Director of International Education.

JAMAICA

Population: 2,348,000   **Capital:** Kingston   **Language:** English
Monetary Unit: Jamaican dollar   **Government:** Parliamentary state
(British monarch and Jamaican prime minister)   **Religion:** 71% Protestant
Households With Television: 2%

UNIVERSITY

University of the West Indies
Mona
Kingston 7

FURTHER INFORMATION

Consulate General of Jamaica
866 Second Avenue
New York, NY 10017
(212) 935-9000

Embassy of Jamaica
1850 K Street, NW
Suite 355
Washington, DC 20006
(202) 452-0660

More Than One City

■ **ROGER WILLIAMS COLLEGE**
  Bristol, RI 02809
  (401) 253-1040

PROGRAM: The Tropical Ecology of Jamaica Program is a spring semester, undergraduate program that concentrates on local marine biology, tropical reef ecology, and the general ecology of this Caribbean island. On-campus preorientation.

ADMITTANCE REQUIREMENTS: Open admission.

TEACHING METHODS: Small classes (approximately seven students) are taught by Roger Williams faculty. Field trips represent a major part of the class activities.

EVALUATION: Periodic exams and papers graded by Roger Williams faculty.

CREDITS OFFERED: Three semester course credits.

HOUSING: Local housing is arranged by the college.

DATES: Approximately early January through May.

COSTS: $975, includes tuition, room and board, round-trip transportation, and local travel.

YEAR ESTABLISHED: 1978.

NUMBER OF STUDENTS IN 1985:   10.

APPLY: During the preceding semester. Dr. Mark Gould, Department of Natural Science.

NOTE: Interfuture (535 Fifth Avenue, Suite # 3103, New York, NY 10017) sponsors individual research projects designed to be carried out by undergraduates. Participants investigate selected programs affecting the future of internationalism, the habitat, or the individual and society. In cooperation with the Association of Caribbean Universities and Research Institutions.

Kingston

■ **THE AMERICAN UNIVERSITY**
Washington, DC 20016
(202) 885-3800

PROGRAM: A Semester in the Caribbean is a liberal arts/social science program held in cooperation with the University of the West Indies. Courses include history, fine arts, languages, political science, etc. Field trips to local sites are often scheduled. Preorientation at American University (usually over a weekend) and onsite.

ADMITTANCE REQUIREMENTS: Juniors and seniors with a GPA of at least 3.0.

TEACHING METHODS: Students are accompanied by a resident professor from American University who schedules seminars with public officials in addition to his or her own lectures. Foreign faculty members complement these lectures and teach specialized courses. Students also intern two days a week with one of the many local government or private organizations.

EVALUATION: Regular exams, midterms and finals, in addition to short seminar papers.

CREDITS OFFERED: 15 to 17 semester hours.

HOUSING: A combination of possibilities from local apartments to living with local families.

DATES: Fall semester: September to December; spring semester: January to May.

COSTS: Tuition: $4,100 per semester; room and board: $2,000 per semester. Scholarships from American University available.

YEAR ESTABLISHED: 1985.

NUMBER OF STUDENTS IN 1985: 30.

APPLY: Rolling admissions; apply 6 to 8 months prior to start of semester. Dr. David C. Brown, Dean, Washington Semester and Study Program Abroad.

■ **UNIVERSITY OF MIAMI**
Coral Gables, FL 33124
(305) 284-4087

PROGRAM: Field Study in Jamaica is a five-week undergraduate and graduate program held in cooperation with the University of the West Indies. Courses cover geography, geology, climatology, sociology, anthropology, history, and urban studies. Students visit urban squatter settlements, sugar plantations, rum factory, bauxite mine, peasant farm, and limestone caves. Three weeks of initial coursework are held in Miami, followed by two weeks in Jamaica.

ADMITTANCE REQUIREMENTS: "Any university student is welcome."

TEACHING METHODS: Special lectures given by both Miami and University of the West Indies faculty; also, seminars, lectures, and field trips; in English.

EVALUATION: Examinations by University of Miami faculty.

CREDITS OFFERED: 3 to 6 semester hours.

HOUSING: Dormitories.

DATES: June 25 through August 1.

COSTS: Tuition and room and board: $696 (three credits); $1,392 (six credits). Plus $595 for round-trip air fare from Miami and local transportation in Jamaica. Does not include personal expenses.

YEAR ESTABLISHED: 1986.

NUMBER OF STUDENTS IN 1986:   10.

APPLY: By June 1. Dr. Thomas D. Boswell, Department of Geography.

PUERTO RICO

Population: 3,287,00   **Capital:** San Juan   **Languages:** Spanish and English
Monetary Unit: U.S. dollar   **Government:** Self-governing commonwealth
associated with the United States (U.S. president and Puerto Rican governor)
Religion: 85% Roman Catholic   **Households With Television:** 8%

SELECTED COLLEGES AND UNIVERSITIES

Inter-American
University of Puerto Rico
P.O. Box 1293
Hato Rey, PR 00936
(809) 758-8000

Universidad de Puerto Rico
Ponce de Leon Avenida, Stop 38,
Rio Piedras, PR 00931
(809) 758-3350

Both schools are accredited by the Middle States Association of Colleges and Universities and offer courses in both Spanish and English.

FURTHER INFORMATION

Economic Development Administration
Tourism Division
1290 Avenue of the Americas
New York, NY 10017
(212) 245-1200

San Juan

■ **STATE UNIVERSITY OF NEW YORK AT OSWEGO**
   Oswego, NY 13126
   (315) 341-2118

PROGRAM: SUNY at Oswego's University of Puerto Rico Exchange is a semester or full-academic-year undergraduate program. Students take regular classes at the university's Rio Piedras campus. Courses cover the humanities, social sciences, political science, business administration, and education.

ADMITTANCE REQUIREMENTS: Sophomore standing, 2.5 GPA, and Spanish language proficiency.

TEACHING METHODS: Courses are taught by the UPR faculty.

EVALUATION: Based on work in class, papers and final exams.

CREDITS OFFERED: 12 to 15 semester hours per semester.

HOUSING: Students live in UPR dormitories.

DATES: Fall semester: mid-August through mid-December; spring semester: mid-January through mid-May.

COSTS: $1,950 per semester; $3,550 for full academic year. Includes tuition, room and board, local field trips, and round-trip transportation from New York. Does not cover personal expenses, travel and SUNY tuition and fees ($687.50 per semester for New York residents; $1,612.50 for nonresidents.)

YEAR ESTABLISHED: 1984.

NUMBER OF STUDENTS IN 1985:   5.

APPLY: By April 1 for fall semester; November 1 for spring semester. Dr. José R. Pérez, Director, International Education, Overseas Academic Programs.

Mayagüez

■ **STATE UNIVERSITY OF NEW YORK AT OSWEGO**
Oswego, NY 13126
(315) 341-2118

PROGRAM: Business Administration Exchange with the University of Puerto Rico-Mayagüez is a semester or full-academic-year undergraduate program designed for those interested in refining their Spanish competencies with a specific focus on Latin American business practices and terminology. Courses cover economics, law, industrial relations, management, statistics, computer data processing, and taxation.

ADMITTANCE REQUIREMENTS: Sophomore standing, 2.5 GPA with at least 12 credits in business administration and Spanish language proficiency.

TEACHING METHODS: Courses are taught by the UPR faculty.

EVALUATION: Based on work in class, papers and final exams.

CREDITS OFFERED: 12 to 18 credit hours per semester.

HOUSING: The university housing office assists students in finding housing in the community.

DATES: Fall semester: mid-August through mid-December; spring semester: mid-January through mid-May.

COSTS: Tuition is free for SUNY students. Non-SUNY students: NY State residents, $687.50; nonresidents, $1,612.50. Does not include room and board, local field trips, and round-trip transportation from New York, or personal expenses.

YEAR ESTABLISHED: 1964.

NUMBER OF STUDENTS IN 1985:   10.

APPLY: By April 1 for fall semester; November 1 for spring semester. Dr. José R. Pérez, Director, International Education, Overseas Academic Programs.

PART FOUR

EUROPE

7.

Europe

MORE THAN ONE COUNTRY

■ **ANTIOCH COLLEGE**
P.O. Box 404
Yellow Springs, OH 43587
(513) 767-1031

PROGRAM: The European Term in Comparative Urban Studies is held in cooperation with the Great Lakes College Association and offers a three-month multidisciplinary program in which students explore the similarities and differences between selected cities in Yugoslavia, the Netherlands, and England. Students carry out their own approved research project in a particular comparative study. Two- to three-day orientation in Philadelphia.

ADMITTANCE REQUIREMENTS: Good academic standing, two years of undergraduate study, and "academic experience in social sciences and concern about the issues important to cities and urban life."

CREDITS OFFERED: 20 quarter credits.

TEACHING METHODS: Students participate as a group accompanied by an academic director and two teaching assistants. Students meet with urban specialists and discuss and observe each city then spend the final month in England completing their individual field research project.

EVALUATION: By academic director, based on research project and individual participation.

HOUSING: In a pension or hotel in Yugoslavia and the Netherlands; with local families or in flats when in London.

COSTS: $4,925 includes tuition, room and board, round-trip transportation from New York, and field-related travel. Does not cover room and board during independent study period or personal expenses.

DATES: September 16 through December 5.

YEAR ESTABLISHED: 1973.

NUMBER OF STUDENTS IN 1985: 31.

APPLY: By March 1. International study offices at Antioch or any GLCA campus.

■ **ASSOCIATED COLLEGES OF THE MIDWEST**
   18 South Michigan Avenue, Suite 1010
   Chicago, IL 60603
   (313) 264-5000

PROGRAM: The Arts of London and Florence is a spring semester undergraduate program that divides equally between the two major cities spending eight weeks in each. Participants study the Italian language and culture, architecture, art, history, literature, music, theater, and Renaissance studies.

ADMITTANCE REQUIREMENTS: Sophomores and above in good academic standing with some background in the humanities. No language requirement, but knowledge of Italian is recommended.

CREDITS OFFERED: 16 semester hours.

TEACHING METHODS: Students participate as a group and are instructed by both U.S. and foreign faculty members in each city. Instruction is in English.

EVALUATION: By course instructors based on class work, papers, and examinations.

HOUSING: In a pension when in Florence and with local families or in flats in London.

COSTS: $1,350 includes tuition, room and some board. Does not cover round-trip transportation, some meals, and personal expenses.

DATES: February 3 through May 30.

YEAR ESTABLISHED: 1971.

NUMBER OF STUDENTS IN 1985: Not available.

APPLY: By October 1. Christine Swanson, or participating institutions.

■ **BALDWIN-WALLACE COLLEGE**
Berea, OH 44017
(216) 826-2231

PROGRAM: Seminar in Europe combines a three-week preorientation on the Baldwin-Wallace campus with a seven-week cultural/academic tour of Greece, Italy, Austria, Germany, France, and England. The program concentrates on the humanities and includes visits "to the sites of major importance in the development of Western culture." Includes an introduction to "the field of intercultural communications," with an emphasis on American values and how they are influenced by other cultures.

ADMITTANCE REQUIREMENTS: Any student of an accredited institution in good academic standing.

TEACHING METHODS: Seminar is conducted in English by American faculty members. Includes a variety of readings with emphasis on the classics, trips to museums, regional sites, field trips, etc. A diary must be kept.

EVALUATION: By program leaders, based upon term paper, graded diary, and class participation.

CREDITS OFFERED: 1 quarter (12 semester hours) credit.

HOUSING: In first-class hotels.

DATES: Offered every other year. 1987: March 30 to April 17 on Baldwin-Wallace campus; April 22 to June 8 European tour.

COSTS: Regular Baldwin-Wallace college tuition and room and board, plus approximately $1,700 (includes all tour expenses from New York and daily meal allowance of $7.00). Financial aid available from Baldwin-Wallace College.

YEAR ESTABLISHED: 1975.

NUMBER OF STUDENTS IN 1985: 35.

APPLY: By October 1. Dorothy Hunter, International Studies Office.

■ **INSTITUTE OF EUROPEAN STUDIES**
223 West Ohio Street
Chicago, IL 60610
(313) 944-1750

PROGRAM: The European Economic Community Program is either a spring or fall semester undergraduate program that incorporates extensive visits to Belgium, France, and West Germany, as well as ten days of program-related travel in Belgium, France, and Luxembourg. Students study German, economics, history, and political science as they relate to the questions and problems of the EEC. Three-day orientation in Freiberg.

ADMITTANCE REQUIREMENTS: Juniors and seniors in good academic standing with some background in the economics, contemporary European history, or comparative government. No language requirement, but knowledge of German is helpful.

CREDITS OFFERED: 15 semester hours.

TEACHING METHODS: Students participate as a group and are instructed by both U.S. and foreign faculty members in each city. Instruction is in English.

EVALUATION: By course instructors, based on class work, papers, and examinations.

HOUSING: Students live in furnished rooms.

COSTS: $3,875 includes tuition and room and board. Does not cover round-trip transportation or personal expenses. Scholarships are available.

DATES: Fall program: September 10 through mid-December; spring program: January 15 through May 30.

YEAR ESTABLISHED: 1981.

NUMBER OF STUDENTS IN 1985: Not available.

APPLY: For fall program by May 1; spring by November 15.

■ **ROGER WILLIAMS COLLEGE**
Bristol, RI 02809
(401) 253-1040, ext. 2247

PROGRAM: The Great Cities Program is a four-week undergraduate excursion to several of Europe's "great cities." The history of the particular city as well as the cultural institutions of the host country are explored in some depth. Students select programs based on which country they would like to visit. Countries include Great Britain, Israel, France, and Greece.

ADMITTANCE REQUIREMENTS: None.

TEACHING METHODS: Students are taught by Roger Williams faculty with some lectures by local experts; lectures are in English. Field trips to museums, historic and archaeological sites, plays, concerts, tours, etc.

EVALUATION: By Roger Williams College instructors, based on papers, exams, students' journals, etc.

CREDITS OFFERED: Students take two courses totaling 6 semester hours.

HOUSING: Students stay in hotels.

DATES: In January. The London tour alternates years with Israel and Paris. (London scheduled for 1987, 1989, etc.) Greece is in late May through mid-July.

COSTS: Vary. The 1987 London program will be approximately $1,400, including round-trip transportation, room and board, and local travel.

YEAR ESTABLISHED: 1983.

NUMBER OF STUDENTS IN 1985: 10.

APPLY: By November 1 for January programs; mid-April for Greece program. Late applications accepted if space is available. Dr. Charles A. Watson, Division of the Humanities.

■ **SANTA BARBARA CITY COLLEGE**
   721 Cliff Drive
   Santa Barbara, CA 93109
   (805) 965-0581

PROGRAM: Centers of European Art is a fall semester undergraduate program held in Paris, Amsterdam, and Florence. Courses cover the history and development of art from pre-Christian times through the present. Two-to five-day period of orientation on the SBCC campus.

ADMITTANCE REQUIREMENTS: Acceptable academic credentials plus 12 units of college credit including freshman level English and a basic drawing course.

TEACHING METHODS: Students attend regular classes often conducted by SBCC professors and occasional guest lecturers. Courses are supplemented with field trips to local museums and cultural and historic sites. Some independent study.

EVALUATION: By class professors, based upon papers and periodic examinations. Students also complete evaluation forms upon completion of the program and comment on faculty, facilities, group leaders, and program in general.

CREDITS OFFERED: 16 semester hours.

HOUSING: Students live in international student facilities similar to dormitories.

DATES: Dates vary from year to year. Approximately from mid-September to mid-December.

COSTS: $3,500 including tuition, room and board, round-trip transportation, and local travel.

YEAR ESTABLISHED: 1984.

NUMBER OF STUDENTS IN 1985: 40.

APPLY: By mid-November. Mr. John Romo, Dean of Instructional Services.

■ **UNIVERSITY OF THE PACIFIC**
McGeorge School of Law
3200 Fifth Avenue
Sacramento, CA 95817
(916) 739-7195

PROGRAM: The International Law Internship program is a fall semester post-juris doctor program consisting of six weeks of concentrated study in Salzburg, Austria, followed by a two-and-a-half-month internship experience with a private law firm or company legal department. Participants have a choice of twenty countries in which to intern, including most European countries, Egypt, Hong Kong, and Taiwan. In addition to the semester program, McGeorge School of Law conducts four summer programs in London, Edinburgh, Salzburg, and Budapest.

ADMITTANCE REQUIREMENTS: Law school graduate and admission to the bar.

CREDITS OFFERED: 5 units of academic credit toward master of law.

HOUSING: Students are responsible for their own arrangements.

DATES: August 18 through December 19.

COSTS: Tuition: $3,180. Does not include room and board, transportation, or personal expenses.

YEAR ESTABLISHED: 1974.

NUMBER OF STUDENTS IN 1985:   Not available.

APPLY: January 15. Robert Taylor, Assistant to the Director.

■ **WASHINGTON AND LEE UNIVERSITY**
Lexington, VA
(703) 463-8721

PROGRAM: Washington and Lee offers two spring semester, undergraduate multicountry programs: The Classical World; and Theatre in London and Paris. The classics program splits between Athens and Rome with courses covering Greek art, special independent study projects, and all levels of Greek, Latin, and Italian. The theater program emphasizes contemporary English and French drama with visits to London, Bath, and Paris. Program-related travel. Three-day orientation in the U.S.

ADMITTANCE REQUIREMENTS: Sophomores, juniors, and seniors in good academic standing with minimum of 2.0 GPA. No language requirement.

CREDITS OFFERED: 6 credits.

TEACHING METHODS: Students participate as a group and are instructed by U.S. faculty members in each city. Instruction is in English.

EVALUATION: By course instructors, based on class work, papers, and examinations.

HOUSING: Students live in apartments and furnished rooms.

COSTS: Classics: $1,350; Theatre: $2,000. Includes tuition, room and board, and program-related travel. Does not cover round-trip transportation or personal expenses.

DATES: April 21 through June 2 (Classics); May 30 (Theatre).

YEAR ESTABLISHED: 1977.

NUMBER OF STUDENTS IN 1985: Not available.

APPLY: By November 15. Mario Pellicciaro (Classics) or Albert Gordon (Theatre).

8.

Western Europe

AUSTRIA

Population: 7,552,000   **Capital:** Vienna   **Language:** German
Monetary Unit: Schilling   **Government:** Federal multiparty republic (president
and chancellor)   **Religion:** 84% Roman Catholic
Households With Television: 33%

SELECTED COLLEGES AND UNIVERSITIES

Austro-American Society
Stallburggasse 2
1010 Vienna

*Courses in German and English
cover German language and
Austrian civilization.*

Federal Ministry of Science
and Research
Minoritenplaz 5
1014 Vienna 1.

*Broad variety of undergraduate and
graduate courses. Offers scholarships.*

Orff Institute, Mozarteum Academy
of Music and Dramatic Arts
Frohnburgweg 55
5020 Salzburg

*Courses in music and music educa-
tion; in English.*

University of Applied Arts in Vienna
Stubenring 3
1010 Vienna

*Courses in architecture, design, art
teacher education, textiles, etc., in
German. Entrance exam required.*

University of Innsbruck
Innrain 52
6020 Innsbruck

*Courses in Germanics and history.
Offers scholarships.*

University of Vienna
Dr Karl Lueger-Ring 1
1010 Vienna

Broad variety of courses; in German.

FURTHER INFORMATION

Embassy of Austria
2343 Massachusetts Avenue, NW
Washington, DC 20008
(202) 483-4474

Austrian Institute
11 East 52nd Street
New York, NY 10022
(212) 759-5165

Consulate General of Austria
31 East 69th Street
New York, NY 10021
(212) 737-6400

Austrian National Tourist Office
545 Fifth Avenue
New York, NY 10017
(212) 944-6880

Bregenz

■ **WAGNER COLLEGE**
631 Howard Avenue
Staten Island, NY 10301
(800) 221-1010 or (718) 390-3107

PROGRAM: The Bregenz Study Program is a single-semester, full-academic year, or summer undergraduate program with courses offered in art history, economics, comparative economic studies, education, English, German, history, philosophy, and interdisciplinary seminars; fall and spring ski trips — fall trip to France, spring trip to Italy. Orientation in the U.S. and Austria.

ADMITTANCE REQUIREMENTS: Sophomores, juniors, and seniors in good academic standing with minimum of 2.5 GPA. No language requirement.

CREDITS OFFERED: 12 to 18 semester hours per semester; 3 to 6 credits for summer program.

TEACHING METHODS: Students are taught in English by an Austrian faculty.

EVALUATION: By course instructors, based on class work, papers, and examinations.

HOUSING: Students live with local families.

COSTS: $5,475 per semester; $10,350 for the full academic year. Includes tuition, room and board, round-trip transportation from New York, and program-related travel.

DATES: Fall semester: early-September through mid-December; spring semester: mid-January through late-May.

YEAR ESTABLISHED: 1962.

NUMBER OF STUDENTS IN 1985: 35.

APPLY: No application deadline. Ms. Ruth A. Perri.

Graz

■ **STATE UNIVERSITY OF NEW YORK AT BINGHAMTON**
Binghamton, NY 13901
(607) 777-2417

PROGRAM: The SUNY Binghamton Graz Program is a single-semester or full-academic-year undergraduate program held in cooperation with the Karl Franzen Universitaet Graz with a strong focus on the German language, Austrian history, and European culture and history. Local travel and field trips to cultural and historic sites. One-day orientation in Binghamton and several onsite sessions in Graz.

ADMITTANCE REQUIREMENTS: 3.0 GPA with "preference given to juniors and seniors."

TEACHING METHODS: Special courses are taught in German by the faculty at the Karl Franzen Universitaet Graz.

EVALUATION: By university faculty and group leaders, based on periodic papers, exams, and finals.

CREDITS OFFERED: 16 semester hours.

HOUSING: Students live with families or in dormitories.

DATES: September 15 through May 20.

COSTS: Tuition: $675 New York residents; $1,600 nonresidents; room and board: $2,600 to $3,000. Does not include round-trip transportation or personal expenses.

YEAR ESTABLISHED: 1969.

NUMBER OF STUDENTS IN 1985: Not available.

APPLY: By March 1. Chairman, Department of German.

■ **UNIVERSITY OF MINNESOTA**
  Extension Classes Offices of Study Abroad (ECOSA)
  202 Wesbrook Hall
  77 Pleasant Street SE
  Minneapolis, MN 55455
  (612) 373-1855

PROGRAM: German and Austrian Studies in Graz is a fall quarter under-graduate and graduate opportunity to study the German language, Austrian studies, and general German studies at Karl Franzen Universitaet. Additional courses are also offered by UM's program director. One-day orientation in the U.S. and Vienna.

ADMITTANCE REQUIREMENTS: Students in good academic standing with at least three quarters of college-level German.

TEACHING METHODS: Students are taught by both U.S. and foreign faculty.

EVALUATION: By course instructors, based upon class work, papers, and final exam.

CREDITS OFFERED: 12 to 14 quarter credits each period.

HOUSING: Students live with Austrian families.

DATES: September 1 through December 9.

COSTS: $2,389 includes tuition for three courses, room and board, and program-related travel. Does not include round-trip transportation or personal expenses.

YEAR ESTABLISHED: 1984.

NUMBER OF STUDENTS IN 1985: 19.

APPLY: January 1. Jody Jensen, ECOSA.

Innsbruck

■ **UNIVERSITY OF NOTRE DAME**
420 Administration Building
Notre Dame, IN 46556
(219) 239-5882

PROGRAM: The University of Notre Dame Program in Innsbruck is a full-academic-year undergraduate program held in cooperation with the University of Innsbruck. Students begin with a four-week orientation and intensive language program in Salzburg, then spend the remainder of the academic year studying at the University of Innsbruck. Courses cover the German language, history, and literature; Austrian history; economics; philosophy; and, theology. Program-related travel complements the courses.

ADMITTANCE REQUIREMENTS: Most students are sophomores, but juniors may participate with approval of major department and dean. 2.5 GPA and 3.0 in German; knowledge of German language. "A limited number of students from other institutions may be accepted if space permits."

TEACHING METHODS: Most courses are taught by professors from the University of Innsbruck. Some courses are in German; some in English.

EVALUATION: By onsite directors appointed among Notre Dame faculty, based upon class work, papers, and exams.

CREDITS OFFERED: At least 15 semester hours per semester.

HOUSING: Students live with Austrian students in dormitories.

DATES: Fall semester: August 16 through mid-December; spring semester: mid-January through June 12.

COSTS: $5,158 per semester includes tuition, room and board, program-related travel, and round-trip transportation from New York.

YEAR ESTABLISHED: 1964.

NUMBER OF STUDENTS IN 1985:   24.

APPLY: By February 1. Dr. Isabel Charles, Assistant Provost, Director, Foreign Studies Programs.

Salzburg

■ **AMERICAN INSTITUTE OF FOREIGN STUDY (AIFS)**
102 Greenwich Avenue
Greenwich, CT 06830
(800) 243-4567 or (203) 869-9090

PROGRAM: AIFS is a national, for-profit organization specializing in comprehensive overseas academic year, semester, and summer study programs. The AIFS program at the University of Salzburg is a full-academic-year, fall, or spring semester experience in which students are enrolled at the university. No campus, as such, exists. Instead it is made up of several buildings, ancient and modern, spread all over the city. AIFS lectures and seminars take place in a site in Nonntal, about fifteen minutes from the center of town. Advanced students can take a wide range of courses at the university with German students. Regular courses cover intensive German, history of art, German and Austrian history, mass communications, musicology, and political science. Program includes visits to local historic sites and museums. Four-week orientation and intensive German in Munich.

ADMITTANCE REQUIREMENTS: College freshmen, sophomores, juniors, and seniors with a 2.5 GPA. No language requirements.

TEACHING METHODS: Students must take a 4-credit intensive German course. Most seminars are taught in German, but English courses are also available.

EVALUATION: By faculty, based upon class work, papers, and periodic exams.

OFFERED: A minimum of 12 semester hours. Most students take 15 semester hours per semester.

HOUSING: Students live with local families and have two meals a day with their families.

DATES: Fall semester: October 6 through January 30; spring semester: March 2 through June 30.

COSTS: $5,150 per semester, includes tuition, room and board, program-related travel and one-way transportation from New York. Does not cover local travel and personal expenses.

YEAR ESTABLISHED: 1972.

NUMBER OF STUDENTS IN 1985: 28.

APPLY: Applications filled on first-come basis. "It is expected that all full-year or fall semester places will be filled by June 1; places for spring semester are kept open until November 15."

■ **UNIVERSITY OF CONNECTICUT**
Storrs, CT 06268
(203) 486-3178

PROGRAM: The Junior Year Abroad is held in cooperation with the universities of New Hampshire, Maine, Rhode Island, Vermont, and the University of Salzburg. Undergraduates can enroll for a single semester or the full academic year and attend regular classes at the University of Salzburg. Field trips to local sites and Eastern Europe. Mandatory orientation from September 15 through September 30 in Austria.

ADMITTANCE REQUIREMENTS: Juniors and seniors in good academic standing with at least intermediate college level German (3.0 GPA) and an overall 2.5 GPA.

TEACHING METHODS: Students are taught in German by the faculty at the University of Salzburg.

EVALUATION: By course instructors, based upon class work, papers and final exam.

CREDITS OFFERED: Up to 16 semester hours per semester.

HOUSING: Students live in dormitories or with Austrian families.

DATES: Fall semester: October 1 through January 31; spring semester: March 1 through June 30.

COSTS: Full program: $4,920 includes tuition, room and board, and program-related travel. Does not include round-trip transportation or personal expenses.

YEAR ESTABLISHED: 1970.

NUMBER OF STUDENTS IN 1985: 10.

APPLY: By April 15. Dr. Herbert Lederer. U-137, Department of Modern Languages.

■ **UNIVERSITY OF THE REDLANDS**
1200 East Colton Avenue
Redlands, CA 92373
(714) 793-2121

PROGRAM: The Salzburg Semester is a single-semester undergraduate pro-
gram with courses offered in art history, economics, European history,
Austrian history and culture, music appreciation, German, and general
humanities-based electives. Two major trips each year: twenty-one days to
Greece and Italy; fourteen days to Vienna, Prague, and Berlin. Orientation in
Austria.

ADMITTANCE REQUIREMENTS: Juniors and seniors in good academic
standing with minimum of 3.0 GPA. No language requirement, but preference is given to those with at least one semester of college German and to
students from institutions that will accept transcript courses.

CREDITS OFFERED: 11 to 15 semester units per semester.

TEACHING METHODS: Students are taught in English by both U.S. and
Austrian faculty. Americans are not integrated with local students.

EVALUATION: By course instructors, based on class work, papers, and
exams.

HOUSING: Students live in a pension leased exclusively for the program.

COSTS: $6,700 per semester; includes tuition, room and board, round-trip
transportation from New York, and program-related travel.

DATES: Fall semester: early September through mid-December; spring
semester: early February through late May.

YEAR ESTABLISHED: 1961.

NUMBER OF STUDENTS IN 1985:   30.

APPLY: Fall semester by March 1; spring semester by October 1. Ben
Dillow, Dean, Special College Programs, Ext. 4450.

Vienna

■ *Vienna is very conservative and at times very private. For the most part it is a very inviting place. It is also a very safe city. However, Vienna is expensive. Stay clear of shopping in the first district and visit the sixth. The two best places are Mariahilferstrasse (an endless street of stores where the locals shop) and Favoritenstrasse.*

- Stephanie Abbajay, Toledo, Ohio

■ *The best bargain in Vienna is standing room at any opera, play or musical event. For a dollar you can see practically anything. The best place to hang out is any café; you can sit, write letters or talk to friends all afternoon. The best places to eat are the gästhauses. The best place to shop is along Mariahilferstrasse.*

- Margaret Riley, Gambier, Ohio

■ *The program was well organized. But most remarkable was the overall efficiency of the Austro-American Institute.*

- Stephanie Abbajay, Toledo, Ohio

■ **BEAVER COLLEGE**
Glenside, PA 19038
(215) 572-2901

PROGRAM: Beaver College offers a pair of programs in Vienna: Soviet and East European Studies, and a regular academic experience concentrating on German and Austrian studies, art history, music, history, and East European studies. The Soviet program emphasizes Russian language, art, history, music, and political science with a concentration on Soviet and East European studies. The Soviet program is given during the fall semester; the general program is either a single-semester or a full-academic-year program. Students attend special classes at the Austro-American Institute of Education. The Soviet course offers travel to the Soviet Union and Czechoslovakia; the regular program offers three weeks to Eastern Europe and Turkey. Onsite orientation.

ADMITTANCE REQUIREMENTS: Sophomores, juniors, and seniors with a 2.8 GPA.

TEACHING METHODS: Students take special courses arranged by the Austro-American Institute.

EVALUATION: By course faculty, based upon class work and periodic exams.

CREDITS OFFERED: 15 to 16 semester hours per semester.

HOUSING: Students live with local families.

DATES: Soviet Studies: September 10 through December 15; general program: fall semester, September 14 through mid-December; spring semester, February 4 through May 17.

COSTS: Approximately $5,000 per semester includes tuition, room and board, and transportation from New York to Austria. Does not cover local travel or personal expenses.

YEAR ESTABLISHED: 1971.

NUMBER OF STUDENTS IN 1985: 100.

APPLY: For fall semester: June 15; spring semester: November 15. College Center for Education Abroad.

■ **BRIGHAM YOUNG UNIVERSITY**
Study Abroad Programs
204 HRCB
Provo, UT 84602
(801) 378-3308

PROGRAM: BYU Study in Vienna is a single-semester or full-academic-year undergraduate and graduate program offering courses in German, art, comparative history, humanities, music, religion, and political science.

ADMITTANCE REQUIREMENTS: Good academic standing with a 3.0 GPA requested. One semester of college German. Adherence to BYU standards.

TEACHING METHODS: Students attend special courses at BYU's own university center and are taught in English by a U.S. faculty. They are not integrated with Austrian students.

EVALUATION: Based on periodic exams. Evaluation determined by program director.

CREDITS OFFERED: A maximum of 24 semester hours.

HOUSING: Students live in the university center.

DATES: Fall semester: approximately mid-June through mid-December; spring semester: mid-January through early-June.

COSTS: Approximately $5,100 includes tuition, room and board, and program-related travel. Does not cover round-trip transportation or additional personal travel.

YEAR ESTABLISHED: 1964.

NUMBER OF STUDENTS IN 1985: 32.

APPLY: Six months prior to start of program.

■ **DEPAUW UNIVERSITY**
DePauw University
Greencastle, IN 46135
(317) 658-4736

PROGRAM: Music in Vienna is a single-semester undergraduate program with courses covering applied music counterpoint, orchestration, conducting, and composition, as well as a blend of general liberal courses and program-related travel.

ADMITTANCE REQUIREMENTS: Sophomores and above in good academic standing with one year of college of German and a 2.5 GPA.

TEACHING METHODS: Students take special courses arranged for the group and taught in English by the faculties at the Austro-American Institute of Education and the Austrian Institute of East and Southeastern European Studies.

EVALUATION: By course faculty, based upon papers and periodic exams.

CREDITS OFFERED: 15 to 16 semester hours.

HOUSING: Students live with local families.

DATES: September 1 through December 17.

COSTS: $5,300 includes tuition, room and board, and program-related travel. Does not cover round-trip transportation, local travel, and personal expenses.

YEAR ESTABLISHED: 1984.

NUMBER OF STUDENTS IN 1985: Not available.

APPLY: By April. Dr. Darrell LaLone, Director of Off-Campus Study.

■ **INSTITUTE OF EUROPEAN STUDY (IES)**
223 West Ohio Street
Chicago, IL 60610
(312) 944-1750

PROGRAM: IES is a nonprofit organization with formal relationships with more than forty American colleges and universities. Study in Vienna is a single-semester or full-academic-year program devoted to German studies; art history, anthropology, music, sociology, business, etc. Internships are available at local international corporations; program includes field trips. One-week orientation in Austria.

ADMITTANCE REQUIREMENTS: Juniors and seniors only. Acceptable college record and recommendations.

TEACHING METHODS: Students take special courses in English arranged for the group.

EVALUATION: By faculty, based upon class work and periodic and final exams. Most courses require a research paper.

CREDITS OFFERED: 15 semester hours per semester.

HOUSING: Students live with local families.

DATES: Fall semester: late August through mid-December; spring semester: mid-January through late May.

COSTS: $6,350 per year, $3,950 per semester, includes tuition, room and board, and program-related travel. Some IES scholarship aid available.

YEAR ESTABLISHED: 1950.

NUMBER OF STUDENTS IN 1985: 42.

APPLY: For fall semester by April 1; spring semester by November 15.

■ *From orientation to the quality of instruction, everything was well run. The program allowed for a great deal of independence, yet was there for support if it was needed.*
>   - Julie Creal, Gambier, Ohio

■ **STATE UNIVERSITY OF NEW YORK AT BROCKPORT**
Office of International Education
Brockport, NY 14420
(716) 395-2119

PROGRAM: The SUNY American International Schools Program in Vienna is a one-semester or academic-year undergraduate program designed for those interested in teaching. Courses cover elementary and secondary education with student teaching opportunities. Four-day orientation in U.S. and Austria.

ADMITTANCE REQUIREMENTS: Seniors who have completed prerequisites for precertification student teaching.

TEACHING METHODS: Students attend special courses taught in English by foreign faculty.

EVALUATION: By university faculty and group leaders based on periodic papers, observation, exams and finals.

CREDITS OFFERED: 15 semester hours.

HOUSING: Students may live in apartments or with families.

DATES: Fall semester: September 1 through mid-December; spring semester: mid-January to May 31.

COSTS: Approximately $3,000 per semester. Includes tuition, room and board, and program-associated travel. Does not cover round-trip transportation, local travel, and personal expenses. Financial aid is available.

YEAR ESTABLISHED: 1985.

NUMBER OF STUDENTS IN 1985:   20.

APPLY: Fall semester by April 1; spring semester by November 1. Dr. John Perry.

■ **UNIVERSITY OF DELAWARE**
Newark, DE 19716
(302) 451-2591

PROGRAM: The Vienna Semester Program is a spring undergraduate session that offers courses in German, art history, economics, music, theater, with an option for independent study; program-related travel to Germany, Hungary, and, Czechoslovakia. Two-day orientation in U.S. and Vienna.

ADMITTANCE REQUIREMENTS: Sophomore and above with a 3.0 GPA, recommendations of major advisor. Some knowledge of German recommended.

TEACHING METHODS: Students do not take courses in a foreign school but are taught independently by both U.S. and local faculty at the Austro-American Institute. Lectures, field trips, and some independent study.

EVALUATION: By U.S. and foreign faculty, based upon class work, papers, and exams.

CREDITS OFFERED: 15 semester hours.

HOUSING: With local families.

DATES: Approximately February 1 through mid-May.

COSTS: Approximately $3,900; covers tuition, room and board, course-related travel. Does not include round-trip transportation and personal expenses.

YEAR ESTABLISHED: 1976.

NUMBER OF STUDENTS IN 1985: 35.

APPLY: By October 15. Chairman, Department of Language and Literature.

BELGIUM

Population: 9,858,000   **Capital:** Brussels   **Languages:** Dutch, French, and German   **Monetary Unit:** Belgian franc   **Government:** Constitutional monarchy (king and prime minister)   **Religion:** 92% Roman Catholic
Households With Television: 30%

SELECTED COLLEGES AND UNIVERSITIES

Belgian American Education
Foundation
11, rue d'egmont
1050 Bruxelles

Academic year, all disciplines.

Université Catholique de Louvain
Halles Universitaires
1348 Louvain-la-Neuve

Academic year, all disciplines.

Free University Brussels
Pleinlaan 2,
1050 Bruxelles

*Academic year; graduate and under-
graduate; liberal arts and strong
sciences.*

FURTHER INFORMATION

Belgian/American Educational
Foundation
195 Church Street
New Haven, CT 06510
(203) 777-5765

Consulate General of Belgium
50 Rockefeller Plaza, Room 1104
New York, NY 10020
(212) 586-5110

Embassy of Belgium
3330 Garfield Street, NW
Washington, DC 20008
(202) 333-6900

Belgian National Tourist Office
745 Fifth Avenue
New York, NY 10501
(212) 758-8130

Ministerie de la Communauté
Française
Avenue de Cortenberg, 158
B-140 Brussels

Commission for Educational Exchange
Between the United States, Belgium,
and Luxembourg
21, rue du Marteu
1040 Brussels

Brussels

■ THE AMERICAN UNIVERSITY
Washington, DC 20016
(202) 885-3800

PROGRAM: Semester in Brussels is a liberal arts/social science program
held in cooperation with the Institute of European Studies. Courses include
history, fine arts, languages, political science, etc. Field trips to major cities in
central Europe are often scheduled. Preorientation at American University
(usually over a weekend) and onsite.

ADMITTANCE REQUIREMENTS: Juniors and seniors with a 3.0 GPA average or better.

TEACHING METHODS: Students are accompanied by a resident professor from American University who schedules seminars with public officials in addition to his or her own lectures. Foreign faculty members complement these lectures and teach specialized courses. Students also intern two days a week with one of the many local government or private organizations.

EVALUATION: Regular exams, midterms and finals, in addition to short seminar papers.

CREDITS OFFERED: 15 to 17 semester hours.

HOUSING: A combination of possibilities from local apartments to living with local families.

DATES: First semester: September to December; second semester: January to May.

COSTS: Tuition: $4,100 per semester; room and board: $2,000 per semester. Scholarships from American University available.

APPLY: Rolling admissions. Apply 6 to 8 months prior to start of semester. Dr. David C. Brown, Dean, Washington Semester and Study Program Abroad.

■ **BOSTON UNIVERSITY**
    755 Commonwealth Avenue
    Boston, MA 02215
    (617) 353-2987

PROGRAM: Boston University offers a pair of graduate programs in cooperation with the Vrije Universiteit: a master of science in computer information systems, and a master of science in management. Both programs offer optional language study and internship opportunities. Summer program also available.

ADMITTANCE REQUIREMENTS: Graduate students with a mathematics background for the computer information program; no language requirement.

TEACHING METHODS: Students attend special courses and seminars and do independent study projects; taught in English by the Vrije Universiteit faculty.

EVALUATION: By course faculty, based upon papers and final exams.

CREDITS OFFERED: 48 credits.

HOUSING: Students are responsible for their own housing.

DATES: September 1 through August 1.

COSTS: $450 per course. Does not cover room and board, transportation, or personal expenses. Some scholarships available.

YEAR PROGRAM ESTABLISHED: 1972.

NUMBER OF STUDENTS IN 1985: 37.

APPLY: By June 1. Dr. William Pendergast, Associate Dean, Overseas Programs.

Leuven

■ **MICHIGAN STATE UNIVERSITY**
108 Center for International Programs
East Lansing, MI 48824
(517) 353-8920

PROGRAM: MSU's Landscape Architecture Experience is a single-semester undergraduate program devoted solely to this single discipline. Orientation in the U.S. and onsite.

ADMITTANCE REQUIREMENTS: For juniors and senior landscape architecture students with acceptable academic credentials, references, and recommendation from advisor. No language requirement.

TEACHING METHODS: Students take special courses arranged for the group and taught by both U.S. and local foreign faculty in English.

EVALUATION: By course faculty, based upon papers and exams.

CREDITS OFFERED: 12 credit hours.

HOUSING: Students live in dormitories.

DATES: September 26 through December 4.

COSTS: Approximately $2,100, includes tuition, room and some meals, and program-related travel. Does not include round-trip transportation or personal expenses.

YEAR ESTABLISHED: 1981.

NUMBER OF STUDENTS IN 1985: 20.

APPLY: By August 2. Dr. Charles A. Gliozzo, Office of Overseas Study.

DENMARK

Population: 5,112,000   Capital: Copenhagen   Language: Danish
Monetary Unit: Krone   Government: Parliamentary constitutional monarch
(queen and prime minister)   Religion: 92% Evangelical Lutheran
Households With Television: 39%

SELECTED COLLEGES AND UNIVERSITIES

Danish Institute
Kultorvet 2
1175 Copenhagen K

Professionals and graduate students; seminars on design, architecture and special education. Courses in English and French.

University of Copenhagen
DIS Study Division
Vestergade 9
1456 Copenhagen K

Undergraduates; academic year or semester; general studies, architecture and design, and international business. Courses in English.

University of Copenhagen
Frue Plads
DK-1168 Copenhagen K

Courses in Danish.

FURTHER INFORMATION

Danish Tourist Board
75 Rockefeller Plaza
New York, NY 10017
(212) 949-2333

Embassy of Denmark
3200 Whitehaven Street, NW
Washington, DC 20008
(202) 363-6315

Danish Information Office
280 Park Avenue
New York, NY 10017
(212) 223-4545

Central Student Advisory Service
at the University of Copenhagen
Krystalagade 25
DK-1150 Copenhagen K

- *The best way to travel around Denmark is by bicycle. The roads are in great condition, and it's an easy and fun way to meet people. Go off the beaten track, and be sure to stop by Svendborg (on Fyn) and Nysted (on Lolland).*

  - Ellen Leerburger, Scarsdale, New York

Copenhagen

■ THE AMERICAN UNIVERSITY
Washington, DC 20016
(202) 885-3800

PROGRAM: Semester in Copenhagen is a liberal arts/social science program held in cooperation with Denmark's International Study Program. Students may attend for both fall and spring semesters. Courses include history, fine arts, languages, political science, etc. Field trips to Moscow are scheduled. Preorientation at American University (usually over a weekend) and onsite.

ADMITTANCE REQUIREMENTS: Juniors and seniors with a 3.0 GPA or better.

TEACHING METHODS: Students are accompanied by a resident professor from American University who schedules seminars with public officials in addition to his or her own lectures. Foreign faculty members complement these lectures and teach specialized courses. Students also intern two days a week with one of the many local government or private organizations.

EVALUATION: Regular exams, midterms and finals, in addition to short seminar papers.

CREDITS OFFERED: 15 to 17 semester hours.

HOUSING: A combination of possibilities from local apartments to living with local families.

DATES: First semester: early September through mid-December; second semester: late January through late May.

COSTS: Tuition: $4,100 per semester; room and board: $2,000 per semester. Scholarships available.

YEAR ESTABLISHED: 1975.

NUMBER OF STUDENTS IN 1985:   30.

APPLY: Rolling admissions. Apply 6 to 8 months prior to start of semester to: Dr. David C. Brown, Dean, Washington Semester and Study Program Abroad.

■ **THE CALIFORNIA STATE UNIVERSITY**
400 Golden Shore
Long Beach, CA 90802
(213) 590-5655

PROGRAM: The CSU International Program in Denmark, held in cooperation with the University of Copenhagen, is a full-academic-year undergraduate and graduate opportunity to study at the Danish university. Students select from the wide range of university course offerings with an emphasis on architecture and business supplemented by special CSU programs. One-week orientation in Copenhagen.

ADMITTANCE REQUIREMENTS: Must be enrolled at a CSU campus. Juniors and above, including graduate students, 2.75 GPA (3.0 for business majors). No language requirement.

TEACHING METHODS: Students take a combination of regular academic courses and supplemental program-sponsored courses taught by foreign faculty.

EVALUATION: By foreign faculty and CSU resident director, based upon periodic and final examinations.

CREDITS OFFERED: 30 semester hours per year or 45 quarter units.

HOUSING: In dormitories and private apartments.

DATES: Full year from August 21 to July 29.

COSTS: Tuition: $0 (residents); $3,600 (nonresidents); room and board: $5,500. Does not include round-trip transportation and living expenses (estimated at $4,130 per year).

YEAR ESTABLISHED: 1970.

NUMBER OF STUDENTS IN 1985: 33.

APPLY: By February 1. Dr. Kibbey M. Horne, Director of International Programs.

■ **DENMARK'S INTERNATIONAL STUDY (DIS) PROGRAM AT THE UNIVERSITY OF COPENHAGEN**
Kattesundet 3
DK-1458
Copenhagen K, DENMARK

PROGRAM: The DIS undergraduate program offers full-year, one-semester, or summer programs "within three different lines of study: liberal arts (general studies), international business, and architecture and design." Students work closely with their Danish professors both in class and on independent projects. Faculty-student ratio is 1:5; lecture classes average about thirty-five students. One-week orientation in Copenhagen includes a crash course in Danish.

ADMITTANCE REQUIREMENTS: Junior and seniors with a 3.0 GPA, approval from home institution. No language requirement.

TEACHING METHODS: Classes, which may be scattered about Copenhagen, are taught in English by Danish professors, program includes lectures, seminars, independent study, group work, study tours, and field trips.

EVALUATION: By Danish faculty, based upon papers, exams, projects, and class work.

CREDITS OFFERED: 12 to 16 semester hours per semester.

HOUSING: Students live in dormitories or with Danish families.

DATES: Fall semester: August 26 through December 16; spring semester: January 20 through May 22.

COSTS: Per semester. Tuition: $3,390 (Liberal Arts); $3,990 (International Business and Architecture and Design). Covers local field trips, study tours, insurance, fees. Room and board: $535 (with a family); $360 (in a dormitory). Does not include round-trip transportation or personal expenses. Some financial grants available for academically qualified.

YEAR ESTABLISHED: 1959.

NUMBER OF STUDENTS IN 1985: 257.

APPLY: Fall semester: April 1; spring and summer semesters: November 1. Local college study abroad office or Nancy F. Lunderskov, Administrative Assistant.

■ **OREGON STATE SYSTEM OF HIGHER EDUCATION (OSSHE)**
   Foreign Study Programs
   International Education
   Oregon State University
   Corvallis, OR
   (503) 754-3006

PROGRAM: The OSSHE Denmark MBA Program is a single-semester graduate program held in cooperation with Copenhagen School of Economics and Business Administration, the University of Copenhagen, Portland State University, and the University of Oregon. The program combines advanced international management with independent study projects. Approximately forty foreign and Danish students in total program. One-day orientation in Oregon.

ADMITTANCE REQUIREMENTS: Graduate student in good standing, recommendation of advisor. No language requirement.

TEACHING METHODS: Classes, seminars, and independent study in English by Danish faculty and guest lecturers.

EVALUATION: By American and university faculty, based on periodic and final exams.

CREDITS OFFERED: The equivalent of one term of graduate credit.

HOUSING: Students live in university dormitories or with families.

DATES: Approximately late August through mid-December.

COSTS: $1,842 for Oregon residents; $2,270 for nonresidents, includes tuition, room and board, field trips, and fees. Does not include round-trip transportation, local travel, or personal expenses.

YEAR ESTABLISHED: 1985.

NUMBER OF STUDENTS IN 1985: 2.

APPLY: By March 15. At participating OSSHE school, or Irma Wright, Office of International Education.

■ **PRATT INSTITUTE**
School of Art & Design
200 Willoughby Avenue
Brooklyn, NY 11205
(718) 636-3598

PROGRAM: Pratt's Architecture and Design in Copenhagen is a twelve-week summer session for both graduates and undergraduates held in cooperation with Denmark International Study (DIS), the University of Copenhagen, the Danish Royal Academy, and Washington State University. Emphasis is on architecture (structural and landscape), industrial design, interior design, communications design, and fashion merchandising. Orientation in Copenhagen.

ADMITTANCE REQUIREMENTS: Sophomores and above with a 3.0 GPA. No language requirement.

TEACHING METHODS: Participants attend regular classes taught in English by Danish faculty; includes local field trips plus a four-day Denmark and seven-day Stockholm-Helsinki study tour.

EVALUATION: By Danish faculty, based upon periodic exams, presentations, and finals.

CREDITS OFFERED: 16 semester hours for undergraduate students; 12 for graduates.

HOUSING: Students usually live with Danish families, but may live in student residence complexes with shared kitchens.

DATES: Approximately May 26 through August 19.

COSTS: $4,945 includes tuition, room and board, round-trip transportation from New York, and all field trips and tours. Does not include personal expenses. Some scholarships available.

YEAR ESTABLISHED: 1974.

NUMBER OF STUDENTS IN 1985: 34.

APPLY: Before May 1. Professor George P. Schmidt, Jr., Pratt/Copenhagen in Denmark Coordinator.

FRANCE

Population: 55,406,000   **Capital:** Paris   **Language:** French
Monetary Unit: Franc   **Government:** Republic (president and prime minister)
Religion: 76% Roman Catholic   **Households With Television:** 91%

SELECTED COLLEGES AND UNIVERSITIES

Centre Universitaire d'Avignon
3, Rue do Rempart de l'Oulle
F-8400 Avignon

École du Louvre
34, Quai du Louvre
75001 Paris

Institut Catholique de Paris
31, Rue de la Fonderie
75270, Paris

Courses in classics and the social sciences in French.

Université de Caen
Esplanade de la Paix
F-14031 Caen

Université de la Sorbonne
Place du Maréchal-de-Lattre-Tassigny
75116 Paris

Requires an entrance examination.

Université de Paris-I
58, Boulevard Arago
75013 Paris

Université de Provence
1, Place Victor-Hugo
F-13331 Marceille

FURTHER INFORMATION

Consulate General of France
934 Fifth Avenue
New York, NY 10017
(212) 606-3600

Embassy of France
4101 Reservoir Road, NW
Washington, DC 20007
(202) 944-6000

French Government Tourist Office
610 Fifth Avenue
New York, NY 10020
(212) 757-1125

French Cultural Services
972 Fifth Avenue
New York, NY 10021
(212) 570-4400

Publishes brochures listing schools and data on admissions, financial aid, etc.

Centre National des Oeuvres
Universitaires et Scolaires (CNOUS)
69, Quai d'Orsay
F-75007 Paris

Provides general information and a list of regional schools.

- *I was surprised to discover how different the French were; and I loved the opportunity to discover these differences. Definitely get a Eurail pass. Also, budget your money well in advance or it will be gone in no time. My particular French program gave me a chance to go to Italy, Provence, and Paris at no additional expense. Take advantage of every opportunity. Assert yourself to get as much out of your situation as possible.*

  - Cathy Bond, Misenheimer, North Carolina

Aix-en-Provence

■ **THE CALIFORNIA STATE UNIVERSITY**
The California State University
400 Golden Shore
Long Beach, CA 90802
(213) 590-5655

PROGRAM: The CSU International Program in France, held in cooperation with the University of Provence, is a full-academic-year undergraduate and graduate opportunity to study at the French university. Students select from the wide range of university course offerings supplemented by special CSU programs. One-week orientation in Aix-en-Provence.

ADMITTANCE REQUIREMENTS: Must be enrolled at a CSU campus. Juniors and above including graduate students; 2.75 GPA. Two years of college French or the equivalent.

TEACHING METHODS: Students take a combination of regular academic courses and supplemental program-sponsored courses taught by foreign faculty.

EVALUATION: By foreign faculty and CSU resident director, based upon periodic and final exams.

CREDITS OFFERED: 30 semester hours per year or 45 quarter units.

HOUSING: In dormitories and private apartments.

DATES: Approximately early September to mid-June.

COSTS: Tuition: $0 for residents; $2,500 nonresidents; room and board: $2,500. Does not include round-trip transportation or living expenses (estimated at approximately $2,505 per year).

YEAR ESTABLISHED: 1963.

NUMBER OF STUDENTS IN 1985: 56.

APPLY: By February 1. Dr. Kibbey M. Horne, Director of International Programs.

■ **COLLEGE CONSORTIUM FOR INTERNATIONAL STUDIES (CCIS)**
866 United Nations Plaza, Room 511
New York, NY 10017
(212) 308-1556

PROGRAM: CCIS is a nonprofit organization that sponsors and organizes several dozen foreign-study programs for member colleges who grant degree credit. The French Program is a single-semester, full-academic-year, or summer program offered in cooperation with Miami-Dade Community College and the University of Aix-Marseille. Students attend classes at the Institute for American Studies under the auspices of the University of Aix-Marseille. Courses cover French (required), French and European studies, geography, studio arts, and general liberal arts and social sciences courses; program-related field trips. Orientation in France.

ADMITTANCE REQUIREMENTS: Sophomore and above (but will accept some freshmen) with 2.5 GPA and acceptable academic credentials.

TEACHING METHODS: Courses, in English and French, are taught by institute professors associated with French universities.

EVALUATION: By course instructors and project leaders.

CREDITS OFFERED: 12 to 15 semester hours per semester.

HOUSING: Students live with local families.

DATES: Fall semester: September 16 through January 26; spring semester: February 1 through May 30.

COSTS: $2,365 per semester includes tuition. Does not cover room and board, local travel, round-trip transportation, or personal expenses.

YEAR ESTABLISHED: Not available.

NUMBER OF STUDENTS IN 1985: 80.

APPLY: Fall semester by August 15; spring semester by November 22.

■ **STATE UNIVERSITY OF NEW YORK AT BINGHAMTON**
Binghamton, NY 13903
(607) 777-2588

PROGRAM: French and Mediterranean Studies is a spring semester undergraduate program held at the Collège Catholique. The program was formerly associated with the Université de Provence but the directors decided to use the classroom facilities at the collège (a local junior-senior high school) rather than pass on to students "what we considered an exorbitant fee ... for providing classrooms at unpopular hours and the dubious privilege of giving participants access to university cafeterias, at double the price charged the French students." The program continues to offer courses on French civilization, history, literature, and political science taught by members of the faculty of the Université de Provence. Two-week orientation in Aix-en-Provence.

ADMITTANCE REQUIREMENTS: Sophomores and above with a 3.0 GPA in the humanities and at least five college semesters of French.

TEACHING METHODS: Specific courses are taught to the group in French by members of the université faculty. Brief field trips to regional sites complements the program.

EVALUATION: By French faculty in cooperation with the resident director, based upon periodic exams, compositions, and a final exam.

CREDITS OFFERED: 14 to 18 semester hours.

HOUSING: Some students live with French families, others live in private houses, apartments, or furnished rooms.

DATES: Approximately January 20 to May 20.

COSTS: Tuition: $690 (New York residents); $1,600 (nonresidents); room and board: $1,750. Does not include round-trip transportation local travel, or personal expenses.

YEAR ESTABLISHED: 1973.

NUMBER OF STUDENTS IN 1985: 20.

APPLY: By November 1. John Lakich, Department of Romance Languages.

■ **VANDERBILT UNIVERSITY**
College of Arts & Sciences
Box #6327-B
Nashville, TN 37235
(615) 371-1224

PROGRAM: Vanderbilt in France is a single-semester, full-academic-year, or summer-session undergraduate program taught by professors of the Université de Provence or other French institutions. Courses cover advanced conversation and composition, phonology, French civilization, La Provence, art, literature, existential and French philosophy, architecture, etc. Some weekend excursions.

ADMITTANCE REQUIREMENTS: 3.0 GPA and "sufficient knowledge of French to pursue studies successfully."

TEACHING METHODS: Students attend special courses at an independent study center. Classes are taught in French.

EVALUATION: By course professors, based upon class work, papers, and exams.

CREDITS OFFERED: From 12 to 18 semester hours per semester.

HOUSING: Students live in rooms rented by local French families. They usually live with another Vanderbilt student, are responsible for their own meals, and are completely independent from the French family.

DATES: Fall semester: August 27 through December 20; spring semester: January 30 through May 16.

COSTS: $4,650 per semester includes tuition, board, and some program activities. Does not cover round-trip transportation, meals (which range from $750 to $850 per semester), or personal expenses (estimated at approximately $450 per semester).

YEAR ESTABLISHED: 1962.

NUMBER OF STUDENTS IN 1985: 65.

APPLY: By March 15 for fall semester; October 15 for spring semester. Overseas Office.

Angers

■ **UNIVERSITY OF NOTRE DAME**
420 Administration Building
Notre Dame, IN 46556
(219) 239-5882

PROGRAM: Stage Université Notre-Dame en France (SUNDEF) is a full-academic year undergraduate program held in cooperation with the International Center for French Studies of the Université Catholique de l'Ouest. Courses cover French language, history, and literature; government; theology; philosophy; and the history of the arts. Program-related travel and one month intensive French in September.

ADMITTANCE REQUIREMENTS: Most students are sophomores, but juniors may participate with approval of major department and dean. 2.5 GPA and 3.0 in French. Knowledge of French language. "A limited number of students from other institutions may be accepted if space permits."

TEACHING METHODS: All courses are taught in French by professors from the Université Catholique de l'Ouest.

EVALUATION: By onsite directors appointed among Notre Dame faculty, based upon class work, papers, and exams.

CREDITS OFFERED: At least 15 semester hours per semester.

HOUSING: Students live in dormitories or with local families.

DATES: Fall semester: August 30 through mid-December; spring semester: mid-January through June 6.

COSTS: $5,158 per semester includes tuition, room and board, program-related travel and round-trip transportation from New York.

YEAR ESTABLISHED: 1966.

NUMBER OF STUDENTS IN 1985: 42.

APPLY: By February 1. Dr. Isabel Charles, Assistant Provost, Director, Foreign Studies Programs.

Avignon

■ **COLLEGE CONSORTIUM FOR INTERNATIONAL STUDIES (CCIS)**
866 United Nations Plaza, Room 511
New York, NY 10017
(212) 308-1556

PROGRAM: CCIS is a nonprofit organization that sponsors and organizes several dozen foreign study programs for member colleges that grant degree credit. The Avignon Program is a single-semester, full-academic-year, or summer program offered in cooperation with Miami-Dade Community College and the University of Avignon. Students attend classes at the Institute for American Universities. Courses cover French (required), French and European studies, fine arts, and general liberal arts and social sciences courses; program-related field trips. Orientation in France.

ADMITTANCE REQUIREMENTS: Sophomore and above (but will accept some freshman) with 2.5 GPA and acceptable academic credentials.

TEACHING METHODS: Courses, in English and French, are taught by institute professors associated with French universities.

EVALUATION: By course instructors and project leaders.

CREDITS OFFERED: 12 to 15 semester hours per semester.

HOUSING: Students live with local families.

DATES: Fall semester: September 16 through January 22; spring semester: January 26 through May 30.

COSTS: $2,365 per semester includes tuition. Does not cover room and board, local travel, round-trip transportation, or personal expenses.

YEAR ESTABLISHED: Not available.

APPLY: Fall semester by August 15; spring semester: November 22.

NUMBER OF STUDENTS IN 1985:   Not available.

■ **NORTHWEST INTERINSTITUTIONAL COUNCIL ON STUDY ABROAD (NICSA)**
Oregon State University
International Education
Corvallis, OR 97331
(503) 754-2394

PROGRAM: The NICSA Program is held in cooperation with the University of Washington, Washington State University, Western Washington University, Central Washington University, Eastern Washington University, Boise State University, University of Alaska - Fairbanks, University of Oregon, Oregon State University, and Portland State University. This is a one-term, undergraduate program although students may elect to enroll for more than a single term. The courses are designed around a general liberal arts curriculum emphasizing history, economics, political science, language, art, literature, English, theater, geography, etc. Excursions play an important role, taking place on a weekly basis; one long (two- to three-day) excursion each term. There is a three-hour orientation on the individual campuses prior to departure and a one-day onsite orientation.

ADMITTANCE REQUIREMENTS: A minimum 2.0 GPA plus good academic standing. Two terms college French or the equivalent.

TEACHING METHODS: Students attend a special center for Americans set up by NICSA. All classes are taught in English by either foreign or various northwestern regional-school faculty members.

EVALUATION: By professors, based on class work, papers, and periodic exams.

CREDITS OFFERED: 15 or 20 credits (quarter hours) per term.

HOUSING: Students live with local families arranged by an onsite homestay coordinator.

DATES: Fall term: September 15 through December 15; winter term: January 3 through March 20; spring term: April 1 through June 15.

COSTS: $1,895, including tuition, room and board, books, and local travel. Does not cover round-trip transportation or personal expenses. Nonresident students attending Oregon State University for one term pay resident tuition.

YEAR ESTABLISHED: 1963.

NUMBER OF STUDENTS IN 1985: 120.

APPLY: Fall term by June 1; winter term by October 15; spring term by January 3. American Heritage Association, P.O. Box #425, Lake Oswego, OR 97034 (503) 635-3703, or Judy Van Dyck or Ann Ferguson, International Education, OSU.

■ **UNIVERSITY OF WASHINGTON**
Foreign Study Office
572 Schmitz Hall, PA-10
Seattle, WA 98195
(206) 543-9272

PROGRAM: The French Program is a fall, winter, or spring undergraduate program designed to serve as "an introduction to France through literature, arts, social sciences, French language, and excursions. A two-term stay is considered ideal." The program includes a three-day stay in Paris and allows a one-week study break commencing with a trip to Nice, Grenoble, or Toulouse. Onsite orientation.

ADMITTANCE REQUIREMENTS: Sophomore standing, at least two quarters college-level French, and acceptable academic credentials.

TEACHING METHODS: Courses are taught in English by visiting Northwest faculty and resident French faculty.

EVALUATION: By course faculty member, based upon papers and exams.

CREDITS OFFERED: A full quarter term per quarter.

HOUSING: Students live with local families.

DATES: Approximately, fall term: late August through late November; winter term: early December through late February; spring semester: early March through late May.

COSTS: $2,300 per term includes tuition and room and board. Does not cover round-trip transportation, local travel, or personal expenses.

YEAR ESTABLISHED: 1968.

NUMBER OF STUDENTS IN 1985:   42.

APPLY: Approximately four months prior to start of term. David Fenner, Advisor.

Beaune

■ **UNIVERSITY OF MONTANA**
Missoula, MT 59812
(406) 243-6800, ext. 2980

PROGRAM: The French Program is a fall quarter undergraduate experience that combines study with working in the wine harvest in the Burgundy region in exchange for room and board. Visits to museums and other cultural attractions during a one-week Paris stay is part of the program. On-campus orientation preceding quarter.

ADMITTANCE REQUIREMENTS: Sophomores or above, acceptable academic record, five quarters college French, plus recommendations.

TEACHING METHODS: Students are taught in French by local instructors. Onsite visits and field trips complement program.

EVALUATION: By local professors, based upon class work, papers, and exams.

CREDITS OFFERED: Between 12 and 18 quarter hours depending on courses.

HOUSING: With local families.

DATES: Approximately September to November.

COSTS: Approximately $1,700, includes tuition, room and board, and course-related travel. Does not cover round-trip transportation or personal expenses.

YEAR ESTABLISHED: 1973.

NUMBER OF STUDENTS IN 1985: 15.

APPLY: By March 1. Dr. O. W. Rolfe, Liberal Arts, Room #150.

Besançon

■ **STATE UNIVERSITY OF NEW YORK AT NEW PALTZ**
New Paltz, NY 12561
(914) 257-2233

PROGRAM: The SUNY Besançon Program is a single-semester or full-academic-year undergraduate and graduate program held in cooperation with the University of Besançon. The program emphasis is on the French language and culture, and includes field trips to various cultural and historic sites. SUNY also offers a six-week summer session (6 to 9 semester hours credit) for undergraduates and "outstanding high school seniors." One-day orientation in New Paltz.

ADMITTANCE REQUIREMENTS: Juniors, seniors, and graduate students with a minimum of two years of college-level French or the equivalent.

TEACHING METHODS: Students attend special courses, including intensive language training, in French taught by a French faculty.

EVALUATION: By French faculty, based upon periodic exams, finals, and depending on the level of the course, a term paper.

CREDITS OFFERED: A minimum of 12, maximum of 18 semester hours per semester.

HOUSING: Students live in dormitories at the University of Besançon.

DATES: Approximately, fall semester: September 25 through January 10; spring semester: January 20 through May 30.

COSTS: Fall semester $1,605, spring semester, $1,750, includes tuition, room and board, and program-related field trips. Nonresidents add approximately $925 per semester. Does not cover round-trip transportation or personal expenses (estimated at approximately $400 per semester).

YEAR ESTABLISHED: 1971.

NUMBER OF STUDENTS IN 1985: 10.

APPLY: For fall semester and academic year by April 1; spring semester by November 1. Dr. Rudolf R. Kossmann, Director, Office of International Education.

■ UNIVERSITY OF KANSAS
Lawrence, KA 66045
(913) 864-3742

PROGRAM: The University of Kansas offers a full academic year at the Institut Universitaire de Technologie. The program is particularly aimed at students in engineering, business, journalism, and the natural sciences, as well as those studying the French language. Students may also enroll in courses at the Centre de Linguistique Appliquee at an extra cost. All participants must take a support class in French grammar, composition, and conversation.

ADMITTANCE REQUIREMENTS: Juniors and above with a minimum of 60 semester hours, 3.0 GPA, French proficiency, plus recommendations.

TEACHING METHODS: Students take regular classes at the university taught in French by local faculty.

EVALUATION: By local professors, based upon class work, papers, and exams.

CREDITS OFFERED: Between 24 and 36 semester hours per year.

HOUSING: In a modern student apartment complex four miles from the university. Students receive a monthly meal stipend.

DATES: Approximately October 1 through June 30.

COSTS: $4,100 includes annual tuition and room and board. Does not cover Kansas enrollment fees, round-trip transportation, local travel, or personal expenses.

YEAR ESTABLISHED: 1985.

NUMBER OF STUDENTS IN 1985: 20.

APPLY: By March 1. Office of Study Abroad, 203 Lippincott.

Cannes

■ **AMERICAN INSTITUTE OF FOREIGN STUDY (AIFS)**
102 Greenwich Avenue
Greenwich, CT 06830
(800) 243-4567 or (203) 869-9090

PROGRAM: AIFS is a national for-profit organization specializing in comprehensive overseas academic-year, one-semester, and summer study programs. The AIFS program at the Collège International de Cannes is either a fall or spring semester program. AIFS students take courses at the college along with other foreign students. AIFS courses, taught in English, cover French language, art, literature, and political life; French history; computer science; international business; acting; cinema; and marine biology. Program includes a five-day trip to Paris and a three-day weekend to Provence.

ADMITTANCE REQUIREMENTS: High school graduates; college freshman and above with a with a 2.5 GPA. No language requirement.

TEACHING METHODS: Most students in the special AIFS courses are Americans; faculty is predominantly French. Students must take an intensive French course.

EVALUATION: By faculty, based upon class work, papers, and periodic exams.

CREDITS OFFERED: The minimum course load is 12 credit hours; the maximum is 18.

HOUSING: Students live in single or double rooms at the college.

DATES: Fall semester: September 9 through December 20; spring semester: February 4 through May 30.

COSTS: $4,449 includes tuition, room and board, program-related travel, and one-way transportation from New York. Does not cover local travel or personal expenses.

YEAR ESTABLISHED: 1983.

NUMBER OF STUDENTS IN 1986: 68.

APPLY: Applications filled on first-come basis. "It is expected that all full-year or fall-semester places will be filled by June 1; places for spring semester are kept open until November 15."

- *The Collège International de Cannes gave me an opportunity to learn about people from many different countries. Unfortunately, I lived in a dorm where it was too easy not to speak French and not to mingle with the French. Next time I'd stay in a home where I could get more involved with the French way of life.*

- Cathy Bond, Misenheimer, North Carolina

■ **COLBY COLLEGE**
Waterville, ME 04901
(207) 872-3168

PROGRAM: Colby's Junior Year in France, with the participation of Washington University in St. Louis, is divided into two sessions: a preliminary six weeks in Paris and a full academic year at the Université de Caen. The program is designed to be a total immersion in French life and culture. Students are expected to speak only French while in France. The academic program includes a variety of "core" courses including: thème et version, la stylistique, pré-romantisme et romantisme, histoire européenne moderne, la litérature, poétique française, etc. Regional travel is integrated into the program.

ADMITTANCE REQUIREMENTS: The program is generally limited to college juniors, however a limited number of sophomores or seniors may be admitted. Acceptable academic record and a solid background in French are essential.

TEACHING METHODS: All classes are in French and conducted by members of the faculty at the Université de Caen.

EVALUATION: By the faculty at the Université de Caen, based upon class work, periodic tests, and final exams.

CREDITS OFFERED: 30 semester hours per year, which includes 6 credits of required preliminary course work in Paris.

HOUSING: Students live in the university dormitories.

DATES: Approximately early September through May.

COSTS: $8,900 includes tuition, room and board, round-trip transportation from New York, and local group excursions.

YEAR ESTABLISHED: 1980.

NUMBER OF STUDENTS IN 1985: 35.

APPLY: By January 15. Elizabeth C. Todrank, Foreign Study Coordinator.

■ **KALAMAZOO COLLEGE**
1200 Academy Street
Kalamazoo, MI 49007
(616) 383-8470

PROGRAM: The Kalamazoo French program is designed for students who have enough language aptitude and training (minimum: 4 units in French) to enable them, after a short intensive period of language study, to handle college-level courses conducted in French. Held in cooperation with the Université de Caen and the Institute for American Universities in Aix-en-Provence. Students may also attend schools in Clermont-Ferrand, Strasbourg, Aix-en-Provence. Assignment to site location is made according to student's language ability (Caen being most advanced, then Clermont-Ferrand, Strasbourg, Aix-en-Provence). Courses cover French language, history, civilization, and literature. Orientation: two hours a week during preceding term at Kalamazoo.

ADMITTANCE REQUIREMENTS: Enrollment at Kalamazoo College in term prior to departure. Ten semester hours of college French or the equivalent.

TEACHING METHODS: Students attend regular academic courses, lectures, seminars, and tutorials in French taught by host-country instructors. Some special courses in English.

EVALUATION: By individual instructors, based upon class work, papers, and exams. Recorded by Kalamazoo only as "pass/fail."

CREDITS OFFERED: Maximum 30 quarter hours credit; 20 in Aix-en-Provence.

HOUSING: With local families, except school dormitories in Strasbourg.

DATES: Approximately mid-September to mid-March.

COSTS: $7,064 includes tuition, room and board, some regional travel, and round-trip transportation from New York. Does not cover the cost of one term at Kalamazoo at $3,532 or personal travel and living expenses.

YEAR ESTABLISHED: 1963.

NUMBER OF STUDENTS IN 1985: 30.

APPLY: By May 1. Dr. Joe K. Fugate, Director, Office of Foreign Study.

Dijon

■ **STETSON UNIVERSITY**
Box #8412
DeLand, FL 32720
(904) 734-4121, ext. 211

PROGRAM: The Stetson University Abroad Program is held in cooperation with the University of Dijon with undergraduate courses concentrating on the French language, literature, civilization, history, art, etc. Students can elect to attend for a single semester or the full academic year. Onsite presession orientation.

ADMITTANCE REQUIREMENTS: Completion of sophomore year (or 60 semester hours) plus two years of French or the equivalent. Language department recommendation.

TEACHING METHODS: Courses are conducted in French by members of the faculty at the University of Dijon.

EVALUATION: Final examination given by local faculty.

CREDITS OFFERED: Upper-level semester credits vary depending upon course load.

HOUSING: Students live in the dormitories at the Foyer International d'Étudiants.

DATES: Fall semester: September 1 through mid-December; spring semester: mid-January through June 10.

COSTS: $8,800 includes tuition, room and board, local travel, orientation, insurance, and international student I.D. card.

YEAR ESTABLISHED: 1964.

NUMBER OF STUDENTS IN 1985: 13.

APPLY: Fall semester only or full academic year, March 15; spring semester, October 15. Office of International Exchange and Off-Campus Programs.

Grenoble

■ **AMERICAN INSTITUTE OF FOREIGN STUDY (AIFS)**
102 Greenwich Avenue
Greenwich, CT 06830
(800) 243-4567 or (203) 869-9090

PROGRAM: AIFS is a national for-profit organization specializing in comprehensive overseas academic-year, semester, and summer study programs. The AIFS program at the Université de Grenoble is a full academic year, fall, or spring semester experience in which students are enrolled in the university's Centre Universitaire d'Études Françaises where foreign students take special courses in English. Advanced students can take a wide range of courses at the university with French students. Regular courses cover intensive French; history of art in France; French history, political life, and literature; economics; French cinema; international business, and international relations. Program includes visits to local historic sites and museums, as well as a three-day trip to Provence. Optional field trips to Paris and Italy. Three-week orientation and intensive French at Antibes (fall semester); two-week orientation at Cannes (spring semester).

ADMITTANCE REQUIREMENTS: College freshman juniors, and seniors with a 2.5 GPA. No language requirements.

TEACHING METHODS: Students must take a 6-credit intensive French course. Most seminars are taught in French, but two are also offered in English.

EVALUATION: By faculty, based upon class work, papers, and periodic exams.

CREDITS OFFERED: A minimum of 12 semester hours. Most students take 15 semester hours per semester.

HOUSING: Students live with local families and have two meals a day with their families.

DATES: Fall semester: September 30 through January 24; spring semester: January 20 through May 22.

COSTS: Fall semester: $4,695; spring semester: $4,595, includes tuition, room and board, program-related travel, and one-way transportation from New York. Does not cover local travel or personal expenses.

YEAR ESTABLISHED: 1986.

NUMBER OF STUDENTS IN 1986: 13.

APPLY: Applications filled on first-come basis. "It is expected that all full-year or fall-semester places will be filled by June 1; places for spring semester are kept open until November 15."

■ **BOSTON UNIVERSITY**
   143 Bay State Road
   Boston, MA 02215
   (617) 353-9888

PROGRAM: Boston University Study Abroad in Grenoble is a single-semester or full-academic-year undergraduate program, held in cooperation with the University of Grenoble and the University of Grenoble Center for Foreigners, offering courses concentrating on the French language, culture, and civilization. Program-related travel to local sites of historic and cultural interest. Two-week onsite orientation.

ADMITTANCE REQUIREMENTS: Good academic standing and at least one semester of college French for beginning programs; five semesters for advanced programs.

TEACHING METHODS: Students attend special courses arranged for the group and taught in French by the faculty of the University of Grenoble and the University of Grenoble Center for Foreigners.

EVALUATION: By course faculty, based upon papers and periodic exams.

CREDITS OFFERED: 16 semester hours per semester.

HOUSING: Students live with local families.

DATES: Fall semester: early September through mid-December; spring semester: early January through late May.

COSTS: Approximately $7,265 per semester includes tuition, room and board, and transportation from New York to Grenoble. Does not include return transportation or personal expenses.

YEAR ESTABLISHED: 1983.

NUMBER OF STUDENTS IN 1985: 73.

APPLY: Fall semester: February 28; spring semester: October 9. Study Abroad Office.

■ **UNIVERSITY OF CONNECTICUT**
  241 Glenbrook Road
  Storrs, CT 06268
  (203) 486-2141

PROGRAM: International Marketing in Grenoble is a recently inaugurated spring-semester program held in cooperation with the five other New England state universities and the University of Grenoble II. Courses cover international marketing; international finance and capital markets; French culture, society, and economy; and a fourth course that varies each year. One-week orientation in Grenoble.

ADMITTANCE REQUIREMENTS: Upper division undergraduates majoring in business administration, economics, or appropriate social science discipline. Good academic standing and completion of at least introductory course in marketing, finance, and micro-economics.

TEACHING METHODS: Four special classes in English are held at the University of Grenoble. Three are taught by Grenoble faculty; one by resident director. Additional courses may be taken at the university.

EVALUATION: By course professors, based upon exams.

CREDITS OFFERED: 12 semester hours plus language credit if selected.

HOUSING: Students have single rooms in university dormitories.

DATES: Early January through the third week of May.

COSTS: $3,150 per semester includes tuition, and room and breakfast during orientation week, transportation to Grenoble, and program-related travel. Does not include return transportation or personal expenses (estimated at $1,000).

YEAR ESTABLISHED: 1986.

NUMBER OF STUDENTS IN 1986: 21.

APPLY: By October 1. Dr. Ronald J. Patten, School of Business Administration, U-41D.

■ **STATE UNIVERSITY OF NEW YORK AT POTSDAM**
College of Arts and Sciences
Pierrepont Avenue
Potsdam, NY 13676
(315) 267-2654

PROGRAM: The Grenoble Study Program is a spring semester or academic-year undergraduate program held in cooperation with the Université de Grenoble and the State University of New York's University Centers at Albany and Buffalo. In addition to the traditional French language, literature, and civilization courses given at the université, there are opportunities for participation in student teaching, work-study programs, and independent study options. One or two extensive trips per year depending on program funds. Many local field trips. One-day orientation in Buffalo and a week in Grenoble.

ADMITTANCE REQUIREMENTS: Juniors and above (although "qualified sophomores will be considered"), 2.75 GPA with a 3.0 GPA in French, and completion of intermediate-level French.

TEACHING METHODS: Students attend regular courses at the Université de Grenoble or special language programs offered by the Centre Universitaire d'Étude Française. All classes are in French; foreign students are integrated with local students. Tutorials and independent study options.

EVALUATION: By French faculty under direction of the French academic program director.

CREDITS OFFERED: 13 to 18 semester hours per semester.

HOUSING: Students live with local families.

DATES: Fall semester: September 28 through January 19; spring semester: January 20 through May 25.

COSTS: Tuition and tours: $1,350 for the academic year for New York residents; $3,200 for nonresidents. $675 for a semester for New York residents; $1,600 for nonresidents. Room, breakfast, round-trip transportation from New York, contingency fee, and administrative fee: $2,500 for the academic year; $1,319 for the spring semester.

YEAR ESTABLISHED: 1971.

NUMBER OF STUDENTS IN 1985: 30.

APPLY: Academic year by March 15; spring semester by October 15. Potsdam students: Dr. Jane Edwards, Carson 215/217, SUCP. All others: International Education Office, SUNY Buffalo-Amherst campus, Buffalo, NY 14261.

■ **SWARTHMORE COLLEGE**
  Swarthmore, PA 19081
  (215) 447-7160

PROGRAM: Swarthmore in Grenoble is a single-semester or full-year undergraduate program. Students may concentrate in intermediate or advanced French, German or Italian languages or may take courses in literature, the humanities, economics, or social sciences. Two-week onsite orientation including language refresher course and field trips.

ADMITTANCE REQUIREMENTS: Sophomore or above. 3.0 GPA plus 3 semesters college French or the equivalent.

TEACHING METHODS: Students attend special courses designed for foreigners and taught by both U.S. and local faculty as well as regular courses offered by the University of Grenoble taught in French.

EVALUATION: Papers and exams given by course instructors.

CREDITS OFFERED: 4 credits per semester.

HOUSING: Students live with local families.

DATES: Approximately September 15 through mid-December; January 10 through early June.

COSTS: Approximately $6,800 per term including tuition, room and board. Does not include round trip transportation, personal expenses, or local transportation.

YEAR ESTABLISHED: 1972.

NUMBER OF STUDENTS IN 1985:   Limited to 20 students.

APPLY: By March 15th for fall term; October 15 for spring term. George Muskos.

Lille

■ **ARIZONA STATE UNIVERSITY**
Academic Services Building, Room #110
Tempe, AZ 85287
(692) 965-6611

PROGRAM: Arizona Program in France is an undergraduate program held under the auspices of the Institut Supérieur de Culture Français Contemporaine of the Faculté Libre in Lille. Students may elect any courses given by the institut. They cover French language and linguistics, literature, culture, philosophy, history, geography, law, archaeology, political life in France, music, etc. Special French courses are required. Preorientation in Lille.

ADMITTANCE REQUIREMENTS: Sophomore standing with at least intermediate-level French or the equivalent and two letters of recommendations.

TEACHING METHODS: Students are instructed in French by professors from the Institut Supérieur de Culture Français Contemporaine.

EVALUATION: Papers and exams given by French instructors.

CREDITS OFFERED: A minimum course load of 12 semester hours is required.

HOUSING: Students live with French families.

DATES: Approximately October 1 through mid-December.

COSTS: Students pay regular registration fee to their Arizona university in addition to a program fee of $2,800, which covers tuition in France and room and board. Does not cover round-trip transportation, personal expenses (estimated at $200 a month minimum), or local travel.

YEAR ESTABLISHED: Not available.

NUMBER OF STUDENTS IN 1985: Not available.

APPLY: By March 1. Dr. Losse, Department of Foreign Languages.

Lyons

■ **OREGON STATE SYSTEM OF HIGHER EDUCATION (OSSHE)**
Foreign Study Programs
International Education
Oregon State University
Corvallis, OR
(503) 754-3006

PROGRAM: OSSHE Study in France — Lyons is a new undergraduate and graduate exchange program held in cooperation with Lyon II, Lyon III, Catholic University, Friends of the Universities of Lyon, and the member schools of OSSHE (Eastern Oregon State College, Oregon Institute of Technology, Portland State University, Southern Oregon State University, University of Oregon, and Western Oregon State College). The program concentrates on French language studies, history, fine arts, political science, business, education, and agriculture. For students sufficient in French some or all classes may be taken at the université. Graduate study is also offered. One-day orientation in Oregon and a three-week period of orientation in France.

ADMITTANCE REQUIREMENTS: Junior standing or above. Minimum 2.75 GPA (3.0 in French), letters of recommendation, and personal interview.

TEACHING METHODS: Taught in French by faculty members from the local universities. Some special courses for Americans are offered. Most classes are integrated. Lectures, seminars, and independent study complemented by some travel to regional museums and cultural sites.

EVALUATION: By university faculty, based on periodic and final exams.

CREDITS OFFERED: The equivalent of attending an American school for two full semesters or three terms of a trimester program.

HOUSING: Students live in university dormitories.

DATES: Approximately mid-September through mid-June.

COSTS: Final costs not established as yet. For similar program in Poitiers resident undergraduates pay $3,888; nonresidents $6,591. (Prices may be several hundred dollars less depending on the housing option chosen.) Includes tuition, room and board, and some local travel. Does not include round-trip transportation or personal expenses (which will probably range from $2,150 to $3,800).

YEAR ESTABLISHED: 1986.

NUMBER OF STUDENTS IN 1986: Not available.

APPLY: By February 15. French department at member OSSHE school, or Irma Wright, Office of International Education.

Montpellier

■ **COLLEGE OF WILLIAM AND MARY**
Office of International Studies
Williamsburg, VA 23185
(804) 253-4354

PROGRAM: William and Mary offers two programs: a full-academic-year program in conjunction with the University of North Carolina, Chapel Hill, and the Université Paul Valéry; and a Summer in France in cooperation with the Université Paul Valéry. The full-year program offers a complete complement of academic courses except studio art. The five-week summer program offers courses specializing in the French language, literature, and civilization. Travel to local historic and cultural sites is part of both programs. Onsite preorientation.

ADMITTANCE REQUIREMENTS: Open to all undergraduates who hold good academic standing at their home institution plus two years of college French or the equivalent.

TEACHING METHODS: Regular courses for the full-year program are taught in French by university faculty members. Students are fully integrated. Summer students are taught by a U.S. faculty. Seminar-sized classes. Both class and onsite lectures, seminars, and ateliers.

EVALUATION: By faculty based upon papers, periodic tests, and a final exam.

CREDITS OFFERED: Full year program: 30 semester hours; summer session: 6 semester hours.

HOUSING: Students for the full year can live with local families, apartments, or in dormitories; summer students live in single rooms in dormitories at the Université Paul Valéry.

DATES: Full year: approximately August 27 through June 15; summer: approximately June 26 through August 2.

COSTS: Tuition and room and board: full year, $5,800; summer, $2,100. Estimated living expenses: full year, $1,500; summer, $200. Round-trip transportation not included. Scholarships available to William and Mary students.

YEAR ESTABLISHED: 1978.

NUMBER OF STUDENTS IN 1985: 48.

APPLY: By March 1. Ms. Carolyn V. Blackwell, Director.

■ **UNIVERSITY OF MINNESOTA**
  Extension Classes Offices of Study Abroad (ECOSA)
  202 Wesbrook Hall
  77 Pleasant Street SE
  Minneapolis, MN 55455
  (612) 373-1855

PROGRAM: French in Montpellier is a spring quarter opportunity to take French language courses administered by the Service Commun Interuniversitaire des Étudiants Étrangers attached to the Université Paul Valéry. The basic program includes three courses, choosing from: intermediate French, French composition and conversation, themes in French literature, history of Southern French civilization, or French literature in English translation. Additional courses are also offered by UM's program director. Five-day orientation in Paris.

ADMITTANCE REQUIREMENTS: Students in good academic standing. No established GPA required. One year of previous language or course work.

TEACHING METHODS: Students are taught by both U.S. and foreign faculty in groups consisting only of other Americans.

EVALUATION: By course instructors, based upon class work, papers, and final exams.

CREDITS OFFERED: 12 to 14 quarter credits each period.

HOUSING: Students live with French families.

DATES: April 1 through June 8.

COSTS: $2,389 includes tuition for three courses, room and board, and program-related travel. Does not include round-trip transportation or personal expenses.

YEAR ESTABLISHED: 1984.

NUMBER OF STUDENTS IN 1985: 25.

APPLY: January 1. Jody Jensen, ECOSA.

■ **WESTERN KENTUCKY UNIVERSITY**
  Bowling Green, KY 42101
  (502) 745-5907

PROGRAM: The Western Kentucky University in France Program, held in cooperation with the Université Paul Valéry, is a full-academic-year undergraduate experience in which Americans are enrolled in the French university with the opportunity to take any courses offered French students. The université has a rich liberal arts curriculum. The month of September is devoted to language study and cultural orientation in Montpellier.

ADMITTANCE REQUIREMENTS: Junior standing with a 2.5 GPA, and a minimum of two years of college French or the equivalent.

TEACHING METHODS: Americans are fully integrated with French students at the université. There are no special courses for foreigners. All courses are in French.

EVALUATION: By université faculty. Grades are processed by a French faculty member acting as a coordinator to convert French grades into an appropriate alphabetical equivalent.

CREDITS OFFERED: 30 semester hours per year.

HOUSING: Students have individual rooms in the université dormitory.

DATES: September 1 through June 15.

COSTS: $5,200 for Western Kentucky students; $5,450 for all others. Includes tuition, room and board, round-trip transportation, and all fees.

YEAR ESTABLISHED: 1971.

NUMBERS OF STUDENTS IN 1985: limited to 10.

APPLY: By March 1. Dr. James C. Babcock, Department of Modern Languages.

■ **WEST CHESTER UNIVERSITY**
West Chester, PA 19383
(215) 436-2700

PROGRAM: West Chester's JYA Program in Montpellier is a full-year undergraduate program held in cooperation with the Université Paul Valéry. Following a placement exam, students elect any courses offered at the université. Some travel to regional sites. Full-month orientation in Montpellier.

ADMITTANCE REQUIREMENTS: Juniors only with at least two years of college French, a 3.0 GPA in French, and two letters of recommendation, one of which is from a French professor.

TEACHING METHODS: Students attend regular classes at the université together with local students. All classes are in French. American students are also required to attend special classes ("recyclage") under the supervision of the resident director.

EVALUATION: Written and oral examinations at the université, plus a separate written evaluation by local professors and a personal evaluation by the resident director.

CREDITS OFFERED: Normally 30 semester hours per year; 36 with permission of the director.

HOUSING: Students are encouraged to stay with French families, but may elect to live in private dormitory rooms.

DATES: Early September to mid-June.

COSTS: $6,000 includes tuition, room and board, round-trip transportation from New York, and program-related travel. Does not include personal expenses (estimated at $1,200 per year) or breakfast from October through June.

YEAR ESTABLISHED: 1963.

NUMBER OF STUDENTS IN 1985: 20.

APPLY: By March 31. Roger J. Brown, Campus Director, JYA Box #9 Main West Chester University.

Nantes

■ **HIRAM COLLEGE**
   Hiram, OH 44234
   (216) 569-5160

PROGRAM: Hiram's French Quarter offers a ten-week undergraduate program in which students select courses from a menu covering language, literature, and civilization. Presession orientation at Hiram and a few days in France. Material mailed to students who can't attend the Hiram session.

ADMITTANCE REQUIREMENTS: A minimum 2.5 GPA with recommendations from your own advisor plus two additional teachers. A language requirement varies from program to program.

TEACHING METHODS: Students attend regular classes or seminars taught by a French faculty. Lectures and seminars are integrated with local field trips.

EVALUATION: By programs leaders and students, based upon papers and exams.

CREDITS OFFERED: Up to 15 quarter hours per quarter.

HOUSING: Students live with local French families.

DATES: The program is offered every three years. Next program scheduled for the spring quarter, 1989; approximately March 31 to June 3.

COSTS: Approximately $4,700 including tuition, room and board, local travel, and fees. Does not cover round-trip transportation or local expenses.

YEAR ESTABLISHED: 1972.

NUMBER OF STUDENTS IN 1986: 10.

APPLY: By December 1. Charles L. Adams, Director, Extra Mural Studies.

■ **INSTITUTE OF EUROPEAN STUDY (IES)**
223 West Ohio Street
Chicago, IL 60610
(312) 944-1750

PROGRAM: IES is a nonprofit organization with formal relationships with more than forty American colleges and universities. The institute maintains ten undergraduate academic centers throughout the world which provide semester or full-academic-year programs. The IES Nantes program, held in cooperation with the University of Nantes, is a semester or full-academic-year program with two components: courses offered through the institute and courses at the University of Nantes. The institute offers art history, French language and literature, economics, history, political science, and theater production. For qualified students there is a wide range of courses available at the university as well as teaching internships. One-week orientation in Nantes.

ADMITTANCE REQUIREMENTS: Juniors and seniors only. Two years college French or the equivalent. Faculty recommendations and an application essay. 85 percent of all students have had a GPA between 2.80 and 3.75.

TEACHING METHODS: Students attend regular university courses with French students. All courses are taught in French. Classes are supplemented by trips to local museums and historic sites.

EVALUATION: By faculty, based upon class work and periodic and final exams. Most courses require a research paper.

CREDITS OFFERED: A maximum of 18; minimum of 15 credit hours per semester.

HOUSING: The institute arranges housing in French homes. Two students often share a room. Breakfast and two meals per week are provided. The student is responsible for other eating arrangements. Full-year students may apply to live in the university dormitory, but space is limited.

DATES: Fall semester: September 17 through January 23; spring semester February 2 through May 29.

COSTS: $6,200 per year; $3,850 per semester. Includes tuition, room and board, and program-related field trips. Does not include round-trip transportation, local travel, or personal expenses (estimated at $2,000 per year). Some IES scholarship aid available; $1,500 for full-year students, $750 for semester students.

YEAR ESTABLISHED: 1967.

NUMBER OF STUDENTS IN 1985:   50.

APPLY: Fall semester by May 1; spring semester by November 15.

■ **KENYON COLLEGE**
   Gambier, OH 43022
   (614) 427-2244

PROGRAM: Kenyon's France Program is a six-month, undergraduate program held in cooperation with Earlham College. A summer program is also available. The six-month program offers courses in history, fine arts, language, political science, and economics. It is designed for those who have completed intensive French. Students spend two weeks as an apprentice to a French artisan in the Rodez area, studying any one of several arts or crafts. Onsite orientation.

ADMITTANCE REQUIREMENTS: Open to students at Kenyon and Earlham and, on a space-available basis, those from schools affiliated with the Great Lakes College Association. Acceptable academic credentials and recommendations.

TEACHING METHODS: All courses are taught in French either by accompanying faculty member or faculty member from France. Americans are not integrated with French students. Travel to local sites supplements class work.

EVALUATION: By course professors, based upon class work, periodic exams, etc.

CREDITS OFFERED: 2½ Kenyon units.

HOUSING: Students live with local families.

DATES: Approximately, late June through early December.

COSTS: Based upon costs at sponsoring institution. Kenyon: Tuition and room and board: $7,054. Does not include round-trip transportation, local travel, or personal expenses.

YEAR ESTABLISHED: 1980.

NUMBER OF STUDENTS IN 1985: 12.

APPLY: By February 15. Off-campus Studies Office.

Nice

■ **PENNSYLVANIA STATE UNIVERSITY**
  Office of Education Abroad Programs
  222 Boucke Building
  University Park, PA 16802
  (814) 865-7681

PROGRAM: Pennsylvania State offers a pair of single-semester undergraduate programs at the Institut Universitaire de Technologie of the Université de Nice. Nice I is a fall semester program designed for business administration majors with little background in the French language. The initial three weeks are devoted to intensive language training, followed by a choice of three 3-credit courses covering the European business community, comparative economics, etc. Nice II is a spring-semester program designed for students majoring in the "French/business option" and is conducted by faculty members from the institut. Orientation at Penn State.

ADMITTANCE REQUIREMENTS: Juniors and seniors with a 2.5 GPA, good academic standing, and "must show evidence of maturity, stability, adaptability, self-discipline and a strong academic motivation." Some specific course prerequisites.

TEACHING METHODS: Students take specially designed courses at the institut. Nice I courses are in English; Nice II in French.

EVALUATION: By course instructors, based upon class work, papers, and exams.

CREDITS OFFERED: Nice I: 15 credits; Nice II: 16 credits.

HOUSING: Students live in regular IUT dormitories.

DATES: Nice I: third week in September through third week in December; Nice II: mid-January through mid-May.

COSTS: Students pay the same as at the University Park Campus. 1986-87 tuition per semester was $2,250 for state residents; $5,150 for nonresidents; room and board: $2,750 per semester. Plus a $100 nonrefundable program fee.

YEAR ESTABLISHED: Nice I: 1981; Nice II: 1982.

NUMBER OF STUDENTS IN 1985: Nice I: 19; Nice II: 20.

APPLY: Nice I by March 1; Nice II by October 15.

■ **UNIVERSITY OF VERMONT**
513 Waterman Building
Burlington, VT 05405
(802) 656-3131

PROGRAM: The Vermont Overseas Study Program is a full-academic-year experience held in cooperation with the Université de Nice. Students take regular classes at the université, which includes courses on: French language and literature; history; fine arts; geography; cinema; foreign languages; political science; economics; psychology; sociology; business administration; and education. The program offers the unique opportunity to teach English in French public schools. Three week presession orientation in Nice.

ADMITTANCE REQUIREMENTS: A good working knowledge of French and completion of at least 12 hours of advanced intermediate French courses.

TEACHING METHODS: Students are enrolled in regular classes and are fully integrated with French students. All courses are in French. Supervised practice teaching of English in French public schools is optional.

EVALUATION: By French faculty, based upon class work, papers, and final exams. Grades are converted to "American system" by resident director.

CREDITS OFFERED: 30 to 33 semester hours per academic year.

HOUSING: Most students live in the residence halls at the université. However, students may elect to live with families or private apartments.

DATES: Late September through early June.

COSTS: $7,950 includes tuition, room, cash allowance for food, round-trip transportation from Montréal, and program-related excursions. Living and personal travel expenses (approximately $1,000 to $1,500) are extra.

YEAR ESTABLISHED: 1967.

NUMBER OF STUDENTS IN 1985: 30.

APPLY: By March 15. Susan Quinn, Program Coordinator.

Orleans

■ **SAINT LOUIS UNIVERSITY**
221 North Grand Boulevard
Saint Louis, MO 63110
(800) 325-6666

PROGRAM: Saint Louis University in France is a full-year undergraduate program held in cooperation with the Université d'Orleans. Courses cover history, fine arts, political science, French language and literature, English literature, geography, and some business courses. Two-week orientation in Orleans.

ADMITTANCE REQUIREMENTS: Sophomores and above with a 2.5 GPA with a 3.0 in French and at least three semesters of college French. Recommendations from college dean and major professor.

TEACHING METHODS: Students attend both special and regular courses at the université taught in French by foreign faculty. All classes are integrated with local students.

EVALUATION: By foreign faculty, based upon class work, papers and exams.

CREDITS OFFERED: Full semester year (follows French educational system).

HOUSING: Students can live in university dormitories, with local families, or in furnished rooms.

DATES: September 10 through June 10.

COSTS: For the full year. Tuition: $3,700, room and board approximately $2,700. Does not include round-trip transportation, local or trip-related travel, or personal expenses.

YEAR ESTABLISHED: 1983.

NUMBER OF STUDENTS IN 1985: 20.

APPLY: By July 1. Office of Admissions.

Paris

- *I adore Paris. I dream about going back to find work. It's a people city; people walk everywhere. Sit and people watch in cafés and enjoy the abundance of culture all around you. It's great to live in the 4th, 6th, 7th, or 15th Arrondisements because there is always something going on: great clubs, cafés, galleries and shopping. Don't miss the boulevards Saint Michel and Saint Germain, Le Marais, and, Les Halles. Also the weekly open markets at Clignancourt.*

  - Carol Ann Blinken, New York, New York

- *Student restaurants are very cheap; but you get what you pay for.*

  - Matthew S. Holland, Lincoln, Massachusetts

■ **ACADEMIC YEAR ABROAD**
17 Jansen Road
New Paltz, NY 12561
(914) 255-8103

PROGRAM: Academic Year Abroad (AYA) sponsors programs for both undergraduate and graduate students in cooperation with the Université de Paris-Sorbonne, Institut d'Études Politiques, and the Institut de Phonétique. Most university subjects are taught in French. Except for language courses, classes are composed of students from throughout Europe. Although there is no fixed pattern of travel, excursions are planned throughout the year. Program also includes a one-month presession orientation.

ADMITTANCE REQUIREMENTS: Competence in the language, though students may be accepted to begin the language; consent of home institution; acceptable academic record.

TEACHING METHODS: Varies with each subject.

EVALUATION: Grades given by the foreign professor.

CREDITS OFFERED: 16 semester hours per semester.

HOUSING: Optional, although AYA does provide housing in local homes when so elected by the student.

DATES: First term: early to mid-September through end of January; second term: end of January through May 30.

COSTS: Room and board $3,800; tuition $3,000. Estimated living expenses $1,000. Students bring financial aid from home institutions.

YEAR ESTABLISHED: 1961.

NUMBER OF STUDENTS IN 1985: 12.

APPLY: Dr. Stuart H. L. Degginger, Professor, SUNY New Paltz.

■ **ALMA COLLEGE**
  Alma, MI 48801
  (517) 463-7247

PROGRAM: Alma College Program of Studies in France is held in coopera-tion with Alliance Française. This program is not in a structured academic setting such as most American schools. Because language courses are offered on a monthly basis and those in literature and civilization on a term basis, students may participate in the Alma program for virtually any period of time. Courses specialize in French language and culture. One-week onsite orientation with the director.

ADMITTANCE REQUIREMENTS: Sophomore and above with a minimum 2.0 GPA, in good academic standing, with letters of recommendation..

TEACHING METHODS: Small classes, usually six to nine students, in French are complemented with visits to local sites and independent study. Direct involvement with French staff and local residents is encouraged and expected.

EVALUATION: Foreign faculty in conjunction with the resident director plus papers and periodic exams.

CREDITS OFFERED: Up to 15 hours per semester.

HOUSING: All students reside in French homes.

DATES: Fall semester: September 1 through January 30; spring semester: February 1 through May 29.

COSTS: Fall semester: $5,450; spring semester: $4,775. Includes round-trip transportation from New York, room and board, plus basic texts and cultural activities. Students can earn money by working "au pair" for their families.

YEAR ESTABLISHED: 1963.

NUMBER OF STUDENTS IN 1985: 115.

APPLY: Two months prior to departure. Alda Dyal Chand, Director, International Education.

■ **THE AMERICAN COLLEGE IN PARIS (ACP)**
31 Avenue Bosquet
75007 Paris, France

PROGRAM: The American College in Paris is an independent, four-year, coeducational college of arts and sciences located in the seventh arrondissement, a five-minute walk from the Eiffel Tower. The school is fully accredited by the Middle States Association of Colleges and Schools and confers BA degrees in half a dozen fields and a BS degree in computer sciences. The school offers more than 250 courses and a wide range of electives. Credits are easily transferable. The school also provides a year-round travel program to complement courses of study. Approximately half the students are American; 15 percent French; and the remainder from sixty other countries.

ADMITTANCE REQUIREMENTS: Students are accepted on a competitive basis based on college or precollege record: a combined SAT score of 1000, a 2.30 to 2.80 GPA, and two academic recommendations. Transfer students are welcomed.

TEACHING METHODS: Regular classes are taught at the college's facilities, plus an exchange agreement with the Sorbonne. Faculty is half American, half European. Student-faculty ratio is 13:1. Classes, seminars, and independent study programs are conducted in English. Local travel complements educational program.

EVALUATION: By college faculty, based on the same standards as any U.S. college.

CREDITS OFFERED: 15 to 16 credit hours per semester.

HOUSING: The college arranges for students to live in studio flats or apartments in Paris. Students also have the option of living with a French family. The college does not maintain dormitory facilities.

DATES: Fall semester: September to mid-January; spring semester: February to mid-June; summer session: June and July.

COSTS: Tuition and fees: $7,750 per year; room and board: $4,220 per year; estimated living expenses: $3,320 per year. Does not include round-trip transportation or travel within Europe. There are a limited number of ACP scholarships available.

YEAR ESTABLISHED: 1962.

NUMBER OF STUDENTS IN 1985: 1,000.

APPLY: Fall semester by July 31; spring semester by December 15. Mrs. Janice Pfeiffer, Director of Admissions.

■ **AMERICAN INSTITUTE OF FOREIGN STUDY (AIFS)**
   102 Greenwich Avenue
   Greenwich, CT 06830
   (800) 243-4567 or (203) 869-9090

PROGRAM: AIFS is a national for-profit organization specializing in comprehensive overseas academic-year, semester, and summer study programs. The AIFS program at the University of Paris is a full-academic-year or single-semester program. AIFS students take courses at the Sorbonne, organized for foreign students by the Cours de Civilisation Française de la Sorbonne. In addition, students with a French background can take courses at other institutions in Paris. An honors program for French majors is also offered. Special AIFS courses, taught in English, cover French (required), French literature in translation, history, music, photography, politics, and business. Three weeks of intensive French orientation in Antibes (fall semester) or Cannes (spring semester).

ADMITTANCE REQUIREMENTS: College freshmen, sophomores and juniors with a 2.5 GPA. No language requirement. For honors program: juniors, seniors, and graduate students with two years of college French or the equivalent.

TEACHING METHODS: Most students in the special AIFS courses are Americans; faculty is predominantly French. Students attend special courses at the Sorbonne, which are taught in English. Honors program students are taught in French.

EVALUATION: By faculty, based upon class work, papers and periodic exams.

CREDITS OFFERED: Approximately 18 semester hours per semester.

HOUSING: Students live with families and receive breakfast. Other meals are obtained in university cafeterias or elsewhere in Paris.

DATES: Fall semester: October 30 through January 30; spring semester: February 1 through May 30.

COSTS: Full academic year: $8,895; fall semester or spring semester: $4,995 — includes tuition, room and board, program-related travel, and one-way transportation from New York. Does not cover local travel or personal expenses.

YEAR ESTABLISHED: 1972.

NUMBER OF STUDENTS IN 1986: 112.

APPLY: Applications filled on first-come basis. "It is expected that all full-year or fall-semester places will be filled by June 1; places for spring semester are kept open until November 15."

■ **BRIGHAM YOUNG UNIVERSITY**
Study Abroad Programs
204 HRCB
Provo, UT 84602
(801) 378-3308

PROGRAM: Spring Term in Paris offers courses in the French language, literature, and civilization. Local field trips to historic and cultural sites are part of the program.

ADMITTANCE REQUIREMENTS: Good academic standing with a 3.0 GPA requested. Adherence to BYU standards.

TEACHING METHODS: Classes are taught by BYU faculty in classrooms designated for the purpose. No foreign schools are involved.

EVALUATION: Based on periodic exams. Evaluation determined by program director.

CREDITS OFFERED: From 6 to 9 credit hours.

HOUSING: Students live in hotels, hostels, or facilities arranged by BYU.

DATES: Approximately April through June.

COSTS: Approximately $1,800 includes tuition, room and board, and local travel. Does not cover round-trip transportation and additional travel.

YEAR ESTABLISHED: 1975.

NUMBER OF STUDENTS IN 1985: 24.

APPLY: By February. Professor Keith Slade, Department of French and Italian.

■ **CENTRAL COLLEGE**
Pella, IA 50219
(515) 628-5287

PROGRAM: Central's Paris Program offers students several academic options depending upon the individual's interests and linguistic ability. Students fluent in French may enroll in the Cours de Civilisation Française de la Sorbonne. Those who do not qualify for the lecture courses enroll in a heavy concentration of French language courses including classes in civilization. Other offerings cover: history, art, business, political science, geography, music, philosophy, etc. Students who elect to stay for the full year may also attend the Institut Catholique. This very popular, well-organized program is limited to eighty students. Two- to three-day orientation in Paris.

ADMITTANCE REQUIREMENTS: Minimum 2.5 GPA (3.0 in French), recommendations, and essay.

TEACHING METHODS: Those not attending the Sorbonne take special classes designed for foreign students taught by French professors. Lectures and seminars in French are complemented by local field trips.

EVALUATION: By French faculty. Resident director sends grades to home institution.

CREDITS OFFERED: 16 to 20 semester hours per semester.

HOUSING: Most students live in dormitories with French roommates. Other options include single rooms or with French families.

DATES: Fall semester: early September through mid-January; spring semester: early-February through mid-May. Students at the Institut Catholique attend from September through June.

COSTS: Approximately, Sorbonne: 35 credit hours @ $8,900; 19 hours @ $5,700; 16 hours @ $4,700. Institut Catholique: from $8,900 to $9,200. Includes tuition, room and board, fees, and some excursions. Does not cover round-trip transportation or personal expenses. Several $500 merit scholarships are available.

YEAR ESTABLISHED: 1966.

NUMBER OF STUDENTS IN 1985: 80.

APPLY: By April 15 for fall semester or full year; November 1 for spring semester. Mrs. Barbara Butler, Coordinator of International Studies.

■ **COLLEGE OF SAINT TERESA**
Winona, MN 55987
(507) 454-2930, ext. 257

PROGRAM: The Autumn Abroad Program is a single-semester undergraduate opportunity that "emphasizes cultural understanding, language growth, and life styles." Students study at the Alliance Française and also have the opportunity to travel and study in other European countries as well. Four-day orientation both at College of Saint Teresa and in Paris.

ADMITTANCE REQUIREMENTS: Juniors and above with a 2.5 GPA and one year of college French or the equivalent.

TEACHING METHODS: Students take a full academic load of five courses in language, civilization, and culture taught by Alliance instructors. Most courses are in French.

EVALUATION: Based upon academic work and conference between student, local instructor, and CST director.

CREDITS OFFERED: 15 semester hours.

HOUSING: Students live with French families.

DATES: August 31 through November 24.

COSTS: Approximately $3,000 includes tuition, room and board, and program-related travel. Does not cover round-trip transportation or personal expenses.

YEAR ESTABLISHED: 1973.

NUMBER OF STUDENTS IN 1985:   Not available.

APPLY: By February 15. Nancy Edstrom, French Department.

■ **COLUMBIA UNIVERSITY**
   419 Lewisohn Hall
   New York, NY 10027
   (212) 280-2559

PROGRAM: The Reid Hall Programs in Paris are for undergraduates inter-ested in a single semester, full year, or summer term. Held in cooperation with the University of Paris, the program concentrates on the French language, civilization, and culture, including courses in art history, history, political science, etc. A one-week orientation period in Paris precedes the program.

ADMITTANCE REQUIREMENTS: 3.0 or better in French, overall good aca-demic standing, and strong letters of recommendation.

TEACHING METHODS: Columbia University conducts classes in French taught by a French faculty. Students qualified to take classes in the French university system are placed directly into the system, not in special classes for foreign students. Coursework includes lectures, field trips, seminars, individual research, and work with French tutors leading to a thesis.

EVALUATION: Exams and papers graded by French faculty.

CREDITS OFFERED: 12 semester hour credits per semester; minimum of 4 courses per semester.

HOUSING: Students can choose to live in dormitories, private homes, local apartments, or with friends or relatives.

DATES: Fall semester: September 2 through December 20; spring semes-ter: January 19 through May 23. Classes in the French university system run from October through June.

COSTS: Tuition: $5,140 per semester; room and board: $1,500 to $2,000 per semester; estimated living expenses: approximately $500 to $1,000 per semester. Does not include round-trip transportation. Does cover a one-week field trip to Normandy and the cost of local trips to museums, galleries, etc.

YEAR ESTABLISHED: 1964.

NUMBER OF STUDENTS IN 1985: 100.

APPLY: For fall semester by April 1; spring semester by October 1. Karen Sudol, Reid Hall Programs in Paris.

■ **INSTITUTE OF EUROPEAN STUDY (IES)**
223 West Ohio Street
Chicago, IL 60610
(312) 944-1750

PROGRAM: IES is a nonprofit organization with formal relationships with more than forty American colleges and universities. The institute maintains ten undergraduate academic centers throughout the world, which provide semester or full-academic-year programs. The IES Paris program, held in cooperation with the Sorbonne and other Parisian universities, is a semester or full-academic-year program. The institute's Paris center is located in the Montparnasse quarter. The program has two components: courses offered through the institute and courses available at local universities. Students with a high proficiency in French may select courses in any undergraduate field from the cooperating Parisian universities. There is also the opportunity for teaching internships in French high schools, in adult evening courses, or unpaid internships with French business firms. One-week orientation in Paris. Summer program also available.

ADMITTANCE REQUIREMENTS: Juniors and seniors only. Two years college French or the equivalent. Faculty recommendations and an application essay. 85 percent of all students have had a GPA between 2.80 and 3.75.

TEACHING METHODS: Students attend regular university courses with French students. All courses are taught in French. Classes are supplemented by trips to local museums and historic sites.

EVALUATION: By faculty, based upon class work and periodic and final exams. Most courses require a research paper.

CREDITS OFFERED: A maximum of 18; minimum of 15 credit hours per semester.

HOUSING: The institute arranges housing in French homes. Two students often share a room.

DATES: Fall semester: September 15 through January 23; spring semester February 2 through May 25.

COSTS: $6,450 per year; $4,000 per semester. Includes tuition, room and board, and program-related field trips. Does not include round-trip transportation, local travel, or personal expenses (estimated at $2,000 per year.) Some IES scholarship aid available; $1,500 for full year students, $750 for semester students.

YEAR ESTABLISHED: 1962.

NUMBER OF STUDENTS IN 1985: 100.

APPLY: Fall semester by February 15; spring semester by September 25.

■ **MIDDLEBURY COLLEGE**
  Middlebury, VT 05753
  (802) 388-3711

PROGRAM: Middlebury College School in France offers undergraduates "long-standing, highly respected, and *serious*" courses in literature, French language, culture, and civilization. An MA program is available in French language and literature. Courses are held at the University of Paris.

ADMITTANCE REQUIREMENTS: The equivalent of five semesters in French and a B average; (for MA a "better than B average" is required.)

TEACHING METHODS: French faculty. All courses, written papers, and exams are in French. Extensive travel, field trips, and cultural exchanges complement the program.

EVALUATION: Faculty-student conferences, term papers, finals, etc.

CREDITS OFFERED: Full semester or full year credit.

HOUSING: Students live in apartments, hostels, or with local families.

DATES: Approximately September 15 through June 10. Students can take a full-year program or fall or spring semester program.

COSTS: Tuition: Full year: $4,900; semester: $2,500; room and board: approximately: $2,000 per semester; round-trip travel to school: approximately $600. Local travel in Europe not included. Some scholarships available.

YEAR ESTABLISHED: 1949.

NUMBER OF STUDENTS IN 1985: 60.

APPLY: Rolling admissions. Dean of French School.

■ **NEW YORK UNIVERSITY**
19 University Place
New York, NY 10003
(212) 598-2262

PROGRAM: New York University in France operates several programs from their own center on the Rue de Passy. Their full-year undergraduate and graduate students take courses both at the center as well as at several Paris universities, Sciences Po, École du Louvre, etc. Summer students study at the center. Undergraduates in the Junior Year in Paris program and summer students elect courses concentrating on the French language, culture, and civilization. Full-year graduate students choose one of two tracks: an MA in French literature or in French language and civilization. The summer graduate program consists of three 3-week intensive courses. Various preorientation sessions depending upon program.

ADMITTANCE REQUIREMENTS: Summer undergraduate program: 2.5 GPA and good academic standing; prior French not required. Junior Year: Juniors with a 3.0 GPA (seniors with special permission) and French proficiency beyond the intermediate level. Graduate summer: French major "or strong minor" and recommendation from present or former professors. Graduate year: Admission to M.A. candidacy, French major or "strong minor." Also, accepts qualified nondegree matriculants.

TEACHING METHODS: All courses at the center are taught by NYU professors and visiting professors; French faculty at the universities. Most courses are in French.

EVALUATION: By NYU professors, visiting faculty, or French university professors. In most cases NYU and foreign faculty collaborate on student evaluation and grading.

CREDITS OFFERED: Undergraduate Summer: 8 NYU credits = 2 semester courses; Junior Year: 32 NYU credits = 4 courses per semester; Graduate Summer: students may take 1,2,3 courses @ 4 NYU credits per course; Full-Year Graduate: 4 normal courses per semester for 16 NYU credits.

HOUSING: Most undergraduate students stay as paying "guests" with French families (summer students usually stay in a French "foyer") and often opt for an "au pair" arrangement. Students may make their own living arrangements in Paris.

DATES: Summer Undergraduate: July 1 through mid-August; Summer Graduate: late June through mid-August; Junior Year: Early September through mid-June; Graduate Year: late September through early June.

COSTS: Summer Undergraduate: tuition, $1,250, room and board, $725; Junior Year: tuition, $5,000, room and board, $450-550 per month; Summer Graduate: $218 per point of credit for each 4-credit course; Graduate Year: Tuition, $5,000, room and board, $450-550 per month. "There are a modest number of partial tuition scholarships for MA degree candidates only."

YEAR ESTABLISHED:		NUMBER OF STUDENTS IN 1985:	
Summer Undergraduate:	1972	Summer Undergraduate:	79
Summer Graduate:	1974	Summer Graduate:	18
Junior Year:	1969	Junior Year:	150
Graduate Year:	1969	Graduate Year:	33

APPLY: Summer Undergraduate by May 1; summer graduate by June 1; Junior Year by May 15; Graduate Year by June 1 (financial aid applicants earlier.) Ms. Rosalyn McWatters, Director, NYU in France Programs.

■ **NORTHERN ILLINOIS UNIVERSITY**
   DeKalb, IL 60115
   (815) 753-0304

PROGRAM: NIU's French Internship Program is a one-semester or full-academic-year undergraduate and graduate program held in cooperation with École Européene des Affairs and Educational Programs Abroad. Students combine internships with members of the French National Assembly with courses covering French culture, politics, and literature. Optional travel program and a week orientation in Paris.

ADMITTANCE REQUIREMENTS: Juniors and above including graduate students with a 3.0 GPA and fluency in French.

TEACHING METHODS: Students take courses taught in French by the faculty at École Européene des Affairs.

EVALUATION: By faculty, based upon class work and course exams.

CREDITS OFFERED: 15 semester hours per semester.

HOUSING: Students live in apartments, furnished rooms, or with local families.

DATES: Fall semester: early September through mid-December; spring semester: mid-January through mid-June.

COSTS: $3,800 per semester includes tuition and room and board. Does not cover round-trip transportation, program-related travel, or personal expenses.

YEAR ESTABLISHED: 1981.

NUMBER OF STUDENTS IN 1985:   18.

APPLY: By June 1 for fall semester; November 1 for spring. Judith Muasher.

■ **SKIDMORE COLLEGE**
  Saratoga Springs, NY 12866
  (518) 584-5000, ext. 2654

PROGRAM: Skidmore's Junior Year in France program offers undergraduates a choice of attending for a semester, the full academic year, or for a summer session. The program is held in cooperation with the Université de Paris IV (Sorbonne) and offers a basic selection of liberal arts courses including: language, political science, economics, literature, history, studio art, history of art, linguistics, etc. At least two excursions outside of Paris are included in the program, as well as special field experiences in the areas of a student's major. A preorientation session is conducted in both Paris and Cesarges.

ADMITTANCE REQUIREMENTS: Juniors or seniors with a 3.0 GPA and good academic standing, plus advanced knowledge of French. (Semester students can be at an early intermediate stage.) No language prerequisite for summer program.

TEACHING METHODS: Students attend regular classes at the Université de Paris IV, which include regular classes and special discussion sections taught by local faculty specially hired for program participants. Courses are in French but tutors are available for those who need special help. Courses include onsite trips and field trips to banks, local businesses, museums, etc.

EVALUATION: By foreign faculty members and group leaders, based upon both periodic and final exams.

CREDITS OFFERED: Up to 16 semester hours for the academic year; up to 6 semester hours for the summer term.

HOUSING: Students live in private homes or apartments.

DATES: Fall semester: September 10 through mid-December; spring semester: mid-January through May 25; summer term: June 28 through August 10.

COSTS: For the full academic year: $13,500 includes tuition, room and board, round-trip transportation, and all local travel. (At least two excursions outside Paris each semester.) Scholarships available for Skidmore students only.

YEAR ESTABLISHED: 1969.

NUMBER OF STUDENTS IN 1985:   27.

APPLY: By February 15 for the fall term or full year; October 15 for the spring term. Dr. Lynne L. Gelber, Coordinator, Skidmore Junior Year Programs Abroad.

■ **SMITH COLLEGE**
Northampton, MA 01063
(413) 584-2700

PROGRAM: Smith College Junior Year in Paris is one of the oldest foreign-study programs in existence. This full-academic-year undergraduate program offers courses in intermediate and advanced French language and literature, art, economics, history, philosophy, political science, psychology, as well as the full curriculum offering at the University of Paris. Field trips to Chartres, Arles, Avignon, and the Riviera. Six-week orientation in Paris.

ADMITTANCE REQUIREMENTS: Juniors with a 3.0 GPA and two years of college French or the equivalent.

TEACHING METHODS: All instruction is in French. Students attend special courses arranged for the group or may enroll and attend regular classes at the École des Beaux-Arts, Institut d'Études Politiques, Sorbonne, or Institut d'Art et Archeologie.

EVALUATION: By course faculty, based upon papers and final exams.

CREDITS OFFERED: 32 semester hours per year.

HOUSING: Students live with French families.

DATES: Fall semester: September 1 through mid-December; spring semester: late January through June 15.

COSTS: $13,760 per year includes tuition, room and board. Does not include round-trip transportation, local travel, or personal expenses.

YEAR ESTABLISHED: 1925.

NUMBER OF STUDENTS IN 1985: 41.

APPLY: By February 1. Patricia C. Olmsted, Committee on Study Abroad. (Extension 4920).

■ **STATE UNIVERSITY OF NEW YORK AT BROCKPORT**
Office of International Education
Brockport, NY 14420
(716) 395-2119

PROGRAM: The Paris Social Sciences Program is a semester or academic year undergraduate experience that offers a varied selection of courses with an emphasis on history, political science, and economics, combined with an intensive study of the French language and literature. Local travel and trips to cultural and historic sites, as well as a field trip to Hungary and a seminar course involving travel to London and Bonn complement the program.

ADMITTANCE REQUIREMENTS: "Exceptional sophomores," juniors and above with a 2.5 GPA and approval of major advisor.

TEACHING METHODS: Students attend special courses arranged for the group and taught by an American faculty. Americans are not integrated with local students. Classes are complemented with field trips, social science seminars, and independent study projects.

EVALUATION: By university faculty and group leaders, based on periodic papers, exams, and finals.

CREDITS OFFERED: 15 semester hours per semester.

HOUSING: Students are responsible for their own housing.

DATES: Fall semester: early September through mid-December; spring semester: mid-January to early May.

COSTS: Approximately $688 per semester (for residents); $1,613 (for nonresidents). Includes tuition and program-associated travel. Does not cover room and board (approximately $1,800), round-trip transportation, local travel, or personal expenses. Financial aid is available.

YEAR ESTABLISHED: 1975.

NUMBER OF STUDENTS IN 1985: 33.

APPLY: Fall semester by April 1; spring semester by November 1. Dr. John Perry, Director, Office of International Education.

■ **STATE UNIVERSITY OF NEW YORK AT OSWEGO**
Oswego, NY 13126
(315) 341-2118

PROGRAM: SUNY at Oswego's French Language and Civilization is a semester or full-academic-year undergraduate program. Courses are under the auspices of the University of Paris-Sorbonne as part of the Cours de Civilisation Francaise. Six hours of language courses and two hours of phonetics courses are required. Students also select courses covering art history, literature, geography, history, philosophy, political science, music history, and stylistics.

ADMITTANCE REQUIREMENTS: 2.7 GPA and completion of at least six hours advanced French.

TEACHING METHODS: Courses are in French and taught by French faculty.

EVALUATION: Based on work in class, papers, and final exams. Grades are converted to U.S. equivalents by SUNY and sent to students' home institution.

CREDITS OFFERED: Up to 16 semester hours per semester.

HOUSING: Students live in dormitories located in the Latin Quarter.

DATES: Fall semester: early October through mid-January; spring semester: early February through mid-June.

COSTS: $2,400 per semester; $4,300 for full academic year. Includes tuition, room and board, local field trips, and round-trip transportation from New York. Does not cover personal expenses, travel, or SUNY tuition and fees ($687.50 per semester for New York residents; $1,612.50 for nonresidents.)

YEAR ESTABLISHED: 1969.

NUMBER OF STUDENTS IN 1985:   30.

APPLY: By April 15 for fall semester; November 15 for spring semester. Dr. José R. Pérez, Director, International Education, Overseas Academic Programs.

■ **SWEET BRIAR COLLEGE**
Sweet Briar, VA 24595
(804) 381-6109

PROGRAM: Sweet Briar College's Junior Year in France is a full-year program held in cooperation with the Universities of Paris I, III, IV, and VII, Institute d'Études Politiques, École de Louvre, Institut Catholique, etc. This program is one of the oldest foreign-study programs; a continuation of the University of Delaware Junior Year in France program founded in 1923. It is considered by many to be a model for subsequent programs. Since 1948 more than 3,900 students from 243 colleges and universities have participated. Special courses for American students are given in: language, literature and civilization, and the arts. For other fields of study, students can take regular courses at the various Paris universities covering: anthropology, art history and archeology, cinema studies, communications, economics, environment, history, language and linguistics, literature and civilization, music, philosophy, religion, political science, and psychology. A month-long onsite orientation held in Tours in cooperation with the Université François-Rabelais, consists of conversation and composition classes, plus a general initiation to French life and culture. Students can receive "recommendation for three hours credit" for a successful completion of this part of the program.

ADMITTANCE REQUIREMENTS: For college juniors with at least two years of college French, or the equivalent (normally including a literature course), a 3.0 GPA in college French and a general average of 2.85, recommendation by department chairman and college dean.

TEACHING METHODS: Americans take regular academic courses with French students at the universities and other institutions of higher learning, as well as special courses designed for the program. All lectures are in French. The lectures and discussion sections vary according to the various French institutions.

EVALUATION: Depends upon the course and institution. Regular exams are given with French students. French grades are transposed into American grades by the resident director according to a fixed scale.

CREDITS OFFERED: 30 semester hours.

HOUSING: Students usually live in private houses with local families.

DATES: Tuesday after Labor Day through May 31.

COSTS: $10,750 for the full academic year. Includes tuition, room and board, and excursion to Tours for orientation. Does not include round-trip transportation, and additional living expenses (estimated at approximately $1,500 to $2,000 for the full year). Scholarships are available from the Junior Year in France program. (In 1985, students received approximately $50,000 in scholarship aid.)

YEAR ESTABLISHED: 1948.

NUMBER OF STUDENTS IN 1985: 118.

APPLY: By February 21. Professor Emile Langlois, Director, Junior Year in France.

■ **TUFTS UNIVERSITY**
  Medford, MA 02155
  (617) 381-3152

PROGRAM: Tufts in Paris, a full-year undergraduate program, is completely integrated into the French university system. Program participants spend the academic year at the University of Paris III or IV. Students take regular university courses. Those interested in political science and economics may attend the Institut d'Études Politiques. Program has an enrollment of 20 to 30 students. Students must take one course per semester taught by Tufts academic advisor. One-week orientation in Talloires.

ADMITTANCE REQUIREMENTS: Good academic standing plus two years of college French or the equivalent.

TEACHING METHODS: In French. Regular classes, seminars, and independent study projects given by the universities. Fully integrated with French students.

EVALUATION: By French professors from the universities.

CREDITS OFFERED: 16 semester hours per semester.

HOUSING: Students must live with local families.

DATES: Fall semester: Last week in September through mid-January; spring semester: mid-January through late May.

COSTS: $7,075 per semester. Covers tuition, room and board, round-trip transportation, and some local travel. Does not cover personal expenses.

YEAR ESTABLISHED: 1965.

NUMBER OF STUDENTS IN 1985: 27.

APPLY: By February 1. Dean Christopher Gray, Director, Tufts Programs Abroad, Ballou Hall.

■ **UNIVERSITY OF ILLINOIS**
Department of French
1425 University Hall M/C 180
Box #4348
Chicago, IL 60680
(312) 996-3221

PROGRAM: The Illinois Program in Paris is an academic-year undergraduate and graduate program held in cooperation with the University of Paris III, University of Paris IV (Cours de Civilisation de la Sorbonne). The program emphasizes French literature, civilization, and language; political science; and business French. A few political internships in the Assemblée Nationale and French political party headquarters are available. Teaching internships are open to all; business and political internships are competitive. A three- to six-week orientation period in Paris is dependent upon the French institutions' beginning dates.

ADMITTANCE REQUIREMENTS: 3.5 GPA with three courses in French beyond the first two years of French language study. "Want students with emotional maturity."

TEACHING METHODS: Regular classes for foreigners taught by French institutions and regular courses for French students. Americans may be integrated with other non-French students as well as French students. All courses are in French.

EVALUATION: By local faculty, based upon "some midterm exams," class quizzes, papers, and final examinations.

CREDITS OFFERED: From 35 to 60 quarter hours depending on the individual. The average is 45 quarter hours.

HOUSING: Students may live in dormitories, independently arranged, or may acquire au pair jobs in exchange for their room and board.

DATES: Mid-September through mid-May.

COSTS: $7,312 includes tuition, double room in dormitory, "modest" food allowance, round-trip transportation from Chicago (not collected if student elects to arrange own travel), and "cultural activities." $5,200 includes round-trip transportation, tuition, and two weeks room and board to allow student to secure au pair position (approximately 12 hours per week work in exchange for a room) or independent housing.

YEAR ESTABLISHED: 1972.

NUMBER OF STUDENTS IN 1985: 24.

APPLY: By March 15.

■ **UNIVERSITY OF SOUTHERN CALIFORNIA**
Overseas Studies, CES 109
University Park
Los Angeles, CA 90089
(213) 746-2500

PROGRAM: USC Year in Paris is an undergraduate program concentrating on liberal arts and humanities; held in cooperation with Sweet Briar College and the University of Paris. Special courses for American students are given in: language, literature, and civilization, and the arts. For other fields of study, students can take regular courses at the various Paris universities covering: anthropology, art history and archaeology, cinema studies, communications, economics, environment, history, language and linguistics, literature and civilization, music, philosophy, religion, political science, and psychology. Onsite orientation.

ADMITTANCE REQUIREMENTS: Sophomores and above in good academic standing with at least two years of college French or the equivalent.

TEACHING METHODS: Courses are taught in French by U.S. and foreign faculty members. Americans may attend regular classes at various Parisian universities, integrated with local students.

EVALUATION: By course faculty member, based upon class work, papers, and periodic exams.

CREDITS OFFERED: 30 semester hours.

HOUSING: Students can live with private families or in furnished apartments.

DATES: Approximately, early September through late May.

COSTS: Approximately, $10,500 covers tuition, room and board, program-related travel. Does not include round-trip transportation or personal expenses. Some scholarships are available.

YEAR ESTABLISHED: 1984.

NUMBER OF STUDENTS IN 1985: 10.

APPLY: By February 1.

■ **WESLEYAN UNIVERSITY**
300 High Street
Middletown, CT 06457
(203) 347-9411, ext. 2271

PROGRAM: The Wesleyan Program in Paris is a semester or full-year undergraduate program in which students have the opportunity to attend classes in Reid Hall, an American classroom building, or take courses under a French faculty at Paris VII or Paris XII. The humanities are emphasized, however, students attending Paris VII may concentrate on the natural and behavioral sciences.

ADMITTANCE REQUIREMENTS: 3.0 GPA and five semesters of college-level French.

TEACHING METHODS: Courses are taught in French by a foreign faculty. Local field trips and weekend excursions complement the program.

EVALUATION: By French faculty, based upon periodic exams, papers, etc.

CREDITS OFFERED: A maximum of 15 semester hours per semester.

HOUSING: Students are given a list of facilities used by former students and, following a visit, decide for themselves.

DATES: Fall semester: August 29 through December 12; spring semester: January 9 through May 8.

COSTS: Tuition $5,430; room and board: approximately $3,000. Does not include round-trip transportation or local travel not associated with the program.

YEAR ESTABLISHED: 1960.

NUMBER OF STUDENTS IN 1985: 50.

APPLY: For fall semester by March 30; spring semester by October 27. Wesleyan Program in Paris.

Pau

■ **CARLETON COLLEGE**
   Northfield, MN 55057
   (507) 663-4000

PROGRAM: The program at the University of Pau is an undergraduate, spring-semester program that offers students the opportunity to take classes in the French language and culture plus their choice of additional courses from the curriculum of the University of Pau. Included in the program is a five-day group trip to Paris and Chartres, a ski trip in the Pyrenees, and frequent day trips to local sites. Onsite orientation.

ADMITTANCE REQUIREMENTS: Sophomores and above with at least two years of college French or the equivalent plus a strong academic record.

TEACHING METHODS: All classes are in French. Literature courses are taught by an accompanying member of the Carleton faculty; language courses for foreign nationals are taught by a French faculty through the institute at the University of Pau. For all other courses, students take regular classes at the university with their French counterparts. In each class taken at the university, an American student is paired with a French student "tutor."

EVALUATION: By French faculty and group leaders, based on class work, periodic exams, and final exams.

CREDITS OFFERED: From 24 to 29 semester hours; (30 to 36 Carleton credits).

HOUSING: Students live with private families.

DATES: Approximately January 5 through June 8.

COSTS: $7,920 includes tuition, room and board, and local travel. Does not include round-trip transportation or personal expenses.

YEAR ESTABLISHED: 1974.

NUMBER OF STUDENTS IN 1985:   14.

APPLY: Rolling admissions. Andrea Iseminger, Director, Off-campus Studies.

■ **UNIVERSITY OF NEVADA–RENO**
Reno, NV 89557
(702) 784-4854

PROGRAM: French Studies in Pau is a single-semester or full-academic-year undergraduate or graduate program held in cooperation with Boise State University, the University of Nevada, Las Vegas, the University of the Basque Country, and the University of Pau. Courses include French, all levels of the Basque language, geography, history, literature, and Basque studies. The program includes ten days of travel to Brussels, Paris, and southern France. Two-day orientation in Pau.

ADMITTANCE REQUIREMENTS: Sophomores and above in good academic standing with some knowledge of French.

TEACHING METHODS: Students take special courses arranged for the group and taught in French and English by a French faculty. Some special courses for foreigners are given at the University of Pau.

EVALUATION: By French faculty, based upon papers and examinations.

CREDITS OFFERED: Up to 28 credits per year; 16 graduate credits.

HOUSING: Students may elect to live in apartments, furnished rooms or with local families.

DATES: Approximately, fall semester: September 1 to December 16; spring semester: January 6 through June 1.

COSTS: $2,000 per semester includes tuition and round-trip transportation. Does not cover room and board, program-related travel, or personal expenses.

YEAR ESTABLISHED: 1985.

NUMBER OF STUDENTS IN 1985:   Not available.

APPLY: By May 15 for fall semester; December 1 for spring. Dr. Carmelo Urza, University Studies in the Basque Country Consortium, University of Nevada Library, Reno.

Poitiers

■ **OREGON STATE SYSTEM OF HIGHER EDUCATION (OSSHE)**
 Foreign Study Programs
 International Education
 Oregon State University
 Corvallis, OR
 (503) 754-3006

PROGRAM: The OSSHE Study in France is an undergraduate and graduate program held in cooperation with the Université de Poitiers and the member schools of OSSHE (Eastern Oregon State College, Oregon Institute of Technology, Portland State University, Southern Oregon State University, University of Oregon, and Western Oregon State College). The program concentrates on French language studies. For students sufficient in French some or all classes may be taken at the université. Graduate study is also offered. One-day orientation in Oregon and three-week period of orientation in France.

ADMITTANCE REQUIREMENTS: Junior standing or above. Minimum 2.75 GPA (3.0 in French), letters of recommendation, and personal interview.

TEACHING METHODS: Taught in French by faculty members of the université. Some courses are in English. Americans are integrated with local students. Lectures, seminars, and independent study complemented by some travel to regional museums and cultural sites.

EVALUATION: By university faculty, based on periodic and final exams.

CREDITS OFFERED: The equivalent of attending an American school for two full semesters or three terms of a trimester program.

HOUSING: Students live in boarding houses, private dwellings, or small apartment buildings.

DATES: Approximately mid-September through mid-June.

COSTS: Resident undergraduates: $3,888; nonresidents: $6,591. (Prices may be several hundred dollars less depending on the housing option chosen.) Includes tuition, room and board, and some local travel. Does not include round-trip transportation or personal expenses (which will probably range from $2,150 to $3,800).

YEAR ESTABLISHED: 1967.

NUMBER OF STUDENTS IN 1985: 35.

APPLY: By February 15. French department at member OSSHE school or Irma Wright, Office of International Education.

Rennes

■ **BELOIT COLLEGE**
Beloit, WI 53511
(608) 365-3391

PROGRAM: The World Outlook Seminar undergraduate program offers a semester in France in cooperation with the Université de Haute Bretagne and the French department at Grinnell College. The program stresses language, contemporary literature, history, theater, art and architecture. Presession orientation is held at Beloit.

ADMITTANCE REQUIREMENTS: B average, two years of French for those taking language courses, and good academic standing.

TEACHNG METHODS: Students attend special courses, unless their language proficiency is high, taught by foreign faculty. Lectures, independent study, and field trips complement classroom work. A U.S. academic leader accompanies group.

EVALUATION: Papers, examinations given by foreign teachers.

CREDITS OFFERED: 16 semester hours.

HOUSING: With local families.

DATES: Approximately January 2 through April 30.

COSTS: Tuition: $3,900; room and board: $1,700; travel to/from Europe: approximately $600.

YEAR ESTABLISHED: 1964.

NUMBER OF STUDENTS IN 1985:   21.

APPLY: By November 30. World Affairs Center.

Rouen

■ **THE EXPERIMENT IN INTERNATIONAL LIVING**
Kipling Road
Brattleboro, VT 05301
(800) 451-4465

PROGRAM: The College Semester Abroad program is designed to allow students to become immersed in a foreign culture by living with a local family and exploring individual personal and educational interests under professional guidance. The Rouen-International Business program covers: intensive language training, international business courses taken at the École Supérieure de Commerce, seminar on French institutions, and international business field work. Orientation in Brattleboro, Paris, and Rouen.

ADMITTANCE REQUIREMENTS: Sophomore standing or above and acceptable academic credentials. One and a half years of college French or the equivalent plus a year of either business studies or economic.

TEACHING METHODS: Americans are fully integrated with French students at the école. Students work directly with their American instructors/advisors in planning and evaluating their individual program. "The semester builds from the more structured language training and lectures and discussions on local life and culture to the independent study project."

EVALUATION: By individual students and their instructor/advisors, based on independent project, papers, reports, and exams. Periodic meetings during the program and for several days at the conclusion.

CREDITS OFFERED: Up to 16 semester hours.

HOUSING: Students live as family members with their host families.

DATES: Approximately September through December.

COSTS: $6,300 includes tuition, room and board, all fees and local travel, and round-trip transportation from Brattleboro, Vermont.

YEAR ESTABLISHED: 1962.

NUMBER OF STUDENTS: 13.

APPLY: By May 15. Admissions Office, College Semester Abroad.

Strasbourg

■ **BRETHREN COLLEGES ABROAD**
  P.O. Box #184
  Manchester College
  North Manchester, IN 46962
  (219) 982-2141, ext. 238

PROGRAM: Brethren Colleges Abroad Program in France is held in cooperation with L'Institut International d'Études Françaises, l'Université des Science Humaines, and Bridgewater College, Elizabethtown College, Juniata College, McPherson College, and the University of La Verne in the United States. The program is available for a semester or the full academic year. Courses include: philosophy, religion, political science, psychology, biology, economics, geography, history, French language and literature, art, music, English literature, and German. Orientation and a five-week intensive language course are given onsite followed by a week in Paris.

ADMITTANCE REQUIREMENTS: Sophomore and above with a 3.0 GPA and two years of college-level French or the equivalent.

TEACHING METHODS: Americans are fully integrated with French students. Both special and regular college courses. Course work is complemented with field trips, and travel to museums and regional sites.

EVALUATION: Director in France and professors determine grades from papers, periodic exams, and finals.

CREDITS OFFERED: 15 to 16 semester hours.

HOUSING: Students live in dormitories or with local families.

DATES: Fall semester: September 1 through January 31; spring semester: February 5 through June 10.

COSTS: $5,800 per semester. Includes tuition, room and board, and round-trip transportation. Does not cover personal expenses or local travel.

YEAR ESTABLISHED: 1963.

NUMBER OF STUDENTS IN 1985:   36.

APPLY: By April 1 for fall semester; November 1 for spring semester. Dr. Allen C. Deeter or Mrs. Helga Walsh.

■ **PENNSYLVANIA STATE UNIVERSITY**
Office of Education Abroad Programs
222 Boucke Building
University Park, PA 16802
(814) 865-7681

PROGRAM: Academic Year at Institut International d'Études Françaises at the Université de Strasbourg is a full-academic-year program. The program begins with a four-week intensive language training course after which students enroll in specially selected full-year courses in advanced French language, French literature, French civilization, French art, French politics, and/or European political community. Students also have the opportunity for observing Council of Europe activities. Orientation at Penn State.

ADMITTANCE REQUIREMENTS: Juniors and seniors with a 2.5 GPA, good academic standing, and "must show evidence of maturity, stability, adaptability, self-discipline, and a strong academic motivation." Some specific course prerequisites. Two years of college French or the equivalent.

TEACHING METHODS: Students take courses at the institut. All lectures are in French. Americans are integrated with local students.

EVALUATION: By course instructors based upon classwork, papers, and exams.

CREDITS OFFERED: A minimum of 27 and a maximum of 36 credits per year in addition to language course.

HOUSING: Students either live in dormitories or in private rooms in Strasbourg.

DATES: Early September through mid-June.

COSTS: Students pay the same as at the University Park Campus. 1986-87 tuition per semester was $2,250 for state residents; $5,150 for nonresidents; room and board: $2,750 per semester. Plus a $100 nonrefundable program fee.

YEAR ESTABLISHED: 1962.

NUMBER OF STUDENTS IN 1985: 17.

APPLY: By March 1.

■ **ROSARY COLLEGE**
  7900 West Division Street
  River Forest, IL 60305
  (312) 366-2490

PROGRAM: Rosary in Strasbourg is a full-year undergraduate program with courses in political and economic social conditions, French, German, and an international business internship.

ADMITTANCE REQUIREMENTS: Sophomores and above with acceptable academic record. Two years of either college level French or German are recommended.

TEACHING METHODS: Students take special courses taught by American and French faculty. Intensive language study. Internship program. Students are not integrated with other foreign students.

EVALUATION: Periodic exams and papers.

CREDITS OFFERED: Up to 16 semester hours per semester, depending upon course load.

HOUSING: Students can stay with families or in dormitories.

DATES: Approximately, early September through mid-May.

COSTS: Tuition: $2,950; room and board: $1,835. Includes local travel but not round-trip transportation or personal expenses.

YEAR ESTABLISHED: 1987.

NUMBER OF STUDENTS IN 1985: Not available.

APPLY: By March 15. Sister Nona Mary Allard, Associate Academic Dean.

Toulon

■ **COLLEGE CONSORTIUM FOR INTERNATIONAL STUDIES (CCIS)**
866 United Nations Plaza, Room 511
New York, NY 10017
(212) 308-1556

PROGRAM: CCIS is a nonprofit organization that sponsors and organizes several dozen foreign study programs for member colleges who grant degree credit. The Toulon Program is a single-semester, full-academic-year, or summer program offered in cooperation with Miami-Dade Community College and the University of Toulon. Students attend classes at the Institute for American Universities under the auspices of the University of Toulon. Courses cover French (required), business administration, marketing, European trade and finance. Orientation in France. Program-related field trips.

ADMITTANCE REQUIREMENTS: Sophomore and above (but will accept some freshman), with 2.5 GPA, knowledge of French, and acceptable academic credentials.

TEACHING METHODS: Courses, in French, are taught by institute professors associated with French universities.

EVALUATION: By course instructors and project leaders.

CREDITS OFFERED: 12 to 15 semester hours per semester.

HOUSING: Students live with local families.

DATES: Fall semester: September 16 through January 22; spring semester: February 1 through May 30.

COSTS: $2,365 per semester includes tuition. Does not cover room and board, local travel, round-trip transportation, or personal expenses.

APPLY: Fall semester by August 15; spring semester: November 22.

Toulouse

■ **THE EXPERIMENT IN INTERNATIONAL LIVING**
Kipling Road
Brattleboro, VT 05301-0676
(800) 451-4465

PROGRAM: The College Semester Abroad program is designed to allow students to become immersed in a foreign culture by living with a local family and exploring individual personal and educational interests under professional guidance. The Toulouse Program covers: intensive language training at the Université of Toulouse-Mirail, seminar on French life and culture, history and politics, geography and economics, art and architecture, social anthropology, social/cultural field work, and an independent study project. Orientation in Brattleboro and Paris.

ADMITTANCE REQUIREMENTS: Sophomore standing or above and acceptable academic credentials. One and a half years of college French or the equivalent.

TEACHING METHODS: Americans are fully integrated with French students at the université. Students work directly with their American instructors/advisors in planning and evaluating their individual program. "The semester builds from the more structured language training and lectures and discussions on local life and culture to the independent study project."

EVALUATION: By individual students and their instructor/advisors, based on independent project, papers, reports, and exams. Periodic meetings during the program and for several days at the conclusion.

CREDITS OFFERED: Up to 16 semester hours.

HOUSING: Students live as family members with their host families.

DATES: Approximately, fall semester: September through December; spring semester: January through May.

COSTS: $5,900 includes tuition, room and board, all fees and local travel, and round-trip transportation from Brattleboro, Vermont.

YEAR ESTABLISHED: 1962.

NUMBER OF STUDENTS IN 1985: Not available.

APPLY: For fall semester by May 15; spring semester by November 15. Admissions Office, College Semester Abroad.

Tours

■ **BOWLING GREEN STATE UNIVERSITY**
Department of Romance Languages
Bowling Green, OH 43403
(419) 372-2531

PROGRAM: The Academic Year in France is an undergraduate program that begins with a month of intensive language study at the Sorbonne in Paris then moves to Tours where classes are held at the Institut d'Études Françaises de Touraine. Courses emphasize French language, history, literature, art, and history. Visits to cultural sites is an important part of the program. A teacher's workshop and summer graduate program are also offered. No preorientation.

ADMITTANCE REQUIREMENTS: Acceptable academic record. Knowledge of French is most important.

TEACHING METHODS: All courses are in French. Professors are from the French universities in Paris and Tours. Small classes and seminars.

EVALUATION: By French professors, based upon class work, papers, and exams.

CREDITS OFFERED: 15 semester hours per semester.

HOUSING: Students live with French families in Tours. In Paris they stay at the Maison des Lycéennes.

DATES: Fall semester: September 1 through December 16; spring semester: January 5 through May 9.

COSTS: $5,550 for both semesters. Covers tuition, room and board, some local travel. Non-Ohio students also pay a nonresident fee of $2,775. Does not include round-trip transportation or personal expenses.

YEAR ESTABLISHED: 1962.

NUMBER OF STUDENTS IN 1985: Not available.

APPLY: By March 15. Drs. Michael or Lenita Locey, Program Directors.

■ **RUTGERS, THE STATE UNIVERSITY OF NEW JERSEY**
Milledoler Hall, Room 205
New Brunswick, NJ 08903
(201) 932-7787

PROGRAM: Junior Year in France is a full-year academic undergraduate program. Students attend both regular classes at the Université François Rabelais and special supplementary tutorial courses. Students select from the regular université catalog, which offers a broad selection of liberal arts courses. A six-week presession concentrating on advanced French language and civilization is held at the Sorbonne in Paris.

ADMITTANCE REQUIREMENTS: Good academic standing and, "at a minimum, students should have completed coursework through first year literature and preferably advanced grammar courses" in French.

TEACHING METHODS: Students attend regular classes with French students. Rutgers offers a limited number of special courses for program participants. All courses are in French.

EVALUATION: By course instructors, based upon class work, papers, and exams.

CREDITS OFFERED: 30 semester hours per year including Paris presession.

HOUSING: Students stay in single rooms in university residence halls—"at either Grandmont or Sanitas." Each student receives a monthly meal allowance equivalent to three meals a day.

DATES: Approximately, September 17 to mid-June.

COSTS: $5,472 New Jersey residents; $6,926 nonresidents. Includes tuition, room and board (except 27 days of holidays), round-trip transportation from New York, and group excursions. Does not cover personal expenses.

YEAR PROGRAM ESTABLISHED: 1966.

NUMBER OF STUDENTS IN 1985: 40.

APPLY: By March 1. Director, Rutgers' Junior Year Abroad.

■ **STATE UNIVERSITY OF NEW YORK AT BROCKPORT**
Office of International Education
Brockport, NY 14420
(716) 395-2119

PROGRAM: The Multilevel French Language Immersion program is a one-semester or academic-year undergraduate program held in cooperation with the Institut d'Études Françaises de Touraine. The program concentrates on French language, literature, and civilization courses given at the institut. Local travel and field trips to cultural and historic sites complement the program.

ADMITTANCE REQUIREMENTS: Juniors and above with a 2.5 GPA and completion of intermediate-level French.

TEACHING METHODS: Students attend regular courses at the institut. All classes are in French taught by institut faculty. Americans are integrated with local students.

EVALUATION: By French faculty and group leaders, based on periodic papers, exams, and finals.

CREDITS OFFERED: 15 semester hours per semester.

HOUSING: Students live with local families.

DATES: Fall semester: October 1 through January 4; spring semester: January 20 through March 12.

COSTS: Approximately, academic year: $2,350 for New York residents; $4,200 for nonresidents. Semester: $1,675 for residents; $2,600 for nonresidents. Includes tuition and room and board. Does not cover round-trip transportation, local travel, or personal expenses.

YEAR ESTABLISHED: 1982.

NUMBER OF STUDENTS IN 1985: 15.

APPLY: Academic year by March 15; spring semester by October 15.

■ **UNIVERSITY OF NORTHERN COLORADO**
Department of Foreign Languages
Greeley, CO 80631
(303) 351-2040

PROGRAM: The French Study Program is a relatively small, intimate study experience of approximately fifteen to twenty students plus a UNC faculty member who serves a both an educator and a group leader. Graduate students are accepted if enrolled in the UNC master's degree program. The program emphasizes French language, culture, and civilization. Students take language courses at L'Institut de Touraine.

ADMITTANCE REQUIREMENTS: Good academic standing plus two quarters of French for lower-division programs; five quarters, or the equivalent, for advanced programs.

TEACHING METHODS: Students attend regular classes at the institut, where they are integrated with French students, as well as special classes taught by U.S. faculty. Courses are in French.

EVALUATION: By UNC instructors, based upon periodic and final exams, journals, papers, and reports.

CREDITS OFFERED: 16 quarter hours.

HOUSING: Students live with local families.

DATES: Approximately March through mid-May.

COSTS: $4,000 includes tuition (out-of-state). room and board, books, one meal a day while traveling, pocket money, and round-trip transportation from Colorado.

YEAR ESTABLISHED: 1969.

NUMBER OF STUDENTS IN 1985:   20.

APPLY: By October 31. Dr. Kathleen Ensz, Chairperson.

THE FEDERAL REPUBLIC OF GERMANY

Population: 60,852,000   **Capital:** Bonn (provisional)   **Language:** German
Monetary Unit: Deutsche Mark   **Government:** Federal multiparty republic
(president and chancellor)   **Religion:** 47% Protestant; 44% Roman Catholic
Households With Television: 75%

SELECTED COLLEGES AND UNIVERSITIES

Goethe Institut
Lenbachplatz 3
Postfach 20 1009
Munchen 2
German language teaching center.

College of Arts
Postfach 12 67 20
1000 Berlin 12
Courses in fine arts, communications, music, etc. Free tuition.

Institute for European History
Alte Universitatsstrasse 19
6500 Mainz
Modern European history. Some courses in English.

Schiller International University
Friedrich-Ebert-Anlage 4
6900 Heidelberg
Business, languages, political science. In English.

Universität Bonn
Nasserstrasse 15
5300 Bonn 1

Universität Hamburg
Edmund-Siemers-Allee 1
2000 Hamburg 13

Universität Regensburg
Postfach 397
8400 Regensburg

FURTHER INFORMATION

Consulate General of the Federal
Republic of Germany
460 Park Avenue
New York, NY 10022
(212) 940-9200

Embassy of the Federal Republic
of Germany
4645 Reservoir Road, NW
Washington, DC 20007
(202) 944-6000

German National Tourist Office
747 Third Avenue
New York, NY 10017
(212) 308-3300

German Information Center
410 Park Avenue
New York, NY 10022
(212) 888-9840
Publishes Higher Education: Federal Republic of Germany.

German Academic Exchange Service
535 Fifth Avenue, Suite #1107
New York, NY 10017
(212) 758-3223
Publishes Academic Studies in the Federal Republic of Germany.

Aachen

■ **MICHIGAN STATE UNIVERSITY**
108 Center for International Programs
East Lansing, MI 48824
(517) 353-8920

PROGRAM: MSU's program in Aachen is devoted exclusively to mechanical engineering. It is a single-semester undergraduate and graduate program held at the technical University of Aachen. Courses cover the complete scope of mechanical engineering topics. Orientation in the U.S.

ADMITTANCE REQUIREMENTS: For sophomores, juniors, seniors, and graduate students majoring in engineering, physics, or mathematics with acceptable academic credentials, references, and recommendation from advisor. No language requirement.

TEACHING METHODS: Students take special courses, lectures, science labs, seminars, and field trips in English arranged for the group and taught by both U.S. and local foreign faculty.

EVALUATION: By course faculty, based upon papers and examinations.

CREDITS OFFERED: 12 to 16 credit hours.

HOUSING: Students live in dormitories and students residence halls.

DATES: March 25 through May 25.

COSTS: Approximately $1,710 includes tuition, room and board, and program-related travel. Does not include round-trip transportation, meals, or personal expenses.

YEAR ESTABLISHED: 1983.

NUMBER OF STUDENTS IN 1985: 11.

APPLY: By February 3. Dr. Charles A. Gliozzo, Office of Overseas Study.

Bayreuth

■ **UNIVERSITY OF NORTHERN COLORADO**
Department of Foreign Languages
Greeley, CO 80631
(303) 351-2040

PROGRAM: The German Study Program is a new, relatively small, intimate study experience of approximately fifteen to twenty students plus a UNC faculty member who serves as both an educator and a group leader. Graduate students are accepted if enrolled in the UNC master's degree program. The program emphasizes German language, culture, and civilization. Students take language courses at the University of Bayreuth.

ADMITTANCE REQUIREMENTS: Good academic standing plus two quarters of German for lower-division programs; five quarters, or the equivalent, for advanced programs.

TEACHING METHODS: Students attend regular classes at the university, where they are integrated with German students, as well as special classes taught by U.S. faculty. Courses are in German.

EVALUATION: By UNC instructors, based upon periodic and final exams, journals, papers, and reports.

CREDITS OFFERED: 16 quarter hours.

HOUSING: Students live with local families.

DATES: Approximately, March through mid-May.

COSTS: $4,000 includes tuition (out-of-state), room and board, books, one meal a day while traveling, pocket money, and round-trip transportation from Colorado.

YEAR ESTABLISHED: 1988.

APPLY: By October 31. Dr. Kathleen Ensz, Chairperson.

Baden-Württemberg

■ **OREGON STATE SYSTEM OF HIGHER EDUCATION (OSSHE)**
Foreign Study Programs
International Education
Oregon State University
Corvallis, OR
(503) 754-3006

PROGRAM: OSSHE Study in Germany is an undergraduate and graduate program held in cooperation with all of the universities and some of the "fuchhochschulen" of Baden-Württemberg and the member schools of OSSHE (Eastern Oregon State College, Oregon Institute of Technology, Portland State University, Southern Oregon State University, University of Oregon, and Western Oregon State College). The program allows the student to select one of the universities in either Konstanz, Hohenheim, Ulm, Freiberg, Tübingen, or Heidelberg to attend; each of which provides a complete range of courses. Graduate study is also offered. One-day orientation in Oregon and a four-week period of orientation in Tübingen.

ADMITTANCE REQUIREMENTS: Junior standing or above. Minimum 2.75 GPA (3.0 in German), letters of recommendation, and personal interview. To commence classes students must also pass the selected German university's entrance examination.

TEACHING METHODS: Taught in German by faculty members of the various universities. Lectures, seminars, and independent study complemented by some travel to regional museums and cultural sites.

EVALUATION: By university faculty, based on periodic and final exams.

CREDITS OFFERED: The equivalent of attending an American school for two full semesters or three terms of a trimester program.

HOUSING: Students live in university dormitories equipped with kitchen facilities.

DATES: Approximately, mid-September through mid-July.

COSTS: Resident undergraduates: $4,420; nonresidents: $7,123. Resident graduates: $5,102; nonresidents $6,388. Includes tuition, room and board, and some local travel. Does not include round-trip transportation or personal expenses.

YEAR ESTABLISHED: 1968.

NUMBER OF STUDENTS IN 1985:   40.

APPLY: By January 31. German department at member OSSHE school, or Irma Wright, Office of International Education.

Berlin (West)

■ **THE EXPERIMENT IN INTERNATIONAL LIVING**
Kipling Road
Brattleboro, VT 05301-0676
(800) 451-4465

PROGRAM: The College Semester Abroad Program is designed to allow students to become immersed in a foreign culture by living with a local family and exploring individual personal and educational interests under professional guidance. The Berlin program covers intensive German language and culture seminar, seminar on East-West relations, and an independent study project.

ADMITTANCE REQUIREMENTS: Sophomore standing or above and acceptable academic credentials. No language prerequisite.

TEACHING METHODS: Students work directly with their American instructors in planning and evaluating their individual program. "The semester builds from the more structured language training and lectures and discussions on local life and culture to the independent study project."

EVALUATION: By individual students and their instructor/advisors based on independent project, papers, reports, and exams. Periodic meetings during the program and for several days at the conclusion.

CREDITS OFFERED: Up to 16 semester hours.

HOUSING: Students live as family members with their host families.

DATES: Approximately, fall semester: September through December; spring semester: January through May.

COSTS: $5,900 includes tuition, room and board, all fees and local travel, and round-trip transportation from New York.

YEAR ESTABLISHED: 1962.

NUMBER OF STUDENTS IN 1985: 13.

APPLY: For fall semester by May 15; spring semester by November 15. Admissions Office, College Semester Abroad.

Bonn

■ **THE AMERICAN UNIVERSITY**
Washington, DC 20016
(202) 885-3800

PROGRAM: Semester in Bonn is a liberal arts/social science program held in cooperation with the University of Bonn. Courses include history, fine arts, languages, political science, etc. Field trips to Brussels and Vienna are often scheduled. Preorientation at American University (usually over a weekend) and onsite.

ADMITTANCE REQUIREMENTS: Juniors and seniors with a "B" average or better.

TEACHING METHODS: Students are accompanied by a resident professor from American University who schedules seminars with public officials in addition to his or her own lectures. Foreign faculty members complement these lectures and teach specialized courses. Students also intern two days a week with one of the many local government or private organizations.

EVALUATION: Regular exams, midterms and finals, in addition to short seminar papers.

CREDITS OFFERED: 15 to 17 semester hours.

HOUSING: A combination of possibilities from local apartments to living with local families.

DATES: First semester: September to December; second semester: January to May.

COSTS: Tuition: $4,100 per semester; room and board: $2,000 per semester. Scholarships from American University available.

YEAR ESTABLISHED: 1984.

NUMBER OF STUDENTS IN 1985:   25.

APPLY: Rolling admissions. Apply 6 to 8 months prior to start of semester. Dr. David C. Brown, Dean, Washington Semester and Study Program Abroad.

■ **KALAMAZOO COLLEGE**
  1200 Academy Street
  Kalamazoo, MI 49007
  (616) 383-8470

PROGRAM: The Bonn Program is designed for students who have enough language aptitude and training (minimum: 4 units German) to enable them, after approximately one month of intensive language study, to enroll in the university courses conducted in German. Courses include: history, religion, art, political science, philosophy, German, psychology, and some sciences. Kalamazoo also offers programs in Hannover, Erlangen, and Münster. Assignments to site location made according to student's language ability. (Bonn most advanced, then Erlangen, Hannover, and Münster.) Orientation: two hours weekly during preceding term at Kalamazoo.

ADMITTANCE REQUIREMENTS: Enrollment at Kalamazoo College in term prior to departure. Ten semester hours of college German or the equivalent.

TEACHING METHODS: Students attend regular academic courses, lectures, seminars, and tutorials in German with host-country students. Special courses are in English.

EVALUATION: By individual instructors, based upon class work, papers, and exams. Recorded by Kalamazoo only as "pass/fail."

CREDITS OFFERED: Maximum 30 quarter hours credit; 20 in Münster.

HOUSING: With local families or, in Bonn, students may elect to live in dormitories.

DATES: Approximately, mid-September to mid-March.

COSTS: $7,064 includes tuition, room and board, and round-trip transportation from New York. Does not cover the cost of one term at Kalamazoo at $3,532 or personal travel and living expenses.

YEAR ESTABLISHED: 1962.

NUMBER OF STUDENTS IN 1985:   43.

APPLY: By May 1. Dr. Joe K. Fugate, Director, Office of Foreign Study.

■ **NORTHERN ILLINOIS UNIVERSITY**
   DeKalb, IL 60115
   (815) 753-0304

PROGRAM: NIU's German Internship Program is a one-semester or full-academic-year undergraduate and graduate program held in cooperation with Bonn University and Educational Programs Abroad. Students combine internships with members of the German Parliament (Bundestag) with courses covering German art and culture, politics and political systems, and history. Program-related travel and a one-week orientation in Germany.

ADMITTANCE REQUIREMENTS: Juniors and above, including graduate students, with a 3.0 GPA and fluency in German.

TEACHING METHODS: Students take courses taught in German by the faculty at Bonn University.

EVALUATION: By faculty, based upon class work and course examinations.

CREDITS OFFERED: 15 semester hours per semester.

HOUSING: Students live in apartments, furnished rooms, or with local families.

DATES: Fall semester: late August through mid-December; spring semester: mid-January through mid-June.

COSTS: $3,500 per semester includes tuition and room and board. Does not cover round-trip transportation, program-related travel, or personal expenses.

YEAR ESTABLISHED: 1981.

NUMBER OF STUDENTS IN 1985:   7.

APPLY: By June 1 for fall semester; November 1 for spring. Judith Muasher.

■ **RIPON COLLEGE**
   300 Seward Street
   P.O. Box #248
   Ripon, WI 54971
   (414) 748-8127

PROGRAM: Ripon College International Study Center at Bonn is either a single-semester or full-academic-year program held in cooperation with the University of Bonn. A full range of both undergraduate and graduate courses are available at this major university. American students take an eight-week orientation at the university consisting primarily of language training and cultural orientation. As part of the program, students take a ten-day field trip to East Germany.

ADMITTANCE REQUIREMENTS: Superior academic record. Some knowledge of the German language is essential.

TEACHING METHODS: All courses are taught at the university in German by members of the University of Bonn faculty. Courses are fully integrated.

EVALUATION:　Based on final examinations and occasional tutorials depending on the course. Evaluation is by German faculty.

CREDITS OFFERED:　A minimum of 16 semester hours per semester.

HOUSING:　Students usually live in the university dormitory, but can live in other facilities by special arrangement with the program director.

DATES:　Fall semester: August 30 through February 15; spring semester: March 1 through July 15.

COSTS:　Per semester: $ 5,600; full year: $11,200. Includes tuition, room and board, round-trip transportation, and all field trips.

YEAR ESTABLISHED:　1966.

NUMBER OF STUDENTS IN 1985:　25.

APPLY:　November 1. Professor James F. Hyde, Jr. Director, International Study Center.

Cologne

■ **NORTHWEST INTERINSTITUTIONAL COUNCIL ON STUDY ABROAD (NICSA)**
Oregon State University
International Education,
Corvallis, OR 97331
(503) 754-2394

PROGRAM:　The NICSA Study Abroad Program is held in cooperation with the University of Washington, Washington State University, Western Washington University, Central Washington University, Eastern Washington University, Boise State University, University of Alaska - Fairbanks, University of Oregon, Oregon State University, and Portland State University. This is a one-semester, undergraduate program although students may elect to enroll for more than a single semester. The courses are designed around a general liberal arts curriculum emphasizing history, economics, political science, language, art, literature, English, theater, geography, etc. Excursions play an important role, taking place on a weekly basis; one long (two- to three-day) excursion each semester. There is a 3-hour orientation on the individual campuses prior to departure and a one-day onsite orientation.

ADMITTANCE REQUIREMENTS: A minimum 2.0 GPA plus good academic standing. Two semesters college German or the equivalent.

TEACHING METHODS: Students attend a special center for Americans set up by NICSA. All classes are taught in English by either foreign or various northwestern regional-school faculty members.

EVALUATION: By professors, based on class work, papers, and periodic exams.

CREDITS OFFERED: 15 or 20 credits (quarter hours) per semester.

HOUSING: Students live with local families arranged onsite by a homestay coordinator.

DATES: Fall semester: September 1 through December 15; spring semester: April 1 through July 15.

COSTS: $1,895, including tuition, room and board, books, and local travel. Does not cover round-trip transportation or personal expenses. Nonresident students attending Oregon State University for one semester pay resident tuition.

YEAR ESTABLISHED: 1963.

NUMBER OF STUDENTS IN 1985:   110.

APPLY: Fall semester by June 1; spring semester by January 3. American Heritage Association, P.O. Box #425, Lake Oswego, OR 97034, (503) 635-3703 or Judy Van Dyck or Ann Ferguson, International Education, OSU.

■ **PENNSYLVANIA STATE UNIVERSITY**
Office of Education Abroad Programs
222 Boucke Building
University Park, PA 16802
(814) 865-7681

PROGRAM: Education Abroad at the University of Cologne is a spring-semester undergraduate program held in cooperation with the Universität zu Köln. Students take special courses, which include a course in the German language and culture, plus 3-credit courses in business administration and economics. Orientation at Penn State.

ADMITTANCE REQUIREMENTS: Juniors and seniors with a 2.5 GPA, good academic standing, and "must show evidence of maturity, stability, adaptability, self-discipline and a strong academic motivation." At least 6 credits in German.

TEACHING METHODS: All classes, except German, are in English. Courses at the Universität zu Köln are taught by regular faculty members. Americans are not integrated with German students.

EVALUATION: By course instructors, based upon class work, papers, and exams.

CREDITS OFFERED: 15 semester hours per semester.

HOUSING: Students live in university residential halls or off-campus.

DATES: Approximately, mid-January through late April.

COSTS: Students pay the same as at the University Park Campus. 1986-87 tuition per semester was $2,250 for state residents; $5,150 for nonresidents; room and board: $2,750 per semester. Plus a $100 nonrefundable program fee.

YEAR ESTABLISHED: 1962.

NUMBER OF STUDENTS IN 1985:   20.

APPLY: By March 1.

■ **UNIVERSITY OF WASHINGTON**
  Foreign Study Office
  572 Schmitz Hall, PA-10
  Seattle, WA 98195
  (206) 543-9272

PROGRAM: The Cologne Program is a fall and spring undergraduate program designed to serve as "an introduction to Germany through courses in literature, arts, social sciences, German language, and excursions. Intensive German language instruction is included during the first three weeks of the semester. Onsite orientation.

ADMITTANCE REQUIREMENTS: Sophomore standing, at least one quarter college-level German, and acceptable academic credentials.

TEACHING METHODS: Courses are taught in English by visiting Northwest faculty and resident German faculty.

EVALUATION: By course faculty member, based upon papers and exams.

CREDITS OFFERED: A full quarter term per quarter.

HOUSING: Students live with local families.

DATES: Approximately, fall semester: early September through mid-December; spring semester: early January through mid-May.

COSTS: $3,000 per semester includes tuition and room and board. Does not cover round-trip transportation, local travel or personal expenses.

YEAR ESTABLISHED: 1978.

NUMBER OF STUDENTS IN 1985:   30.

APPLY: Approximately four months prior to start of semester. David Fenner, Advisor.

Constance

■ **RUTGERS, THE STATE UNIVERSITY OF NEW JERSEY**
Milledoler Hall, Room 205
New Brunswick, NJ 08903
(201) 932-7787

PROGRAM: Junior Year Abroad in Germany is a full-year academic undergraduate program. Students attend regular classes at the University of Constance, which offers a broad selection of liberal arts courses with an emphasis on German language, literature, culture, and European affairs. A six-week presession intensive language and literature course is held at the Universität Konstanz.

ADMITTANCE REQUIREMENTS: Good academic standing and a "thorough knowledge of German is essential. At a minimum, students should have completed coursework through first year literature and preferably advanced grammar courses."

TEACHING METHODS: Students attend regular classes with German students. All courses are in German.

EVALUATION: By course instructors, based upon class work, papers, and exams.

CREDITS OFFERED: 30 semester hours per year including presession.

HOUSING: Students stay in single rooms in university residence halls. Each student receives a monthly meal allowance equivalent to three meals a day. In addition, there are kitchens in the residence halls.

DATES: Approximately, September 4 to mid-July.

COSTS: $5,472 New Jersey residents; $6,926 nonresidents. Includes tuition, room and board (except 45 days at holidays and between semesters), round-trip transportation from New York, and group excursions. Does not cover personal expenses.

YEAR ESTABLISHED: 1975.

NUMBER OF STUDENTS IN 1985: Limited to 30.

APPLY: By March 1. Director, Rutgers' Junior Year Abroad

Erlangen

■ **UNIVERSITY OF KANSAS**
Lawrence, KA 66045
(913) 864-3742

PROGRAM: The University of Kansas offers a full academic year at the Universities of Erlangen-Nüremberg in cooperation with the universities of Arkansas, Minnesota, Missouri, and Nebraska. Students enroll in regular coursework along with German students. Six-week orientation and language crash course in Germany.

ADMITTANCE REQUIREMENTS: Juniors and above with a minimum of 60 semester hours, 3.0 GPA, proficiency in German, plus recommendations.

TEACHING METHODS: Students take regular classes at the universities taught in German by local instructors.

EVALUATION: By local professors, based upon class work, papers, and exams.

CREDITS OFFERED: 30 to 36 semester hours per year.

HOUSING: Students live in university residence halls or student lodgings.

DATES: Approximately, November 1 through July 31.

COSTS: $5,460 includes annual tuition, room and board, orientation program, and field trips. Does not cover round-trip transportation, local travel, or personal expenses.

YEAR ESTABLISHED: 1963.

NUMBER OF STUDENTS IN 1985:   17.

APPLY: By March 10. Office of Study Abroad, 203 Lippincott.

Flensburg

■ **PENNSYLVANIA STATE UNIVERSITY**
Office of Education Abroad Programs
222 Boucke Building
University Park, PA 16802
(814) 865-7681

PROGRAM: Intensive German Language at the Pädagogische Hochschule is a fifteen-week spring undergraduate program conducted at the Pädagogische Hochschule. Four courses are offered: German 1, 2, 3, and a course on German life and letters today. Program includes visits to local sites of historic and cultural interest. Orientation at Penn State.

ADMITTANCE REQUIREMENTS: Juniors and seniors with a 2.5 GPA, good academic standing, and "must show evidence of maturity, stability, adaptability, self-discipline and a strong academic motivation." No previous knowledge of German required.

TEACHING METHODS: Students attend classes four hours per day; five days a week. All courses are taught in German.

EVALUATION: By course instructors, based upon class work, papers, and exams.

CREDITS OFFERED: 15 semester hours.

HOUSING: Students live in residence halls at the Pédagogische Hochschule.

DATES: Approximately, early February through late May.

COSTS: Students pay the same as at the University Park Campus. 1986–87 tuition per semester was $2,250 for state residents; $5,150 for nonresidents; room and board: $2,750 per semester. Plus a $100 nonrefundable program fee.

YEAR ESTABLISHED: 1984.

NUMBER OF STUDENTS IN 1985: 14.

APPLY: By October 15.

Freiberg

■ **INSTITUTE OF EUROPEAN STUDY (IES)**
223 West Ohio Street
Chicago, IL 60610
(312) 944-1750

PROGRAM: IES is a nonprofit organization with formal relationships with more than forty American colleges and universities. The institute offers a pair of programs in Freiberg in cooperation with the University of Freiberg: A semester, full-academic-year, or summer program devoted to German studies; or, a single-semester study of the economic, political, and historic developments of the European Economic Community. The German Study Program offers courses in twentieth-century German art, economics, German history, German language and literature, and political science. Field trips to East Germany and Prague. The European Community Program is designed primarily for economics, political science, international relations, and business majors with field trips to Common Market institutions in Brussels, Luxembourg, Strasbourg, and the OECD in Paris. One-week orientation in Freiberg.

ADMITTANCE REQUIREMENTS: Juniors and seniors only. Two years of college German or the equivalent for the German study program. Faculty recommendations and an application essay. 85 percent of all students have had a GPA between 2.80 and 3.75.

TEACHING METHODS: Students selecting the German study program may attend regular university courses with German students. All courses are taught in German. The Economic Community Program is taught in English at the IES center by a German faculty. Both programs include class work and field trips.

EVALUATION: By faculty, based upon class work and periodic and final exams. Most courses require a research paper.

CREDITS OFFERED: 15 semester hours per semester.

HOUSING: German Study students have their own furnished room in German student residence halls; Economic Community students live in double rooms in a building rented by the institute.

DATES: Fall semester: September 9 through December 20 (Economic Community); or February 13 (German Study); spring semester: EC—January 12 through May 9; German Study—February 23 through July 25. (These dates vary depending upon the student's program. Courses at the IES center end about a month earlier than the university courses.)

COSTS: German Study Program: $5,750 per year; $3,600 per semester. Economic Community Program: $3,875 (semester only). Includes tuition, room and board, and program-related travel (field trips on the Economic Community Program are covered in the tuition; German Study students share the cost). Does not include round-trip transportation, local travel, or personal expenses (estimated at $1,000 per semester). Some IES scholarship aid available; $1,500 for full year students, $750 for semester students.

YEAR ESTABLISHED: German Study: 1962; Economic Community: 1982.

NUMBER OF STUDENTS IN 1985: German Study: 45; Economic Community: 22.

APPLY: For fall semester by May 1; spring semester by November 15.

■ **STETSON UNIVERSITY**
  Box #8412
  DeLand, FL 32720
  (904) 734-4121, ext. 211

PROGRAM: The Stetson University Abroad Program is held in cooperation with the Pädogogische Hochschule with undergraduate courses concentrating on the German language, literature, civilization, history, art, etc. Students can elect to attend for a single semester or the full academic year. Onsite presession orientation.

ADMITTANCE REQUIREMENTS: Completion of sophomore year (or 60 semester hours), plus two years of German or the equivalent and language department recommendation.

TEACHING METHODS: Courses are conducted in German by members of the faculty at the Pädogogische Hochschule.

EVALUATION: Final examination given by local faculty.

CREDITS OFFERED: Upper-level semester credits vary depending upon course load.

HOUSING: Students live in the dormitories at the Internationales Wohnhein.

DATES: Fall semester: September 15 through December; spring semester: mid-January through July 10.

COSTS: $8,800 includes tuition, room and board, local travel, orientation, insurance, and international student I.D. card.

YEAR ESTABLISHED: 1964.

NUMBER OF STUDENTS IN 1985: 13.

APPLY: Fall semester only or full academic year: March 15; spring semester October 15. Office of International Exchange.

■ **UNIVERSITY OF SOUTHERN CALIFORNIA**
  Overseas Studies, CES 109
  University Park
  Los Angeles, CA 90089
  (213) 746-2500

PROGRAM: USC Year in Germany is an undergraduate program concentrating on the natural sciences; held in cooperation with the Institute of European Studies. Onsite orientation.

ADMITTANCE REQUIREMENTS: Sophomores and above in good academic standing with at least two years of college German, or the equivalent.

TEACHING METHODS: Courses are taught in German by U.S. and foreign faculty members.

EVALUATION: By course faculty member, based upon class work, papers, and periodic exams.

CREDITS OFFERED: 30 semester hours.

HOUSING: Students can live with private families or in dormitories.

DATE: Approximately, early September through late May.

COSTS: Approximately, $11,000 covers tuition, room and board, program-related travel. Does not include round-trip transportation or personal expenses. Some scholarships are available.

YEAR ESTABLISHED: 1984.

NUMBER OF STUDENTS IN 1985: 6.

APPLY: By February 1.

Hamburg

■ **BELOIT COLLEGE**
Beloit, WI 53511
(608) 365-3391

PROGRAM: World Outlook Seminar undergraduate program offers a semester in Germany in cooperation with the University of Hamburg. The program stresses language, contemporary literature, history, theater, North German art and architecture. Presession orientation is held at Beloit.

ADMITTANCE REQUIREMENTS: B average, two years of German for those taking language courses and good academic standing.

TEACHING METHODS: Students attend special courses, unless their language proficiency is high, taught by faculty from the University of Hamburg. Lectures, independent study, and field trips complement classroom work. A U.S. academic leader accompanies group.

EVALUATION: Papers and examinations given by German professors.

CREDITS OFFERED: 16 semester hours.

HOUSING: With local families.

DATES: Approximately January 15 through April 30.

COSTS: Tuition: $3,900; room and board: $1,700; travel to/from Europe: approximately $600.

YEAR ESTABLISHED: 1969.

NUMBER OF STUDENTS IN 1985: 12.

APPLY: By November 30. World Affairs Center.

■ **HIRAM COLLEGE**
Hiram, OH 44234
(216) 569-5160

PROGRAM: Hiram's German Quarter offers a ten-week undergraduate program in which students select three courses from a menu including German language, literature, biology, and interdisciplinary studies. Presession orientation at Hiram and a few days in Germany. Material mailed to students who can't attend the Hiram session.

ADMITTANCE REQUIREMENTS: A minimum 2.5 GPA with recommendations from your own advisor plus two additional teachers. A language requirement varies from program to program.

TEACHING METHODS: Students attend regular classes or seminars taught by members of the Hiram faculty. Lectures and seminars are integrated with local field trips. Classes are conducted in a suburban convention center.

EVALUATION: By programs leaders and students, based upon papers and exams.

CREDITS OFFERED: Up to 15 quarter hours per quarter.

HOUSING: Students live at facilities at the suburban convention center.

DATES: The program is offered every three years. Next program scheduled for the spring quarter, 1989.

COSTS: Approximately $4,500 including tuition, room and board, local travel and fees. Does not cover round-trip transportation or local expenses.

YEAR ESTABLISHED: 1967.

NUMBER OF STUDENTS IN 1985: Not available.

APPLY: By January 10. Charles L. Adams, Director, Extra Mural Studies.

■ **SMITH COLLEGE**
Northampton, MA 01063
(413) 584-2700

PROGRAM: Smith College Junior Year in Hamburg is a full-academic-year undergraduate program offering courses in intermediate and advanced German language and literature, mathematics, philosophy, and religion as well as the full curriculum offering at the University of Hamburg. Orientation in Hamburg.

ADMITTANCE REQUIREMENTS: Juniors with a 3.0 GPA and two years of college German or the equivalent.

TEACHING METHODS: All instruction is in German. Students attend special courses arranged for the group or may enroll and attend regular classes at the University of Hamburg.

EVALUATION: By course faculty, based upon papers and final exams.

CREDITS OFFERED: 32 semester hours per year.

HOUSING: Students live within university dormitories.

DATES: Fall semester: September 1 through mid-December; spring semester: late January through July 15.

COSTS: $13,760 per year includes tuition and room and board. Does not include round-trip transportation, local travel, or personal expenses.

YEAR ESTABLISHED: 1982.

NUMBER OF STUDENTS IN 1985: 12.

APPLY: By February 1. Patricia C. Olmsted, Committee on Study Abroad (Extension 4920).

Heidelberg

■ **THE CALIFORNIA STATE UNIVERSITY**
400 Golden Shore
Long Beach, CA 90802
(213) 590-5655

PROGRAM: The CSU International Program in Germany, held in cooperation with Ruprecht-Karls University in Heidelberg and Eberhard-Karls University in Tübingen, is a full-academic-year undergraduate and graduate opportunity to study at either German university. Students select from the wide range of university course offerings supplemented by special CSU programs. One-week orientation in Heidelberg.

ADMITTANCE REQUIREMENTS: Must be enrolled at a CSU campus. Juniors and above including graduate students. 2.75 GPA. Two years of college German or the equivalent, except for those students enrolling in the Learn German in Germany program.

TEACHING METHODS: Students take a combination of regular academic courses and supplemental program-sponsored courses taught by foreign faculty.

EVALUATION: By foreign faculty and CSU resident director, based upon periodic and final exams.

CREDITS OFFERED: 30 semester hours per year or 45 quarter units.

HOUSING: In dormitories and private apartments.

DATES: Approximately, July 23 to July 13.

COSTS: Tuition: $0 (residents); $3,600 (nonresidents); room and board: $2,750. Does not include round-trip transportation and living expenses estimated at approximately $3,385 per year.

YEAR ESTABLISHED: 1963.

NUMBER OF STUDENTS IN 1985: 66.

APPLY: By February 1. Dr. Kibbey M. Horne, Director of International Programs.

■ **COLLEGE CONSORTIUM FOR INTERNATIONAL STUDIES (CCIS)**
866 United Nations Plaza, Room 511
New York, NY 10017
(212) 308-1556

PROGRAM: CCIS is a nonprofit organization that sponsors and organizes several dozen foreign study programs for member colleges who grant degree credit. CCIS offers a pair of undergraduate programs in Heidelberg both in cooperation with Ocean County College (N.J.): general business/liberal arts and an intensive language program. Both are offered six times a year and last for eight weeks. Students attend classes at the Collegium Palatium. The business program offers courses in German (required), German art and culture (required), European Common Market, international business, international law, international marketing, and advertising. The language program concentrates on German language studies. Two-day orientation in Germany with an optional field trip/seminar in East and West Berlin.

ADMITTANCE REQUIREMENTS: Freshman and above with 3.0 GPA and acceptable academic credentials. Some knowledge of German for the business program.

TEACHING METHODS: Special courses for foreigners, in English and German, are taught by professors associated with German universities.

EVALUATION: By course instructors and project leaders.

CREDITS OFFERED: 12 credits per eight-week program.

HOUSING: Students live in dormitories, apartments, or with local families.

DATES: January through March; March through May; May through July; July through September; September through November; and November through January.

COSTS: Approximately, $3,100 per cycle for the business/liberal arts program; $1,195 for the intensive language program. Does not cover room and board, local travel, round-trip transportation, or personal expenses. Berlin excursion $200 extra.

YEAR ESTABLISHED: 1982.

NUMBER OF STUDENTS IN 1985: 9.

APPLY: 45 days prior to the beginning of the cycle.

■ **HEIDELBERG COLLEGE**
   310 East Market Street
   Tiffin, OH 44883
   (419) 448-2256

PROGRAM: The American Junior Year at Heidelberg University is held in cooperation with one of Germany's oldest institutions (founded in 1386). Students attend regular classes at the university and may select any course offered. More than 28,000 students, a tenth of them non-German, attend the university. Many American students supplement their studies with courses in the German language offered by the Institute for German. A trip to East Germany is usually planned during the summer semester. Four-week preliminary course/orientation concentrates on language training plus forty hours of cultural orientation at Heidelberg.

ADMITTANCE REQUIREMENTS: Juniors or seniors with a 3.0 GPA and two years of college German or the equivalent.

TEACHING METHODS: Students who pass the PNDS exam take regular university courses with German students. If necessary, special courses are taught in German by American and university instructors. Some local trips included in tuition.

EVALUATION: By university professors, based upon term papers and final exams.

CREDITS OFFERED: Up to 16 semester hours per semester.

HOUSING: Students may live in university dormitories or choose to live in local rooming houses or with local families.

DATES: Approximately, winter semester: September 1 through late February; summer semester: March 1 through mid-July.

COSTS: Tuition: $6,350 for the full year; room and board: $2,600 for the full year. Does not include round-trip transportation or personal expenses (estimated at $1,000 a year).

YEAR ESTABLISHED: 1958.

NUMBER OF STUDENTS IN 1985: 25.

APPLY: For winter semester by March 15; for summer semester by October 15. The American Junior Year at Heidelberg University.

Kessel

■ ALMA COLLEGE
Alma, MI 48801
(517) 463-7247

PROGRAM: Alma College Program of Studies in Germany is held in cooperation with the Europa-Kelleg. This program is not in a structured academic setting such as most American schools. Rather, teachers and staff "leave enough freedom in the academic environment to allow students to meet their needs through consultation with the director." Courses specialize in German language and culture. One-week orientation with the director onsite.

ADMITTANCE REQUIREMENTS: Sophomores and above with a minimum 2.0 GPA, in good academic standing, with letters of recommendation..

TEACHING METHODS: Small classes, usually six to nine students, in German are complemented with visits to local sites and independent study. Direct involvement with German staff and local residents is encouraged and expected.

EVALUATION: Foreign faculty in conjunction with the resident director plus papers and periodic exams.

CREDITS OFFERED: Up to 15 hours per semester.

HOUSING: All students reside in local homes.

DATES: Summer term: July 1 through August 24; fall semester: September 2 through December 21; winter semester: January 2 through April 26.

COSTS: Summer session: $1,950; fall semester: $4,450; winter semester: $4,450. Includes round-trip transportation from New York, room and board, plus basic texts and cultural activities.

YEAR ESTABLISHED: 1985.

NUMBER OF STUDENTS IN 1985: 1.

APPLY: Two months prior to departure. Alda Dyal Chand, Director, International Education.

Kiel

■ **PENNSYLVANIA STATE UNIVERSITY**
Office of Education Abroad Programs
222 Boucke Building
University Park, PA 16802
(814) 865-7681

PROGRAM: Education Abroad at the Christian-Albrechts University is a spring-semester undergraduate program held in cooperation with Christian-Albrechts University. In 1986, PSU initiated a full-year exchange program with C-A University, in which students are fully integrated into classes and take regular courses with German students. The spring-semester program is specially designed for Pennsylvania State program students. Students take special courses that cover the German language, literature, and culture plus political science. Orientation at Penn State.

ADMITTANCE REQUIREMENTS: Juniors and seniors with a 2.5 GPA, good standing, and "must show evidence of maturity, stability, adaptability, self-discipline and a strong academic motivation." At least 15 credits in German; for the full-year exchange program advanced German is required.

TEACHING METHODS: All classes are in German and are taught by regular faculty members. Americans are not integrated with German students in classes (except the exchange program), but there is "extensive social contact."

EVALUATION: By course instructors, based upon class work, papers, and exams.

CREDITS OFFERED: 15 semester hours per semester.

HOUSING: Students live in university dormitories or with private families.

DATES: Approximately, exchange program: early October through early July; semester program: mid-January through mid-May.

COSTS: Students pay the same as at the University Park Campus. 1986-87 tuition per semester was $2,250 for state residents; $5,150 for nonresidents; room and board: $2,750 per semester. Plus a $100 nonrefundable program fee.

YEAR ESTABLISHED: 1981.

NUMBER OF STUDENTS IN 1985: 13.

APPLY: For exchange program by March 1; semester program by October 15.

Mainz

■ **MIDDLEBURY COLLEGE**
Middlebury, VT 05753
(802) 388-3711

PROGRAM: Middlebury College School in Germany offers undergraduates "long-standing, highly respected, and *serious*" courses in literature, German language, culture, and civilization. An MA program is available in German language and literature. Courses are held at the University of Mainz.

ADMITTANCE REQUIREMENTS: The equivalent of 5 semesters in German and a B average; (for MA a "better than B average" is required.)

TEACHING METHODS: German faculty. All courses, written papers, and exams are in German. Extensive travel, field trips, and cultural exchanges complement the program.

EVALUATION: Faculty-student conferences, term papers, finals, etc.

CREDITS OFFERED: Full semester or full year credit.

HOUSING: Students live in dormitories at the university.

DATES: Approximately, September 15 through June 10. Students can take a full-year program or fall or spring-semester program.

COSTS: Tuition: full year: $4,900; semester: $2,500; room and board: approximately, $2,000 per semester; round-trip travel to school: approximately $600. Local travel in Europe not included. Some scholarships available.

YEAR ESTABLISHED: 1959.

NUMBER OF STUDENTS IN 1985: 60.

APPLY: Rolling admissions. Dean of German School.

Mannheim

■ **UNIVERSITY OF CONNECTICUT**
241 Glenbrook Road
Storrs, CT 06268
(203) 486-2141

PROGRAM: The University of Connecticut Mannheim Program, held in cooperation with the Goethe Institute, University of Mannheim, Hochschule für Musik, Fachhochschule für Technik, and the Fachhochschule für Sozialwesen, is a six-month spring-semester program with an option to extend through July and August and serve an internship at a German company. The program has been developed in special consideration of the needs of students in business, engineering, music and drama, and social work. A student can earn a maximum of 21 credits within a six-month period including 9 to 12 in the German language plus 9 to 12 in a specific field. Field trips to historic and cultural sites are part of the program.

ADMITTANCE REQUIREMENTS: Juniors and above in good academic standing with at least two years of college German or the equivalent.

TEACHING METHODS: Students attend special courses arranged for the group, as well as any of the courses offered by the participating institutions in which Americans are fully integrated with German students. All classes are in German.

EVALUATION: By course professors based upon papers and exams.

CREDITS OFFERED: Up to 21 semester hours.

HOUSING: Students share double rooms in university dormitories with non-U.S. students.

DATES: Early February through early July.

COSTS: $4,500 per semester includes tuition, room and board, and some program-related travel. Does not cover round-trip transportation or personal expenses.

YEAR ESTABLISHED: 1985.

NUMBER OF STUDENTS IN 1985: 7.

APPLY: By October 15. Study Abroad Office, U-207.

Marburg

■ **BRETHREN COLLEGES ABROAD**
P.O. Box #184
Manchester College,
N. Manchester, IN 46962
(219) 982-2141, ext. 238

PROGRAM: Brethren Colleges Abroad is held in cooperation with Philipps-Universität Marburg, and Bridgewater College, Elizabethtown College, Juniata College, McPherson College, and the University of La Verne in the United States. The program is available for a semester or the full academic year. Courses include: German literature, music, sociology, psychology, political science, business, economics, mathematics, sciences, international relations, history, religion, philosophy, English and American literature, and German. Orientation and a five-week intensive language course are given onsite.

ADMITTANCE REQUIREMENTS: Sophomores and above with a 3.0 GPA and two years of college-level German or the equivalent.

TEACHING METHODS: Americans are fully integrated with German students. Both special and regular college courses. Coursework is complemented with field trips and travel to museums and regional sites.

EVALUATION: Director in Germany and professors determine grades from papers, periodic exams, and finals.

CREDITS OFFERED: 15 to 16 semester hours.

HOUSING: Students live in dormitories.

DATES: Fall semester: September 1 through January 31; spring semester: February 5 through July 15.

COSTS: $5,800 per semester. Includes tuition, room and board, and round-trip transportation. Does not cover personal expenses or local travel.

YEAR ESTABLISHED: 1962.

NUMBER OF STUDENTS IN 1985:   27.

APPLY: By April 1 for fall semester and November 1 for spring semester. Dr. Allen C. Deeter or Mrs. Helga Walsh.

■ **MILLERSVILLE UNIVERSITY**
   Millersville, PA 17551
   (717) 872-3011

PROGRAM: The Junior Year in Marburg program is held in cooperation with the Philipps-Universität Marburg/Lahn. Students may elect a semester or full year at either the undergraduate or graduate level. The program is intensive and students are required to speak German at all times. Courses emphasize German language, history, music, fine arts, political science, economics, etc. Students also take excursions to other German cities, including West Berlin, as well as either Austria or Czechoslovakia. There is a six-week onsite orientation.

ADMITTANCE REQUIREMENTS: Junior standing with a 3.0 GPA and two years of college German or the equivalent. The graduate program requires admission to the summer graduate program at Millersville University prior to departure to Marburg.

TEACHING METHODS: Students are expected to immerse themselves in the language. Courses are integrated and taught by regular German faculty members in the 760-year-old university. Participants normally take up to 27 credits (9 courses) per year.

EVALUATION: Periodic exams and finals conducted by German university faculty.

CREDITS OFFERED: A maximum of 18 semester hours per semester.

HOUSING: Students live with German and other international students in the university dormitory.

DATES: Approximately, fall semester: September 1 to mid-December; spring semester: mid-January to June 10.

COSTS: Tuition: $2,000 per semester; room and board: $3,060 per semester. Does not include round-trip transportation, additional educational expenses (estimated at $820 per year), or "pocket money" (estimated at $1,500 per year). Millersville University offers a $1,000 merit scholarship.

YEAR ESTABLISHED: 1963.

NUMBER OF STUDENTS IN 1985:   18.

APPLY: By February 15. Director, Junior Year in Marburg, Department of Foreign Languages.

■ **PENNSYLVANIA STATE UNIVERSITY**
Office of Education Abroad Programs
222 Boucke Building
University Park, PA 16802
(814) 865-7681

PROGRAM: Education Abroad at Philipps-Universität is a full-year undergraduate program held in cooperation with Philipps-Universität and Millersville University. The program begins with a six-week intensive German language session and follows with survey courses covering German history, geography, and contemporary problems. Program includes visits to local sites of historic and cultural interest. Orientation at Penn State.

ADMITTANCE REQUIREMENTS: Juniors and seniors with a 2.5 GPA, good academic standing, and "must show evidence of maturity, stability, adaptability, self-discipline and a strong academic motivation." At least two years of German with a 3.0 average.

TEACHING METHODS: One half of the students' work consists of special courses; the remaining work is done in regular Philipps-Universität classes with German students. All courses are taught in German.

EVALUATION: By course instructors based upon class work, papers, and exams.

CREDITS OFFERED: 12 to 15 semester hours per semester.

HOUSING: Students usually live in university dormitories.

DATES: Approximately, early September through mid-July.

COSTS: Students pay the same as at the University Park Campus. 1986-87 tuition per semester was $2,250 for state residents; $5,150 for nonresidents; room and board: $2,750 per semester. Plus a $100 nonrefundable program fee.

YEAR ESTABLISHED: 1982.

NUMBER OF STUDENTS IN 1985: 2.

APPLY: For first semester: by March 1; second semester by October 15.

Muenster

■ **COLLEGE OF WILLIAM AND MARY**
Office of International Studies
Williamsburg, VA 23185
(804) 253-4354

PROGRAM: William and Mary Summer in Muenster is held in cooperation with Vassar College. The summer session presents a five-week program, including courses specializing in the German language, literature, and civilization and travel to local historic and cultural sites. Onsite preorientation.

ADMITTANCE REQUIREMENTS: Open to all undergraduates who hold good academic standing at their home institution, plus one year of college German or the equivalent.

TEACHING METHODS: Regular courses are taught by a U.S. faculty. Seminar-sized classes. Both class and onsite lectures, seminars.

EVALUATION: By faculty, based upon papers, periodic tests, and a final exam.

CREDITS OFFERED: 6 semester hours.

HOUSING: Students live with host families.

DATES: Approximately, June 3 through July 8.

COSTS: Tuition and room and board: $2,100; estimated living expenses: $200. Round-trip transportation not included. Scholarships available to William and Mary students.

YEAR ESTABLISHED: 1980.

NUMBER OF STUDENTS IN 1985: 28.

APPLY: By February 1. Ms. Carolyn V. Blackwell, Director.

Munich

■ **SLIPPERY ROCK UNIVERSITY**
Slippery Rock, PA 16057
(412) 794-7425

PROGRAM: The Slippery Rock University/Overseas Student Teaching Program is a ten-week, spring-semester program designed to provide student teaching opportunities, in all academic areas, on U.S. military bases. Orientation both at Slippery Rock University and onsite.

ADMITTANCE REQUIREMENTS: For eligible student teachers with a minimum 3.0 GPA.

TEACHING METHODS: Student teachers work with members of the Slippery Rock faculty and a local cooperating teacher.

EVALUATION: By both Slippery Rock faculty and local teacher.

CREDITS OFFERED: 6 semester hours.

HOUSING: Students live on the military bases.

DATES: March 1 through May 10.

COSTS: Students pay the going Slippery Rock University tuition plus $175 administrative fee. Living facilities are provided. Students pay for meals and extra living expenses, approximately $8 to $10 per day.

YEAR ESTABLISHED: 1982.

NUMBER OF STUDENTS IN 1985:   24.

APPLY: By September 1. Stan Kendziorski, Director, International Education.

■ **UNIVERSITY OF WISCONSIN – STEVENS POINT**
208 Old Main
Stevens Point, WI 54481
(715) 346-2717

PROGRAM: Semester in Germany is a fall travel/study undergraduate program. Although the majority of the program is in Munich, the group spends about a month traveling to Trier, Koblenz, Bremen, Berlin (east and west), Dresden, Prague, Vienna, and Klagenfurt. Classes concentrate on the humanities and social sciences including history, political science, European geography, and art history.

ADMITTANCE REQUIREMENTS: Sophomores and above in good academic standing. "Preference is given to students who have had German 101 or its equivalent."

TEACHING METHODS: Students attend courses taught in English arranged for the group. German language courses are offered. Many of the courses are given by the group's program leader.

EVALUATION: By instructors and group leaders, based upon class work, papers, and exams.

CREDITS OFFERED: A minimum of 13 semester hours; maximum of 17.

HOUSING: Students stay in hostels while traveling and dormitories with the group in Munich.

DATES: Approximately, August 25 to December 10.

COSTS: Approximately, $3,175 includes tuition, room and board, and round-trip transportation from Madison. Minnesota students pay a small "reciprocity fee"; non-Wisconsin residents pay a surcharge. Does not cover personal expenses.

YEAR ESTABLISHED: 1970.

NUMBER OF STUDENTS IN 1985: Not available.

APPLY: "Early application is advised." Dr. Helen Cornell, Director, International Programs.

Regensburg

■ **UNIVERSITY OF COLORADO**
Campus Box 123
Boulder, CO 80309
(303) 492-7741

PROGRAM: Study Abroad at Regensburg is a full-academic-year program held in cooperation with the universities of Nebraska, Missouri, Wyoming and Colorado State University and the University of Regensburg. Students take regular classes selected from the Regensburg course catalogue and are fully integrated with German students. Orientation in the U.S. followed by a six-week intensive German language program in Regensburg.

ADMITTANCE REQUIREMENTS: Juniors and seniors with a 3.0 GPA and at least two years of college German or the equivalent.

TEACHING METHODS: Students may select any course from the University of Regensburg catalogue all of which are taught in German.

EVALUATION: By University of Regensburg faculty, based upon class performance, papers, and final exams.

CREDITS OFFERED: 24 to 36 semester hours per year.

HOUSING: Students may elect to live in residence halls or in local rooming houses or apartments.

DATES: September 1 through July 31.

COSTS: $3,756 to $4,560 per year depending upon housing arrangements. Includes tuition, room and board, and some program-related travel. Does not cover round-trip transportation or personal expenses.

YEAR ESTABLISHED: 1969.

NUMBER OF STUDENTS IN 1985:   17.

APPLY: By March 1. Office of International Education.

■ **VANDERBILT UNIVERSITY**
College of Arts & Sciences
Box #6327-B
Nashville, TN 37235
(615) 371-1224

PROGRAM: Vanderbilt-in-Germany is a full-academic-year undergraduate program in which students are enrolled directly in the University of Regensburg. Courses are the regular listings offered German students. Some study tours are offered by the resident director and are part of the program. Intensive German language program (4 credits awarded) and concurrent cultural orientation program precedes university opening.

ADMITTANCE REQUIREMENTS: 3.0 GPA and "sufficient knowledge of German to pursue studies successfully."

TEACHING METHODS: Students attend regular classes at the university. Classes are fully integrated with local students and are taught in German.

EVALUATION: By course professors, based upon class work, papers, and exams.

CREDITS OFFERED: From 12 to 18 semester hours per semester.

HOUSING: Students live in single rooms in the university dormitory and are responsible for their own meals.

DATES: Approximately, September 1 through late July.

COSTS: $4,650 per semester includes tuition, board, and some program activities. Does not cover round-trip transportation, meals (which range from $750 to $850 per semester), or personal expenses (estimated at approximately $450 per semester). Each year Vanderbilt-in-Germany offers a $500 award to "a worthy participant."

YEAR ESTABLISHED: 1971.

NUMBER OF STUDENTS IN 1985: 21.

APPLY: By March 15. Overseas Office.

Tübingen

■ **ANTIOCH COLLEGE**
Box #58
Yellow Springs, OH 45387
(513) 767-1031

PROGRAM: Antioch in Tübingen, held in cooperation with Eberhard-Karls-Universitat, can be experienced for a full academic year or, in some instances, for a single semester. Students select courses at the university in any field, including advanced academic work in all disciplines. The university is known for its theoretical and applied sciences. Language study may be undertaken at East German universities in East Berlin, Dresden, or Leipzig. Five-week combined orientation and language program in Tübingen and Blaubeuren. Semester orientation is shorter.

ADMITTANCE REQUIREMENTS: Two years of undergraduate study and good academic standing. German fluency is also necessary.

TEACHING METHODS: Students experience the German university system. All courses are in German and all classes include German students.

EVALUATION: By foreign faculty members. An Antioch staff member assists American students. Although courses are graded by German standards, a standard record of achievement contains U.S. grades.

CREDITS OFFERED: Depends upon a student's fluency in German. Maximum: the equivalent of 40 Antioch quarter *graduate* or *undergraduate* credits (a full credit load of semester hours) per year.

HOUSING: Students live in the dormitories at Eberhard-Karls-Universitat.

DATES: Fall term: mid-October through mid-February; spring term: mid-April through mid-July.

COSTS: Tuition is approximately $5,650 per year. Not included is round-trip transportation, room and board, or personal expenses (estimated at $400 to $450 per month).

YEAR ESTABLISHED: 1958.

NUMBER OF STUDENTS IN 1985: 12.

APPLY: By January 15. Connie Bauer, Dean.

■ **OREGON STATE SYSTEM OF HIGHER EDUCATION (OSSHE)**
Foreign Study Programs
International Education
Oregon State University
Corvallis, OR
(503) 754-3006

PROGRAM: The OSSHE Spring Intensive German Language Program is held in cooperation with Eberhard-Karls-Universitat and the member schools of OSSHE (Eastern Oregon State College, Oregon Institute of Technology, Portland State University, Southern Oregon State University, University of Oregon, and Western Oregon State College). The program provides intensive language for students who have completed two terms of first-year German. Covers basic grammar, reading, conversation, and German culture. One-day orientation in Oregon.

ADMITTANCE REQUIREMENTS: Minimum 2.5 GPA (3.0 in German), letters of recommendation, and personal interview.

TEACHING METHODS: Taught in German by Eberhard-Karls-Universitat faculty. Lectures, seminars, and independent study complemented by some travel to regional museums and cultural sites.

EVALUATION: By university faculty based on periodic and final exams.

CREDITS OFFERED: One term or 20 trimester hours.

HOUSING: Students live in university dormitories.

DATES: Approximately, April 10 through July 11.

COSTS: $2,000 includes tuition, room and board, and some local travel. Does not include round-trip transportation or personal expenses.

YEAR ESTABLISHED: 1984.

NUMBER OF STUDENTS IN 1985: 10.

APPLY: By January 31. German department at member OSSHE school, or Irma Wright, Office of International Education.

■ **TUFTS UNIVERSITY**
  Medford, MA 02155
  (617) 381-3152

PROGRAM: Tufts in Tübingen, a full-year undergraduate program, is completely integrated into the German university system. Program participants spend the academic year at the Eberhard-Karls Universitat. Students take regular university courses in the following departments: art history, biology, chemistry, economics, French, geology, German, history, philosophy, political science, and psychology. Program has an enrollment of twenty students. Two-week intensive language orientation in Bavarian Alps.

ADMITTANCE REQUIREMENTS: Good academic standing plus two years of college German or the equivalent.

TEACHING METHODS: Regular classes, seminars, and independent study projects given by the universities in German. Fully integrated with German students.

EVALUATION: By German professors from the universities.

CREDITS OFFERED: 16 semester hours per semester.

HOUSING: Students live with German students in dormitories.

DATES: Fall semester: third week in September through mid-February; spring semester: mid-April through mid-July.

COSTS: $7,075 per semester. Covers tuition, room and board, round-trip transportation, and some local travel. Does not cover personal expenses.

YEAR ESTABLISHED: 1965.

NUMBER OF STUDENTS IN 1985: 13.

APPLY: By February 1. Dean Christopher Gray, Director, Tufts Programs Abroad, Ballou Hall.

Zwingenberg

■ **BIOLA UNIVERSITY**
  13800 Biola Avenue
  La Mirada, CA 90639
  (213) 944-0351, ext. 3290

PROGRAM: Biola Abroad is a semester program with a strong emphasis on European studies. Courses include: German language and literature, German and European history and culture, physical education, and Bible/Christian education.

ADMITTANCE REQUIREMENTS: Open to Biola students and those from sponsoring institutions with "near B average and two semesters of college German."

TEACHING METHODS: Lectures and class work is in English; taught by U.S. faculty. Field trips to local regions and neighboring countries supplement class work.

EVALUATION: Three major exams in each subject.

CREDITS OFFERED: 15 semester units.

HOUSING: Students live and study in the residence, and when on field trips, in hotels.

DATES: Approximately, September 15 through December 15.

COSTS: $4,700 includes tuition, room and board, books, round-trip transportation, and all travel costs associated with the program.

YEAR ESTABLISHED: 1973.

NUMBER OF STUDENTS IN 1985: 30.

APPLY: By February. Biola Abroad Office.

GREECE

Population: 10,008,000   **Capital:** Athens   **Language:** Greek
Monetary Unit: Drachma   **Government:** Unitary multiparty republic
(president and prime minister)   **Religion:** 98% Greek Orthodox
Households with Television: 18%

SCHOOLS AND UNIVERSITIES

College Year in Athens
P.O. Box #3476
Kolonaki, Athens

Courses in Greek language and Greek civilization taught in English.

University of Athens
Athens

Entrance examination required. Courses taught in Greek.

University of Thessaloniki
Thessaloniki

Entrance examination required. Courses taught in Greek.

University of Crete
Iraklion

Entrance examination required. Courses taught in Greek.

FURTHER INFORMATION

Consulate General of Greece
69 East 79th Street
New York, NY 10021
(212) 988-5500

Embassy of Greece
2221 Massachusetts Avenue, NW
Washington, DC 20008
(202) 667-3168

Greek National Tourist Organization
645 Fifth Avenue
New York, NY 10022
(212) 421-5777

More Than One City

■ **THE EXPERIMENT IN INTERNATIONAL LIVING**
Kipling Road
Brattleboro, VT 05301
(800) 451-4465

PROGRAM: The College Semester Abroad Program is designed to allow students to become immersed in a foreign culture by living with a local family and exploring individual personal and educational interests under professional guidance. The Greece Program spends four weeks in Athens, seven weeks in Thessaloniki, two weeks at a location appropriate to a field study project, and winds up in Thessaloniki (fall semester) or an Aegean island (spring semester) for a week of program evaluation. Courses cover: intensive language training at the Athens Center, seminar on Greek life and culture, history and politics, geography and economics, art and architecture, social anthropology, social/cultural field work, and an independent study project. One-week orientation in Athens.

ADMITTANCE REQUIREMENTS: Sophomore standing or above and acceptable academic credentials. No language prerequisite.

TEACHING METHODS: Students work directly with their American instructors-advisors in planning and evaluating their individual program. "The semester builds from the more structured language training and lectures and discussions on local life and culture to the independent study project."

EVALUATION: By individual students and their instructor/advisors based on independent project, papers, reports, and exams. Periodic meetings during the program and for several days at the conclusion.

CREDITS OFFERED: Up to 16 semester hours.

HOUSING: Students live as family members with their host families.

DATES: Approximately, fall semester: September through December; spring semester: January through May.

COSTS: $5,800 includes tuition, room and board, all fees and local travel, and round-trip transportation from Brattleboro, Vermont.

YEAR ESTABLISHED: 1985.

NUMBER OF STUDENTS IN 1985: 13.

APPLY: For fall semester by May 15; spring semester by November 15. Admissions Office, College Semester Abroad.

■ **DEPAUW UNIVERSITY**
   Greencastle, IN 46135
   (317) 658-4736

PROGRAM: Mediterranean Studies is a single-semester undergraduate program with courses covering Greek (required), Greek and Near Eastern history, anthropology, archaeology, art, government, literature, philosophy, and religion. Program-related travel to Turkey, Egypt, and Crete.

ADMITTANCE REQUIREMENTS: Sophomores and above in good academic standing with some knowledge of Greek and a 2.5 GPA.

TEACHING METHODS: Students take special courses arranged for the group and taught in English by the both U.S. and Greek faculty.

EVALUATION: By course faculty, based upon papers and periodic examinations.

CREDITS OFFERED: 15 to 16 semester hours.

HOUSING: Students live in apartments.

DATES: Fall semester: September 5 through December 21; spring semester: January 9 through May 22.

COSTS: $5,300 includes tuition, apartment, some meals, and program-related travel. Does not cover round-trip transportation, local travel, and personal expenses.

YEAR ESTABLISHED: 1970.

NUMBER OF STUDENTS IN 1985: 13.

APPLY: For fall semester by April 1; spring semester by October 1. Dr. Darrell LaLone, Director of Off-Campus Study.

■ **SAN FRANCISCO STATE UNIVERSITY**
1600 Holloway Avenue
San Francisco, CA 94132
(415) 469-1371

PROGRAM: Semester in Greece is a recent fall-semester undergraduate and graduate program held in cooperation with the Athens Center. Courses cover both ancient and modern Greek, Greek history and Byzantine culture, archaeology, Greek drama and literature. Field trips to Delphi, Olympia, Corinth, Crete, Epidaurus, and Santorini. Orientation both in U.S. and Athens.

ADMITTANCE REQUIREMENTS: Sophomores and above, including both graduate students and interested post-college "students." 3.0 GPA.

TEACHING METHODS: Students attend special courses, taught in English by both American and Greek faculty, arranged for the group by the Athens Center.

EVALUATION: By faculty, based upon class work, papers, and period examinations.

CREDITS OFFERED: 15 semester hours.

HOUSING: Students live in a pension in Athens.

DATES: September 7 through December 18.

COSTS: $4,000 includes tuition, room and breakfast, and program-related travel. Does not cover round-trip transportation, most meals, or personal expenses.

YEAR ESTABLISHED: 1986.

NUMBER OF STUDENTS IN 1986:   Not available.

APPLY: By June 1. Mary Pierrat, International Travel Study Office.

■ **SOUTHEAST MISSOURI STATE UNIVERSITY**
Cape Giradeau, MO 63701
(314) 651-2562

PROGRAM: The Student/Faculty Exchange Program between the American College of Greece and Southeast Missouri State University is a recently inaugurated single-semester program that offers a broad, multidiscipline selection of courses taught by regular faculty members at the American College of Greece. Orientation on various Missouri campuses prior to departure.

ADMITTANCE REQUIREMENTS: Good academic standing.

TEACHING METHODS: Students take regular courses in English at the American College of Greece.

EVALUATION: By Greek faculty, based upon class work and examinations.

CREDITS OFFERED: Up to 18 semester hours per semester.

HOUSING: Students live in the college residence hall.

DATES: January 10 through May 15.

COSTS: Tuition: $1,000; room and board: $975. Does not include round-trip transportation or living expenses (estimated at $1,500).

YEAR ESTABLISHED: 1986.

NUMBER OF STUDENTS IN 1986: Not available.

APPLY: September 15. Center for International Studies.

■ **UNIVERSITY OF WISCONSIN – STEVENS POINT**
208 Old Main
Stevens Point, WI 54481
(715) 346-2717

PROGRAM: Semester in Greece is a travel/study spring undergraduate program. Although the majority of the program is held in Athens, the group spends about a month traveling to Italy, Turkey, Crete, etc. Classes in Athens are given at the Athens Center and include literature, history, geography, art and archaeology, culture and civilization, and conversational Greek.

ADMITTANCE REQUIREMENTS: Sophomores and above in good academic standing. Knowledge of a foreign language is not required.

TEACHING METHODS: Students attend courses taught in English arranged for the group at the Athens Center. Greek language courses are offered.

EVALUATION: By instructors and group leaders, based upon class work, papers, and exams.

CREDITS OFFERED: A minimum of 13 semester hours; maximum of 17.

HOUSING: Students stay in hostels while traveling and the Hotel Neon Kronos in Athens.

DATES: Approximately January 4 to April 30.

COSTS: Approximately $3,100 includes tuition, room and board, round-trip transportation from Chicago, and program-related travel. Minnesota students pay a small "reciprocity fee"; non-Wisconsin residents pay a surcharge. Does not cover personal expenses.

YEAR ESTABLISHED: 1985.

NUMBER OF STUDENTS IN 1985:   17.

APPLY: "Early application is advised." Dr. Helen Cornell, Director, International Programs.

IRELAND

Population: 3,547,000   **Capital:** Dublin   **Languages:** English, Gaelic
Monetary Unit: Irish pound   **Government:** Unitary multiparty republic
(president and prime minister)   **Religion:** 94% Roman Catholic
Households with Television: 11%

SELECTED COLLEGES AND UNIVERSITIES

National University of Ireland
49 Merrion Square
Dublin 2
For information on University College at Belfield, Dublin, Cork, and Galway.

School of International Education
The National Institute of Higher Education
Limerick

In 1987 NIHE initiated a variety of courses aimed at the "international student." Encourages direct enrollment.

St. Patrick's College
Maynooth
County Kildare

Trinity College
Dublin 1

FURTHER INFORMATION

Consulate General of Ireland
580 Fifth Avenue
New York, NY 10036
(212) 319-2555

Embassy of Ireland
2234 Massachusetts Avenue, NW
Washington, DC 20008
(202) 462-3939

Irish Tourist Board
1157 Third Avenue
New York, NY 10036
(212) 418-0800

Central Applications Office
P.O. Box No 33
Eglinton Street
Galway

For information on undergraduate pro-grams at national universities.

Irish Council for Overseas Students
14 Ely Place
Dublin 2

Advisory service for students from outside the Republic.

Cork

■ **BEAVER COLLEGE**
Glenside, PA 19038
(215) 572-2901

PROGRAM: Irish University Year at University College is a full-academic-year program. Students attend regular classes at University College, Cork, and are fully integrated into the school's academic and social programs. Courses cover applied psychology, archaeology, Celtic civilization, computer sciences, economics, English, European studies, geography, Greek and Roman civilization, history, languages, mathematics, music, political science, natural and physical sciences, etc. Orientation in Dublin.

ADMITTANCE REQUIREMENTS: Juniors and seniors with a 3.0 GPA.

TEACHING METHODS: Students take regular courses, seminars, and tutorials taught by university professors. Americans are fully integrated with Irish students.

EVALUATION: By course faculty, based upon class work and periodic examinations.

CREDITS OFFERED: 15 to 16 semester hours per semester.

HOUSING: Students live in student residences.

DATES: Fall semester: September 21 through December 19; spring semester: January 4 through June 20.

COSTS: Approximately $5,250 per year includes tuition and room. Does not cover meals, round-trip transportation, or personal expenses.

YEAR ESTABLISHED: 1981.

NUMBER OF STUDENTS IN 1985: 15.

APPLY: April 20. Center for Education Abroad.

Dublin

■ **BEAVER COLLEGE**
  Glenside, PA 19038
  (215) 572-2901

PROGRAM: Irish University Year at Trinity College is a full-academic-year program. Students attend regular classes at Trinity College and are fully integrated into the school's academic and social programs. Courses cover applied Gaelic, Greek, Hebrew, Latin, ancient and modern literature, art history, archaeology, Biblical studies, classics, economics, education, English literature and language, history, languages, mathematics, mental and moral sciences, music, natural and physical sciences, etc. Some program-related travel.

ADMITTANCE REQUIREMENTS: Juniors with a 3.0 GPA.

TEACHING METHODS: Students take regular courses, seminars, and tutorials taught by university professors. Americans are fully integrated with Irish students.

EVALUATION: By course faculty, based upon class work and periodic examinations.

CREDITS OFFERED: 15 to 16 semester hours per semester.

HOUSING: Students live in dormitories, student residences, or with local families.

DATES: Fall semester: September 21 through December 19; spring semester: January 4 through June 20.

COSTS: Approximately $5,250 per year includes tuition and room. Does not cover meals, round-trip transportation, or personal expenses.

YEAR ESTABLISHED: 1977.

NUMBER OF STUDENTS IN 1985: 20.

APPLY: January 15. Center for Education Abroad.

■ **THE CATHOLIC UNIVERSITY OF AMERICA**
   Washington, DC 20064
   (202) 635-5000

PROGRAM: The Irish Society and Politics program, held in cooperation with Ireland's Institute of Public Administration, offers upper-level undergraduate and graduate students an opportunity to work as professional aids to members of the Irish Parliament each semester. The program also offers formal courses and tutorials on Irish society and politics, literature, and history.

ADMITTANCE REQUIREMENTS: Sophomores and above with an acceptable academic record.

TEACHING METHODS: Each course is dual level (undergraduate/graduate) and meets once weekly for fourteen weeks.

EVALUATION: By class participation, written work, and periodic exams. Member of Parliament's assessment and program director's review also are considered.

CREDITS OFFERED: Up to 12 semester hours.

HOUSING: With local Irish families.

DATES: Fall: September through December; spring: January through May.

COSTS: Same as semester costs at Catholic University (approximately $4,400), plus room and board.

YEAR ESTABLISHED: 1981.

NUMBER OF STUDENTS IN 1985:   24.

APPLY: By April 1. Professor Charles Dechert, Department of Politics.

■ **COLLEGE CONSORTIUM FOR INTERNATIONAL STUDIES (CCIS)**
866 United Nations Plaza, Rm. 511
New York, NY 10017
(212) 308-1556

PROGRAM: CCIS is a nonprofit organization that sponsors and organizes several dozen foreign study programs for member colleges who grant degree credit. The Dublin program is a single-semester or full-academic-year experience for undergraduates and post-college "students" held in cooperation with Mohegan Community College (Connecticut) and the Institute of Irish Studies in Dublin. The program offers courses in Gaelic; Irish studies, covering history, literature, economics, politics, and theater; Irish/Anglo-Irish studies; and independent studies. Orientation in Dublin. Program-related travel in Ireland.

ADMITTANCE REQUIREMENTS: Sophomores and juniors (but will accept upper-level freshmen, seniors, and post-college students) with 2.5 GPA and acceptable academic credentials.

TEACHING METHODS: Students attend classes taught by Irish faculty at the Institute of Irish Studies.

EVALUATION: By course instructors and project leaders.

CREDITS OFFERED: 12 to 15 semester hours per semester.

HOUSING: Students live with local families.

DATES: Fall semester: September 9 through December 14; spring semester: January 20 through April 26.

COSTS: $2,980 per semester includes tuition, room, and program-related travel. Does not cover local travel, some meals, round-trip transportation, or personal expenses.

YEAR ESTABLISHED: Not available.

NUMBER OF STUDENTS IN 1985:   26.

APPLY: Fall semester by June 1; spring semester by October 15.

■ **ROLLINS COLLEGE**
1000 Holt Avenue
Winter Park, FL 32789
(305) 646-2280

PROGRAM: Rollins Fall Term in Dublin is a one-semester undergraduate program held in cooperation with Ireland's National Institute of Higher Education (NIHE). The program concentrates primarily on Irish studies with courses on Irish art, literature, history, theater, environment, economy, sociology, media, and women's history. One day onsite orientation and city tour.

ADMITTANCE REQUIREMENTS: Minimum 2.5 GPA and good academic standing with approval of the appropriate dean or director at student's home institution.

TEACHING METHODS: Students may enroll in regular classes at NIHE; other courses are taught by Irish faculty especially for students in the program. Field trips to local cultural attractions and various historic sites in Derry, Northern Ireland plus excursions to the Aran Islands complement class lectures and discussions.

EVALUATION: By local faculty, based on class work, papers, and exams.

CREDITS OFFERED: Students take four courses for 16 semester hours or 25 quarter hours credit.

HOUSING: All students live with local families.

DATES: Approximately September through mid-December.

COSTS: $4,820 includes tuition, room and board, local travel and round-trip transportation from New York. Pocket money (estimated at $1,500) not included.

YEAR ESTABLISHED: 1972.

NUMBER OF STUDENTS IN 1985: 16.

APPLY: By April 1. Dr. Patricia Lancaster, Director of International Programs, Box #2712.

Galway

■ **BEAVER COLLEGE**
Glenside, PA 19038
(215) 572-2901

PROGRAM: Irish University Year at University College, Galway, is either a single-semester or a full-academic-year program. Students attend regular classes at University College, and are fully integrated into the school's academic and social programs. Courses cover accounting, archaeology, business studies, economics, English, finance, history, industrial relations, languages, legal science, logic and scientific method, management, marketing, mathematics, physics, organized behavior, psychology, sociology, and political science. Some program-related travel.

ADMITTANCE REQUIREMENTS: Juniors and seniors with a 3.0 GPA.

TEACHING METHODS: Students take regular courses, seminars, and tutorials taught by university professors. Americans are fully integrated with Irish students.

EVALUATION: By course faculty, based upon class work and periodic examinations.

CREDITS OFFERED: 15 to 16 semester hours per semester.

HOUSING: Students live in student residences.

DATES: Fall semester: September 14 through December 19; spring semester: January 4 through June 20.

COSTS: Approximately $5,250 per year includes tuition and room. Does not cover meals, round-trip transportation, or personal expenses.

YEAR ESTABLISHED: 1981.

NUMBER OF STUDENTS IN 1985: 25.

APPLY: April 20. Center for Education Abroad.

Limerick

■ **THE EXPERIMENT IN INTERNATIONAL LIVING**
Kipling Road
Brattleboro, VT 05301
(800) 451-4465

PROGRAM: The College Semester Abroad Program is designed to allow students to become immersed in a foreign culture by living with a local family and exploring individual personal and educational interests under professional guidance. The Ireland program is affiliated with Thomond College in Limerick. Students spend seven weeks in Limerick and five weeks at a location appropriate to a field study project, ending up in either Limerick or Dublin for a week of program evaluation. Courses cover: seminar on Irish life and culture, history and politics, geography and economics, arts and humanities, social anthropology, social/cultural field work, and an independent study project. One-week orientation in Dublin.

ADMITTANCE REQUIREMENTS: Sophomore standing or above and acceptable academic credentials. No language prerequisite.

TEACHING METHODS: Students work directly with their American instructors-advisors in planning and evaluating their individual program. "The semester builds from the more structured language training and lectures and discussions on local life and culture to the independent study project."

EVALUATION: By individual students and their instructor-advisors based on independent project, papers, reports, and examinations. Periodic meetings during the program and for several days at the conclusion.

CREDITS OFFERED: 16 semester hours.

HOUSING: Students live as family members with their host families.

DATES: Approximately, fall semester: September through December; spring semester: January through May.

COSTS: $5,900 includes tuition, room and board, all fees and local travel, and round-trip transportation from Brattleboro, Vermont.

YEAR ESTABLISHED: 1969.

NUMBER OF STUDENTS IN 1985: 13.

APPLY: For fall semester by May 15; spring semester by November 15. Admissions Office, College Semester Abroad.

■ **SLIPPERY ROCK UNIVERSITY**
Slippery Rock, PA 16057
(412) 794-7425

PROGRAM: The Slippery Rock University/Thomond College Exchange is a fall-semester undergraduate program designed only for physical education students. It is held in cooperation with Ireland's Thomond College. Onsite orientation.

ADMITTANCE REQUIREMENTS: At least second-semester sophomore with a minimum 2.5 GPA and permission from major advisor.

TEACHING METHODS: Students attend regular Thomond College courses involving lectures, demonstrations, and participation.

EVALUATION: By Thomond College faculty, based on class work.

CREDITS OFFERED: 12 to 15 semester hours.

HOUSING: Students live in private apartments.

DATES: October 1 through December 20.

COSTS: Students pay the going Slippery Rock University tuition. Room and board vary and are paid directly to the local landlord. Estimated living expenses, approximately $6 per day.

YEAR ESTABLISHED: 1983.

NUMBER OF STUDENTS IN 1985: 6.

APPLY: By March 15. Stan Kendziorski, Director, International Education.

Louisburgh

■ **COLLEGE OF ST. SCHOLASTICA**
1200 Kenwood Avenue
Duluth, MN 55811
(218) 723-6032

PROGRAM: Study Center in Ireland is a spring program designed to allow students to pursue a full quarter's course work in addition to experiencing interculture exchange and travel. Courses cover various liberal arts electives including history, humanities, literature, and the social sciences. Presession orientation during winter quarter at Duluth or by telephone and correspondence.

ADMITTANCE REQUIREMENTS: Open to sophomores and above. Good academic standing plus recommendations by two faculty/staff members of home institution.

TEACHING METHODS: Taught by U.S. faculty. Lectures, discussion, and travel to regional sites. Curriculum is augmented by guest lectures from members of University College Galway, local experts in Irish folk lore, and contemporary local poets and authors. Eight weekend trips are taken by chartered bus, ending the term with a few days' stay in Dublin.

EVALUATION: Periodic quizzes plus a final exam.

CREDITS OFFERED: Four courses, 16 quarter credits.

HOUSING: Students live in village-owned cottages (four students per cottage), shop in the local village, and share the expenses. Linens and household equipment are supplied; students pay for utilities.

DATES: Early March to mid-May.

COSTS: Tuition: $1,892; room and board: $280; bus trips: $320; living expenses: approximately $300. Travel to and from Ireland not included. Federal and state grants and loans if sufficient need.

YEAR ESTABLISHED: 1980.

NUMBER OF STUDENTS IN 1985: 20.

APPLY: By November 15. Sr. Mary Odile Cahoon, Senior Vice President, College of St. Scholastica.

ITALY

Population: 57,291,000   **Capital:** Rome   **Language:** Italian
Monetary Unit: Lira   **Government:** Republic (president and prime minister)
Religion: 83% Roman Catholic   **Households with Television:** 72%

SELECTED COLLEGES AND UNIVERSITIES

European Institute of Design
Via dei Fori Imperiali 1/A
00186 Rome

Courses in architecture, design, photography, illustration taught in English.

Rhode Island School of Design
Piazza Cenci 56
00186 Rome

Fine arts, architecture, painting, sculpture, etc., taught in English.

University of Florence
Via Vittorio Emanuele 64
50134 Florence

University of Milan
Via Festa del Perdono 7
20122 Milan

Universite International de l'Art
Villa Il Ventaglio
Via delle Forbici 24-26
50133 Florence

Courses in music, art restoration, archaeology, etc., taught in Italian.

FURTHER INFORMATION

Consulate General of Italy
690 Park Avenue
New York, NY 10021
(212) 737-9100

Embassy of Italy
1601 Fuller Street, NW
Washington, DC 20009
(202) 328-5500

Italian Cultural Institute
686 Park Avenue
New York, NY 10021
(212) 879-4242

Publishes Higher Education in Italy.

- *For the best food, eat in the inexpensive restaurants (i.e., the trattorias). As for the best shopping: find out where the Italians go, not the tourists.*

  - Barbara del Rosario, Elmsford, New York

- *Italy's culture is very different from America's. Being a woman in Italy isn't easy. It was difficult meeting Italian women and difficult to make just male friends.*

  - Jennifer Carattini, Marymount College

More Than One City

■ AMERICAN INSTITUTE OF FOREIGN STUDY (AIFS)
102 Greenwich Avenue
Greenwich, CT 06830
(800) 243-4567 or (203) 869-9090

PROGRAM: AIFS is a national for-profit organization specializing in comprehensive overseas academic year, semester, and summer study programs. The AIFS program in Italy is a full-academic, fall, winter, or spring- semester program held in cooperation with the Universities of Siena and Florence, and the Fortman Studios in Florence. Each semester consists of four weeks in Siena, ten weeks in Florence, and a week field trip. AIFS students take a month of intensive Italian in Siena followed by courses at the AIFS center at Via Pier Capponi in Florence. AIFS "is able to arrange enrollment for Italian language majors in certain courses at the University of Florence" which require fluent Italian. AIFS course offerings include Italian studies, studio art (at the Fortman Studios), art history, and Italian. Program includes a one-week trip to Rome, Naples, and Venice.

ADMITTANCE REQUIREMENTS: College sophomores and above with a 2.5 GPA, as well as graduate students. No language requirement.

TEACHING METHODS: Most students in the special AIFS courses are Americans; faculty is predominantly Italian. Students must take an intensive Italian course.

EVALUATION: By faculty, based upon class work, papers, and periodic examinations.

CREDITS OFFERED: A minimum of 13 semester hours per semester; a maximum of 16.

HOUSING: In Florence, students live with families or in student residences where they are provided breakfast; other meals are obtained in the student residence or in a student restaurant. In Siena, students stay in a student residence or "family hotel."

DATES: Fall semester: September 1 through December 13; winter semester: January 5 through April 18; spring semester: March 16 through June 27.

COSTS: $4,695 per semester, includes tuition, room and board, program-related travel, and one-way transportation from New York. Does not cover local travel or personal expenses.

YEAR ESTABLISHED: 1982.

NUMBER OF STUDENTS IN 1986: 41.

APPLY: Applications filled on first-come basis. "It is expected that all full-year or fall-semester places will be filled by June 1; places for spring semester are kept open until November 15."

- *In Florence, we studied, along with 62 people who flew over from the States, in an apartment where they changed bedrooms into classrooms. I chose to live in a family situation because I felt I could learn more of the culture. The first day our landlady told us she would rather speak English. The place was very small and we were not allowed to use any of the apartment except our bedrooms.*

  - Barbara del Rosario, Elmsford, New York

■ THE EXPERIMENT IN INTERNATIONAL LIVING
Kipling Road
Brattleboro, VT 05301-0676
(800) 451-4465

PROGRAM: The College Semester Abroad Program is designed to allow students to become immersed in a foreign culture by living with a local family and exploring individual personal and educational interests under professional guidance. Students on the Italian program spend seven weeks in Rome or Siena, five weeks at a location appropriate to a field study project, and a three-week homestay ending up in Siena for a week of program evaluation. Courses cover: seminar on Italian life and culture, history and politics, geography and economics, arts and humanities, social anthropology, methods and techniques of field work, and an independent study project. One-week orientation in Rome and/or Siena.

ADMITTANCE REQUIREMENTS: Sophomore standing or above and acceptable academic credentials. No language prerequisite.

TEACHING METHODS: Students work directly with their American instructors-advisors in planning and evaluating their individual program. "The semester builds from the more structured language training and lectures and discussions on local life and culture to the independent study project."

EVALUATION: By individual students and their instructor-advisors, based on independent project, papers, reports, and exams. Periodic meetings during the program and for several days at the conclusion.

CREDITS OFFERED: 16 semester hours.

HOUSING: Students live as family members with their host families.

DATES: Approximately, fall semester: September through December; spring semester: January through May.

COSTS: $5,900 includes tuition, room and board, all fees and local travel, and round-trip transportation from Brattleboro, Vermont.

YEAR ESTABLISHED: 1972.

NUMBER OF STUDENTS IN 1985: 13.

APPLY: For fall semester by May 15; spring semester by November 15. Admissions Office, College Semester Abroad.

■ **LAKE ERIE COLLEGE**
  Painesville, OH 44077
  (216) 352-3361

PROGRAM: Lake Erie's program in Italy includes stays in both Florence and Perugia. Students may enroll for a single semester, term, or full academic year. The program is open to undergraduates, precollege, or professionals. Students take courses in the Italian language, civilization, independent study projects, or internships.

ADMITTANCE REQUIREMENTS: Any "student" with a serious interest in the Italian culture.

TEACHING METHODS: Special courses for Americans are taught by both local Italian faculty and U.S. faculty.

EVALUATION: By both U.S. and local faculty, based upon classwork and written exams.

CREDITS OFFERED: 12 to 16 semester hours per semester.

HOUSING: Students live with local families or in pensioni.

DATES: September through mid-May. Student may enroll for a single semester, an "Italian" term, or the full academic year.

COSTS: Varies from $2,700 for a ten-week term to $3,800 per semester or $6,900 for the academic year. Includes tuition, room and board and program-related travel. Does not include round-trip transportation, personal travel, or expenses.

YEAR ESTABLISHED: 1965.

NUMBER OF STUDENTS IN 1985: Not available.

APPLY: 60 days prior to start of semester or term. Dr. Egidio Lunardi, ext. 370.

■ **MICHIGAN STATE UNIVERSITY**
108 Center for International Programs
East Lansing, MI 48824
(517) 353-8920

PROGRAM: Social Science in Rome and Venice is a recently initiated spring-semester undergraduate program that combines beginning Italian and a range of social science courses with travel. Orientation in the U.S.

ADMITTANCE REQUIREMENTS: For sophomores, juniors, seniors with a 2.0 GPA. No language requirement.

TEACHING METHODS: Students take special courses, lectures, seminars, and independent study in English arranged for the group and taught by both U.S. and local foreign faculty.

EVALUATION: By course faculty, based upon papers and examinations.

CREDITS OFFERED: 12 credit hours.

HOUSING: Students live in dormitories.

DATES: April 1 through June 1.

COSTS: $1,560 includes tuition, room, and program-related travel. Does not include round-trip transportation, most meals, or personal expenses.

YEAR ESTABLISHED: 1986.

NUMBER OF STUDENTS IN 1986: 20.

APPLY: By April 21. Dr. Charles A. Gliozzo, Office of Overseas Study.

Bologna

■ **THE JOHNS HOPKINS UNIVERSITY**
School of Advanced International Studies (SAIS)
1740 Massachusetts Avenue, NW
Washington, DC 20036
(202) 785-6200

PROGRAM: The Bologna Center offers a graduate program intended as the first of a two-year track leading to an MA in international relations. Intensive courses cover international relations, international economics, history, politics, and language. The program at the Bologna Center provides "corso intensivo"; a one-month language training in Italian for Americans.

ADMITTANCE REQUIREMENTS: Open to students who are first accepted into the programs at SAIS.

TEACHING METHODS: Graduate courses are taught in English by both American and non-American faculty.

EVALUATION: Usually based upon papers and examinations.

CREDITS OFFERED: First part of two-part graduate program at SAIS.

HOUSING: Students are responsible for their own housing with assistance of the center.

DATES: Approximately, mid-September to mid-May.

COSTS: Tuition: $9,700; room and board: $5,000 (approximately). Does not cover round-trip transportation, local travel, or living expenses.

YEAR ESTABLISHED: 1955.

NUMBER OF STUDENTS IN 1985:   60.

APPLY: By February 1. Admissions Office, SAIS.

Florence

- *The location for Art Renaissance Study just couldn't be better.*
                        - Barbara del Rosario, Elmsford, New York

- *Florence is the most interesting and beautiful city in the world. For an artist, it is an infinite source of inspiration. We never found a bad meal, except in the central tourist areas. Shop in the San Lorenzo market. Travel by foot.*
                        - Giorgio Scali, Tufts University

■ **ARIZONA STATE UNIVERSITY**
Academic Services Building, Room #110
Tempe, AZ 85287
(692) 965-6611

PROGRAM: Arizona Program in Italy is an undergraduate program held in cooperation with the University of Arizona and Northern Arizona University. Courses cover Italian language and literature, art of Florence, survey of Western Arts, painting and drawing, the Renaissance, and an option for independent studies. Students must take one course each semester in Italian.

ADMITTANCE REQUIREMENTS: Students must be registered at an Arizona university the semester in attendance.

TEACHING METHODS: Students are instructed by U.S. professors in conjunction with instructors from Italian institutions. All courses, except language, are in English.

EVALUATION: Papers and exams given by U.S. instructors.

CREDITS OFFERED: A minimum course load of 12 semester hours is required.

HOUSING: Students live in "an attractive residence located in the center of Florence."

DATES: Approximately, fall semester: August 29 through December 12; spring semester: January 6 through April 10.

COSTS: Students pay tuition to their Arizona university in addition to a program fee of $3,225, which covers tuition in Italy, room, breakfast and one other meal per day, and three excursions in Tuscany. Does not cover round-trip transportation, personal expenses (estimated at $200 a month minimum), or local travel.

YEAR ESTABLISHED: Not available.

NUMBER OF STUDENTS IN 1985: Not available.

APPLY: One semester in advance. Denis J. Kigin, Director of Summer Sessions.

■ **ASSOCIATED COLLEGES OF THE MIDWEST (ACM)**
   18 South Michigan Avenue; Suite 1010
   Chicago, IL 60603
   (312) 263-5000

PROGRAM: The ACM Florence Program is a sixteen-week, fall-semester undergraduate program held in cooperation with the Linguaviva School of Italian in Florence and is cosponsored by the member colleges of the ACM

(Beloit College, Carleton College, Coe College, Cornell College, Colorado College, Grinnell College, Knox College, Lake Forest College, Lawrence University, Macalester College, Monmouth College, Ripon College, and St. Olaf College). The semester is divided into two parts, with a week-long break. During the first four weeks, students receive intensive instruction in the Italian language and begin a course on contemporary Italy. For the remainder of the semester students continue their initial coursework and select three additional courses: twentieth-century Italy through its literature and cinema; Florentine painters of the Renaissance; literature of the Italian Renaissance; Tuscan Gothic and early Renaissance architecture and sculpture, 1250-1500; topics in Italian art: Mannerism.

ADMITTANCE REQUIREMENTS: Prefer juniors and above with a 2.5 GPA. Permission of academic officer, three recommendations, and courses in literature, fine arts, and history are required. Students from non-ACM colleges must receive credit from their home school for the program or enroll in Beloit College as an "off-campus study participant."

TEACHING METHODS: Courses are in English and are taught by an American faculty member and by a foreign faculty. Class lectures, onsite museum visits and lectures, and group discussions. Trips, as determined by the program director, usually consist of three- to four-day trips plus a five-day trip to Rome.

EVALUATION: By professors, based upon class work, papers, and oral projects.

CREDITS OFFERED: 16 semester hours.

HOUSING: Students live in private homes with local families.

DATES: August 30 through December 11.

COSTS: Tuition is determined by home college or lowest ACM tuition (the greater of the two). Room and board is approximately $1,600. Plan on approximately $1,500 for local expenses. Local travel is included but round-trip transportation and personal travel are at the student's expense.

YEAR ESTABLISHED: 1971.

NUMBER OF STUDENTS IN 1985:   27.

APPLY: By October 15 for early decision; March 15 for regular decision.

- *The program was well organized and Linguaviva is a great school. All the professors were intelligent and warm. They are good teachers and helped us with any problems we had with school, the country or the language. I lived with two friends and an elderly Italian woman who was very friendly and hugged us all the time.*

  - Barbara C. Caufman, Kenyon College

■ BRIGHAM YOUNG UNIVERSITY
Study Abroad Programs, 204 HRCB
Provo, UT 84602
(801) 378-3308

PROGRAM: Spring Term in Italy is a six-week program offering courses in art history and the Italian language and civilization. Local field trips to historic and cultural sites are part of the program.

ADMITTANCE REQUIREMENTS: Good academic standing with a 3.0 GPA requested. Adherence to BYU standards.

TEACHING METHODS: Classes are taught by BYU faculty in classrooms designated for the purpose. No foreign schools are involved.

EVALUATION: Determined by program director, based on periodic exams.

CREDITS OFFERED: From 6 to 9 credit hours.

HOUSING: Students are assigned housing either in hotels, hostels, or private facilities.

DATES: Approximately, May through June.

COSTS: Approximately, $1,800 includes tuition, room and board, two meals a day, and local travel. Does not cover round-trip transportation or additional travel.

YEAR ESTABLISHED: 1975.

NUMBER OF STUDENTS IN 1985: 19.

APPLY: By March. Study Abroad Office.

■ **THE CALIFORNIA STATE UNIVERSITY**
400 Golden Shore
Long Beach, CA 90802
(213) 590-5655

PROGRAM: The CSU International Program in Italy, held in cooperation with the University of Florence, is a full-academic-year undergraduate and graduate opportunity to study at the university. Students select from the wide range of university course offerings focusing most frequently on architecture, art history, history and politics, and Italian language and literature, supplemented by special CSU programs. One-week orientation in Florence.

ADMITTANCE REQUIREMENTS: Must be enrolled at a CSU campus. Juniors and above, including graduate students. 2.75 GPA.

TEACHING METHODS: Students take a combination of regular academic courses and supplemental program-sponsored courses taught by foreign faculty.

EVALUATION: By foreign faculty and CSU resident director, based upon periodic and final examinations.

CREDITS OFFERED: 30 semester hours per year or 45 quarter units.

HOUSING: In dormitories and private apartments.

DATES: Approximately, September 2 through May 30.

COSTS: Tuition: $0 (residents); $3,600 (nonresidents); room and board: $3,425. Does not include round-trip transportation or living expenses (estimated at approximately $3,145 per year).

YEAR ESTABLISHED: 1966.

NUMBER OF STUDENTS IN 1985: 81.

APPLY: By February 1. Dr. Kibbey M. Horne, Director of International Programs.

■ **COLLEGE CONSORTIUM FOR INTERNATIONAL STUDIES (CCIS)**
866 United Nations Plaza, Room 511
New York, NY 10017
(212) 308-1556

PROGRAM: CCIS is a nonprofit organization that sponsors and organizes several dozen foreign study programs for member colleges who grant degree credit. CCIS offers four programs in Florence in cooperation with College of Staten Island and Westchester Community College (New York), including: (1) Film Making, which offers intensive Italian (required); cultural and technical methodology of cinema/film making including directing, filming, editing, set preparation, and animation; and cinematographic semiology, (2) Intensive Italian, which offers language and contemporary Italian studies, (3) Italian Civilization and Culture, which offers all levels of the Italian language, art, history, literature, politics, Renaissance and contemporary Italy, (4) Studio Arts and Art History, which offers Italian language and culture, art history, art restoration, graphic design, history, jewelry, print making, sculpture, and studio art. Orientation in U.S. and Italy. Some program-related travel.

ADMITTANCE REQUIREMENTS: Undergraduates with a 2.5 GPA and acceptable academic credentials. The studio arts program is designed for those majoring in the field.

TEACHING METHODS: Students attend classes taught in English (except language program) by the faculty at the Scuola Lorenzo de Medici.

EVALUATION: By course instructors and project leaders.

CREDITS OFFERED: 12 to 15 semester hours per semester.

HOUSING: Students live in apartments, pensioni, or with local families.

DATES: Fall semester: August 31 through December 30; spring semester: January 10 through May 16.

COSTS: Film making: $1,745; Intensive Italian or Italian civilization: $1,360; Studio arts: $2,020 per semester. Does not include room and board, program-related travel, round-trip transportation, or personal expenses.

YEAR ESTABLISHED: Not available.

NUMBER OF STUDENTS IN 1985: 100.

APPLY: Fall semester by July 15; spring semester December 1.

■ **COLLEGE OF WILLIAM AND MARY**
Office of International Studies
Williamsburg, VA 23185
(804) 253-4354

PROGRAM: William and Mary Summer in Florence is held in cooperation with the Scuola Linguaviva. The summer session presents a five-week program in Italian language at all levels, advanced Italian literature and art history. Travel to local historic and cultural sites (including Rome and Venice) is part of the program.

ADMITTANCE REQUIREMENTS: Open to all undergraduates in good academic standing at their home institution.

TEACHING METHODS: Regular courses are taught in Italian (except art history which is taught in English) by members of the Linguaviva faculty. Both class and onsite lectures, seminars.

EVALUATION: By faculty, based upon papers, periodic tests, and a final examination.

CREDITS OFFERED: 6 semester hours.

HOUSING: Students live in local pensioni, where they receive both breakfast and dinner.

DATES: May 30 through June 30.

COSTS: Tuition, room and board: $1,800; round-trip airfare, approximately: $499; estimated living expenses: $350. Scholarships available to William and Mary students.

YEAR ESTABLISHED: 1980.

NUMBER OF STUDENTS IN 1985:   24.

APPLY: By February 1. Ms. Carolyn V. Blackwell, Director.

■ **FLORIDA STATE UNIVERSITY**
Tallahassee, FL 32306
(904) 644-3272

PROGRAM: The FSU Florence Study Program is held in cooperation with the State University Systems of Florida and is a one- or two-semester or summer course of study featuring the humanities, fine arts, art history, music, and Italian language and culture.

ADMITTANCE REQUIREMENTS: 2.5 GPA and good academic standing. Sophomores and above; will accept high school seniors and above for summer program.

TEACHING METHODS: Students receive regular FSU courses taught in English by an American faculty. A class in Italian is mandatory. Field trips to local cultural sites complement the program.

EVALUATION: By American faculty, based upon class work and examinations.

CREDITS OFFERED: 15 semester hours per semester.

HOUSING: Students can live in a pensione or may locate their own housing.

DATES: Approximately, fall semester: early September to mid-December; spring semester: mid-January to late April; summer session: late June to mid-August.

COSTS: Approximately, tuition: $1,600 per semester; room and board: $1,820 per semester. Does not include round-trip airfare or personal expenses (estimated at $2,500 per semester). Financial and work/study aid available.

YEAR ESTABLISHED: 1966.

NUMBER OF STUDENTS IN 1985: 80

APPLY: Fall semester by June 16; spring semester by October 20. Dr. C.E. Tanzy, FSU Florence/London Programs, 115 WMS.

■ **HARDING UNIVERSITY**
  Searcy, AK 72143
  (501) 268-6161

PROGRAM: Harding University in Florence owns and maintains a modernized, sixteenth-century villa on the outskirts of Florence in which they offer three separate semester programs devoted to the Italian language, archaeology, Bible history, art, music, and literature. Students are also afforded the opportunity to travel extensively throughout Italy, Greece, and Western Europe.

ADMITTANCE REQUIREMENTS: At least twenty-seven hours of college work with a minimum 2.0 GPA and good academic standing.

TEACHING METHODS: Courses are taught by American and Italian Harding University professors. Lectures, seminars, independent study, and field trips to Rome and Greece.

EVALUATION: Regular testing during the semester.

CREDITS OFFERED: 16 hours per semester.

HOUSING: Students live in the Harding-owned villa.

DATES: Fall semester: September through November; spring semester: February through May; summer semester: May through August.

COSTS: Tuition: $101.50 per semester hour; room and board: $1,119 per semester; estimated living expenses: $15.00 per day. Round-trip from Little Rock to Amsterdam, two-month Eurail pass, and field trip to Greece are an extra $1,700.

YEAR ESTABLISHED: 1979.

NUMBER OF STUDENTS IN 1985: 38.

APPLY: Two months prior to semester. Dr. Don Shackelford, Director.

■ **MIDDLEBURY COLLEGE**
Middlebury, VT 05753
(802) 388-3711

PROGRAM: Middlebury College School in Italy offers undergraduates "long-standing, highly respected, and *serious*" courses in literature, Italian language, culture, and civilization. An MA program is available in Italian language and literature. Courses are held at the University of Florence.

ADMITTANCE REQUIREMENTS: The equivalent of five semesters in Italian and a B average; (for MA a "better than B average" is required).

TEACHING METHODS: Italian faculty. All courses, written papers, and exams are in Italian. Extensive travel, field trips, and cultural exchanges complement the program.

EVALUATION: Faculty-student conferences, term papers, finals, etc.

CREDITS OFFERED: Full semester or full year credit.

HOUSING: Students live with families, in pensioni, or in apartments.

DATES: Approximately, September 15 through June 10.

COSTS: Tuition: $4,900 for full year; $2,500 for semester; room and board: approximately $2,000 per semester. Round-trip travel to school: approximately $600. Local travel in Europe not included. Some scholarships available.

YEAR ESTABLISHED: 1960.

NUMBER OF STUDENTS IN 1985:   60.

APPLY: Rolling admissions. Contact Dean of Italian School.

■ **ROSARY COLLEGE**
   7900 West Division Street
   River Forest, IL 60305
   (312) 366-2490

PROGRAM: Rosary in Florence is an undergraduate summer program held in cooperation with Arizona State University. Courses include: Italian, Italian history, Italian cinema, Italian renaissance art, and independent study.

ADMITTANCE REQUIREMENTS: College undergraduates with acceptable academic record.

TEACHING METHODS: Students take special courses taught by American and Italian faculty. Intensive language study. Students are not integrated with other foreign students. Several local day trips are included in the program.

EVALUATION: Periodic exams and papers.

CREDITS OFFERED: Up to 6 semester hours.

HOUSING: Students stay in pensioni.

DATES: June 28 through August 5.

COSTS: $1,195 includes tuition, housing, and three excursions. Does not include meals, round-trip transportation, additional local travel, or personal expenses.

YEAR ESTABLISHED: 1979.

NUMBER OF STUDENTS IN 1985: 18

APPLY: By March 15. Sister Nona Mary Allard, Associate Academic Dean.

■ **RUTGERS, THE STATE UNIVERSITY OF NEW JERSEY**
Milledoler Hall, Room 205
New Brunswick, NJ 08903
(201) 932-7787

PROGRAM: Junior Year in Italy is a full-year academic undergraduate program. Students attend regular classes at the University of Florence (except medicine or law courses), which offers a broad selection of liberal arts courses with an emphasis on Italian language, literature, arts and culture, and European affairs. Most students take courses from the following *facoltà: economia e commercio, architettura, scienze politiche,* and *lettere.* No courses are offered in studio art, music performance, acting, or dancing. A six-week presession consisting of intensive language, grammar, literature, and history is held at the University of Urbino.

ADMITTANCE REQUIREMENTS: Good academic standing is required and a "thorough knowledge of Italian is essential. At a minimum, students should have completed course work through first-year literature and preferably advanced grammar courses."

TEACHING METHODS: Students attend regular classes with Italian students. All courses are in Italian.

EVALUATION: By course instructors, based upon class work, papers, and examinations.

CREDITS OFFERED: 30 semester hours per year including presession.

HOUSING: Students live with local families or in private apartments.

DATES: Approximately, September 16 to mid-June.

COSTS: $6,282 New Jersey residents; $7,820 nonresidents. Includes tuition, room and board (except 23 days at holidays and between semesters), round-trip transportation from New York, and group excursions. Does not cover personal expenses.

YEAR ESTABLISHED: 1970.

NUMBER OF STUDENTS IN 1985: limited to 40.

APPLY: By March 1. Director, Rutgers' Junior Year Abroad.

■ **SMITH COLLEGE**
Northampton, MA 01063
(413) 584-2700

PROGRAM: Smith College Junior Year in Florence, one of the oldest foreign-study programs, is a full-academic-year undergraduate program held in cooperation with the University of Florence and offering courses in intermediate and advanced Italian language and literature, art history, economics, history, music, and political science. Orientation in Italy.

ADMITTANCE REQUIREMENTS: Juniors with a 3.0 GPA and two years of college Italian or the equivalent.

TEACHING METHODS: All instruction is in Italian. Students attend special courses arranged for the group and taught by both U.S. and foreign faculty at the University of Florence.

EVALUATION: By course faculty, based upon papers and final examinations.

CREDITS OFFERED: 32 semester hours per year.

HOUSING: Students live with local families.

DATES: Fall semester: September 10 through mid-December; spring semester: late January through June 10.

COSTS: $13,760 per year includes tuition and room and board. Does not include round-trip transportation, local travel, or personal expenses.

YEAR ESTABLISHED: 1931.

NUMBER OF STUDENTS IN 1985: 14.

APPLY: By February 1. Patricia C. Olmsted, Committee on Study Abroad, ext. 4920.

■ **UNIVERSITY OF ARIZONA**
Tucson, AZ 85721
(602) 621-4819

PROGRAM: Arizona in Italy is a full-year undergraduate program with an optional summer session held in cooperation with Arizona State University and Northern Arizona University. Students take a general range of liberal arts courses with a concentration on Italian language studies, culture and civilization, history, art, economics, and geography. Summer students have a Renaissance studies option. Guided visits to points of interest in Florence and Tuscany are part of the program. Onsite orientation.

ADMITTANCE REQUIREMENTS: For sophomores and above in good standing with their home institution.

TEACHING METHODS: Students attend regular academic and special courses taught by both U.S. and foreign faculty in English; some courses are in Italian. Classes are integrated with foreign students. Field trips complement course of study.

EVALUATION: Based upon student evaluations, reports from the director of each program; periodic and final examinations.

CREDITS OFFERED: 8 semester hours for summer session; 12 semester hours per semester for annual program.

HOUSING: Students live in pensioni.

DATES: Fall semester: early September through mid-December; spring semester: mid-January through late April; summer session: mid-June through late July (six weeks).

COSTS: Students pay regular tuition, if any, to U of A plus approximately $5,000 per semester, room and board. Does not cover round-trip transportation, local travel, or personal expenses.

YEAR ESTABLISHED: 1977.

NUMBER OF STUDENTS IN 1985: 15.

APPLY: By June 1. Eugene von Teuber, Coordinator of International Studies, Room 209, Robert L. Nugent Building.

■ **UNIVERSITY OF CONNECTICUT**
241 Glenbrook Road
Storrs, CT 06268
(203) 486-2141

PROGRAM: Florence Study Program offers two options: a single-semester or full-academic-year undergraduate program held in cooperation with the University of Florence in which students enroll at the university usually taking Italian language, literature, art history, and civilization courses. Alternative courses can be selected if the student has an adequate command of Italian. Or, a Fine Arts Program for students interested in art history, art restoration, museology, and studio art. Students enroll at the Università Internazionale dell'Arte. Six-week intensive Italian is part of the orientation in Italy.

ADMITTANCE REQUIREMENTS: Sophomores and above in good academic standing with a 2.75 GPA and at least two years of college Italian (one year for Fine Arts Program) or the equivalent.

TEACHING METHODS: Students attend special courses arranged for the group as well as any of the courses offered by the University of Florence in which Americans are fully integrated with non-U.S. students. All classes are in Italian.

EVALUATION: By course professors, based upon papers and examinations.

CREDITS OFFERED: 15 semester hours per semester.

HOUSING: Students live in apartments or with local families.

DATES: Fall semester: early September through mid-December; spring semester: mid-January through mid-June.

COSTS: Approximately $6,700 per year (state residents); $9,590 (nonresidents) includes tuition, room and board, round-trip transportation from New York, and program-related travel. Some scholarship aid available.

YEAR ESTABLISHED: Not available.

NUMBER OF STUDENTS IN 1985:   Not available.

APPLY: By April 1. Director, Florence Program.

■ **UNIVERSITY OF MICHIGAN**
  5208 Angell Hall
  Ann Arbor, MI 48106
  (313) 764-4311

PROGRAM: Academic Year in Florence is designed for both undergraduate and graduate students from Michigan and Wisconsin, however, the program regularly accepts approximately ten guest students each semester to complete the total enrollment to forty-five. The academic focus, whose actual classes change each semester, is on Florence, Tuscany, and Italy. The art, history, literature, music, economics, philosophy and politics of Medieval, Renaissance, early modern, and contemporary Italy have been the subjects of recent classes.

ADMITTANCE REQUIREMENTS: 3.0 GPA "evidence of substantial preparation for proposed course of study," and some college-level work in Italian.

TEACHING METHODS: Students take classes at the Villa Corsi Salviati in Sesto a few miles northwest of the city. Tours to local museums and sites are common. Courses are taught in English by senior professors from Michigan and Wisconsin and employ local faculty for art history, language, and political science courses.

EVALUATION: By course instructors, based upon papers, class work, and final exams.

CREDITS OFFERED: Up to 16 semester hours per semester.

HOUSING: Students live and take classes at the Villa Corsi Salviati.

DATES: Approximately, fall semester: early September through mid-December; spring semester: mid-January through late May.

COSTS: Approximately $3,800 to $6,000, depending upon tuition and room and board at home institution. Does not include round-trip transportation.

YEAR ESTABLISHED: 1982.

NUMBER OF STUDENTS IN 1985: 45.

APPLY: By March 15. Center for Western European Studies.

Milan

■ **ACADEMIC YEAR ABROAD (AYA)**
   17 Jansen Road
   New Paltz, NY 12561
   (914) 255-8103

PROGRAM: AYA sponsors programs for both undergraduate and graduate students in cooperation with the Università Luigi Bocconi. Most university subjects are taught in Italian. Except for language courses, classes are composed of students from throughout Europe. Although there is no fixed pattern of travel, excursions are planned throughout the year. Program also includes a one-month presession orientation.

ADMITTANCE REQUIREMENTS: Competence in the language, though students may be accepted to begin the language; consent of home institution; acceptable academic record.

TEACHING METHODS: Varies with each subject.

EVALUATION: Grades given by the foreign professor.

CREDITS OFFERED: 16 semester hours per semester.

HOUSING: Optional, although AYA does provide housing in local homes when so elected by the student.

DATES: First term: early to mid-September through end of January; second term: end of January through May 30.

COSTS: Room and board: $3,800/year; tuition: $3,000/year; estimated living expenses: $1,000/year. Students bring financial aid from home institutions.

YEAR ESTABLISHED: 1961.

NUMBER OF STUDENTS IN 1985: 12.

APPLY: Dr. Stuart H. L. Degginger, Professor, SUNY New Paltz, c/o Academic Year Abroad.

■ **PRATT INSTITUTE**
   School of Art & Design
   200 Willoughby Avenue
   Brooklyn, NY 11205
   (718) 636-3706

PROGRAM: Total Design in Italy is a four-week summer session for both graduate and undergraduates held in cooperation with Domus Academy. Emphasis is on "interior and automotive design, human factors, industrial technology and the history of design in Milan." Orientation with Vieri Salvadori, Dean, School of Art & Design.

ADMITTANCE REQUIREMENTS: Juniors and above (sophomores only with submission of portfolio). Professionals must indicate evidence of professional affiliation.

TEACHING METHODS: Participants attend specialized courses taught by Domus Academy faculty. Special lectures, visits to show rooms, design and production facilities. Field trips to Flos, Benetton, Fiorucci, Fiat, Maserati, and Cassina.

EVALUATION: Students are given letter grades, determined by periodic exams and final design project.

CREDITS OFFERED: 6 semester hours.

HOUSING: Students reside on a double occupancy basis "in a deluxe hotel a five minute walk from the Domus Academy."

DATES: Approximately, July 9 through August 1.

COSTS: $3,100 covers tuition, continental breakfast, double-occupancy hotel room, studio and lecture privileges, round-trip transportation, and local travel.

YEAR ESTABLISHED: 1985.

NUMBER OF STUDENTS IN 1985:   42.

APPLY: By April 1. Dr. Vieri R. Salvadori, Dean.

Pietrasanta

■ **PROVIDENCE COLLEGE**
Providence, RI 02918
(401) 865-2114

PROGRAM: A full-semester summer program devoted to the arts, offers courses in language, literature, history, religion, art history, architecture, sculpture, etc. A trip of approximately five weeks spent traveling in London, Paris, Rome, Florence, and Siena is an integral part of the program.

ADMITTANCE REQUIREMENTS: College juniors with an above average academic record. No language requirement.

TEACHING METHODS: All courses are taught in English by U.S. faculty.

EVALUATION: By faculty review.

CREDITS OFFERED: 6 semester hours.

HOUSING: Students live in local pensioni.

DATES: Approximately, June 12 through August 10.

COSTS: $5,942 per year including tuition, room and board, local travel and round-trip airfare.

YEAR ESTABLISHED: 1970.

NUMBER OF STUDENTS IN 1985: Not available.

APPLY: By January 15. James F. Flanagan, Director, Providence-in-Europe.

Rome

■ **THE AMERICAN UNIVERSITY**
  Washington, DC 20016
  (202) 885-3800

PROGRAM: A Semester in Rome is a liberal arts/social science program held in cooperation with American University in Rome. Courses include history, fine arts, languages, political science, etc. Students may stay for both semesters. Field trips to Greece, Pompeii, and Paestum are often scheduled. Preorientation at American University (usually over a weekend) and onsite.

ADMITTANCE REQUIREMENTS: Juniors and seniors with a "B" average or better.

TEACHING METHODS: Students are accompanied by a resident professor from American University who schedules seminars with public officials in addition to his or her own lectures. Foreign faculty members complement these lectures and teach specialized courses. Students also intern two days a week with one of the many local government or private organizations.

EVALUATION: Regular exams, midterms and finals, in addition to short seminar papers.

CREDITS OFFERED: 15 to 17 semester hours.

HOUSING: A combination of possibilities from local apartments to living with local families.

DATES: First semester: September to December; second semester: January to May.

COSTS: Tuition: $4,100 per semester; room and board: $2,000 per semester. Scholarships from American University available.

YEAR ESTABLISHED: 1974.

NUMBER OF STUDENTS IN 1985:   65.

APPLY: Rolling admissions. Apply six to eight months prior to start of semester to: Dr. David C. Brown, Dean, Washington Semester and Study Program Abroad.

■ **HIRAM COLLEGE**
Hiram, OH 44234
(216) 569-5160

PROGRAM: The John Cabot International College is directly affiliated with Hiram and offers a full complement of undergraduate liberal arts and business courses. A special program, recently added, offers a BA degree in the history, politics, and economy of the Mediterranean region.

ADMITTANCE REQUIREMENTS: A minimum 2.5 GPA with recommendations from your own institution.

TEACHING METHODS: Students attend regular classes taught mostly by foreign faculty members. Although there are no language requirements, most classes are taught in Italian. Americans are fully integrated with other foreign students.

EVALUATION: By professors, based upon same standards as Hiram College.

CREDITS OFFERED: Up to 15 quarter hours per quarter.

HOUSING: Students share local apartments with other students.

DATES: Fall quarter: September 23 to December 5; winter: January 6 to March 20; spring: April 14 to June 14.

COSTS: Students make payments in lire although dollar equivalent is accepted. Approximately, tuition: $1450 per quarter; room and board: $1,400 per quarter; estimated living expenses: $500 per quarter. Does not include round-trip transportation or local travel.

YEAR ESTABLISHED: 1972.

NUMBER OF STUDENTS IN 1985: 100+.

APPLY: At least three months prior to desired quarter. Charles L. Adams, Director, Extramural Studies.

■ **INTERCOLLEGIATE CENTER FOR CLASSICAL STUDIES**
  c/o Stanford Overseas Studies
  P.O. Box L
  Stanford, CA 94305
  (415) 723-2300

PROGRAM: The Intercollegiate Center for Classical Studies is designed for both undergraduate and graduate students from member institutions, but will accept guest students. The academic focus is upon Classical, Renaissance, and Baroque studies, Latin and Greek.

ADMITTANCE REQUIREMENTS: 3.0 GPA and "evidence of substantial preparatory course work completed."

TEACHING METHODS: Students attend courses arranged for the group. Instruction is in Italian and English.

EVALUATION: By course instructors, based upon papers, class work, and final exams.

CREDITS OFFERED: Up to 16 semester hours per semester.

HOUSING: Students may live with families or locate their own facilities.

DATES: Approximately, fall semester: early September through mid-December; spring semester: early February through late May.

COSTS: Approximately $4,000 per semester for tuition, room and board. Does not include round-trip transportation or personal expenses.

YEAR ESTABLISHED: 1965.

NUMBER OF STUDENTS IN 1985: Not available.

APPLY: By April 15 for fall semester; October 15 for spring semester.

■ **LOYOLA UNIVERSITY OF CHICAGO**
Rome Center of Liberal Arts
6525 North Sheridan Road
Chicago, IL 60626
(312) 508-2760

PROGRAM: Loyola University of Chicago/Rome Center of Liberal Arts operates on its own campus on Via Massimi, ten minutes from the Vatican. Students may attend for a semester or the full academic year. Courses include: classical studies, communications, economics, English, finance, fine arts, Greek, history, Italian, business management, Latin, management science, marketing, philosophy, political science, psychology, and theology. There is a preorientation in Chicago and a two-day orientation in Rome.

ADMITTANCE REQUIREMENTS: Acceptable academic credentials plus at least 30 semester hours.

TEACHING METHODS: Most students are Americans. The faculty is predominantly American though there are several Italian scholars at the center. All courses, except languages, are in English and conducted by lecture. Several art history courses are held in local museums.

EVALUATION: All courses feature a typical periodic exam schedule. Several courses require short papers.

CREDITS OFFERED: Depending upon course load, between 12 and 19 hours per semester.

HOUSING: All students must live in the school dormitory unless they are living with a family off-campus.

DATES: Fall semester: late August through early December; spring semester: early January through early May.

COSTS: Tuition: $2,795 per semester; room and board: $2,065 per semester. Does not include round-trip transportation or living expenses ($1,000 to $1,500 per semester).

YEAR ESTABLISHED: 1962.

NUMBER OF STUDENTS IN FALL 1985: 210.

APPLY: For fall semester, March 1; spring semester, October 1. Rome Center Office.

■ **PENNSYLVANIA STATE UNIVERSITY**
Office of Education Abroad Programs
222 Boucke Building
University Park, PA 16802
(814) 865-7681

PROGRAM: Education Abroad in Rome is a spring-semester, fall-semester, or full-academic-year undergraduate program held in affiliation with Temple University. The program is held at the Villa Caproni in central Rome. Courses emphasize Italian art, literature, history, and politics with many classes devoted to the studio arts. Museum visits and tours to local cultural sites complements the class work. Orientation at Penn State.

ADMITTANCE REQUIREMENTS: Juniors and seniors with a 2.5 GPA, good academic standing, and "must show evidence of maturity, stability, adaptability, self-discipline and a strong academic motivation." Some specific course prerequisites. Students registering for Fine Arts sequence must present portfolio for review.

TEACHING METHODS: Students take courses in English taught by both U.S. and local teachers. Classes are not integrated with Italian students.

EVALUATION: By course instructors, based upon class work, papers, and examinations.

CREDITS OFFERED: 12 to 18 semester hours per semester.

HOUSING: Housing is arranged by Temple University in local pensioni.

DATES: Fall semester: mid-September through mid-December; spring semester: mid-January through mid-April.

COSTS: Students pay the same as at the University Park Campus. 1986-87 tuition per semester was $2,250 for state residents; $5,150 for nonresidents; room and board: $2,750 per semester. Plus a $100 nonrefundable program fee.

YEAR ESTABLISHED: 1966.

NUMBER OF STUDENTS IN 1985: 14.

APPLY: Fall semester or full year by March 1; spring semester by October 15.

■ **SAINT MARY'S COLLEGE**
  Notre Dame, IN 46556
  (219) 284-4000

PROGRAM: Saint Mary's College Rome Program is a semester or full-year undergraduate program that is particularly associated with the history, art, and culture of Italy. The school is conducted at the Hotel Tiziano on the Corso Vittorio Emanuele II. Courses, which are all interrelated, cover fine arts, archaeology, Italian literature, contemporary Italian problems, and philosophy. Five-day orientation in Assisi.

ADMITTANCE REQUIREMENTS: 2.5 GPA and successful completion of one year of college Italian or the equivalent.

TEACHING METHODS: Most courses are given in English by an international faculty. In addition to field trips to local cultural sites, the program also includes two weekend trips each semester to southern and northern Italy.

EVALUATION: By local faculty, based upon class work, papers, and examinations.

CREDITS OFFERED: 14 semester hours per semester; 5 of which are in the Italian language.

HOUSING: Women live at the Hotel Tiziano; men at the nearby Pensione Barrett.

DATES: September 19 through May 9.

COSTS: Approximately the same as a student's home campus tuition plus room and board. Estimated living expenses range from $1,900 to $2,500. Round-trip transportation is not included.

YEAR ESTABLISHED: 1970.

NUMBER OF STUDENTS IN 1985:   65.

APPLY: By January 1 for fall semester; August 15 for spring semester. Dr. Peter A. Checca, 145A Regina Hall.

■ **UNIVERSITY OF WASHINGTON**
Foreign Study Office
572 Schmitz Hall, PA-10
Seattle, WA 98195
(206) 543-9272

PROGRAM: Architecture in Rome is a fall and winter undergraduate program designed to "introduce students to the urban history and development of the city of Rome through first-hand studies of its topography and morphology." The spring quarter continues with studio-orientated projects and seminars that offers a multidisciplinary introduction to the art, architecture, and history of Rome. Onsite orientation.

ADMITTANCE REQUIREMENTS: Fall and winter terms: undergraduate and graduate students of architecture and related fields; spring term: junior standing and acceptable academic credentials. Knowledge of Italian recommended but not required.

TEACHING METHODS: Courses are taught in English by Washington College of Architecture faculty.

EVALUATION: By course faculty member, based upon papers and examinations.

CREDITS OFFERED: A full quarter term per quarter.

HOUSING: Students live in pensioni.

DATES: Approximately, fall term: late August through mid-November; winter term: early December through mid-February; spring term: early March through late May.

COSTS: $3,200 per term for resident undergraduates includes tuition, room and board. Does not cover round-trip transportation, local travel, or personal expenses.

YEAR ESTABLISHED: 1969.

NUMBER OF STUDENTS IN 1985: 12.

APPLY: Approximately four months prior to start of semester. David Fenner, Advisor.

Siena

■ **ACADEMIC YEAR ABROAD (AYA)**
17 Jansen Road
New Paltz, NY 12561
(914) 255-8103

PROGRAM: AYA sponsors programs for both undergraduate and graduate students in cooperation with the Scuola di Lingua e Cultura Italiana. Most university subjects are taught in Italian. Except for language courses, classes are composed of students from throughout Europe. Although there is no fixed pattern of travel, excursions are planned throughout the year. Program also includes a one-month presession orientation.

ADMITTANCE REQUIREMENTS: Competence in the language, though students may be accepted to begin the language; consent of home institution; acceptable academic record.

TEACHING METHODS: Varies with each subject.

EVALUATION: Grades given by the foreign professor.

CREDITS OFFERED: 16 semester hours per semester.

HOUSING: Optional, although AYA does provide housing in local homes when so elected by the student.

DATES: First term: early to mid-September through end of January; second term: end of January through May 30.

COSTS: Room and board: $3,800/year; tuition: $3,000/year; estimated living expenses: $1,000/year. Students bring financial aid from home institutions.

YEAR ESTABLISHED: 1961.

NUMBER OF STUDENTS IN 1985: 12.

APPLY: Dr. Stuart H. L. Degginger, Professor, SUNY New Paltz, c/o Academic Year Abroad.

Urbino

■ **STATE UNIVERSITY OF NEW YORK AT NEW PALTZ**
New Paltz, NY 12561
(914) 257-2233

PROGRAM: The SUNY Urbino Program is a single-semester or full-academic-year undergraduate and graduate program held in cooperation with the University of Urbino. The program emphasis is on the Italian language and culture with additional courses in art history and studio art. Part of the program is held in Florence. SUNY also offers an eight-week summer session (6 credits), which is available to undergraduates and high school seniors. One-day orientation in New Paltz.

ADMITTANCE REQUIREMENTS: Juniors, seniors, and graduate students in good academic standing with at least one year of college-level Italian or the equivalent.

TEACHING METHODS: Students take special courses taught by an Italian faculty. Includes lectures, intensive language courses, and regional field trips to historic and cultural sites.

EVALUATION: By Italian faculty, based upon periodic exams, finals and, depending on the level of the course, a term paper.

CREDITS OFFERED: A minimum of 12; maximum of 18 semester hours per semester.

HOUSING: Students live with families in Urbino and in a pensione while in Florence.

DATES: Approximately, fall semester: September 10 through December 23; spring semester: January 25 through May 31.

COSTS: Fall semester: $1,605; spring semester: $1,750, includes tuition, room and board, and program-related field trips. Nonresidents add approximately $925 per semester. Does not cover round-trip transportation or personal expenses (estimated at approximately $400 per semester).

YEAR ESTABLISHED: 1972.

NUMBER OF STUDENTS IN 1985:   25.

APPLY: For fall semester and academic year by April 1; spring semester by November 1. Dr. Rudolf R. Kossmann, Director, Office of International Education.

Venice

■ **COLGATE UNIVERSITY**
Hamilton, NY 13346
(315) 824-1000

PROGRAM: The Venice Study Group is a single-semester undergraduate program that offers courses in the Italian language, Latin, Greek, literature, art history, archaeology, medieval and Renaissance history, and includes a two- to three-week field trip to central and southern Italy. Orientation in the U.S.

ADMITTANCE REQUIREMENTS: Sophomores and above in good academic standing. Classics majors and Colgate students are shown a preference, but others accepted. One year of Italian, Latin, or Greek.

TEACHING METHODS: Students attend special courses arranged for the group and taught in English by both U.S. and Italian faculty.

EVALUATION: By course professors, based upon papers and examinations.

CREDITS OFFERED: 16 semester hours.

HOUSING: Students live in pensioni.

DATES: Approximately, early February through late May.

COSTS: $6,800 includes tuition, housing, round-trip transportation and tour. Does not cover meals or personal expenses.

YEAR ESTABLISHED: 1984.

NUMBER OF STUDENTS IN 1985: 17.

APPLY: By March 14. Professor Rebecca Ammerman, Department of the Classics.

■ **PRATT INSTITUTE**
School of Art & Design
200 Willoughby Avenue
Brooklyn, NY 11205
(718) 636-3598

PROGRAM: Pratt in Venice is a four-week summer session for both graduates and undergraduates held in cooperation with the Università Internazionale dell'Arte. Emphasis is on painting, drawing, and art history. All classes include some field trips; art history is "onsite" once a week. Orientation during preceding semester.

ADMITTANCE REQUIREMENTS: Advanced sophomores and above.

TEACHING METHODS: Participants attend regular classes taught in English by both U.S. and Venetian faculty.

EVALUATION: Portfolio review and a group show for studio classes; papers and class participation for art history students.

CREDITS OFFERED: 7 semester hours.

HOUSING: Students reside "in a good second class pensione with breakfast included."

DATES: Approximately, June 30 through July 31.

COSTS: Tuition: $1,610 for undergraduates; $1,820 for graduates. Room and breakfast; $560. Does not include round-trip transportation, local travel, or personal expenses. Scholarships and assistantships available.

YEAR ESTABLISHED: 1980.

NUMBER OF STUDENTS IN 1985:   20.

APPLY: By March 10. Dr. Diana G. Pechukas, Department of Art History.

LUXEMBOURG

Population: 365,900   **Capital:** Luxembourg   **Languages:** French, German
Monetary Unit: Luxembourg franc   **Government:** Constitutional monarchy
(grand duke and prime minister)   **Religion:** 93% Roman Catholic
Households with Television: 13%

SELECTED UNIVERSITY
Centre Universitaire de Luxembourg
162 A, Avenue de la Faiencerie
1511 Luxembourg

FURTHER INFORMATION

Commission for Educational
Exchange Between the United
States, Belgium, and Luxembourg
21, rue du Marteu
1040 Brussels
Belgium

Consulate General of Luxembourg
801 Second Avenue
New York, NY 10017
(212) 370-9850

Embassy of Luxembourg
2200 Massachusetts Avenue, NW
Washington, DC 20008
(202) 265-4171

Luxembourg Tourist Office
801 Second Avenue
New York, NY 10017
(212) 370-9850

Luxembourg

■ **MIAMI UNIVERSITY**
Langstroth House
Oxford, OH 45056
(513) 529-6841

PROGRAM: Miami University's European Center allows students to concentrate their studies in either the humanities or the social sciences. Courses are organized around themes such as "Culture and Society—Discovering the European Heritage" and "The Uniting of Modern Europe—The Economic and Political Challenge." Although students may attend for one or two semesters, the full-year program is recommended. Courses within the concentrations include history, geography, art history, music, literature, French, German, economics, and political science. Two major field trips each semester. Extensive orientation both prior to departure in Oxford and immediately upon arrival.

ADMITTANCE REQUIREMENTS: At least sophomore status, 2.5 minimum GPA, good discipline record, two references, essay, and interview.

TEACHING METHODS: Miami University maintains its own center and library with courses taught in English by American faculty on assignment as well as by local Luxembourg professors. Lectures, discussions, guest speakers, and extensive visits to European sites. Americans are not integrated with local students.

EVALUATION: Midterm and final exams, graded by American faculty.

CREDITS OFFERED: A minimum of 16 credit hours per semester must be taken.

HOUSING: With local families arranged by the university.

DATES: Early September to early May.

COSTS: Tuition: $2,475 for the full year; room and breakfast: $890 for the full year. Does not include round-trip transportation, travel, and full meal plan. Estimated living expenses $4,880 for full-year program.

YEAR ESTABLISHED: 1968.

NUMBER OF STUDENTS IN 1985: 105.

APPLY: By January 24 of preceding academic year. Dr. Annette Tomarken, MUEC Coordinator.

THE NETHERLANDS

Population: 14,582,000   **Capital:** Amsterdam   **Language:** Dutch
Monetary Unit: Netherlands guilder   **Government:** Constitutional monarchy
(queen and prime minister)   **Religion:** 36% Roman Catholic; 19% Dutch Reformed
Households with Television: 15%

SELECTED COLLEGES AND UNIVERSITIES

University of Amsterdam
Spui 21
1012 WX Amsterdam
*Courses in law and economics
in English.*

University of Rotterdam
Postbus 1738
3000 DR Rotterdam

University of Leiden
Schutterveld 9, 3e Verd
2316 XG Leiden

FURTHER INFORMATION

Embassy of The Netherlands
4200 Linnean Avenue, NW
Washington, DC 20008
(202) 244-5300

Consulate General of
The Netherlands
One Rockefeller Plaza
New York, NY 10020
(212) 246-1429

Publishes University Studies in
the Netherlands.

National Tourist Office of
The Netherlands
437 Madison Avenue
New York, NY 10036
(212) 223-8141

Amsterdam

■ DORDT COLLEGE
Sioux Center, Iowa 51250
(712) 722-3771

PROGRAM: Dordt College in The Netherlands is designed for any under-graduate students with an interest in becoming acquainted with the cultural heritage of The Netherlands. The program, given only in the spring, is held in cooperation with the Free University of The Netherlands. Courses offered include: art, business, Dutch, sociology, and history.

ADMITTANCE REQUIREMENTS: For college sophomores or above, with a 2.5 GPA, and at least a semester of college Dutch or its equivalent.

TEACHING METHODS: Courses, taught by Dordt instructors, are in English with the exception of Dutch language courses. Language skill field trips and museum visits complement class work.

EVALUATION: Periodic and final exams graded by Dordt teachers.

CREDITS OFFERED: 15 credits per semester.

HOUSING: Three weeks are spent with local families; the remainder in student dormitories.

DATES: End of January through mid-May.

COSTS: Tuition: $2,500; room and board: $875; local travel: approximately $600.

YEAR ESTABLISHED: 1976.

NUMBER OF STUDENTS IN 1985: 18.

APPLY: By November 15. Dr. K.J. Boot or Dr. J. Struyk, Department of Foreign Languages, Netherlands Study Program.

Leiden

■ **CENTRAL COLLEGE**
Pella, IA 50219
(515) 628-5287

PROGRAM: Central College's Netherlands Program is a new undergraduate semester or full-academic-year of study under the direction of Dr. William Stronks. The program courses cover: Dutch studies, literature, and culture; urban and regional planning in the Netherlands; history of the Low Countries; international marketing; and modern European history. Orientation in Leiden.

ADMITTANCE REQUIREMENTS: Minimum 2.5 GPA, knowledge of Dutch, recommendations, and essay.

TEACHING METHODS: Special classes for American students are taught in English by Dutch faculty. Lectures and seminars are complemented by local field trips.

EVALUATION: By Dutch professors; resident director sends grades to home institution.

CREDITS OFFERED: 16 semester hours per semester.

HOUSING: Students live in apartments or with local families.

DATES: Fall semester: August 27 through December 13; spring semester: January 19 through May 16.

COSTS: Approximately, both semesters $8,300; one semester, $4,500. Includes tuition, room, fees, and all meals. Does not cover round-trip transportation or personal expenses. Several $500 merit scholarships are available.

YEAR ESTABLISHED: 1986.

NUMBER OF STUDENTS IN 1986: Not available.

APPLY: By April 15 for fall semester or full year; November 1 for spring semester. Mrs. Barbara Butler, Coordinator of International Studies.

Rotterdam

■ **MICHIGAN STATE UNIVERSITY**
108 Center for International Programs
East Lansing, MI 48824
(517) 353-8920

PROGRAM: Business Law in The Netherlands is a single-semester undergraduate and graduate program held at Erasmus University. Courses cover the complete scope of business law and international business. Field trips to points of historic, cultural, and academic interest. Brief orientation in the U.S.

ADMITTANCE REQUIREMENTS: For sophomores, juniors, seniors, and graduate students with acceptable academic credentials, references, and recommendation from advisor. No language requirement.

TEACHING METHODS: Students take special courses, lectures, seminars, and independent study projects in English arranged for the group and taught by both U.S. and Erasmus University faculty.

EVALUATION: By course faculty, based upon papers and examinations.

CREDITS OFFERED: 12 credit hours.

HOUSING: Students live in dormitories and student residence halls.

DATES: April 1 through June 6.

COSTS: $1,900 includes tuition, room, and program-related travel. Does not include round-trip transportation, meals, or personal expenses.

YEAR ESTABLISHED: 1975.

NUMBER OF STUDENTS IN 1985: 23.

APPLY: By February 3. Dr. Charles A. Gliozzo, Office of Overseas Study.

NORWAY

Population: 4,166.000   **Capital:** Oslo   **Language:** Norwegian
Monetary Unit: Krone   **Government:** Constitutional monarchy (king and prime minister)   **Religion:** 88% Lutheran   **Households with Television:** 14%

SELECTED COLLEGES AND UNIVERSITIES

Stavanger College of Education
Box 2521 Ullandhaug
4001 Stavanger

Norwegian language for teachers. Free tuition.

University of Bergen
Nordisk Institutt
Sydneplass 9
5000 Bergen

Courses in Norwegian language and culture taught in Norwegian.

University of Oslo
P.O. Box 10
Blindern
Oslo 3

Courses in Norwegian language, literature, and culture; summer program; many courses in English.

FURTHER INFORMATION

Embassy of Norway
2720 34th Street, NW
Washington, DC 20008
(202) 333-6000

Norwegian National Tourist Office
75 Rockefeller Plaza
New York, NY 10019
(212) 949-2333

Norwegian Information Service
825 Third Avenue
New York, NY 10022
(212) 421-7333

Publishes Foreign Students in Norway *and* The Regional Colleges in Norway.

Oslo

■ **HIGHER EDUCATION CONSORTIUM FOR URBAN AFFAIRS (HECUA)**
HECUA at Hamline University
St. Paul, MN 55104
(612) 646-8831

PROGRAM: The Scandinavian Urban Studies Term (SUST) is an interdisciplinary field-learning program that gives a broad introduction to contemporary Scandinavian with an emphasis on Norway. Study is combined with travel to Denmark, Sweden, Finland, and the USSR. The program is cosponsored by the University of Olso's International summer school and is part of a consortium administered by HECUA for fifteen cooperating colleges and universities in the upper Midwest. Courses cover: urban studies, fine arts, history and language (Norwegian), political science, social science and sociology.

ADMITTANCE REQUIREMENTS: Juniors and seniors in good academic standing, essay, recommendation from home institution.

TEACHING METHODS: Faculty are citizen-residents of the host country. Integration of regular classroom work (lectures, readings, discussions, etc.) with field study in communities and site visits.

EVALUATION: Varies according to program. Expect exams and periodic papers graded by local professors.

CREDITS OFFERED: HECUA programs are equivalent to a full semester load; typically four courses per semester (4-1-4 system) or 16 credit hours.

HOUSING: Dormitories at the University of Oslo—single rooms with shared kitchen. One or two weekend homestays with Oslo family.

DATES: August 25 through December 5.

COSTS: Tuition, room and board, and local field trips $4,300. Estimated living expenses $500 to $700. Travel to and from Oslo, approximately $950, not included. Nonmember college students pay additional $150 administrative fee.

YEAR ESTABLISHED: 1972.

NUMBER OF STUDENTS IN 1985: 13.

APPLY: By March 31. Ms. Jean Leibman, Administrative Associate.

PORTUGAL

Population: 10,250,000   **Capital:** Lisbon   **Language:** Portuguese
Monetary Unit: Escudo   **Government:** Parliamentary state (president and prime minister)   **Religion:** 95% Roman Catholic   **Households with Television:** 6%

SELECTED COLLEGES AND UNIVERSITIES

Fondation Calouste Gulbenkian
Avenida de Berna
1093 Lisboa

University of Lisboa
1200 Lisboa

FURTHER INFORMATION

Consulate General of Portugal
630 Fifth Avenue; Suite 655
New York, NY 10111
(212) 246-4580

Portugese National Tourist Office
548 Fifth Avenue
New York, NY 10036
(212) 354-4403

Embassy of Portugal
2125 Kalorama Road, NW
Washington, DC 20008
(202) 328-8610

- *Don't leave Portugal without a visit to the southern part of the country, the Algarve. Highlights include: Sagres, Lagos, and cataplana (national dish consisting of pork and small clams) in Faro.*

  - Ellen Leerburger, Scarsdale, New York

Lisbon

- **UNIVERSITY OF CONNECTICUT**
  241 Glenbrook Road
  Storrs, CT 06268
  (203) 486-2141

PROGRAM: Portuguese Studies at the University of Lisbon is a single-semester or full-academic-year undergraduate program held in cooperation with the Universidade Classica de Lisboa. Courses concentrate on the Portuguese language. Students who successfully complete the elementary, intermediate, or advanced levels receive a "Certificado de Aproveitamento." Upper-level courses include Portuguese linguistics, history, literature, art, geography, and other liberal arts subjects. Successful upper-level students receive a Diploma of Portuguese Studies.

ADMITTANCE REQUIREMENTS: Sophomores and above in good academic standing, with a 2.50 GPA. No language requirement for beginning courses.

TEACHING METHODS: Students attend special courses arranged for the group and taught by faculty members at the University of Lisbon. All classes are in Portuguese.

EVALUATION: By course professors, based upon papers and examinations.

CREDITS OFFERED: 16 semester hours per semester.

HOUSING: Students are responsible for making their own living arrangements, but may eat at the university canteen.

DATES: Fall semester: early September through mid-December; spring semester: mid-January through mid-June.

COSTS: Annual tuition and fees in Portugal: $250 plus a $290 fee to the University of Connecticut. Estimated room and board: $1,800 per year. Does not include round-trip transportation from New York or local travel.

YEAR ESTABLISHED: 1986.

NUMBER OF STUDENTS IN 1986: 1.

APPLY: For fall semester by March 1; spring semester: October 15. Study Abroad Office.

SPAIN

Population: 38,818,000   **Capital:** Madrid   **Language:** Spanish
Monetary Unit: Peseta   **Government:** Constitutional monarchy (king and prime minister)   **Religion:** 97% Roman Catholic
Households with Television: 26%

SELECTED COLLEGES AND UNIVERSITIES

University of Barcelona
Gran Via 585
Barcelona-7

University of Madrid
Canto Blanco
Madrid-34

University of Granada
Puentezuelas 55
Granada

University of Salamanca
Salamanca

FURTHER INFORMATION

Consulate General of Spain
150 East 58th Street
New York, NY 10015
(212) 355-4080

Spanish National Tourist Office
665 Fifth Avenue
New York, NY 10022
(212) 759-8822

Embassy of Spain
2700 15th Street, NW
Washington, DC 20009
(202) 265-0190

Publishes Study in Spain: General
Information for Foreign University
Students *and* American Programs
in Spain.

■ *To get the most out of your visit to Spain, forget that you are an American. Immerse yourself in all Spain has to offer by becoming friends with Spaniards and not just hanging out with other Americans. Live like the Spanish. It's worth it!*

- Karen M. Gately, Columbia, Maryland

■ *If you have a chance of staying a semester or a year, STAY THE YEAR! I didn't and I regret it.*

- Brian C. Dunning, Somerville, Massachusetts

More Than One City

■ **THE CALIFORNIA STATE UNIVERSITY**
400 Golden Shore
Long Beach, CA 90802
(213) 590-5655

PROGRAM: The CSU International Program in Spain, held at the universities of Madrid and Granada, is a full-academic-year undergraduate and graduate opportunity to study in Spain. Courses at both schools are oriented toward the study of Spanish civilization and society. Granada is noted for its offerings in Moorish, Arabic, and Jewish studies. Four-week language presession in Baeza.

ADMITTANCE REQUIREMENTS: Must be enrolled at a CSU campus. Juniors and above, including graduate students, 2.75 GPA, and two years of college Spanish.

TEACHING METHODS: Students take a combination of regular academic courses in Spanish supplemented with program-sponsored courses, taught by foreign faculty.

EVALUATION: By foreign faculty and CSU resident director, based upon periodic and final examinations.

CREDITS OFFERED: 30 semester hours per year or 45 quarter units.

HOUSING: In dormitories and private apartments.

DATES: Approximately, August 14 through May 30.

COSTS: Tuition: $0 (residents); $3,600 (nonresidents); room and board: $2,300. Does not include round-trip transportation or living expenses (estimated at approximately $2,630 per year).

YEAR ESTABLISHED: 1963.

NUMBER OF STUDENTS IN 1985: 57.

APPLY: By February 1. Dr. Kibbey M. Horne, Director of International Programs.

Barcelona

■ **BRETHREN COLLEGES ABROAD**
P.O. Box #184
Manchester College
North Manchester, IN 46962
(219) 982-2141, ext. 238

PROGRAM: Brethren Colleges Abroad Spanish Program is held in cooperation with the Universidad de Barcelona and Bridgewater College, Elizabethtown College, Juniata College, McPherson College, and the University of La Verne in the United States. Courses cover the humanities and social sciences. Art courses are held in conjunction with the Massasa Art School. Onsite orientation includes three-week intensive language course and a week in Madrid and its surroundings.

ADMITTANCE REQUIREMENTS: For juniors and seniors, with 3.0 GPA and two years college-level Spanish.

TEACHING METHODS: Americans are fully integrated with Spanish students. Both special and regular college courses. Coursework is complemented with field trips, and travel to museums and regional sites.

EVALUATION: Director in Spain and professors determine grades from papers, periodic exams and finals.

CREDITS OFFERED: 15 to 16 semester hours.

HOUSING: Local families and residencias.

DATES: Fall semester: September 1 through December 30; spring semester: January 10 through June 5.

COSTS: $5,800 per semester. Includes tuition, room and board, and round-trip transportation. Does not cover personal expenses or local travel.

YEAR ESTABLISHED: 1962.

NUMBER OF STUDENTS IN 1985:   27.

APPLY: By April 1 for fall semester and November 1 for spring semester. Dr. Allen C. Deeter or Mrs. Helga Walsh.

Caceres

■ **MICHIGAN STATE UNIVERSITY**
108 Center for International Programs
East Lansing, MI 48824
(517) 353-8920

PROGRAM: Spanish Language, Literature, and Culture in Caceres is a spring-term undergraduate program with courses covering the Spanish language, art, music, history, and culture. Brief orientation in the U.S.

ADMITTANCE REQUIREMENTS: For sophomores and above with acceptable academic credentials, and one and a half years college Spanish or the equivalent.

TEACHING METHODS: Students take special courses, lectures, seminars, and language labs in Spanish and English arranged for the group and taught by both U.S. and Spanish faculty.

EVALUATION: By course faculty, based upon papers and examinations.

CREDITS OFFERED: 12 credit hours.

HOUSING: Students live with local families.

DATES: April 2 through June 6.

COSTS: $1,600 includes tuition, room and board, and program-related travel. Does not include round-trip transportation or personal expenses.

YEAR ESTABLISHED: 1981.

NUMBER OF STUDENTS IN 1985: 17.

APPLY: By February 3. Dr. Charles A. Gliozzo, Office of Overseas Study.

Granada

- *One of the most beautiful cities in Spain; the Alhambra and Generalife are the eighth wonder of the world, and should not be missed.*
                                        - Ellen Leerburger, Scarsdale, New York

■ **BELOIT COLLEGE**
Beloit, WI 53511
(608) 365-3391

PROGRAM: World Outlook Program Seminar undergraduate program offers a semester in Spain in cooperation with the University of Granada. The program stresses language, contemporary literature, history, theater, art, and architecture. Presession orientation is held at Beloit.

ADMITTANCE REQUIREMENTS: B average, two years of Spanish for those taking language courses, and good academic standing.

TEACHING METHODS: Students attend special courses, unless their language proficiency is high, taught by foreign faculty. Lectures, independent study, and field trips complement classroom work. A U.S. academic leader accompanies group.

EVALUATION: Papers and examinations given by foreign teachers.

CREDITS OFFERED: 16 semester hours.

HOUSING: With local families.

DATES: Approximately, January 2 through April 30.

COSTS: Tuition: $3,900; room and board: $1,700. Travel to/from Europe: approximately $600.

YEAR ESTABLISHED: 1962.

NUMBER OF STUDENTS IN 1985:   12.

APPLY: By November 30. World Affairs Center.

■ **CENTRAL COLLEGE**
Pella, IA 50219
(515) 628-5287

PROGRAM: Central College's Spain Program offers students several semester or full-year academic options depending upon the individual's interests and linguistic ability. Students fluent in Spanish may enroll in an honors program; those who do not qualify for the advanced courses enroll in the accelerated language and civilization program. Both are taught in cooperation with the University of Granada. Courses cover: Spanish language literature and culture; history, art, business, political science, geography, music, philosophy, etc. Both programs spend ten days in Madrid, where the emphasis is on fine arts, and three weeks orientation in a small Andalusian village outside Granada.

ADMITTANCE REQUIREMENTS: Minimum 2.5 GPA (3.0 in Spanish), recommendations, and essay.

TEACHING METHODS: Those not attending the regular courses at the university take special classes designed for foreign students taught by Spanish professors. Lectures and seminars in Spanish are complemented by local field trips.

EVALUATION: By Spanish faculty. Resident director sends grades to home institution.

CREDITS OFFERED: 16 to 20 semester hours per semester.

HOUSING: Some students live in dormitories with Spanish roommates. Most live with Spanish families.

DATES: Fall semester: early September through mid-January; spring semester: early February through mid-May.

COSTS: Approximately 26 to 32 credit hours @ $8,300; 17 to 20 hours @ $5,500; 14 to 16 hours @ $4,400. Includes tuition, room and board, fees, some excursions. Does not cover round-trip transportation or personal expenses. Several $500 merit scholarships are available.

YEAR ESTABLISHED: 1966.

NUMBER OF STUDENTS IN 1985:   80.

APPLY: By April 15 for fall semester or full year; November 1 for spring semester. Mrs. Barbara Butler, Coordinator of International Studies.

■ **THE EXPERIMENT IN INTERNATIONAL LIVING**
Kipling Road
Brattleboro, VT 05301
(800) 451-4465

PROGRAM: The College Semester Abroad Program is designed to allow under-graduate students to become immersed in a foreign culture by living with a local family and exploring individual personal and educational interests under professional guidance. Students on the Spanish program spend most of their stay in Granada, however, one week is spent in an Andalusian village and another in a location appropriate to a field study project, and the final week evaluating the program in Madrid. Courses cover: intensive language study, seminar on Spanish life and culture, history and politics, geography and economics, arts and humanities, social anthropology, methods and techniques of field work, and an independent study project. One-week orientation in Brattleboro and Madrid.

ADMITTANCE REQUIREMENTS: Sophomore standing or above and acceptable academic credentials. One and a half years college Spanish or the equivalent.

TEACHING METHODS: Students work directly with their American instructor-advisors in planning and evaluating their individual program. Nonlanguage courses are in English. "The semester builds from the more structured language training and lectures and discussions on local life and culture to the independent study project."

EVALUATION: By individual students and their instructor-advisors based on independent project, papers, reports, and examinations. Periodic meetings during the program and for several days at the conclusion.

CREDITS OFFERED: 16 semester hours.

HOUSING: Students live as family members with their host families.

DATES: Approximately, fall semester: September through December; spring semester: January through May.

COSTS: $5,800 includes tuition, room and board, all fees and local travel, and round-trip transportation from Brattleboro.

YEAR ESTABLISHED: 1984.

NUMBER OF STUDENTS IN 1985: 13.

APPLY: For fall semester by May 15; spring semester by November 15. Admissions Office, College Semester Abroad.

■ **UNIVERSITY OF CONNECTICUT**
   241 Glenbrook Road
   Storrs, CT 06268
   (203) 486-2141

PROGRAM: Study Abroad in Spain at the University of Granada is a single-semester or full-academic-year undergraduate program held in cooperation with the universities of New Hampshire and Rhode Island and the University of Granada. The program is held in the Facultad de Traductores e Interpretes of the University of Granada, which receives students from all over Europe. Courses cover Spanish language, literature and culture; linguistics; translation; economics; art history; music appreciation; geography; sociology; political science; history; and architecture. Option for internships and independent study. Two-week orientation in Madrid.

ADMITTANCE REQUIREMENTS: Sophomores and above in good academic standing with a 2.75 GPA and at least five semesters of college Spanish or the equivalent.

TEACHING METHODS: Students attend special courses arranged for the group as well as any of the courses offered by the University of Granada in which Americans are fully integrated with non-U.S. students. All classes are in Spanish.

EVALUATION: By course professors, based upon papers and examinations.

CREDITS OFFERED: 15 semester hours per semester.

HOUSING: Students live with local families.

DATES: Fall semester: August 26 through mid-December; spring semester: mid-January through May 30.

COSTS: Approximately $6,200 per semester includes tuition, room and board, round-trip transportation from New York, and program-related travel. Some scholarship aid available.

YEAR ESTABLISHED: 1985.

NUMBER OF STUDENTS IN 1985: 33.

APPLY: By March 15. Sally Innis Klitz, U-207.

Madrid

- *Madrid is a city full of places to be discovered. The mesones (taverns) along the Arco de Cuchilleros have wonderful tapas and atmosphere, and are great for meeting Spaniards. Also, be sure to visit the less-known art museums and galleries: the Sorolla museum, Ermita de San Antonio de la Florida (great Goya frescoes), Galería Fernando Vijande and Fundación Juan March, which all contain masterpieces in Spanish Art. Finally, be outside as much as possible—the Spaniards are truly themselves on the streets, plazas, and parks. You will be surprised how much you can learn about the Spanish culture from the Madrileños.*

  - Ellen Leerburger, Scarsdale, New York

- *Madrid is a great city; extremely clean and safe. Retiro Park is a wonderful place to "escape" to; for shopping, stay away from Gran Via and Puerta del Sol—they are mostly tourist traps. The small neighborhood shops are much better. To meet young Spaniards, go to bars and restaurants in the Arguelles area, near the university.*

  - Karen Gately, Columbia, Maryland

■ **ACADEMIC YEAR ABROAD (AYA)**
17 Jansen Road
New Paltz, NY 12561
(914) 255-8103

PROGRAM: AYA sponsors programs for both undergraduate and graduate students in cooperation with the Universidad de Madrid Complutense. Most university subjects are taught in Spanish. Except for language courses, classes are composed of students from throughout Europe. Although there is no fixed pattern of travel, excursions are planned throughout the year. Program also includes a one-month presession orientation.

ADMITTANCE REQUIREMENTS: Competence in the language, though students may be accepted to begin the language; consent of home institution; acceptable academic record.

TEACHING METHODS: Varies with each subject.

EVALUATION: Grades given by the foreign professor.

CREDITS OFFERED: 16 semester hours per semester.

HOUSING: Optional, although AYA does provide housing in local homes when so elected by the student.

DATES: First term: early to mid-September through end of January; second term: end of January through May 30.

COSTS: Room and board: $3,800/year; tuition: $3,000/year; estimated living expenses: $1,000/year. Students bring financial aid from home institutions.

YEAR ESTABLISHED: 1961.

NUMBER OF STUDENTS IN 1985: 12.

APPLY: Dr. Stuart H. L. Degginger, Professor, SUNY New Paltz, c/o Academic Year Abroad.

■ **ALMA COLLEGE**
Alma, MI 48801
(517) 463-7247

PROGRAM: Alma College Program of Studies in Spain is held in cooperation with Estudio International Sampere and the University of Madrid. This program is not in a structured academic setting such as most American schools. Rather, teachers and staff at EIS "leave enough freedom in the academic environment to allow students to meet their needs through consultation with the director." Courses specialize in Spanish language and culture. Onsite orientation with the director.

ADMITTANCE REQUIREMENTS: Sophomores and above, with a minimum 2.0 GPA, in good academic standing, with letters of recommendation.

TEACHING METHODS: Small classes, usually six to nine students, in Spanish are complemented with visits to local sites and independent study. Direct involvement with Spanish staff and local residents is encouraged and expected.

EVALUATION: Foreign faculty in conjunction with the resident director, plus papers and periodic exams.

CREDITS OFFERED: Up to 15 hours per semester.

HOUSING: All students reside in Spanish homes.

DATES: Fall semester: September 1 through December 19; spring semester: February 2 through May 22.

COSTS: Fall semester: $4,800; spring semester: $4,850. Includes tuition, room and board, round-trip transportation from New York, plus basic texts and cultural activities.

YEAR ESTABLISHED: 1979.

NUMBER OF STUDENTS IN 1985:   15.

APPLY: Two months prior to departure. Alda Dyal Chand, Director, International Education.

■ **BOSTON UNIVERSITY**
  143 Bay State Road
  Boston, MA 02215
  (617) 353-9888

PROGRAM: Boston University Study Abroad in Madrid is a single-semester or full-academic-year undergraduate program, held in cooperation with the Instituto Internacional en España, offering courses concentrating on the Spanish language, culture, and civilization; art history; economics; history; literature; and politics. Program-related travel to local sites of historic and cultural interest. Two-week onsite orientation.

ADMITTANCE REQUIREMENTS: Sophomores and above in good academic standing, with at least one semester of college Spanish for beginning programs, five semesters for advanced programs.

TEACHING METHODS: Students attend regular courses taught in Spanish by the faculty of the instituto.

EVALUATION: By course faculty, based upon papers and periodic examinations.

CREDITS OFFERED: 16 semester hours per semester.

HOUSING: Students live with local families.

DATES: Fall semester: early September through mid-December; spring semester: early January through late May.

COSTS: Approximately $7,265 per semester includes tuition, room and board, and transportation from New York to Madrid. Does not include return transportation or personal expenses.

YEAR ESTABLISHED: 1983.

NUMBER OF STUDENTS IN 1985: 59.

APPLY: Fall semester: February 28; spring semester: October 9. Study Abroad Office.

■ **HEIDELBERG COLLEGE**
310 East Market Street
Tiffin, OH 44883
(419) 448-2256

PROGRAM: The Heidelberg College in Madrid is held in association with the Colegios Mayores Universitarios de la Complutense. The major course emphasis is on Spanish language, literature, history, and drama. One week of orientation in Madrid.

ADMITTANCE REQUIREMENTS: Juniors or seniors with a 2.5 GPA (3.0 in Spanish), two years of college Spanish or the equivalent, and two letters of recommendation.

TEACHING METHODS: Courses are taught in Spanish by members of the faculty from the Colegios Mayores Universitarios de la Camplutense; includes some local trips.

EVALUATION: By university professors based upon term papers and final examinations.

CREDITS OFFERED: Up to 16 semester hours per semester.

HOUSING: Students may live in private homes, mostly in the Moncloa district.

DATES: Approximately, fall semester: September 3 through December 13; spring semester: January 15 through May 14.

COSTS: Tuition, room and board: $3,250 per semester; $5,900 for the full year. Includes, round-trip transportation from New York and five weekend excursions. Does not cover personal expenses.

YEAR ESTABLISHED: 1985.

NUMBER OF STUDENTS IN 1985: Not available.

APPLY: For fall semester by June 15; for spring semester by October 15. Heidelberg College in Madrid.

■ **HIRAM COLLEGE**
  Hiram, OH 44234
  (216) 569-5160

PROGRAM: Hiram's Spanish Quarter offers a ten-week undergraduate program in which students select three courses from a menu covering Spanish civilization, language, drama, or literature.

ADMITTANCE REQUIREMENTS: A minimum 2.5 GPA with recommendations from your own advisor plus two additional teachers and two to three college-level courses in Spanish or the equivalent.

TEACHING METHODS: Students attend regular classes or seminars taught by a member of the Hiram faculty. On occasion, a course is taught by a foreign professor. The program always includes field trips to regional sites, museums, etc.

EVALUATION: By programs leaders and students.

CREDITS OFFERED: Up to 15 quarter hours per quarter.

HOUSING: Students live with local families.

DATES: The program is offered every three years. Next program: early January to mid-March, 1988.

COSTS: Approximately $4,000 including tuition, room and partial board, local travel and fees. Does not cover round-trip transportation or local expenses. Some IES scholarship aid available; $1,500 for full year students, $750 for semester students.

YEAR ESTABLISHED: 1972.

NUMBER OF STUDENTS IN 1985: 12.

APPLY: By October 10. Charles L. Adams, Director, Extramural Studies.

■ **INSTITUTE OF EUROPEAN STUDY (IES)**
223 West Ohio Street
Chicago, IL 60610
(312) 944-1750

PROGRAM: IES is a nonprofit organization with formal relationships with more than forty American colleges and universities. The institute maintains ten undergraduate academic centers throughout the world, which provide semester or full-academic-year programs. The IES Madrid center offers courses in art history, business, economics, Spanish history, literature, music, political science, sociology and religion, and Spanish language and culture. Qualified full-year students may also enroll directly in courses at the Universidad Complutense. Students may apply for noncredit teaching internships in Spanish high schools. Summer program also available. One week orientation in Madrid.

ADMITTANCE REQUIREMENTS: Juniors and seniors ("exceptionally well-qualified sophomores *may* be considered") with minimum two years of college Spanish or the equivalent, faculty recommendations, and an application essay. 85 percent of all students have had a GPA between 2.80 and 3.75.

TEACHING METHODS: All courses are taught in Spanish by a Spanish faculty, and are supplemented by trips to local museums and historic sites.

EVALUATION: By Spanish faculty, based upon class work, periodic tests, and final exams. Most courses require a research paper.

CREDITS OFFERED: 15 to 18 semester hours per semester.

HOUSING: Students may live with local families or in a university residence hall.

DATES: Fall semester: September 8 through December 19; spring semester: January 19 through May 22.

COSTS: Tuition: $3,800 per semester; room and board: $6,150 per year (add $600 if university residence). Does not include round-trip transportation, local travel, or personal expenses (estimated at $2,850 per year).

YEAR ESTABLISHED: 1964.

NUMBER OF STUDENTS IN 1985: 75.

APPLY: For fall semester by May 1; spring semester by November 15.

■ **KALAMAZOO COLLEGE**
  1200 Academy Street
  Kalamazoo, MI 49007
  (616) 383-8470

PROGRAM: The Madrid Program is designed for students who have enough language aptitude and training (minimum: 3 units Spanish) to enable them to handle college-level courses conducted in Spanish. Held in cooperation with the International Institute in Spain. Courses cover Spanish language, history, art history, literature, and current events. Orientation: two hours weekly during preceding term at Kalamazoo.

ADMITTANCE REQUIREMENTS: Enrollment at Kalamazoo College in term prior to departure. Ten semester hours of college Spanish or the equivalent.

TEACHING METHODS: Students attend regular academic courses, lectures, seminars, and tutorials in Spanish. Taught by host-country instructors; not open to nonprogram students.

EVALUATION: By individual instructors based upon class work, papers, and examinations. Recorded by Kalamazoo only as "pass/fail."

CREDITS OFFERED: 20 quarter hours credit.

HOUSING: With local families.

DATES: Approximately, mid-September to mid-March.

COSTS: $7,064 includes tuition, room and board, some regional travel, and round-trip transportation from New York. Does not cover the cost of one term at Kalamazoo at $3,532 or personal travel and living expenses.

YEAR ESTABLISHED: 1963.

NUMBER OF STUDENTS IN 1985: 30.

APPLY: By May 1. Dr. Joe K. Fugate, Director, Office of Foreign Study.

■ **MIDDLEBURY COLLEGE**
Middlebury, VT 05753
(802) 388-3711

PROGRAM: Middlebury College School in Spain offers undergraduates "long-standing, highly respected, and *serious*" courses in literature, Spanish language, culture, and civilization including art history, cinema, music, etc. An MA program is available in Spanish language and literature. Courses are held at the Instituto International.

ADMITTANCE REQUIREMENTS: The equivalent of five semesters in Spanish and a B average; (for MA a "better than B average" is required).

TEACHING METHODS: Spanish faculty. All courses, written papers, and exams are in Spanish. Extensive travel, field trips, and cultural exchanges complement the program.

EVALUATION: Faculty-student conferences, term papers, finals, etc.

CREDITS OFFERED: Full-semester or full-year credit.

HOUSING: Students live with families or in pensions or apartments.

DATES: Approximately, September 15 through June 10.

COSTS: Tuition: full year $4,900; semester $2,500; room and board: approximately $2,000 per semester. Round-trip travel: approximately $600. Local travel in Europe not included. Some scholarships available.

YEAR ESTABLISHED: 1951.

NUMBER OF STUDENTS IN 1985: 60.

APPLY: Rolling admissions. Contact Dean of Spanish School.

■ *There is no doubt in my mind that Middlebury College attracts the finest faculty available in Spain. (Carlos Bousoño, for example, a famous poet and a member of the Real Academia.) No other program can compare with this faculty. But, in my opinion, that's all the program has going for it. The biggest fault is that classes are not held at the university so there is really no way to make friends with the native students.*

- Name withheld, Medford, Massachusetts

■ **NEW YORK UNIVERSITY**
   19 University Place, Room 409
   New York, NY 10003
   (212) 598-2848

PROGRAM: New York University in Spain is an independent program held at the Instituto Internacional, a national monument. The program specializes in Hispanic literature and languages with side trips to artistic and cultural cities. A summer program is held in Salamanca. One-week orientation in Madrid.

ADMITTANCE REQUIREMENTS: GPA of 3.0 or better, plus advanced language proficiency.

TEACHING METHODS: Courses are taught by a Spanish faculty in Spanish with several special courses given by members of the NYU faculty. Class work complemented by independent study, field trips, and travel to regional sites.

EVALUATION: Periodic exams plus a final exam.

CREDITS OFFERED: 4 semester hours credit per course.

HOUSING: With local families or other private accommodations.

DATES: Fall semester: August 25 through December 18; spring semester: January 12 through May 12.

COSTS: Tuition for full academic year: $5,000; room and board, approximately $2,900; estimated living expenses: $1,800. Not including travel to and from Madrid. "Some scholarships available for outstanding students."

YEAR ESTABLISHED: 1958.

NUMBER OF STUDENTS IN 1985: 235.

APPLY: By August 1 for fall semester; December 1 for spring semester. Professor Salvador Martinez, Director, NYU in Spain.

■ **NORTHERN ILLINOIS UNIVERSITY**
   DeKalb, IL 60115
   (815) 753-0304

PROGRAM: NSU's Spanish Internship program is a one-semester or full-academic-year undergraduate and graduate program held in cooperation with Universidad de Complutense, Universidad Nacional, and Educational Programs Abroad. Students combine internships with law firms, communications' companies, lobbying groups, and members of the Cortes (parliament) with courses covering Spanish art and culture, business, communications, politics, and history. Optional program-related travel; a three-day orientation in Madrid.

ADMITTANCE REQUIREMENTS: Juniors and above, including graduate students, with a 3.0 GPA and fluency in Spanish.

TEACHING METHODS: Students take courses taught in Spanish by the faculty at Universidad de Complutense and Universidad Nacional.

EVALUATION: By faculty, based upon class work and course examinations.

CREDITS OFFERED: 15 semester hours per semester.

HOUSING: Students live in apartments, furnished rooms, or with local families.

DATES: Fall semester: early September through mid-December; spring semester: mid-January through mid-June.

COSTS: $3,500 per semester includes tuition and room and board. Does not cover round-trip transportation, program-related travel, or personal expenses.

YEAR ESTABLISHED: 1983.

NUMBER OF STUDENTS IN 1985: Not available.

APPLY: By June 1 for fall semester; November 1 for spring. Judith Muasher.

■ **PORTLAND STATE UNIVERSITY**
P.O. Box #751
Portland, OR 97207
(503) 229-4081

PROGRAM: The Hispanic Studies Program is a six-week undergraduate and graduate summer session held in cooperation with the Facultad de Filosofia y Letras, University of Madrid. The program emphasizes language, literature, civilization, and the Hispanic culture. Excursions to Cordoba, Seville, Granada, Burgos, Santander, and Picos de Europa complement the session.

ADMITTANCE REQUIREMENTS: Open to all students. Two years of Spanish recommended.

TEACHING METHODS: Special courses are presented by Portland State University in Spanish. Americans are not integrated into regular university classes.

EVALUATION: By the program director, based upon examinations.

CREDITS OFFERED: Up to 12 quarter hour credits for undergraduates; 8 quarter hour credits for graduate students.

HOUSING: Most students stay in apartments with local families.

DATES: July 1 through August 10.

COSTS: Tuition: $837; room and board: $450. Includes program-related travel. Does not cover round-trip transportation or personal expenses.

YEAR ESTABLISHED: 1966.

NUMBER OF STUDENTS IN 1985: 20.

APPLY: No deadline for applications, but early application is suggested. Director, Summer Session.

■ **ROLLINS COLLEGE**
  1000 Holt Avenue
  Winter Park, FL 32789
  (305) 646-2135

PROGRAM: Verano Español is a six-week undergraduate summer program. Students normally elect two courses from the five-course curriculum: language, Spanish art, business Spanish, contemporary Spanish society, and contemporary Spanish literature. Preorientation by a series of four newsletters.

ADMITTANCE REQUIREMENTS: Open to all students with four semesters of college-level Spanish or the equivalent.

TEACHING METHODS: Students are taught by native Spanish faculty. All courses are in Spanish. Trips to local historic sites and museums.

EVALUATION: Based on class work, papers, and a final examination by local faculty.

CREDITS OFFERED: Each course is 5 quarter hours or 3 1/3 semester hours.

HOUSING: All students live with local families.

DATES: June 15 through July 25.

COSTS: $1,995 includes tuition, room and board, local travel, and round-trip transportation from New York. Pocket money (estimated at $300) not included.

YEAR ESTABLISHED: 1960.

NUMBER OF STUDENTS IN 1985: 23.

APPLY: By March 15 (plus one month grace period). Edward E. Borsoi, Verano Español, Box #2702.

■ **SANTA BARBARA CITY COLLEGE**
   721 Cliff Drive
   Santa Barbara, CA 93109
   (805) 965-0581

PROGRAM: Semester in Spain is a spring undergraduate program concentrating on the Spanish language culture. Two- to five-day period of orientation on the SBCC campus.

ADMITTANCE REQUIREMENTS: Acceptable academic credentials plus 12 units of college credit including freshman-level Spanish.

TEACHING METHODS: Students attend regular classes taught by SBCC faculty members. Courses are supplemented with field trips to local museums and cultural and historic sites; some independent study.

EVALUATION: By class professors, based upon papers and periodic examinations. Students also complete evaluation forms upon completion of the program and comment on faculty, facilities, group leaders, and program in general.

CREDITS OFFERED: 15 to 16 semester hours.

HOUSING: Students live in dormitories.

DATES: Dates vary from year to year. Approximately from mid-January to mid-May.

COSTS: Approximately $2,600 including tuition, room and board, and local travel. Does not include round-trip transportation.

YEAR ESTABLISHED: 1987.

NUMBER OF STUDENTS IN 1987: Not available.

APPLY: By mid-November. Mr. John Romo, Dean of Instructional Services.

■ **SAINT LOUIS UNIVERSITY**
   221 North Grand Blvd.
   St. Louis, MO 63110
   (800) 325-6666

PROGRAM: Saint Louis University in Spain is a semester, full-year, or summer undergraduate program (with some graduate courses available in the summer) held on the university's own campus in Madrid. Courses cover art history, history, political science, theology, philosophy, Spanish literature, languages, sociology, computer science, natural science, and some business courses, and local field trips to museums and cultural sites. Each semester there are three trips to Spanish cities available at an extra cost. Two-week orientation in Madrid.

ADMITTANCE REQUIREMENTS: Sophomores and above with a 2.0 GPA. No language requirement. However, if planning to take courses taught in Spanish, you need four semesters of college Spanish. Recommendations from college dean and major professor.

TEACHING METHODS: Students attend special courses taught in English and Spanish by both U.S. and foreign faculty. All classes are integrated with local students.

EVALUATION: By both American and foreign faculty, based upon class work, papers, and examinations.

CREDITS OFFERED: Full semester year (follows Spanish educational system).

HOUSING: Students can live in University of Madrid dormitories or with local families.

DATES: Fall semester: September 1 to December 22; spring semester: January 7 to May 22; summer session: June 25 to July 25.

COSTS: For the full year: tuition $3,700; room and board approximately $2,700. Does not include round-trip transportation, local or trip-related travel, or personal expenses.

YEAR ESTABLISHED: 1969.

NUMBER OF STUDENTS IN 1985:   525.

APPLY: For fall by August 1; for spring by December 1; for summer by June 1. Office of Admissions.

■ **SKIDMORE COLLEGE**
  Saratoga Springs, NY 12866
  (518) 584-5000, ext. 2654

PROGRAM: Skidmore Junior Year in Spain offers undergraduates a choice of attending for a semester or the full academic year. The program is held in cooperation with the Universidad Autónoma de Madrid and offers a basic selection of liberal arts courses including: language, political science, economics, literature, history, studio art, history of art, linguistics, etc. At least two excursions outside of Madrid are included in the program, as well as special field experiences in the areas of a student's major. A preorientation session is conducted in both Madrid and Toledo.

ADMITTANCE REQUIREMENTS: Juniors or seniors with a 3.0 GPA and good academic standing plus advanced knowledge of Spanish.

TEACHING METHODS: Students attend regular classes at the Universidad Autónoma de Madrid as well as special discussion sections taught by local faculty specially hired for program participants. Courses are in Spanish, but tutors are available for those who need special help. Courses include onsite trips and field trips to banks, local businesses, museums, etc.

EVALUATION: By foreign faculty members and group leaders, based upon both periodic and final exams.

CREDITS OFFERED: Up to 16 semester hours for the academic year.

HOUSING: Students live in private homes or apartments.

DATES: Fall semester: September 10 through mid-December; spring semester: mid-January through May 25.

COSTS: Full academic year: $13,500 includes tuition, room and board, round-trip transportation, and all local travel (at least two excursions outside Madrid each semester). Scholarships available for Skidmore students only.

YEAR ESTABLISHED: 1969.

NUMBER OF STUDENTS IN 1985: 15.

APPLY: By February 15 for the fall term or full year; October 15 for the spring term. Dr. Lynne L. Gelber, Coordinator, Skidmore Junior Year Programs Abroad.

■ **STETSON UNIVERSITY**
Box #8412
DeLand, FL 32720
(904) 734-4121, ext. 211

PROGRAM: The Stetson University Abroad Program is held in cooperation with the University of Madrid with undergraduate courses concentrating on the Spanish language, literature, civilization, history, art, etc. Students can elect to attend for a single semester or the full academic year. Onsite presession orientation.

ADMITTANCE REQUIREMENTS: Completion of sophomore year (or 60 semester hours) plus two year of Spanish or the equivalent; language department recommendation.

TEACHING METHODS: Courses are conducted in Spanish by members of the faculty at the University of Madrid.

EVALUATION: Final examination given by local faculty.

CREDITS OFFERED: Upper-level semester credits vary depending upon course load.

HOUSING: Students live with local families.

DATES: Fall semester: September 1 through mid-December; spring semester: mid-January through May 31.

COSTS: $8,800 includes tuition, room and board, local travel, orientation, insurance, and international student I.D. card.

YEAR ESTABLISHED: 1964.

NUMBER OF STUDENTS IN 1985:   13.

APPLY: Fall semester only or full academic year: March 15; spring semester October 15. Office of International Exchange and Off-Campus Programs.

■ **TUFTS UNIVERSITY**
  Medford, MA 02155
  (617) 381-3152

PROGRAM: Tufts in Madrid is a full-year undergraduate program held in cooperation with the University of Madrid and the Universidad Autónoma de Madrid, located 15 kilometers from the center of the city. In addition to the wide range of university courses available, students take two special courses in Spanish language and civilization. Two-week orientation in Madrid.

ADMITTANCE REQUIREMENTS: Good academic standing, plus two years of college Spanish or the equivalent.

TEACHING METHODS: Classes, seminars and independent study projects; in Spanish.

EVALUATION: By Spanish professors from the universidad.

CREDITS OFFERED: 16 semester hours per semester.

HOUSING: Students must live with local families.

DATES: Fall semester: third week in September through mid-December; spring semester: early January through early May.

COSTS: $7,075 per semester covers tuition, room and board, round-trip transportation, and some local travel. Does not cover personal expenses.

YEAR ESTABLISHED: 1979.

NUMBER OF STUDENTS IN 1985:   30.

APPLY: By February 1 for fall semester and full-year program; October 15 for spring semester. Dean Christopher Gray, Director, Tufts Programs Abroad, Ballou Hall.

■ **UNIVERSITY OF SOUTHERN CALIFORNIA**
University Park
Los Angeles, CA 90089
(213) 746-2500

PROGRAM: USC Semester in Spain is a fall or spring undergraduate program concentrating on liberal arts and humanities with an emphasis on the Spanish language and culture. One-week orientation in Barcelona and three days in Madrid.

ADMITTANCE REQUIREMENTS: Sophomores and above in good academic standing with at least a semester of Spanish.

TEACHING METHODS: Courses are designed for the group and are taught in English by foreign faculty members. Americans are not integrated with local students.

EVALUATION: By course faculty member, based upon class work, papers and periodic examinations.

CREDITS OFFERED: 16 semester hours per semester.

HOUSING: Students live in apartments or with local families.

DATES: Fall semester: August 29 through December 16; spring semester: January 10 through May 11.

COSTS: Approximately: $5,800 covers tuition, room and board, program-related travel. Does not include round-trip transportation or personal expenses. Some work/study grants available.

YEAR ESTABLISHED: 1975.

NUMBER OF STUDENTS IN 1985: 136.

APPLY: For fall semester by April 1; spring semester by December 1.

■ **UNIVERSITY OF WISCONSIN – STEVENS POINT**
208 Old Main
Stevens Point, WI 54481
(715) 346-2717

PROGRAM: Semester in Spain is a fall undergraduate travel/study program. Although the majority of the program is held in Madrid, the group spends about a month traveling to Toledo, Avila, El Escorial, Granada, Cordoba, Seville, "and perhaps Valencia." Classes in Madrid are given through the Centre for International Studies and include art history, European history, political science, philosophy, business, economics, computer science, and language courses.

ADMITTANCE REQUIREMENTS: Sophomores and above in good academic standing. "Preference is given to students who have had Spanish 101 or its equivalent."

TEACHING METHODS: Students attend courses taught in English arranged for the group. Spanish language courses are offered.

EVALUATION: By instructors and group leaders, based upon class work, papers, and examinations.

CREDITS OFFERED: A minimum of 13 semester hours; maximum of 17.

HOUSING: Students stay in hostels while traveling and pensions or with families in Madrid.

DATES: Approximately, August 25 to December 23.

COSTS: Approximately $3,100 includes tuition, room and board, and round-trip transportation from Madison. Minnesota students pay a small "reciprocity fee"; non-Wisconsin residents pay a surcharge. Does not cover personal expenses.

YEAR ESTABLISHED: 1970.

NUMBER OF STUDENTS IN 1985: 19.

APPLY: "Early application is advised." Dr. Helen Cornell, Director, International Programs.

■ **VANDERBILT UNIVERSITY**
College of Arts & Sciences
Box #6327-B
Nashville, TN 37235
(615) 371-1224

PROGRAM: Vanderbilt in Spain is a single-semester, full-academic-year, or summer-session undergraduate program offered in cooperation with the Facultad de Filosofía y Letras of the University of Madrid. Courses cover intensive Spanish; phonology; Spanish history, literature, and art; Spain in Modern Europe; and independent study opportunities. Some weekend excursions.

ADMITTANCE REQUIREMENTS: 3.0 GPA and "sufficient knowledge of Spanish to pursue studies successfully."

TEACHING METHODS: Students attend special courses at the university designed for non-Spanish students. Classes are taught in Spanish.

EVALUATION: By course professors, based upon class work, papers, and examinations.

CREDITS OFFERED: From 12 to 18 semester hours per semester.

HOUSING: Students live with Spanish families, usually with another Vanderbilt student.

DATES: Fall semester: August 30 through December 18; spring semester: February 1 through June 6.

COSTS: $4,650 per semester includes tuition, room and board, and some program activities. Does not cover round-trip transportation or personal expenses (estimated at approximately $450 per semester). A $500 award is offered each year to a "worthy participant in the fall semester program."

YEAR ESTABLISHED: 1966.

NUMBER OF STUDENTS IN 1985:   35.

APPLY: By March 15 for fall semester; October 15 for spring semester. Overseas Office.

■ **WESLEYAN UNIVERSITY**
   300 High Street
   Middletown, CT 06457
   (203) 347-9411, ext. 2271

PROGRAM: The Vassar-Wesleyan-Colgate Program in Spain is a semester or full-year undergraduate program held in cooperation with Vassar and Colgate Colleges, in which students have the opportunity to attend classes at Madrid's Instituto Internacional. The humanities are highlighted, with an emphasis on Spanish life, language, and culture. Three-week orientation in Santiago de Compostela from August 3 through August 29.

ADMITTANCE REQUIREMENTS: 3.0 GPA and four semesters of college-level Spanish.

TEACHING METHODS: Courses are taught in Spanish by a foreign faculty. Local field trips and weekend excursions complement the program.

EVALUATION: By Spanish faculty, based upon periodic exams, papers, etc.

CREDITS OFFERED: A maximum of 15 semester hours per semester.

HOUSING: Students are assigned housing.

DATES: Fall semester: September 12 through December 17; spring semester: January 12 through May 17.

COSTS: $7,400 August through December; $6,700 January through May. Includes tuition and room and board. Does not include round-trip transportation or local travel not associated with the program.

YEAR ESTABLISHED: 1960.

NUMBER OF STUDENTS IN 1985: 55.

APPLY: For fall semester by March 30; spring semester by October 27. Vassar-Wesleyan-Colgate Program in Spain.

Salamanca

■ **AMERICAN INSTITUTE OF FOREIGN STUDY (AIFS)**
102 Greenwich Avenue
Greenwich, CT 06830
(800) 243-4567 or (203) 869-9090

PROGRAM: AIFS is a national for-profit organization specializing in comprehensive overseas academic-year, semester, and summer study programs. The AIFS program at the Universidad de Salamanca is a full-academic-year, fall- or spring-semester program. All AIFS students matriculate at the university. Those fluent in Spanish may enroll in virtually any course offered within the Facultades de Letras & Historias; others take courses designed especially for American students taught in Spanish and validated by the university. Courses cover Spanish (required), art history, economics, history, languages, literature, politics, and international marketing. Honors program also available for the full academic year only. Three-week orientation including intensive Spanish at Salamanca and a week in Andalusia.

ADMITTANCE REQUIREMENTS: College freshman and above as well as graduate students, with a 2.5 GPA, and two years high school or one year college Spanish (two years for honors program) or the equivalent.

TEACHING METHODS: Students take either special or regular courses at the university depending upon their proficiency in Spanish. All students must take a Spanish language course.

EVALUATION: By faculty, based upon class work, papers, and periodic examinations.

CREDITS OFFERED: A minimum of 15 semester hours per semester.

HOUSING: Students live with local families.

DATES: Fall semester: August 31 through January 27; spring semester: February 1 through May 30.

COSTS: $3,250 per semester. Includes tuition, room and board, program-related travel, and one-way transportation from New York. Does not cover local travel or personal expenses.

YEAR ESTABLISHED: 1973.

NUMBER OF STUDENTS IN 1986: 67.

APPLY: Applications filled on first-come basis. "It is expected that all full-year or fall-semester places will be filled by June 1; places for spring semester are kept open until November 15."

■ **COLBY COLLEGE**
Waterville, ME 04901
(207) 872-3168

PROGRAM: Colby in Salamanca is an undergraduate program held in cooperation with the Universidad de Salamanca. Students are permitted to enroll in or audit any course at the university but are encouraged to enroll in a special core curriculum of courses in art, history, literature, and social or political science. The program is designed as a full academic year, with full-year courses. Students who elect to remain for one semester will have their midyear grade count as the final semester grade. Four-week onsite orientation.

ADMITTANCE REQUIREMENTS: The program is generally limited to college juniors, however a limited number of sophomores or seniors may be admitted. Acceptable academic record and at least one course in college Spanish beyond the intermediate level.

TEACHING METHODS: All classes are in Spanish and conducted by members of the faculty at the Universidad de Salamanca. An advanced grammar and composition course is available to American students.

EVALUATION: By the faculty at the Universidad de Salamanca, based upon class work and periodic and final tests.

CREDITS OFFERED: 30 semester hours per year.

HOUSING: Students live in the university dormitories during orientation period and then can choose either to remain in the dormitories or to live with families in private homes during the academic year.

DATES: Academic year runs from October 1 to May 31 (exams are taken during the first week in June) with a midyear break in February.

COSTS: $8,300 includes tuition, room and board, round-trip transportation from New York, and local group excursions.

YEAR ESTABLISHED: 1984.

NUMBER OF STUDENTS IN 1985:   11.

APPLY: By April 1. Elizabeth C. Todrank, Foreign Study Coordinator.

■ **PENNSYLVANIA STATE UNIVERSITY**
Office of Education Abroad Programs
222 Boucke Building
University Park, PA 16802
(814) 865-7681

PROGRAM: Education Abroad at the University of Salamanca is a spring-semester undergraduate program with courses covering advanced oral Spanish, advanced written Spanish, culture and civilization of modern Spain, and Spanish art history. Orientation at Penn State.

ADMITTANCE REQUIREMENTS: Juniors and seniors with a 2.5 GPA, good academic standing, and "must show evidence of maturity, stability, adaptability, self-discipline and a strong academic motivation." A minimum of 15 semester hours in college Spanish or the equivalent.

TEACHING METHODS: Students take specially designed courses at the university taught in Spanish by university faculty members. Classes are not integrated with Spanish students.

EVALUATION: By course instructors, based upon class work, papers, and examinations.

CREDITS OFFERED: 15 semester hours.

HOUSING: Students live with families in Salamanca.

DATES: Mid-January through mid-May.

COSTS: Students pay the same as at the University Park Campus. 1986-87 tuition per semester was $2,250 for state residents; $5,150 for nonresidents; room and board: $2,750 per semester. Plus a $100 nonrefundable program fee.

YEAR ESTABLISHED: 1963.

NUMBER OF STUDENTS IN 1985: 17.

APPLY: By October 15.

■ **UNIVERSITY OF MONTANA**
Missoula, MT 59812
(406) 243-6800, ext. 5702

PROGRAM: The Spanish Program is a spring-semester undergraduate program that divides time between Salamanca and Madrid. Classes are held at the Colegio de España in Salamanca. Visits to museums and other cultural attractions are part of the program. On-campus orientation preceding quarter.

ADMITTANCE REQUIREMENTS: Sophomores or above, with acceptable academic record, two quarters college Spanish, plus recommendations.

TEACHING METHODS: Students are taught in English and Spanish by both U.S. and by local Spanish instructors. Onsite visits and field trips complement program.

EVALUATION: By local professors, based upon class work, papers, and examinations.

CREDITS OFFERED: Between 12 and 18 quarter hours depending on courses.

HOUSING: With local families.

DATES: Approximately early January to June.

COSTS: Approximately, $2,200 includes tuition, room and board, and course-related travel. Does not cover round-trip transportation or personal expenses.

YEAR ESTABLISHED: 1973.

NUMBER OF STUDENTS IN 1985: 15.

APPLY: By October 31. Dr. Anthony Beltramo, Liberal Arts Room #148.

■ **WESTERN ILLINOIS UNIVERSITY**
   Macomb, IL 61455
   (309) 298-1615

PROGRAM: The Western Illinois Salamanca Experience is a fall-semester undergraduate program held in cooperation with the Colegio de España. Students attend the colegio and select five courses from the school's curriculum. A six-day tour of Andulusia and four-day visit to Madrid are part of the program.

ADMITTANCE REQUIREMENTS: 2.5 GPA, good academic standing, and at least three years of high school or one year of college Spanish.

TEACHING METHODS: Courses are taught by the faculty at the Colegio de España. Field trips and independent study complement the program.

EVALUATION: By course instructors, based upon class work, papers, and examinations.

CREDITS OFFERED: 15 semester hours.

HOUSING: Students live with local families,

DATES: Approximately, September 5 through December 15.

COSTS: $2,555 per semester. Includes tuition, room and board, program-related travel, and round-trip transportation from Chicago. Does not cover personal expenses.

YEAR ESTABLISHED: 1984.

NUMBER OF STUDENTS IN 1985: 14.

APPLY: No application deadline. Dr. Scott Helwig, Dept. of Foreign Languages and Literature.

San Sebastián

■ **UNIVERSITY OF NEVADA – RENO**
University Studies in the Basque Country Consortium
Reno, NV 89557
(702) 784-4854

PROGRAM: University Studies in the Basque Country Consortium is a single-semester or full-academic-year undergraduate or graduate program held in cooperation with Boise State University, the University of Nevada-Las Vegas, and the Universidad del Pais Vasco (University of the Basque Country). Courses cover all levels of both the Spanish and Basque language, culture, and civilization; anthropology; cuisine; economics; folk dance; history; literature; music; political science; teacher education; and independent study. The program includes a week of travel within Spain, including a stay in Fuenterrabia. One-week orientation in Spain.

ADMITTANCE REQUIREMENTS: Sophomores and above in good academic standing with some knowledge of Spanish.

TEACHING METHODS: Students take special courses arranged for the group and taught in Spanish and English by the faculty at the University of the Basque Country.

EVALUATION: By Spanish faculty, based upon papers and examinations.

CREDITS OFFERED: Up to 30 semester hours per year; 16 graduate credits.

HOUSING: Students may elect to live in dormitories or with local families.

DATES: Approximately, fall semester: September 3 to December 16; spring semester; January 6 through May 20.

COSTS: $4,861 per semester includes tuition, program-related travel, and round-trip transportation. Does not cover room and board or personal travel or expenses.

YEAR ESTABLISHED: 1982.

NUMBER OF STUDENTS IN 1985: Not available.

APPLY: By May 15 for fall semester; December 1 for spring. Dr. Carmelo Urza, University Studies in the Basque Country Consortium, University of Nevada Library, Reno.

Seville

- *Seville is the most beautiful, romantic city I have ever seen. The best way to travel is by walking! However, be careful with your valuables. Seville, along with Barcelona, is one of the petty theft capitals of Spain.*

  - Harry Brigham, Chestnut Hill, Massachusetts

- *Be sure to wander around the narrow streets in the Santa Cruz area. Part of the fun is looking in at people's patios, and also getting lost. Don't worry, though, you can always look up and find the Giralda to regain your bearings.*

  - Ellen Leerburger, Scarsdale, New York

■ BROWARD COMMUNITY COLLEGE
International Education Institute
1000 Coconut Creek Boulevard
Coconut Creek, FL 33066
(305) 973-2206

PROGRAM: Semester in Spain is held in cooperation with the College Consortium for International Studies (CCIS) and the University of Seville. Courses include Spanish language, literature, history, government, and business administration. An equestrian studies program is also offered. Students with a proficiency in the language take courses taught in Spanish. A half-day orientation is available in Fort Lauderdale, Florida.

ADMITTANCE REQUIREMENTS: 2.5 GPA; no previous study of Spanish is required, as introductory Spanish is available.

TEACHING METHODS: Lectures, field trips, museum visits, and independent study.

EVALUATION: By foreign faculty, based upon periodic exams, oral participation, and final exams.

CREDITS OFFERED: 15 to 18 semester hours per term.

HOUSING: With local families or in "residencias."

DATES: Fall: September through December; Spring: January through May.

COSTS: Tuition: $1,000; room and board: approximately $1,000; travel to/from Seville: $700; estimated living expenses: $300. Local travel extra.

YEAR ESTABLISHED: 1979.

NUMBER OF STUDENTS IN 1985: 40.

APPLY: For Fall term by August 15; for spring term by December 1 to: Dr. William Greene, Director of International Education

■ **STATE UNIVERSITY OF NEW YORK AT NEW PALTZ**
New Paltz, NY 12561
(914) 257-2233

PROGRAM: The SUNY Seville Program is a single semester or full academic year undergraduate and graduate program held in cooperation with the University of Seville. The program's emphasis is on the Spanish language and culture. SUNY also offers an eight week summer session (6 credits) in Seville and Oviedo. One day orientation in New Paltz.

ADMITTANCE REQUIREMENTS: Juniors, seniors and graduate students in good academic standing with at least two year college-level Spanish or the equivalent.

TEACHING METHODS: Students take special courses taught in Spanish by a Spanish faculty. Includes lectures, intensive language courses and regional field trips to historic and cultural sites.

EVALUATION: By Spanish faculty, based upon periodic exams, finals and, depending on the level of the course, a term paper.

CREDITS OFFERED: A minimum of 12 and maximum of 18 semester hours per semester.

HOUSING: Students live in family-owned boarding houses or local apartments; some come unfurnished.

DATES: Fall semester: Approximately September 16 through January 24; Spring semester: Approximately January 15 through June 13.

COSTS: Fall semester: $1,605; spring semester: $1,750 includes tuition, room and board, and program-related field trips. Non-state residents add approximately $925 per semester. Does not cover round-trip transportation and personal expenses estimated at approximately $400 per semester.

YEAR ESTABLISHED: 1969.

NUMBER OF STUDENTS IN 1985: 25.

APPLY: For fall semester and academic year by April 1; spring semester by November 1. Dr. Rudolf R. Kossmann, Director, Office of International Education.

- **SWEET BRAIR COLLEGE**
  Sweet Briar, VA 24595
  (804) 381-6295

PROGRAM: Sweet Briar College's Junior Year in Spain is a single semester or full year program held in cooperation with the University of Seville. Special courses for American students are given in: language, history, international relations, geography, economics, political science, Latin American studies, anthropology, and art history. For other fields of study, students can take regular courses at the University of Seville. A month long onsite orientation consists of conversation and composition classes, usually two or three excursions (Granada, Cordoba, Rhonda, etc.), and lectures presented by faculty members from the university, curators from museums or historical sites.

ADMITTANCE REQUIREMENTS: For college juniors or first semester seniors with at least two years of college Spanish (one course beyond the intermediate level), a 3.0 GPA. in college Spanish and a general average of 2.85, recommendation by department chairman and college dean.

TEACHING METHODS: Students have three options: take special courses for "foreign students" taught by the faculty at the University of Seville; enroll in regular university courses, thus allowing American students the opportunity to integrate with Spanish students; or a combination of both. All lectures are in Spanish.

EVALUATION: Depends upon the course and options chosen. A mid-term exam may be given, but generally there is only a final. Tutorials are provided for students enrolled in regular University of Seville courses.

CREDITS OFFERED: Five units per semester; nine for the full year program.

HOUSING: Students usually live in private houses with local families or widows. If available, men enrolled for the year have the option of living in a residencia.

DATES: Fall semester: September 2 through January 2; spring semester: January 31 through May 31.

COSTS: $5,500 per semester; $8,200 for the full academic year. Includes tuition, room and board, and excursions during orientation. Does not include round-trip transportation, and additional living expenses estimated at approximately $100 per month.

YEAR ESTABLISHED: 1983.

NUMBER OF STUDENTS IN 1985: 13.

APPLY: Fall and full year program by March 15; spring semester by October 15. Professor Antonia Taylor, Director, Junior Year in Spain.

■ **TRINITY CHRISTIAN COLLEGE**
2065 Laraway Lake Drive
Grand Rapids, MI 49506
(616) 949-3051

PROGRAM: Semester in Spain is a single-semester undergraduate program that concentrates exclusively on the Spanish language. Courses cover grammar, composition, and conversation. Some travel to regional sites, museums, etc. One-day orientation in Seville.

ADMITTANCE REQUIREMENTS: 2.0 GPA and good academic standing.

TEACHING METHODS: A dozen instructors, most of whom are Spanish, use the tutorial method in small classes.

EVALUATION: By instructors, based upon periodic and final exams.

CREDITS OFFERED: 16 semester hours.

HOUSING: Students live with local families.

DATES: Approximately, fall semester: September 1 to December 20; spring semester: February 1 to June 1.

COSTS: $3,670 includes tuition, room and board, round-trip transportation from Detroit, program-related travel.

YEAR ESTABLISHED: 1978.

NUMBER OF STUDENTS IN 1985: 133.

APPLY: Fall semester by August 1; spring semester by January 3. Semester in Spain.

■ **UNIVERSITY OF WISCONSIN – PLATTEVILLE**
Institute for Study Abroad Programs
1 University Plaza
Platteville, WI 53818
(608) 342-1726

PROGRAM: The Seville Study Center is a semester or full year undergraduate program held in cooperation with the Spanish-American Institute of International Education. The emphasis is on liberal arts with courses on the Spanish language, art, history, government and culture; economics and business administration; sociology; and special courses devoted to equestrian studies. Four field trips are included in the program with optional travel opportunities offered weekly. Orientation in Seville.

ADMITTANCE REQUIREMENTS: Sophomore or above with a 2.5 GPA. Fluency in Spanish is not required.

TEACHING METHODS: Students take courses specially designed for American students and taught in English by an American and Spanish faculty. The Spanish-American Institute also accepts students who are taught in Spanish and integrated directly into regular classes.

EVALUATION: By course faculty, based upon class work, papers, and examinations.

CREDITS OFFERED: 15 semester hours per semester.

HOUSING: All students live with "carefully-screened" Spanish families.

DATES: Fall semester: September 2 through December 12; spring semester: January 13 through May 22.

COSTS: $2,495 per semester (Wisconsin and Minnesota residents); $2,795 (nonresidents). Includes tuition, room and board, and program-related field trips. Does not cover round-trip transportation or personal expenses, estimated at about $200 a month.

YEAR ESTABLISHED: 1984.

NUMBER OF STUDENTS IN 1985: 80.

APPLY: Fall semester by April 30; spring semester by December 1. Institute for Study Abroad Programs, 308 Warner Hall.

Toledo

■ **UNIVERSITY OF MINNESOTA**
Extension Classes Offices of Study Abroad
202 Wesbrook Hall
77 Pleasant Street SE
Minneapolis, MN 55455
(612) 373-1855

PROGRAM: The International Program in Toledo is a semester, full-year or summer program cosponsored by the José Ortega y Gasset Foundation and is open to both undergraduate and graduate students. Courses cover anthropology and archaeology, art history, economics, geography, history, interdisciplinary studies, culture, linguistics, literature, political science, and the Spanish language. A two-week field trip to southern Spain is scheduled every semester.

ADMITTANCE REQUIREMENTS: Students in good academic standing (no established GPA required) with two years of previous language or coursework or the equivalent.

TEACHING METHODS: Students are taught by both U.S. and foreign faculty in groups consisting only of other Americans. With the exception of the English language courses, all courses are taught in English and require two years of college English.

EVALUATION: By course instructors, based upon class work, papers, and final examination.

CREDITS OFFERED: 12 to 14 quarter credits each period.

HOUSING: Students choose between living with a local family or at the San Juan de la Penitencia Residence, a renovated sixteenth-century convent.

DATES: Fall semester: September 7 to December 14; spring semester: January 18 to May 9; summer program: June 15 to July 27.

COSTS: $3,725 per semester; $1,450 for summer program. Includes tuition, room and board, and program-related travel. Does not include round-trip transportation or personal expenses. The José Ortega y Gasset Foundation offers a $500 academic scholarship and work/study grants.

YEAR ESTABLISHED: 1982.

NUMBER OF STUDENTS IN 1985: 120.

APPLY: For fall semester by July 15; spring semester by December 1; summer program by April 15. Jody Jensen, ECOSA.

SWEDEN

Population: 8,361,000   **Capital:** Stockholm   **Language:** Swedish
Monetary Unit: Swedish krona   **Government:** Constitutional monarchy (king and prime minister)   **Religion:** 90% Church of Sweden
Households With Television: 22%

SELECTED COLLEGES AND UNIVERSITIES

University of Stockholm
106 91 Stockholm
Some courses in English.

Uppsala University
P.O. Box #256
751 05 Uppsala
Some courses in English.

FURTHER INFORMATION

Consulate General of Sweden
825 Third Avenue
New York, NY 10022
(212) 751-5900

Embassy of Sweden
600 New Hampshire Avenue, NW
Suite 1200
Washington, DC 20037
(202) 944-5600

Swedish Information Service
825 Third Avenue
New York, NY 10022
(212) 751-5900
Publishes Studying in Sweden.

Lund

■ **COLLEGE CONSORTIUM FOR INTERNATIONAL STUDIES (CCIS)**
866 United Nations Plaza, Room 511
New York, NY 10017
(212) 308-1556

PROGRAM: CCIS is a nonprofit organization that sponsors and organizes several dozen foreign study programs for member colleges that grant degree credit. The Lund program is a single-semester or full-academic-year undergraduate program held in cooperation with Kingsborough Community College (New York) and the University of Lund. Fall courses cover the Swedish language, society, and culture (required) with internships in: international marketing, preschool education, recreation, and rehabilitation. Spring courses cover: Swedish, architecture, ecology, economy, political science, Scandinavian fine arts, social sciences, social welfare, and urban planning.

ADMITTANCE REQUIREMENTS: Freshman, sophomores, and juniors with a 2.5 GPA and acceptable academic credentials; knowledge of Swedish is helpful.

TEACHING METHODS: Students attend classes at the University of Lund with Swedish students.

EVALUATION: By course instructors and project leaders.

CREDITS OFFERED: 12 to 15 semester hours per semester.

HOUSING: Students live in university dormitories.

DATES: Fall semester: September 1 through December 17; spring semester: February 1 through May 29.

COSTS: $1,685 per semester. Does not include room and board, program-related travel, round-trip transportation, or personal expenses.

YEAR ESTABLISHED: Not available.

NUMBER OF STUDENTS IN 1985: Not available.

APPLY: Fall semester by June 1; spring semester by October 1.

Uppsala

■ **THE CALIFORNIA STATE UNIVERSITY**
400 Golden Shore
Long Beach, CA 90802
(213) 590-5655

PROGRAM: The CSU International Program in Sweden, held at Uppsala University, is a full-academic-year undergraduate and graduate opportunity to study at Sweden's oldest university. Participating students elect courses from five overall curriculum options: biochemistry, international communication studies, fresh-water ecology, international development studies, and Soviet and East European studies. Six-week language presession in Sigtuna.

ADMITTANCE REQUIREMENTS: Must be enrolled at a CSU campus. Juniors and above, including graduate students, with a 2.75 GPA.

TEACHING METHODS: Students take a combination of regular academic courses taught mostly in English with some Swedish lectures later in the program.

EVALUATION: By foreign faculty and CSU resident director, based upon periodic and final examinations.

CREDITS OFFERED: 30 semester hours per year or 45 quarter units.

HOUSING: In dormitories and private apartments.

DATES: Approximately, July 18 through June 6.

COSTS: Tuition: $0 (residents); $3,600 (nonresidents); room and board: $3,200. Does not include round-trip transportation or personal expenses (estimated at approximately $3,615 per year).

YEAR ESTABLISHED: 1964.

NUMBER OF STUDENTS IN 1985: 28.

APPLY: By February 1. Dr. Kibbey M. Horne, Director of International Programs.

Växjö

■ **UNIVERSITY OF MINNESOTA**
Extension Classes Offices of Study Abroad
202 Wesbrook Hall
77 Pleasant Street SE
Minneapolis, MN 55455
(612) 373-1855

PROGRAM: Swedish in Växjö is a spring-quarter opportunity to study the Swedish language and culture and to explore the roots of Swedish emigration. Courses cover the Swedish language, Sweden today, and Swedish emigration.

ADMITTANCE REQUIREMENTS: Students in good academic standing; no established GPA required.

TEACHING METHODS: Students are taught by both U.S. and foreign faculty in groups consisting only of other Americans.

EVALUATION: By course instructors, based upon class work, papers, and final examination.

CREDITS OFFERED: 12 to 13 quarter credits.

HOUSING: Students live with Swedish families.

DATES: April 1 through June 8.

COSTS: $2,407 includes tuition for four courses and room and board (two meals a day). Does not include round-trip transportation or personal expenses.

YEAR ESTABLISHED: 1984.

NUMBER OF STUDENTS IN 1985: 20.

APPLY: February 15. Jody Jensen, ECOSA.

SWITZERLAND

Population: 6,556,000   **Capital:** Bern   **Language:** French, German, and Italian
Monetary Unit: Swiss franc   **Government:** Federal state (president)
Religion: 48% Roman Catholic; 44% Protestant   **Households with Television:** 22%

SELECTED COLLEGES AND UNIVERSITIES

University of Geneva
19, Place des Augustins
1205 Geneva

University of Lausanne
1015 Lausanne

FURTHER INFORMATION

Consulate General of Switzerland
444 Madison Avenue
New York, NY 10022
(212) 728-2560

Embassy of Switzerland·
2900 Cathedral Avenue, NW
Washington, DC 20008
(202) 745-7900

Swiss National Tourist Office
608 Fifth Avenue
New York, NY 10020
(212) 757-5944

Office Central Universitaire Suisse
Sophienstrasse 2,
8032 Zurich
Publishes Universites en Suisse,
un petit Guide.

Fribourg

■ **PROVIDENCE COLLEGE**
Providence, RI 02918
(401) 865-2114

PROGRAM: In consortium with LaSalle University of Philadelphia, Providence College is recognized by the University of Fribourg as a partner in the American College Program and listed in Fribourg's catalogue. Students take the same courses that European students take; basically a liberal arts curriculum. A three-session orientation program at Providence College is followed by a two-week onsite orientation.

ADMITTANCE REQUIREMENTS: College juniors with a 3.0 GPA, intermediate level French or German, and permission of major advisor or dean of college.

TEACHING METHODS: Students take regular courses at the university and also within the American College Program, taught by both U.S. and foreign faculty. Courses are offered in both French and German with a limited number of courses in English.

EVALUATION: By foreign faculty, based upon class work and final exams.

CREDITS OFFERED: 15 semester hours per semester; 30 credits per year.

HOUSING: Students have their own furnished rooms in private homes.

DATES: Approximately September 25 through July 1.

COSTS: $5,500 per year including tuition, housing, and round-trip air fare. Does not include meals (estimated at $300 per month) or personal expenses such as local travel, etc. (estimated at $1,500 for the ten-month program).

YEAR ESTABLISHED: 1960.

NUMBER OF STUDENTS IN 1985: 65.

APPLY: By March 31. James F. Flanagan, Director, Providence-in-Europe.

Geneva

■ **COLGATE UNIVERSITY**
Hamilton, NY 13346
(315) 824-1000

PROGRAM: The Geneva Study Group is a single-semester undergraduate program that offers courses in the French language, philosophy, political science, and history. Internships with international organizations are optional. Field trip to Belgium, France, and central Switzerland. Orientation in the U.S.

ADMITTANCE REQUIREMENTS: Sophomores and above in good academic standing. Colgate students are shown a preference, but others accepted. One year of college French or the equivalent and one course in international relations.

TEACHING METHODS: Students attend special courses arranged for the group and taught in English by both U.S. and Swiss French faculty.

EVALUATION: By course professors, based upon papers and examinations.

CREDITS OFFERED: 16 semester hours.

HOUSING: Students live in dormitories or with local families.

DATES: Approximately, early September through mid-December.

COSTS: $6,500 includes tuition, housing, round-trip transportation, and program-related travel. Does not cover meals or personal expenses.

YEAR ESTABLISHED: 1978.

NUMBER OF STUDENTS IN 1985:   20.

APPLY: By February 10. Professor Roland Blum, Department of Philosophy.

■ **SMITH COLLEGE**
   Northampton, MA 01063
   (413) 584-2700

PROGRAM: Smith College Junior Year in Geneva, one of the oldest foreign study programs, is a full-academic-year undergraduate program held in cooperation with the University of Geneva and offering courses in intermediate and advanced French language and literature, art history, economics, history, international law and relations, psychology, religion, and political science. Five-week orientation in Paris.

ADMITTANCE REQUIREMENTS: Juniors with a 3.0 GPA and two years of college French or the equivalent.

TEACHING METHODS: All instruction is in French. Students attend special courses arranged for the group and taught by both U.S. and foreign faculty or may attend regular courses at the University of Geneva.

EVALUATION: By course faculty, based upon papers and final examinations.

CREDITS OFFERED: 32 semester hours per year.

HOUSING: Students live in university dormitories.

DATES: Fall semester: September 5 through mid-December; spring semester: late January through July 15.

COSTS: $11,600 per year includes tuition. Does not include round-trip transportation, local travel, room and board, or personal expenses.

YEAR ESTABLISHED: 1946.

NUMBER OF STUDENTS IN 1985:   29.

APPLY: By February 1. Patricia C. Olmsted, Committee on Study Abroad, Extension 4920.

Lugano

■ **COLLEGE CONSORTIUM FOR INTERNATIONAL STUDIES (CCIS)**
866 United Nations Plaza, Room 511
New York, NY 10017
(212) 308-1556

PROGRAM: CCIS is a nonprofit organization that sponsors and organizes several dozen foreign study programs for member colleges who grant degree credit. The Lugano program is a single-semester or full-academic-year undergraduate program held in cooperation with Westchester Community College (New York) and Franklin College (Lugano). Courses cover all levels of French, German, and Italian, as well as broad liberal arts and humanities courses emphasizing European studies. Orientation in Switzerland. Two-week program-related travel in Europe with an optional spring trip to the Soviet Union.

ADMITTANCE REQUIREMENTS: Freshman, sophomores, and juniors with a 2.5 GPA and acceptable academic credentials. No language requirement.

TEACHING METHODS: Students take courses, mostly in English, taught by the faculty of Franklin College.

EVALUATION: By course instructors.

CREDITS OFFERED: 12 to 15 semester hours per semester.

HOUSING: Students live in local furnished apartments.

DATES: Fall semester: late August through mid-December; spring semester: mid-January through mid-May.

COSTS: $3,500 per semester. Does not include room and board, program-related travel, round-trip transportation, or personal expenses.

YEAR ESTABLISHED: Not available.

NUMBER OF STUDENTS IN 1985: Not available.

APPLY: Fall semester by August 1; spring semester by December 15.

Zurich

■ **THE EXPERIMENT IN INTERNATIONAL LIVING**
Kipling Road
Brattleboro, VT 05301
(800) 451-4465

PROGRAM: The College Semester Abroad Program is designed to allow under-graduate students to become immersed in a foreign culture by living with a local family and exploring individual personal and educational interests under professional guidance. Students on the Switzerland program spend most of their stay in Zurich, however, part of the semester is spent at a location appropriate to a field study project. The final week is spent evaluating the program in Ticino. Courses cover: intensive language study, seminar on Swiss life and culture, history and politics, geography and economics, arts and humanities, social anthropology, methods and techniques of field work, and an independent study project. One-week orientation in Zurich.

ADMITTANCE REQUIREMENTS: Sophomore standing or above and acceptable academic credentials. No language requirement.

TEACHING METHODS: Students work directly with their American instructor-advisors in planning and evaluating their individual program. Nonlanguage courses are in English. "The semester builds from the more structured language training and lectures and discussions on local life and culture to the independent study project."

EVALUATION: By individual students and their instructor-advisors, based on independent project, papers, reports, and examinations. Periodic meetings during the program and for several days at the conclusion.

CREDITS OFFERED: 16 semester hours.

HOUSING: Students live as family members with their host families.

DATES: Approximately, fall semester: September through December; spring semester: January through May.

COSTS: $6,300 includes tuition, room and board, all fees and local travel, and round-trip transportation from Brattleboro, Vermont.

YEAR ESTABLISHED: 1985.

NUMBER OF STUDENTS IN 1985: 13.

APPLY: For fall semester by May 15; spring semester by November 15. Admissions Office, College Semester Abroad.

THE UNITED KINGDOM
England

Population: 47,111,700   **Capital:** London   **Language:** English
Monetary Unit: Pound sterling   **Government:** Constitutional monarchy
(British monarch and prime minister)   **Religion:** 57% Anglican
Households With Television: 97%

SELECTED SCHOOLS AND UNIVERSITIES

City of London Polytechnic
117 Houndsditch
London EC3A 7BU
Offers special business studies courses for foreigners.

London School of Economics and Political Science
Houghton Street
London WC2 2AE
Both graduate and undergraduate programs.

University of Bath
Claverton Down
Bath BA2 7AY

University of Birmingham
PO Box 363
Birmingham B15 2TT
Strong graduate programs in science and technology and education.

University of Bristol
Senate House
Bristol BS8 1TH

University of Cambridge
The Old Schools
Cambridge CB2 1TT

University of Essex
Wivenhoe Park
Colchester CO4 3SQ

University of Exeter
Northcote House
The Queens Drive
Exeter EX4 4QJ

University of Leeds
Leeds LS 9JT

University of London
Senate House, Malet Street
London WC1E 7HU
Offers broad curriculum in both sciences and social sciences.

University of Manchester
Oxford Road
Manchester M13 9PI

University of Oxford
Wellington Square
Oxford OX1 2JD

University of York
Heslington, York YO1 5DD

University of Sussex
Sussex House, Falmer
Brighton BN1 9RH

*Special graduate program in
Development Studies.*

FURTHER INFORMATION

British Information Services
845 Third Avenue
New York, NY 10022
(212) 752-8440

British Council
10 Spring Gardens
London SW1A 2BN

Publishes Higher Education in the
United Kingdom.

Consulate General of the
United Kingdom
845 Third Avenue
New York, NY 10022
(212) 752-8400

Universities Central Council
on Admissions
PO Box 28
Cheltenham, Glos GX50 1HY

Publishes excellent free guide, How to
Apply for Admissions to a University.

Embassy of the United Kingdom
3100 Massachusetts Avenue
Washington, DC 20008
(202) 462-1340

Central Bureau for Educational
Visits and Exchanges
43 Dorset Street,
Seymour Mews House
London WC1E 7B2

British Tourist Office
680 Fifth Avenue
New York, NY 10019
(212) 581-4700

*Publications are primarily for British
students, but are also helpful to
Americans.*

- *A BritRail Youth Pass is a must; gets you everywhere for cheap. However, the American Youth Hostel card is a waste of $20. There are thousands of hostels not included in the AYH association that are better with fewer boisterous Americans. Lyme Regis and Glastonberry are a definite must to visit.*

  - Margaret M. Silver, Brooklyn, New York

- *The people are not like Americans. Just because the same language is being spoken many people take it for granted that the British customs and lifestyle are the same as in America. There will be similarities, but openness to new experience is the best attitude to have.*

  - Marian L. Pollock, Greensboro, North Carolina

- *You can always expect to have many adventures while studying and traveling in England. Always try to travel extensively and make the best of your year abroad.*

  - Laurance Tolliver, Washington, D.C.

More Than One City

■ **LAKE ERIE COLLEGE**
Painesville, OH 44077
(216) 352-3361

PROGRAM: Lake Erie's tour of British Equestrian Centers is one of the few foreign-study programs that features equestrian studies. The program is open to undergraduates, graduates, or professionals. Students visit sites in Aston Park, Moat House, Yorkshire, Waterstock, and Wellington, and study dressage, combined training, stadium jumping, or independent study projects. Internships available.

ADMITTANCE REQUIREMENTS: Any "student" with a serious interest in horsemanship.

TEACHING METHODS: Courses are taught by local British faculty and include lectures, demonstrations, and individual instruction.

CREDITS OFFERED: College credit is available.

HOUSING: Students live with local families or in local onsite cottages.

DATES: September through mid-May. Student may enroll for a single semester, a "British" term, or the full academic year.

COSTS: Vary from $2,900 to $7,300 depending upon duration and options selected. Includes tuition and room and board. Does not include round-trip transportation or personal expenses.

YEAR ESTABLISHED: 1973.

NUMBER OF STUDENTS IN 1985: Not available.

APPLY: 60 days prior to start of semester or term. Dr. Egidio Lunardi, ext. 370.

■ **MARYMOUNT COLLEGE**
Tarrytown, NY 10591
(914) 631-3200, ext. 222

PROGRAM: Marymount College Study Abroad Program is a broad and varied opportunity to study for either a semester or the full year at one or more of several schools in the United Kingdom. The program is held in cooperation with City University (London), Kings College (London), London School of Economics, Middlesex Polytechnic, Polytechnic of Central London, Queen Elizabeth College, Queen Mary College, University College, London College of Fashion, London College of Furniture, University of Essex, University of Kent at Canterbury, University of Lancaster, University of St. Andrews, and the University of York. In addition to the full range of arts and science courses offered at the various universities and polytechnic institutes, Marymount also offers a drama program taught by staff from the Royal Academy of the Dramatic Arts and the London Academy of Music and Dramatic Arts. One or two weekend trips are offered each semester with a longer trip (usually to the Soviet Union) available over the major holiday. Also offered is an internship program in London, Paris, and Bonn held in cooperation with the European Parliament. A preorientation of five days in London is required (one evening at Marymount is optional). Two weeks of intensive language training is given in Paris and Bonn to those in the internship program.

ADMITTANCE REQUIREMENTS: Open to juniors and seniors with a 3.0 GPA or better, plus permission of a dean and department chairman. The internships in Paris and Bonn require language proficiency.

TEACHING METHODS: With the exception of the drama and internship programs, students attend regular courses at the foreign institution, fully integrated with foreign students. The drama program is also staffed by foreign faculty members. Under the internship program, students work in a foreign agency or firm and take courses taught by the foreign faculty.

EVALUATION: Varies with each program. Usually papers and examinations given by foreign faculty.

CREDITS OFFERED: 15 to 16 semester hours per semester.

HOUSING: Students may elect to live in university dormitories, Marymount housing, or with local families.

DATES: Vary from college to college. Usually the fall semester runs from mid-September through mid-December; the spring semester from mid-January to early June.

COSTS: Vary from $4,300 to $5,050 per semester including travel to and from Europe, tuition, room and board. Weekend trips are partially subsidized by the college; the Soviet trip costs about $400. Financial aid available in terms of Pell grants, regent scholarships, etc.

YEAR ESTABLISHED: 1924.

NUMBER OF STUDENTS IN 1985: 189.

APPLY: By January 15 for the fall semester; October 1 for the spring semester. Gloria Kenny, Campus Study Abroad Director.

■ **UNIVERSITY OF KANSAS**
  Lawrence, KA 66045
  (913) 864-3742

PROGRAM: The University of Kansas offers programs for a semester or the full academic year at the Universities of Essex, Exeter, Hull and Reading (England); St. Andrews, Stirling and Strathclyde-Glasgow (Scotland) (fall option only); and Aberystwth (Wales). Students enroll in regular course work along with British students.

ADMITTANCE REQUIREMENTS: Juniors and above with a minimum of 60 semester hours, 3.0 GPA, plus recommendations. Initial selection made by Kansas University; final selection is made by British universities.

TEACHING METHODS: Students take regular classes at the universities taught by local instructors.

EVALUATION: By local professors, based upon class work, papers, and examinations.

CREDITS OFFERED: 30 to 36 semester hours per year.

HOUSING: Students live in university residence halls or flats on campus.

DATES: Approximately, fall semester: mid-September through December; spring semester: January through June.

COSTS: Approximately—Essex: $6,100; Exeter: $5,900; Reading: $6,500; St. Andrews: $8,910 (sciences), $7,350 (arts); Stirling: $6,950; Strathclyde: $5,750 (arts), $6,800 (sciences). Includes annual tuition and room and board (Essex cost excludes food). Does not cover round-trip transportation, local travel, or personal expenses.

APPLY: By February 25. Office of Study Abroad, 203 Lippincott.

Arundel

■ **NEW ENGLAND COLLEGE**
Henniker, NH 03242
(603) 428-2211

PROGRAM: New England College operates a branch campus in an eighteenth-century manor house near Duke of Norfolk Castle 55 miles southeast of London. The program is primarily for undergraduates, but a limited number of graduate courses in education are offered. Students can attend for a semester of a full four-year program. Courses include: art, biology, communications, computer science, economics, elementary education, engineering, environmental sciences, geology, history, mathematics, philosophy, physical education, psychology, public administration, sociology, and theater.

ADMITTANCE REQUIREMENTS: The same admission standards as New England College. Students from other schools can take courses for transfer credit with a 2.0 GPA. No foreign language requirement.

TEACHING METHODS: Students take a full load of five courses taught by English and visiting American faculty. Classes are multinational with approximately half non-Americans. Small lecture classes, field trips, and labs.

EVALUATION: By attending professors, based upon class work, papers and exams.

CREDITS OFFERED: Each course is a 3-semester-hour course; labs are 4 semester hours.

HOUSING: Students can elect to live in dormitories, local flats, or room and board establishments.

DATES: Fall semester: August 28 through December 20; spring semester: January 11 through May 8; summer term: May 18 through July 26.

COSTS: Tuition: $7,110 for full year; room and board: $3,250 for full year. Does not include round-trip transportation. Estimated living expenses $1,000 per year. Some financial aid available.

YEAR ESTABLISHED: 1971.

NUMBER OF STUDENTS IN 1985: 250.

APPLY: Rolling admissions. R. W. Phalunas, Director of Admissions.

Bradford

■ **THE CALIFORNIA STATE UNIVERSITY**
400 Golden Shore
Long Beach, CA 90802
(213) 590-5655

PROGRAM: The CSU International Program in England, held at the recently founded (1966) University of Bradford, is a full-academic-year undergraduate and graduate opportunity to study in a moderate-sized industrial city in the north of England. Of the 5,000 students attending the university, some 70 percent are enrolled in scientific or technical subjects. Americans, however, take courses in five subject areas: economics, geography, history, literature, and politics. One-week onsite orientation.

ADMITTANCE REQUIREMENTS: Must be enrolled at a CSU campus. Juniors and above, including graduate students, with a 3.0 GPA.

TEACHING METHODS: Students take a combination of regular academic courses supplemented with program-sponsored courses, taught by foreign faculty.

EVALUATION: By foreign faculty and CSU resident director, based upon periodic and final examinations.

CREDITS OFFERED: 30 semester hours per year or 45 quarter units.

HOUSING: In dormitories and private apartments.

DATES: Approximately, September 26 through June 27.

COSTS: Tuition: $0 (residents); $3,600 (nonresidents); room and board: $1,850. Does not include round-trip transportation or living expenses (estimated at $2,130 per year).

YEAR ESTABLISHED: 1969.

NUMBER OF STUDENTS IN 1985: 22.

APPLY: By February 1. Dr. Kibbey M. Horne, Director of International Programs.

Bristol

■ **BEAVER COLLEGE**
Glenside, PA 19038
(215) 572-2901

PROGRAM: British University Year at the University of Bristol is a full-academic-year program in which students are fully integrated into regular classes at the university. Courses cover the regular university scope with an emphasis on the humanities, natural and social sciences, law, English, and drama. Orientation in London.

ADMITTANCE REQUIREMENTS: Juniors and seniors with a 3.0 GPA; if a student plans to continue courses at Bristol beyond the single academic year or if drama or English specialties are elected, a higher GPA is required.

TEACHING METHODS: Students take regular courses, seminars, and tutorials taught by University of Bristol professors.

EVALUATION: By Bristol faculty, based upon class work and periodic examinations.

CREDITS OFFERED: 30 to 33 semester hours per year.

HOUSING: Students live in university dormitories and student residences.

DATES: The academic year runs from mid-September to late June.

COSTS: $7,815 per year includes tuition, room, transportation to London, and program-related travel. Does not cover meals, return transportation, or personal expenses.

YEAR ESTABLISHED: 1974.

NUMBER OF STUDENTS IN 1985: 15.

APPLY: March 20. Center for Education Abroad.

Cambridge

■ **AMERICAN INSTITUTE OF FOREIGN STUDY (AIFS)**
102 Greenwich Avenue
Greenwich, CT 06830
(800) 243-4567 or (203) 869-9090

PROGRAM: AIFS is a national, for-profit organization specializing in comprehensive overseas academic year, semester, and summer study programs.
The AIFS program at Cambridge University's Homerton College enables
students to take either a four-year undergraduate course leading to the
Bachelor of Education degree of the University of Cambridge; a single-year
liberal arts or education undergraduate course of study; or, a one-year
graduate course designed to provide teaching qualifications for holders of
degrees in arts or sciences. Courses cover biological sciences, chemistry,
drama, education, English literature, fine arts, geography, history, mathematics, music, physics, and religious studies.

ADMITTANCE REQUIREMENTS: Full-year students only. Freshman must
have a minimum average combined CEEB mathematics and verbal SAT
scores of 600. Others, a 3.2 GPA.

TEACHING METHODS: Americans are fully integrated with British students and take regular courses at Homerton College including "a personal-
ized form of individual teaching for each student given by the Fellows and
Lecturers of the College."

EVALUATION: By Homerton College faculty, based upon class work, papers,
and periodic examinations.

CREDITS OFFERED: AIFS students normally obtain about 34 credit hours
each year.

HOUSING: Students live in residence halls at the college and are provided
twelve meals each week.

DATES: Fall term: September 25 through December 11; winter term: January 12 through March 21; spring term: April 21 through June 24.

COSTS: $9,950 includes tuition, room and some board, and one-way trans-
portation from New York. Does not cover local travel or personal expenses.

YEAR ESTABLISHED: 1978.

NUMBER OF STUDENTS IN 1985:   20.

APPLY: By July 15.

■ **COLLEGE OF WILLIAM AND MARY**
  Office of International Studies
  Williamsburg, VA 23185
  (804) 253-4354

PROGRAM: William and Mary Summer in Cambridge is held in cooperation with Christ's College, Cambridge University. The summer session presents a six-week program in a varied curriculum that alternates each summer. It usually includes English literature, government, and economics. Travel to local historic and cultural sites is part of the program.

ADMITTANCE REQUIREMENTS: Open to all undergraduates who hold good academic standing at their home institution.

TEACHING METHODS: Regular courses are taught by a U.S. faculty with British guest lecturers. Seminar-sized classes. Both class and onsite lectures, seminars.

EVALUATION: By faculty, based upon papers, periodic tests, and a final examination.

CREDITS OFFERED: Six semester hours.

HOUSING: Students live in single rooms at Christ's College dormitories.

DATES: Approximately July 1 through August 10.

COSTS: Tuition, room and board: $2,100; estimated living expenses: $450. Round-trip transportation not included. Scholarships available to William and Mary students.

YEAR ESTABLISHED: 1974.

NUMBER OF STUDENTS IN 1985: 40.

APPLY: By March 1. Ms. Carolyn V. Blackwell, Director.

■ **HIRAM COLLEGE**
Hiram, OH 44234
(216) 569-5160

PROGRAM: Hiram offers two programs in Cambridge. Education in England provides a ten-week undergraduate program in which students select three courses in elementary education and have the opportunity to have direct field experience or student teach in British elementary schools. The Cambridge Quarter offers courses in British history, literature, and an interdisciplinary course. Also courses may be available in biology and theater. Presession orientation at Hiram and a few days in England. For those unable to attend Hiram, material is mailed to student's campus.

ADMITTANCE REQUIREMENTS: A minimum 2.5 GPA with recommendations from your own advisor plus two additional teachers.

TEACHING METHODS: Students attend regular classes or seminars. Courses in Education in England are taught by members of the Hiram faculty; all Cambridge Quarter classes are taught by British faculty. Lectures and seminars are integrated with local field trips.

EVALUATION: By programs leaders and students, based upon papers and examinations.

CREDITS OFFERED: Up to 15 quarter hours per quarter.

HOUSING: Students live in local flats.

DATES: Education in England is offered every other year. Next session: early September to mid-November, 1987. Cambridge Quarter is an annual program from approximately September 7 through November 15.

COSTS: Education in England: approximately $4,000 including tuition, room and two meals, local travel, and fees. Cambridge Quarter: tuition, $2,639; room and board, $830. Does not cover round-trip transportation or local expenses.

YEAR ESTABLISHED: Education in England, 1972; Cambridge Quarter, 1970.

NUMBER OF STUDENTS IN 1985: Education in England, 12; Cambridge Quarter, 18.

APPLY: By April 1. Charles L. Adams, Director, Extramural Studies.

■ **SANTA BARBARA CITY COLLEGE**
721 Cliff Drive
Santa Barbara, CA 93109
(805) 965-0581

PROGRAM: Spring Semester in Cambridge is an undergraduate program held in cooperation with Cambridgeshire College of Arts and Technology. Courses cover: history, English literature, fine arts, political science, etc. Two-to five-day orientation on the SBCC campus.

ADMITTANCE REQUIREMENTS: Acceptable academic credentials plus 12 units of college credit, including freshman-level English.

TEACHING METHODS: Students attend regular classes often conducted by SBCC professors and occasional guest lecturers. Courses are supplemented with field trips to local museums and cultural and historic sites; some independent study.

EVALUATION: By class professors, based upon papers and periodic examinations. Students also complete evaluation forms at the end of the program and comment on faculty, facilities, group leaders, and program in general.

CREDITS OFFERED: 16 semester hours.

HOUSING: Students live with local families.

DATES: Dates vary from year to year. Approximately from mid-January to mid- May.

COSTS: $2,600 including tuition, room and board, round-trip transportation, and local travel.

YEAR ESTABLISHED: 1983.

NUMBER OF STUDENTS IN 1985: 40.

APPLY: By mid-November. Mr. John Romo, Dean of Instructional Services.

■ **UNIVERSITY OF SOUTHERN CALIFORNIA**
  Overseas Studies, CES 109
  University Park
  Los Angeles, CA 90089
  (213) 746-2500

PROGRAM: USC Year in England is an undergraduate program concentrating on liberal arts and humanities. Courses include: American studies, anthropology, biology, classics, fine arts, political science, international relations, mathematics, religion, English, etc. Held in cooperation with the University of Kent. Three-day onsite orientation.

ADMITTANCE REQUIREMENTS: Sophomores and above in good academic standing.

TEACHING METHODS: Courses are taught by foreign faculty members. Americans attend regular classes at the university and are integrated with local students.

EVALUATION: By course faculty member, based upon class work, papers, and periodic examinations.

CREDITS OFFERED: 32 semester hours.

HOUSING: Students live in dormitories or furnished apartments.

DATES: Approximately, early October through mid-June.

COSTS: Approximately: $9,500 covers tuition, room and board, program-related travel. Does not include round-trip transportation or personal expenses. Some scholarships are available.

YEAR ESTABLISHED: 1981.

NUMBER OF STUDENTS IN 1985: 26.

APPLY: By February 1.

Cheltenham

■ **BRETHREN COLLEGES ABROAD**
P.O. Box #184
Manchester College
N. Manchester, IN 46962
(219) 982-2141, ext. 238

PROGRAM: Brethren Colleges Abroad Program in England is held in cooperation with the College of St. Paul and Mary, and Bridgewater College, Elizabethtown College, Juniata College, McPherson College, and the University of La Verne in the United States. The program is available for a semester or the full academic year. Courses include: teacher education, creative arts, English, geography, geology, history, mathematics, religious studies, science, physical education, and recreation studies. Onsite orientation.

ADMITTANCE REQUIREMENTS: Sophomore and above with a 3.0 GPA.

TEACHING METHODS: Americans are fully integrated with British students. Both special and regular college courses. Course work is complemented with field trips and travel to museums and regional sites.

EVALUATION: Director in England and professors determine grades from papers, periodic exams, and finals.

CREDITS OFFERED: 15 to 16 semester hours.

HOUSING: Students live in dormitories or with local families.

DATES: Fall semester: September 12 through December 10; spring semester: January 2 through April 5.

COSTS: $4,375 per semester. Includes tuition, room and board, round-trip transportation from New York, and program-related travel.

YEAR ESTABLISHED: 1978.

NUMBER OF STUDENTS IN 1985:   36.

APPLY: By April 1 for fall semester; November 1 for spring semester. Dr. Allen C. Deeter or Mrs. Helga Walsh.

Chichester

■ **PENNSYLVANIA STATE UNIVERSITY**
Office of Education Abroad Programs
222 Boucke Building
University Park, PA 16802
(814) 865-7681

PROGRAM: The Student Teaching Practicum in Early Childhood Education at Chichester is a fall- or spring-semester program held in cooperation with the Sussex Institute of Higher Education in Chichester in affiliation with Bishop Otter and Bognor Regis College. Students complete a practicum in early childhood education and gain direct experience with the British educational system through supervised teaching on the nursery, kindergarten, and primary level. Orientation at Penn State.

ADMITTANCE REQUIREMENTS: Juniors and seniors with a 2.5 GPA, good academic standing, and "must show evidence of maturity, stability, adaptability, self-discipline and a strong academic motivation." Participants must be admitted to Penn State's elementary teacher preparation program and must meet all standard student teaching prerequisites.

TEACHING METHODS: Student teaching is carried out in a local school school under supervision of the faculty of the West Sussex Institute.

EVALUATION: By course instructors, based upon observations and examinations.

CREDITS OFFERED: Practicum in student teaching, 12 credits; professional development practicum, 3 credits.

HOUSING: Students live in university dormitories.

DATES: Approximately, fall semester: early September through mid-December; spring semester: mid-January through mid-May.

COSTS: Students pay the same as at the University Park Campus. 1986-87 tuition per semester was $2,250 for state residents; $5,150 for nonresidents; room and board: $2,750 per semester. Plus a $100 nonrefundable program fee.

YEAR ESTABLISHED: 1968.

NUMBER OF STUDENTS IN 1985: 36.

APPLY: Fall semester by March 1; spring semester by October 15.

Colchester

■ **BEAVER COLLEGE**
Glenside, PA 19038
(215) 572-2901

PROGRAM: British University Year at the University of Essex is a full-academic-year program in which students are fully integrated into regular classes at the university. Courses cover the regular university scope with an emphasis on art history, biology, computer sciences, economics, electrical engineering, political science, literature, philosophy, physics, and sociology. Orientation in Colchester.

ADMITTANCE REQUIREMENTS: Juniors and seniors with a 3.0 GPA (3.3 for a science or engineering tract).

TEACHING METHODS: Students take regular courses, seminars, and tutorials taught by University of Essex professors.

EVALUATION: By Essex faculty, based upon class work and periodic examinations.

CREDITS OFFERED: 30 to 33 semester hours per year.

HOUSING: Students live in university dormitories.

DATES: The academic year runs from mid-September to late June.

COSTS: $8,250 per year includes tuition, room, transportation to London, and program-related travel. Does not cover meals, return transportation, or personal expenses.

YEAR ESTABLISHED: 1982.

NUMBER OF STUDENTS IN 1985: 5.

APPLY: April 20. Center for Education Abroad.

■ **UNIVERSITY OF CONNECTICUT**
241 Glenbrook Road
Storrs, CT 06268
(203) 486-2141

PROGRAM: University of Essex Junior Year in Social Sciences or Engineering Computer Sciences is a nine-month, three-trimester program held in cooperation with the University of Essex. Students are full members of the university student body and select any subjects offered in the school's catalogue. Courses include government, sociology, history, literature, economics, philosophy, electrical engineering, computer science, biology, chemistry, language and linguistics, mathematics, art history, and law. One-day orientation in Connecticut; four days in Colchester.

ADMITTANCE REQUIREMENTS: Sophomores and above in good academic standing. Specific prerequisites for engineering courses.

TEACHING METHODS: Students attend regular classes at the university and are fully integrated with British students. Seminars and tutorials rarely consist of more than ten students.

EVALUATION: By course professors, based upon papers and examinations.

CREDITS OFFERED: Trimester system. Students earn a maximum of 32 academic credits.

HOUSING: Students are housed on campus. Each student has a study-bedroom and shares a kitchen and bathroom with other residents of the apartment.

DATES: October 1 through June 15.

COSTS: $6,200 for state residents (slightly higher for nonresidents). Engineering and computer science students pay an additional $1,300. Covers tuition, room and board, and round-trip transportation from New York.

YEAR ESTABLISHED: 1983.

NUMBER OF STUDENTS IN 1986: 12.

APPLY: By March 1. Sally Innis Klitz, Study Abroad Office, U-207.

Durham

■ **INSTITUTE OF EUROPEAN STUDY (IES)**
223 West Ohio Street
Chicago, IL 60610
(312) 944-1750

PROGRAM: IES is a nonprofit organization with formal relationships with more than forty American colleges and universities. The institute maintains ten undergraduate academic centers throughout the world which provide semester or full-academic-year programs. The IES Durham Program, held in cooperation with the University of Durham, is for the full academic year only. Students enroll in the university for three complete British terms and elect courses from more than thirty different disciplines covering the humanities, social sciences, natural sciences, mathematics, education, engineering, etc. One-week orientation in Durham.

ADMITTANCE REQUIREMENTS: Juniors and seniors only. Faculty recommendations and an application essay. 85 percent of all students have had a GPA between 2.80 and 3.75.

TEACHING METHODS: Students attend regular university courses with British students. Classes are supplemented by trips to local museums and historic sites.

EVALUATION: By faculty, based upon class work and periodic and final exams. Most courses require a research paper.

CREDITS OFFERED: The recommended course load is 30 semester hours for the entire academic year.

HOUSING: Every student is a member of one of eleven residential colleges. (One college is in a thirteenth-century castle). Students are housed in one of these colleges, usually in single or double rooms.

DATES: Michaelmas term: October 4 through December 10; Epiphany term: January 15 through March 18; Easter term: April 23 through June 24.

COSTS: $8,500 per year. Includes tuition, room and board, and program-related field trips. Does not include round-trip transportation, local travel, or personal expenses (estimated at $2,500 per year). Up to $3,000 in IES scholarship aid is available.

YEAR ESTABLISHED: 1968.

NUMBER OF STUDENTS IN 1985:   47.

APPLY: By February 15.

Exeter

■ **KENYON COLLEGE**
   Gambier, OH 43022
   (614) 427-2244

PROGRAM: Kenyon's Exeter Program is a full-year, undergraduate program held in cooperation with Exeter University. The program, designed primarily for English majors, offers two courses in English literature and a third course in any other field.

ADMITTANCE REQUIREMENTS: Open to all English majors in their junior year, attending a school affiliated with the Great Lakes College Association. Acceptable academic credentials and recommendations.

TEACHING METHODS: Students attend regular classes at Exeter University and are fully integrated with English students. Travel to local sites supplements class work.

EVALUATION: By professors at Exeter University, based upon class work, periodic exams, etc.

CREDITS OFFERED: 4 Kenyon units.

HOUSING: Students live in Exeter University dormitories or may rent local flats.

DATES: Approximately early October through early June.

COSTS: Based upon costs at sponsoring institution. The following figures are for Kenyon. Tuition: $8,583; room and board: $1,440. Does not include round-trip transportation, local travel or personal expenses (estimated at $1,525).

YEAR ESTABLISHED: 1975.

NUMBER OF STUDENTS IN 1985: 20.

APPLY: By February 21. Off-campus Studies Office.

■ **PENNSYLVANIA STATE UNIVERSITY**
Office of Education Abroad Programs
222 Boucke Building
University Park, PA 16802
(814) 865-7681

PROGRAM: Education Abroad at the University of Exeter is a spring undergraduate program. Students take courses specially designed for Americans taught by University of Exeter faculty. Subjects cover political science, economics, sociology/human development, and contemporary British culture and civilization. Program often includes visits to local sites of historic and cultural interest. Orientation at Penn State.

ADMITTANCE REQUIREMENTS: Juniors and seniors with a 2.5 GPA, good academic standing, and "must show evidence of maturity, stability, adaptability, self-discipline and a strong academic motivation."

TEACHING METHODS: Students take four 3-credit courses, which are team taught with about five instructors per course, each lecturing in his or her own area of expertise.

EVALUATION: By course instructors, based upon class work, papers, and examinations.

CREDITS OFFERED: 12 semester hours.

HOUSING: Students live in school dormitories.

DATES: Approximately, mid-January through late April.

COSTS: Students pay the same as at the University Park Campus. 1986-87 tuition per semester was $2,250 for state residents; $5,150 for nonresidents; room and board: $2,750 per semester. Plus a $100 nonrefundable program fee.

YEAR ESTABLISHED: 1975.

NUMBER OF STUDENTS IN 1985:   25.

APPLY: By October 15.

Grantham

■ **UNIVERSITY OF EVANSVILLE**
1800 Lincoln Avenue
Evansville, IN 47714
(812) 479-2146

PROGRAM: Evansville's Harlaxton College Program is a semester, full-year, or summer session which provides a wide range of degree offerings. British studies and archaeology are new programs held in conjunction with the University of Leicester. Basic undergraduate courses cover: accounting, economics, literature, composition, computer science, mathematics, art and art history, natural and physical sciences, anthropology, geography, French, German, religion, and music. Also available: a limited number of nursing clinicals in community health, internships in business and law offices, and student teaching positions. On-campus orientation prior to departure. Students from out-of-area are sent video tapes.

ADMITTANCE REQUIREMENTS: Freshman must be "acceptable" to Evansville admission's department. Sophomores and above in good academic standing with home school advisor's and dean's permission.

TEACHING METHODS: Most faculty members are British. Courses include lectures, laboratories, archaeological digs, class work, and independent study.

EVALUATION: By local professors, based upon class work, papers, and examinations.

CREDITS OFFERED: Approximately 15 semester hours per semester.

HOUSING: Women stay in a Victorian manor house; men live next door in a college block.

DATES: Fall semester: August 30 through December 10; spring semester: January 3 through April 15.

COSTS: $4,662 per semester includes tuition and room and board. Does not cover round-trip transportation, local travel, field trips, or personal expenses. Financial aid and work/study grants are available.

YEAR ESTABLISHED: 1971.

NUMBER OF STUDENTS IN 1985: 173.

APPLY: By June 1 for fall semester and full year; November 1 for spring semester. Suzy Lantz, Harlaxton Coordinator.

Guildford

■ **BEAVER COLLEGE**
Glenside, PA 19038
(215) 572-2901

PROGRAM: British University Year at the University of Surrey is a full-academic-year program in which students are fully integrated into regular classes at the university. Courses cover the regular university scope with an emphasis on dance, economics, electrical, chemical, civil and mechanical engineering, political science, modern languages, linguistics, music, literature, philosophy, physics, psychology, and sociology. Orientation in London.

ADMITTANCE REQUIREMENTS: Juniors and seniors with a 3.0 GPA (3.3 for a science or engineering tract).

TEACHING METHODS: Students take regular courses, seminars, and tutorials taught by University of Surrey professors.

EVALUATION: By Surrey faculty, based upon class work and periodic examinations.

CREDITS OFFERED: 30 to 33 semester hours per year.

HOUSING: Students live in university dormitories.

DATES: The academic year runs from mid-September to late June.

COSTS: $7,815 per year includes tuition, room, transportation to London, and program-related travel. Does not cover meals, return transportation, or personal expenses.

YEAR ESTABLISHED: 1972.

NUMBER OF STUDENTS IN 1985:   15.

APPLY: By April 20. Center for Education Abroad.

Lancaster

■ **BEAVER COLLEGE**
Glenside, PA 19038
(215) 572-2901

PROGRAM: The Beaver program at the University of Lancaster is a single-semester or full-academic-year program in which students are fully integrated into regular classes at the university. Courses cover the regular university scope with an emphasis on business administration, electronic, chemical, civil and mechanical engineering, political science, modern languages, linguistics, music, literature, philosophy, physics, psychology, and sociology. Orientation in London.

ADMITTANCE REQUIREMENTS: Juniors and seniors with a 3.0 GPA.

TEACHING METHODS: Students take regular courses, seminars, and tutorials taught by University of Lancaster professors.

EVALUATION: By Lancaster faculty, based upon class work and periodic examinations.

CREDITS OFFERED: 30 to 33 semester hours per year.

HOUSING: Students live in university dormitories and student residences.

DATES: Fall semester: September 14 through December 12; spring semester: December 28th through May 29.

COSTS: $8,250 per year; fall semester: $4,080; spring semester: $5,485. Includes tuition, room, transportation to London, and program-related travel. Does not cover meals, return transportation, or personal expenses.

YEAR ESTABLISHED: 1969.

NUMBER OF STUDENTS IN 1985: 25.

APPLY: April 20. Center for Education Abroad.

Leeds

■ **PENNSYLVANIA STATE UNIVERSITY**
Office of Education Abroad Programs
222 Boucke Building
University Park, PA 16802
(814) 865-7681

PROGRAM: Pennsylvania State University offers three different programs in cooperation with the University of Leeds: a three-term exchange program in which Americans take regular courses at the University of Leeds as a regular member of the school's student body; a spring semester program that concentrates on civil engineering; and a fall semester program devoted to architectural engineering with courses in architectural and structural design, and architectural history. Orientation at Penn State.

ADMITTANCE REQUIREMENTS: Juniors and seniors with a 2.5 GPA, good academic standing, and "must show evidence of maturity, stability, adaptability, self-discipline and a strong academic motivation." The exchange program requires a 3-credit course dealing with British literature, history, politics, or art. The civil engineering and architecture programs require some prior academic subject-related experience.

TEACHING METHODS: Students on the exchange program enroll in regular courses. The architecture and civil engineering programs include specially designed academic sessions consisting of lectures, design studies, directed field trips, and term reports.

EVALUATION: By course instructors, based upon class work, papers, and examinations.

CREDITS OFFERED: Exchange program: 24 credits; architectural engineering program: 13 credits; civil engineering: 12 to 15 credits.

HOUSING: Students live at University of Leeds residence halls.

DATES: Approximately, exchange program: early September through the third week in June; civil engineering program: January 12 through March 20; architectural engineering: late September through mid-December.

COSTS: Students pay the same as at the University Park Campus. 1986-87 tuition per semester was $2,250 for state residents; $5,150 for nonresidents; room and board: $2,750 per semester. Plus a $100 nonrefundable program fee.

YEAR ESTABLISHED: Exchange, 1984; civil engineering, 1985; architectural engineering, 1977.

NUMBER OF STUDENTS IN 1985:   Exchange, 5; civil engineering, 10; architectural engineering, 15.

APPLY: Exchange and architectural engineering program by March 1; civil engineering by October 15.

■ **VANDERBILT UNIVERSITY**
College of Arts & Sciences
Box #6327-B
Nashville, TN 37235
(615) 371-1224

PROGRAM: Vanderbilt in England is a full-academic-year undergraduate program in which students are enrolled directly at the University of Leeds with the identical status of attending British students. Courses are the regular listings offered British students. Some study tours are offered by the resident director and are part of the program.

ADMITTANCE REQUIREMENTS: Juniors and above with a 3.0 GPA and letters of recommendation.

TEACHING METHODS: Students attend regular classes at the university which are fully integrated with local students. "Instruction is given through lectures, tutorials and 'practical classes.' Tutors monitor students' progress throughout the year in preparation for the final exam on which the grade is based."

EVALUATION: By course professors and tutors, based upon final examinations.

CREDITS OFFERED: 30 semester hours per year.

HOUSING: Students live in university residence halls or, on occasion, in university flats. Some halls serve two meals a day; some three. Students living in university flats are responsible for providing their own meals.

DATES: Approximately, October 1 through late July. The school year consists of three terms with vacation periods of approximately four weeks between terms.

COSTS: $9,300 per semester includes tuition and some program activities. Does not cover round-trip transportation, room and board (which varies depending upon choice of university housing), and personal expenses (estimated at approximately $450 per term).

YEAR ESTABLISHED: 1973.

NUMBER OF STUDENTS IN 1985: 22.

APPLY: By February 15. Overseas Office.

Lincolnshire

■ **MANSFIELD UNIVERSITY**
Mansfield, PA 16933
(717) 662-4000

PROGRAM: Introduction to British Education is a twenty-five-day summer program designed for graduate students in education or undergraduate seniors in the final year of a college program. The program combines education courses with a cultural component. Students work directly with British children and teachers. Two-week preorientation at Mansfield.

ADMITTANCE REQUIREMENTS: Graduate level or in-service teachers. Also available to education students in their final year.

TEACHING METHODS: Students participate and observe in British primary and secondary schools. Seminars with professors and British educators.

EVALUATION: There are no exams. Evaluation is by observation, discussion of the program, and preparing a paper.

CREDITS OFFERED: 3 or 6 credits, depending on course of study.

HOUSING: Students live in a college dormitory and spend one week at the Cathedral Hostel.

DATES: Last week in June through the third week of July.

COSTS: Tuition: $82 per credit; room and board: approximately $750. Does not include round-trip transportation, local travel, or expenses.

YEAR ESTABLISHED: 1974.

NUMBER OF STUDENTS IN 1985:   26.

APPLY: By March 1. Dr. John C. Heups, Department of Education.

London

- *The best way to travel in London is to buy a tube pass. It usually costs about 15 pounds a month and provides an unlimited use of the underground and buses. Two excellent pubs which provide dinner for a reasonable rate are The Bunch of Grapes in Knightsbridge and Dickens' Inn near the Tower of London. As for shopping, Harrods is the place. Also, at Laura Ashley you can buy their clothes at more than a third less than in America.*

  - Virginia A. Corey, Weston, Massachusetts

■ **AMERICAN INSTITUTE OF FOREIGN STUDY (AIFS)**
102 Greenwich Avenue
Greenwich, CT 06830
(800) 243-4567 or (203) 869-9090

PROGRAM: AIFS is a national for-profit organization specializing in comprehensive overseas academic-year, semester, and summer study programs. AIFS offers two London programs. One for college students; one for high school students (described below). The AIFS college program at Richmond College is a two-year AA degree program; four-year BA degree program; full-academic year program; or single-semester program in which students are fully integrated into the college's academic, social, athletic, and cultural life. The college was founded in 1843, and until 1972, was a part of London University. At that time it was reincorporated as an American private international college affiliated with AIFS. Courses cover biological sciences, business administration, chemistry, computer sciences, drama, economics, engineering, English, fine arts, French, history, mathematics, music, philosophy, political science, physics, psychology, sociology, Spanish, and studio art. Ongoing orientation in London during the first weeks of the semester.

ADMITTANCE REQUIREMENTS: College freshman and above with a 2.5 GPA.

TEACHING METHODS: Most students are Americans; faculty is predominantly British. Freshman and sophomores live at and attend the Richmond Hill campus; juniors and seniors live at and attend the Kensington campus.

EVALUATION: By college faculty, based upon class work, papers, and periodic examinations.

CREDITS OFFERED: Approximately 15 semester hours per semester.

HOUSING: Students live in single or double rooms in residence halls or may elect to live with local families.

DATES: Fall semester: September 1 through December 12; spring semester: January 12 through May 13.

COSTS: Full academic year: $8,895; fall or spring semester: $4,795. Includes tuition, room and board, and one-way transportation from New York. Does not cover local travel or personal expenses.

YEAR ESTABLISHED: 1972.

NUMBER OF STUDENTS IN 1985:   1,100.

APPLY: Applications filled on first-come basis. "It is expected that all full-year or fall-semester places will be filled by June 1; places for spring semester are kept open until November 15."

- *Richmond's program was fairly well organized but on weekends there were not any planned activities. This allowed students to travel wherever they pleased. The professors' enthusiasm in their subjects was immense. The quality of education was different because many classes were not held in classroom environments. This was fun. The food was quite a shock because of its bland taste. Overall it consisted mainly of fruits and vegetables.*

    - Marian L. Pollock, Greensboro, North Carolina

- *Richmond was much stronger academically than I anticipated. The faculty is excellent. However, we were a bit surprised to find Richmond is an American college. It was never clear that there weren't any British students there; it was made up of very conservative middle Americans from little colleges you never heard of.*

    - Name withheld, Washington, D.C.

■ **THE AMERICAN UNIVERSITY**
Washington, DC 20016
(202) 885-3800

PROGRAM: A Semester in London is a liberal arts/social science program held in cooperation with Birkbeck College, University of London. Courses include history, fine arts, languages, political science, etc. Field trips to Brussels and Stratford are often scheduled. Preorientation at American University (usually over a weekend) and onsite.

ADMITTANCE REQUIREMENTS: Juniors and seniors with a "B" average or better.

TEACHING METHODS: Students are accompanied by a resident professor from American University who schedules seminars with public officials in addition to his or her own lectures. Foreign faculty members complement these lectures and teach specialized courses. Students also intern two days a week with one of the many local government or private organizations.

EVALUATION: Regular exams, midterms and finals, in addition to short seminar papers.

CREDITS OFFERED: 15 to 17 semester hours.

HOUSING: A combination of possibilities from local apartments to living with local families.

DATES: Fall semester: September to December; spring semester: January to May.

COSTS: Tuition: $4,100 per semester; room and board: $2,000 per semester. Scholarships from American University available.

YEAR ESTABLISHED: 1974.

NUMBER OF STUDENTS IN 1985: 120.

APPLY: Rolling admissions. Apply six to eight months prior to start of semester. Dr. David C. Brown, Dean, Washington Semester and Study Program Abroad.

■ **ANTIOCH COLLEGE**
Box ACBS
Yellow Springs, OH 45387
(513) 767-1031

PROGRAM: Antioch London, held in cooperation with the University of London, can be experienced for a full academic year or for the fall, winter, or spring term. Each term, students participate in a directed field study, which may be a research project, a job or internship, or volunteer work in a student's area of interest. Although primarily an undergraduate program, an MA degree can be achieved in Psychology of Therapy & Counseling or Creative Writing. Undergraduate courses include: creative writing, psychology, economics, and British studies covering art and architecture, literature, history, media studies, political science, economics and sociology. Five-day orientation in London.

ADMITTANCE REQUIREMENTS: Two years of undergraduate study and good academic standing.

TEACHING METHODS: Students take courses under the supervision of a U.S. academic director. Most faculty members are non-American. Classes are small and tend toward seminars and tutorials.

EVALUATION: By foreign faculty members.

CREDITS OFFERED: The equivalent of 20 Antioch quarter graduate or undergraduate credits (a full credit load of semester hours).

HOUSING: Students are assisted in obtaining housing with families in rented rooms or shared flats. Housing is provided for the first few days.

DATES: Fall term: September 15 through December 12; winter term: January 5 through April 5; spring term: April 27 through June 19.

COSTS: Tuition is approximately $3,050 per term or $6,100 for the full academic year. Does not include round-trip transportation, room and board, or personal expenses (estimated at $400 to $450 per month).

YEAR ESTABLISHED: 1970.

NUMBER OF STUDENTS IN 1985: 25.

APPLY: By March 30 for fall term or academic year. Connie Bauer, Dean.

■ **ARIZONA STATE UNIVERSITY**
Academic Services Building, Room #110
Tempe, AZ 85287
(692) 965-6611

PROGRAM: London Semester is an undergraduate program held in cooperation with the University of Arizona, Northern Arizona University, and the American Institute of Foreign Study. Although the course selection varies from semester to semester, the basic emphasis is always on Britain's history, culture, and place in the Western World. All students are required to take the course, British Life and Culture. Optional orientation tour of Europe prior to start of program is available for $350.

ADMITTANCE REQUIREMENTS: Students must be registered at ASU the semester in attendance. 2.0 GPA and at least 25 semester hours.

TEACHING METHODS: Students are instructed by U.S. professors at the University of London's Student Union. There is no integration with British students. Guest lecturers from London for British Life and Culture course.

EVALUATION: Papers and exams given by U.S. instructors.

CREDITS OFFERED: A minimum course load of 12 semester hours is required.

HOUSING: Students live in off-campus dormitories.

DATES: Approximately, fall semester: August 29 through December 12; spring semester: January 6 through April 10.

COSTS: Arizona residents: $3,320; nonresidents: $4,747. Includes tuition and room and board. Does not cover round-trip transportation, personal expenses (estimated at $200 a month minimum) or local travel.

YEAR ESTABLISHED: 1981.

NUMBER OF STUDENTS IN 1985:   30.

APPLY: One semester in advance. Denis J. Kigin, Director of Summer Sessions.

■ **BALL STATE UNIVERSITY**
Muncie, IN 47306
(317) 285-6261

PROGRAM: Ball State's London Center offers a nine-week undergraduate liberal arts program, with a different speciality available each quarter, followed by a three-week optional tour of the continent. Limited to forty-five students.

ADMITTANCE REQUIREMENTS: At least one quarter (or semester) of college and a 2.5 GPA.

TEACHING METHODS: Students attend regular classes at the center taught by Ball State and visiting British professors. Also field trips, concerts, and visits to local cultural and historic sites.

EVALUATION: By attending faculty, based upon class work, papers, and examinations.

CREDITS OFFERED: Generally students take three courses (but may take four) for 12 hours of credit per quarter.

HOUSING: Students live in a London hotel, which also contains classrooms and kitchen facilities.

DATES: Approximately, fall quarter: August 30 to November 22; winter quarter: November 29 to February 28; spring quarter: March 7 to May 23.

COSTS: Tuition: $1,464 (for three 12-hour quarters); room and board: 1,738 (for three quarters). Includes continental tour during third quarter. Does not cover round-trip transportation, local travel, or personal expenses.

YEAR ESTABLISHED: 1972.

NUMBER OF STUDENTS IN 1985: 37.

APPLY: Dr. Mark Popovich, On-Campus Coordinator, London Center.

■ **BEAVER COLLEGE**
Glenside, PA 19038
(215) 572-2901

PROGRAM: Beaver operates more than a dozen separate programs in London in cooperation with the London School of Economics, University of London, and the City of London Polytechnic. Programs range from a full academic year to single semester and parliamentary internships. Students interested in broad humanities programs may enroll at Queen Marys College or University College at the University of London; science and engineering students may investigate programs at Royal Holloway and Bedford New College, University of London; a fall semester studio art program is held at Sir John Cass Faculty of Fine Art; a fall pre-law semester is offered at the London School of Economics, etc. Orientation in London.

ADMITTANCE REQUIREMENTS: Juniors and seniors with a 3.0 GPA (3.3 for a science or engineering tract).

TEACHING METHODS: Students take regular courses, seminars, and tutorials taught by university professors. In most cases, Americans are fully integrated with British students.

EVALUATION: By course faculty, based upon class work and periodic examinations.

CREDITS OFFERED: 15 to 16 semester hours per semester.

HOUSING: Students live in university dormitories or with local families.

DATES: The academic year runs from mid-September to late June.

COSTS: Vary depending upon school and program. Approximately $4,800 per semester includes tuition, room, transportation to London, and program-related travel. Does not cover meals, return transportation, or personal expenses.

YEAR ESTABLISHED: 1972.

NUMBER OF STUDENTS IN 1985: 600.

APPLY: Fall semester by April 20; spring semester by October 5. Center for Education Abroad.

■ **BOSTON UNIVERSITY**
143 Bay State Road
Boston, MA 02215
(617) 353-9888

PROGRAM: Boston University offers four specific internship programs for both undergraduate and graduate students: art/architecture, business/ economics, journalism/mass communications, and politics/parliament. Courses for each internship concentrate in that program's specific area of coverage; internships provide students the opportunity to work with architectural firms, banks and multinational corporations, newspapers and radio-TV stations, and with Members of Parliament and political parties. Summer session. Two-day orientation in London.

ADMITTANCE REQUIREMENTS: 3.0 GPA, essay or portfolio, and recommendations.

TEACHING METHODS: Students attend special courses arranged for the group and taught by British faculty.

EVALUATION: By course faculty, based upon papers and periodic examinations.

CREDITS OFFERED: 16 semester hours per semester.

HOUSING: Students live in rented flats or with local families.

DATES: Fall semester: September 8 to December 22; spring semester: January 19 through April 27.

COSTS: Approximately $4,500 per semester includes tuition and housing. Does not cover meals, round-trip transportation, or personal expenses.

YEAR ESTABLISHED: 1986.

NUMBER OF STUDENTS IN 1985: 385.

APPLY: At least two months prior to start of semester. Dr. Timothy Perkins, London Internship Programme.

■ **BRIGHAM YOUNG UNIVERSITY**
Study Abroad Programs
204 HRCB
Provo, UT 84602
(801) 378-3308

PROGRAM: BYU offers two six-week summer programs and a six-month program. There are two summer programs. The first, Family Studies in England, is held at the London School of Economics. Students study the "effects of socializing agents on children"; they stay in London but also spend five days with English families. The second program, England Design, offers students various design and photography courses. The two-term program offers courses in the humanities, European studies, history, political science, English literature, religion, etc.

ADMITTANCE REQUIREMENTS: Good academic standing with a 3.0 GPA requested. Adherence to BYU standards.

TEACHING METHODS: In the Family Program, students are exposed "to peoples and places of London and Britain and also have time to explore on their own in small groups." The other programs "adapt the content of each course to the European environment."

EVALUATION: Determined by program director, based on periodic exams.

CREDITS OFFERED: From 6 to 9 semester hours for the summer programs; 17 credit hours for the two-month program.

HOUSING: Students are assigned housing in hotels, hostels, or private facilities.

DATES: Summer term: approximately, June 20 through mid to late-August; six-month term: approximately, June to December.

COSTS: Approximately $2,000 (English Families); $2,600 (Design); $5,095 (six-month program). Includes tuition, room and breakfast, local travel. Does not cover round-trip transportation or additional travel.

YEAR ESTABLISHED: 1975.

NUMBER OF STUDENTS IN 1985: 38.

APPLY: By April. Alvin Price, Professor of Family Science; Wally Barruss, Associate Professor, Design; Dr. Marion J. Bentley (six-month program).

■ **THE CATHOLIC UNIVERSITY OF AMERICA**
Washington, DC 20064
(202) 635-5000

PROGRAM: The Parliamentary Internship Program, held in cooperation with the English-Speaking Union, offers upper-level undergraduate and graduate students an opportunity to work as full-time research assistants to Members of Parliament for a ten-week period in early summer. The internship involves a close relationship with the working legislator/sponsor and possible involvement in areas such as constituency relations, representation, and party liaison, etc.

ADMITTANCE REQUIREMENTS: Sophomores and above with an acceptable academic record.

TEACHING METHODS: In addition to the actual working with the selected MP, students attend lectures, tours, and special programs focused on British government, society, and history.

EVALUATION: By review of daily log maintained by the student plus an oral exam based on the intern's readings and experience. Member of Parliament's assessment and program director's review are also considered.

CREDITS OFFERED: 6 semester hours.

HOUSING: Students may live with local families, in special student accommodations, or share apartments with fellow interns.

DATES: Mid-May through July.

COSTS: $1,800 plus an $600 fee which is returned to the students in pounds sterling to be used for lodging and basic living costs during the program. Round-trip transportation not included.

YEAR ESTABLISHED: 1967.

NUMBER OF STUDENTS IN 1985:   18.

APPLY: Fall semester by April 1; spring semester by December 1. Professor Charles Dechert, Department of Politics.

- *My MP and I got along extremely well. He was open, fond of Americans, and swapping stories over tea was common procedure. . . . He thought it essential that I see his constituency and the work he does on his own home ground.*
                                                          - Name withheld, Chicago, Illinois

■ **CENTRAL COLLEGE**
   Pella, IA 50219
   (515) 628-5287

PROGRAM: Central College's London Study Program offers undergraduate students either a semester or full academic year of study and/or the opportunity to serve an internship in such areas as business, communications, social work, health care, etc. A broad range of liberal arts courses are presented at the North London Polytechnic and cover: British studies, literature, and culture and history, art, business, political science, theater, music, philosophy, etc. Three-day orientation in London.

ADMITTANCE REQUIREMENTS: Minimum 2.5 GPA, recommendations, and essay.

TEACHING METHODS: Special classes for American students are taught by British faculty. Lectures and seminars are complemented by local field trips.

EVALUATION: By British faculty. Resident director sends grades to home institution.

CREDITS OFFERED: 16 to 20 semester hours per semester.

HOUSING: Students live in a five-story Georgian rowhouse.

DATES: Fall semester: September through December; spring semester: early January through May.

COSTS: Approximately, $8,300 for both semesters (9 months); $4,500 for one semester (4½ months). Includes tuition, room, fees, excursions, and two meals a day. Does not cover round-trip transportation, one meal a day, or personal expenses. Several $500 merit scholarships are available.

YEAR ESTABLISHED: 1974.

NUMBER OF STUDENTS IN 1985: 28.

APPLY: By April 15 for fall semester or full year; November 1 for spring semester. Mrs. Barbara Butler, Coordinator of International Studies.

■ **ELON COLLEGE**
Elon College, NC 27244
(919) 584-2354

PROGRAM: Elon offers a fall semester in London in cooperation with Guilford College. Students take formal courses in history, fine arts, political science, literature, economics, etc. For nonresidents of Elon, optional readings supplement a preorientation session at the college.

ADMITTANCE REQUIREMENTS: Acceptable academic record.

TEACHING METHODS: Lectures and travel to local sites.

EVALUATION: By group leaders and faculty based on class work and exams.

CREDITS OFFERED: Full semester credit or 3 semester hours per course.

HOUSING: Students live in dormitories and local hotels.

DATES: Approximately early September through mid-December.

COSTS: $1,750 includes tuition and room and board. Round-trip transportation and local travel are not included.

YEAR ESTABLISHED: Not available.

NUMBER OF STUDENTS IN 1985: Not available.

APPLY: By June 1. Dr. Bill Rich, Box # 2207.

■ **FLORIDA STATE UNIVERSITY**
Tallahassee, FL 32306
(904) 644-3272

PROGRAM: The FSU London Study Program is held in cooperation with the State University Systems of Florida and is a one- or two-semester or summer course of study featuring the humanities, business, theater, political science, history, sociology, etc.

ADMITTANCE REQUIREMENTS: 2.5 GPA and good academic standing. Sophomores and above; will accept high school seniors and above for summer program.

TEACHING METHODS: Students take courses at the American Study Center taught by an American faculty. A Parliament course is taught by a member of Parliament. Field trips to local cultural sites complement the program.

EVALUATION: By American faculty, based upon class work and examinations.

CREDITS OFFERED: 15 semester hours per semester.

HOUSING: Students can live at the Queensberry Court Hotel or may locate their own housing.

DATES: Approximately, fall semester: early September to mid-December; spring semester: mid-January to late April; summer session: late June to mid-August.

COSTS: Approximately, tuition (depends on in-state or out-of-state residence); room and board: $2,820 per semester includes round-trip airfare. Does not include personal expenses (estimated at $2,000 per semester). Financial and work/study aid available.

YEAR ESTABLISHED: 1971.

NUMBER OF STUDENTS IN 1985: 106.

APPLY: Fall semester by May 30; spring semester by October 20. Dr. C.E. Tanzy, FSU Florence/London Programs, 115 WMS.

■ **INSTITUTE OF EUROPEAN STUDY (IES)**
223 West Ohio Street
Chicago, IL 60610
(312) 944-1750

PROGRAM: IES is a nonprofit organization with formal relationships with more than forty American colleges and universities. The institute maintains ten undergraduate academic centers throughout the world which provide semester or full academic year programs. The IES London center, in Bloomsbury Square, offers students the option to choose a social science or humanities tract. Full year students may select a different tract each semester. All courses are taught by a British faculty. The majority of social science professors are from the London School of Economics and Political Science; humanities from Birkbeck College. Students may apply for a nonpaying business or parliamentary internship program. Summer program also available. Five-day orientation in London.

ADMITTANCE REQUIREMENTS: Juniors and seniors ("exceptionally well qualified sophomores *may* be considered"). Faculty recommendations and an application essay. 85 percent of all students have had a GPA between 2.80 and 3.75.

TEACHING METHODS: Lectures and field trips. Tutorials are required unless waived by home institution.

EVALUATION: By British faculty, based upon class work and periodic and final exams. Most courses require a research paper.

CREDITS OFFERED: 15 to 18 semester hours per semester.

HOUSING: Students arrange for their own housing.

DATES: Fall semester: August 26 through December 12; spring semester: January 12 through May 8.

COSTS: $2,800 per semester for tuition. Does not include room and board (estimated at $2,800 per semester), round-trip transportation, or personal expenses. Some IES scholarship aid available: $1,500 for full year students, $750 for semester students.

YEAR ESTABLISHED: 1974.

NUMBER OF STUDENTS IN 1985: 100.

APPLY: For fall semester by May 1; spring semester by November 15.

■ **ITHACA COLLEGE**
Ithaca, NY 14850
(607) 274-3306

PROGRAM: The Ithaca College London Center is the college's own facility in London. The undergraduate program is basically a liberal arts curriculum offering courses in fine arts, international business, communications, political science, drama, theater, economics, and the social sciences. The program also offers students the opportunity to experience internships in business, economics, social services, and communications. Presession orientations in both Ithaca and in London.

ADMITTANCE REQUIREMENTS: Sophomores and above with a 2.75 GPA and permission of home school advisor and dean.

TEACHING METHODS: Classes are taught at the center by British faculty. Seminars, independent study, and travel to regional sites, museums, theater, etc., complement class work.

EVALUATION: By British faculty, based upon periodic and final examinations.

CREDITS OFFERED: 12 to 18 semester hours per semester.

HOUSING: Students are responsible for their own housing, but the center's staff assists in placement in local flats or with local families.

DATES: Approximately, fall semester: early September through mid-December; spring semester: mid-January through mid-May.

COSTS: Tuition and program-related travel: $3,823 per semester. Does not cover room and board (estimated at $2,000 per semester), round-trip transportation, or personal expenses.

YEAR ESTABLISHED: 1973.

NUMBER OF STUDENTS IN 1985: 185.

APPLY: Fall semester by April 1; spring semester by November 1. Director, Office of International Programs.

■ **NEW HAMPSHIRE COLLEGE**
2500 North River Road
Manchester, NH 03104
(603) 668-2211, ext. 387

PROGRAM: The London Semester is held in cooperation with the Polytechnic of North London. Students attend the institute with British students. Courses cover business, the humanities, social sciences, and the natural sciences. New Hampshire College also operates a pilot program with Lansdowne College in London which offers small classes and a flexible academic course of study.

ADMITTANCE REQUIREMENTS: Acceptable academic record plus recommendations.

TEACHING METHODS: Classes are held at the cooperating college.

EVALUATION: By cooperating college faculty.

CREDITS OFFERED: Up to 30 credits per year.

HOUSING: Students stay in the Royal National Hotel in central London.

DATES: Approximately, September through December or January through May.

COSTS: Same tuition as home institution.

YEAR ESTABLISHED: Not available.

NUMBER OF STUDENTS IN 1985: Not available.

APPLY: By March 1. Dr. James Grace, Program Coordinator or Dr. Richard Erskine, Associate Academic Dean.

■ **NORTHEASTERN UNIVERSITY**
College of Arts and Sciences
360 Huntington Ave.
Boston, MA 02115
(617) 437-5278

PROGRAM: The London Writers' Workshop is a two-week intensive fiction-writing course designed for writers and teachers of writing.

ADMITTANCE REQUIREMENTS: Open to anyone interested in the "craft of writing short fiction."

TEACHING METHODS: Instruction is by professional writers and instructors of fiction. Guest instructors are "noted" authors. Intensive workshops teach the writing process. Students write short works which are critiqued in class.

EVALUATION: If credit is desired, two projects are required: one work of fiction written during the course of the workshop; another written after the conclusion of the workshop.

CREDITS OFFERED: 6 quarter hours.

HOUSING: Students can live at the Forum Hotel in South Kensington.

DATES: Usually the second and third weeks of July.

COSTS: Tuition: $1,080; room and board: $38 night double occupancy; plus round-trip transportation and local living expenses.

YEAR ESTABLISHED: 1983.

NUMBER OF STUDENTS IN 1985:   40.

APPLY: By May 21. Suzanne Robblee, Program Coordinator.

■ **NORTHWEST INTERINSTITUTIONAL COUNCIL ON STUDY ABROAD (NICSA)**
Oregon State University
International Education,
Corvallis, OR 97331
(503) 754-2394

PROGRAM: The NICSA Study Abroad Program is held in cooperation with the University of Washington, Washington State University, Western Washington University, Central Washington University, Eastern Washington University, Boise State University, University of Alaska - Fairbanks, University of Oregon, Oregon State University, and Portland State University. This is a one-term, undergraduate program, although students may elect to enroll for more than a single term. The courses are designed around a general liberal arts curriculum emphasizing history, economics, political science, language, art, literature, English, theater, geography, etc. Excursions play an important role, taking place on a weekly basis; one long (two- to three-day) excursion each term. There is a three-hour orientation on the individual campuses prior to departure and a one-day onsite orientation.

ADMITTANCE REQUIREMENTS: A minimum 2.0 GPA plus good academic standing.

TEACHING METHODS: Students attend a special center for Americans set up by NICSA. All classes are taught by a either foreign or various northwestern regional-school faculty members.

EVALUATION: By professors based on class work, papers, and periodic exams.

CREDITS OFFERED: 15 or 20 credits (quarter hours) per term.

HOUSING: Students live with local families arranged by an onsite homestay coordinator.

DATES: Fall term: September 15 through December 15; winter term: January 3 through March 20; spring term: April 1 through June 15.

COSTS: $2,195 including tuition, room and board, books, and local travel. Does not cover round-trip transportation or personal expenses. Nonresident students attending Oregon State University for one term pay resident tuition.

YEAR ESTABLISHED: 1963.

NUMBER OF STUDENTS IN 1985:   220.

APPLY: Fall term by June 1; winter term by October 15; spring term by January 3. American Heritage Association, P.O. Box #425, Lake Oswego, OR 97034 (503) 635-3703, or Judy Van Dyck or Ann Ferguson, International Education, OSU.

■ **ROGER WILLIAMS COLLEGE**
Bristol, RI 02809
(401) 253-1040

PROGRAM: The London Theater Program is a fall-semester, undergraduate program designed for "serious theater students" concentrates on "fine arts in theater." (This program is required of all Roger Williams College theater majors.) Students combine class activities with visits to many of the current London theatrical presentations as well as visits to St. Albans, Greenwich, Canterbury, Stratford-upon-Avon, Windsor, Hampton Court, and a tour of Britain. Courses include: British theater and its cultural influences, theater of Shakespeare, theater design workshop, seminar in directing problems, and the history of architecture. Four-day preorientation session in London.

ADMITTANCE REQUIREMENTS: Open to theater majors with permission and satisfactory recommendation of student's home campus academic advisor or department chairman.

TEACHING METHODS: Small classes (approximately seven students) are taught by British faculty. Includes attendance of more than sixty plays, concerts, etc.

EVALUATION: Periodic exams and papers graded British faculty.

CREDITS OFFERED: 15 semester hours.

HOUSING: Students live in local hotels, which provide breakfast. An evening meal allowance is distributed weekly.

DATES: September 17 through December 7.

COSTS: Tuition $2,922; room and board: $1,745. Estimated additional living expenses: approximately $500. Does not include round-trip transportation. However, all tours and local travel (including a one-week BritRail pass) included.

YEAR ESTABLISHED: 1971.

NUMBER OF STUDENTS IN 1985: 28.

APPLY: By June 1 (but often accepts late applications). Mr. William Grandgeorge, Chairman, Theater Department.

■ **ROGER WILLIAMS COLLEGE**
  Bristol, RI 02809
  (401) 253-1040

PROGRAM: The Law in London Program is a two-week, late-spring undergraduate course that concentrates in various aspects of British law including comparative legal studies, juvenile justice, etc. A one-day intensive preorientation session is held in Bristol, Rhode Island.

ADMITTANCE REQUIREMENTS: Open to any college-level student with a satisfactory academic record.

TEACHING METHODS: This is a special program for American students taught by both Roger Williams' and local faculty. There is no integration with British students. Lectures and visits to local sites.

EVALUATION: Final paper graded by the course instructor.

CREDITS OFFERED: 3 semester hours.

HOUSING: Students live in local hotels.

DATES: May 25 through June 7.

COSTS: Tuition: $250; room and board: $912. Estimated additional living expenses: approximately $150. Does not include round-trip transportation. However, all local travel is included.

YEAR ESTABLISHED: 1984.

NUMBER OF STUDENTS IN 1985: 15.

APPLY: By March 1. Mr. Thomas E. Wright, Bristol Ferry Road, Bristol, RI 02809.

■ **ROSARY COLLEGE**
7900 West Division Street
River Forest, IL 60305
(312) 366-2490

PROGRAM: Rosary in London is a fall semester undergraduate program directed toward British life and culture. Students take tutorials that cover trends in the history, art, and literature of Britain. Students "log at least 200 hours of contact with British life and culture at museums, theaters, historic homes and churches, libraries and London events."

ADMITTANCE REQUIREMENTS: Sophomores and above with acceptable academic record.

TEACHING METHODS: Students take special courses taught by an American faculty and English tutors. Students are not integrated with British students.

EVALUATION: Periodic exams with a major paper in tutorial.

CREDITS OFFERED: Up to 16 semester hours depending upon course load.

HOUSING: Students stay in private homes.

DATES: September 1 through December 10.

COSTS: Tuition: $2,950; room and board: $1,700. Includes a ten-day English excursion. Round-trip transportation and personal expenses not included.

YEAR ESTABLISHED: 1971.

NUMBER OF STUDENTS IN 1985:   21.

APPLY: By February 1. Sister Nona Mary Allard, Associate Academic Dean.

■ **SOUTHEAST MISSOURI STATE UNIVERSITY**
   Cape Giradeau, MO 63701
   (314) 651-2562

PROGRAM: The Missouri London Program is a single-semester or summer program held in cooperation with the University of Missouri in Rolla, St. Louis, Columbia, and Kansas City; Southwest Missouri State University, Springfield; and Central Missouri State University, Warrensburg. The program offers a broad, multidiscipline selection of courses taught by regular Missouri faculty members. Orientation on various Missouri campuses prior to departure.

ADMITTANCE REQUIREMENTS: Good academic standing.

TEACHING METHODS: Students are not integrated with British students and are taught by visiting members of the various Missouri University faculties.

EVALUATION: By U.S. faculty, based upon class work and examinations.

CREDITS OFFERED: Up to 18 semester hours per semester; 6 semester hours for the summer sessions.

HOUSING: Students live in a leased facility.

DATES: Summer programs from June 10 to July 9 or from July 9 to August 7; fall semester: August 22 through December 5; spring semester: January 9 through May 24.

COSTS: Tuition: $1,000 per semester; room and board: $3,595 per semester. Does not include round-trip transportation or living expenses (estimated at $1,500 per semester).

YEAR ESTABLISHED: 1983.

NUMBER OF STUDENTS IN 1985:   40.

APPLY: Three months prior to start of course. Center for International Studies.

■ **STATE UNIVERSITY OF NEW YORK AT BINGHAMTON**
  Binghamton, NY 13901
  (607) 777-2417

PROGRAM: The SUNY Binghamton Semester in London program is a spring-semester undergraduate program with a strong focus on literature, writing, and theater. Local travel and field trips to cultural and historic sites are supplemented by extensive theater visits. One-day orientation in Binghamton and several onsite sessions in London.

ADMITTANCE REQUIREMENTS: 3.0 GPA with "preference given to juniors and seniors."

TEACHING METHODS: Faculty from SUNY-Binghamton teach courses especially designed to take advantage of the London setting. Students attend classes with British students.

EVALUATION: By university faculty and group leaders based on periodic papers, exams, and finals.

CREDITS OFFERED: 16 semester hours.

HOUSING: Students live together in either a hotel or in dormitories until they locate their own flats or rooming houses.

DATES: January 15 through May 20.

COSTS: Tuition: $675 state residents; $1,600 nonresidents; room and board: $2,600 to $3,000. Does not include round-trip transportation or personal expenses.

YEAR ESTABLISHED: 1973.

NUMBER OF STUDENTS IN 1985: 68.

APPLY: By November 1. Carol Fischler, Assistant to the Chairman, Department of English.

■ **STATE UNIVERSITY OF NEW YORK AT BROCKPORT**
Office of International Education
Brockport, NY 14420
(716) 395-2119

PROGRAM: The SUNY-Brockport London Program is a one-semester or academic-year undergraduate program held in cooperation with Brunel University. The program offers a varied selection of courses with an emphasis on history, political science, sociology, and criminal justice. Local travel and field trips to cultural and historic sites complement the program. Two-day orientation in London.

ADMITTANCE REQUIREMENTS: "Exceptional sophomores," juniors, and above with a 2.5 GPA and approval of major advisor.

TEACHING METHODS: Students attend special courses at the university arranged for the group. Both U.S. and foreign faculty. Americans are integrated with local students.

EVALUATION: By university faculty and group leaders, based on periodic papers, exams, and finals.

CREDITS OFFERED: 15 semester hours per semester.

HOUSING: Students may live in university dormitories or select their own flats or rooming houses.

DATES: Fall semester: early September through mid-December; spring semester: mid-January to early May.

COSTS: Approximately, $3,000 per semester. Includes tuition, room and board, and program-associated travel. Does not cover round-trip transportation, local travel, or personal expenses. Financial aid is available.

YEAR ESTABLISHED: 1972.

NUMBER OF STUDENTS IN 1985: 40.

APPLY: Fall semester by April 1; spring semester by October 1.

■ **STATE UNIVERSITY OF NEW YORK AT NEW PALTZ**
New Paltz, NY 12561
(914) 257-2233

PROGRAM: The SUNY-New Paltz-Middlesex Program is a single-semester or full-academic-year undergraduate and graduate program held in cooperation with Middlesex Polytechnic. The program emphasis is on liberal arts with courses covering: art history, American studies, drama and theater studies, history, law, history of ideas, philosophy, psychology, geography, English, and art studio courses in the School of Art and Design. One-day orientation in New Paltz.

ADMITTANCE REQUIREMENTS: Juniors, seniors, and graduate students in good academic standing.

TEACHING METHODS: Students attend regular university courses taught by the resident British faculty.

EVALUATION: By university faculty, based upon periodic exams, finals, and depending on the level of the course, a term paper.

CREDITS OFFERED: A minimum of 12; maximum of 18 semester hours per semester.

HOUSING: Students live in dormitories at the university or in local flats.

DATES: Approximately, fall semester: September 30 through January 20; spring semester: February 10 through June 6.

COSTS: Fall semester: $1,605; spring semester: $1,750. Includes tuition, room and board, and program-related field trips. Nonstate residents add approximately $925 per semester. Does not cover round-trip transportation or personal expenses (estimated at approximately $400 per semester).

YEAR ESTABLISHED: 1984.

NUMBER OF STUDENTS IN 1985: 10.

APPLY: For fall semester and academic year by April 1; spring semester by November 1. Dr. Rudolf R. Kossman, Director, Office of International Education.

■ **STATE UNIVERSITY OF NEW YORK AT OSWEGO**
Oswego, NY 13126
(315) 341-2118

PROGRAM: SUNY at Oswego offers a pair of London programs: International Broadcasting and Humanities. Both are semester or full-academic-year undergraduate programs. International Broadcasting is designed for students to gather insight into the social, political and cultural conditions which have created and perpetuated British systems of broadcasting. Courses cover: business in broadcasting in U.K./Europe; survey of British broadcasting; twentieth-century British history; dramatic theory and criticisim; a director's seminar, etc. The Humanities Program covers art, music, theater, and literature with a major emphasis on British works. Neither program is affiliated with a British university. SUNY at Oswego also offers a six-week summer program devoted to contemporary British culture.

ADMITTANCE REQUIREMENTS: Sophomores or above with a 2.5 GPA. Students interested in the broadcasting program should have from 6 to 12 hours in communications or broadcasting courses.

TEACHING METHODS: Courses are taught by both U.S. and British faculty with many guest lecturers.

EVALUATION: Based on work in class, papers, and final exams.

CREDITS OFFERED: 12 to 15 semester hours.

HOUSING: Students stay "in SUNY-approved accommodations in a nice London residential area."

DATES: Fall semester: early September through mid-December; spring semester: mid-January through mid-May.

COSTS: $2,400 per semester; $4,300 for full academic year. Includes tuition, room and breakfast, local field trips, and round-trip transportation from New York. Does not cover personal expenses, travel, and SUNY tuition and fees ($687.50 per semester for New York residents; $1,612.50 for nonresidents).

YEAR ESTABLISHED: 1966.

NUMBER OF STUDENTS IN 1985: 64.

APPLY: By April 10 for fall semester; November 1 for spring semester. Dr. José R. Pérez, Director, International Education, Overseas Academic Programs.

■ **TUFTS UNIVERSITY**
Medford, MA 02155
(617) 381-3152

PROGRAM: Tufts in London is a one- or two-semester undergraduate program held in cooperation with Westfield College, a constituent college of the University of London. Students participate in both Tufts courses (i.e., international economics, European organizations, English architecture, internships in media and Parliament, etc.) and Westfield courses (a more general, liberal arts curriculum covering language study, history, drama, art, etc.). Three-week orientation in London.

ADMITTANCE REQUIREMENTS: Good academic standing plus a 3.0 GPA in major.

TEACHING METHODS: Students may choose regular classes from Westfield catalogue as well as special courses designed by Tufts. Classes, seminars, and independent study projects.

EVALUATION: By British and Tufts professors, based upon class work, papers, and examinations.

CREDITS OFFERED: 16 semester hours per semester.

HOUSING: Students must live in Westfield College residences.

DATES: Fall semester: August 28 through December 11; spring semester: January 8 through April 21.

COSTS: $7,075 per semester. Covers tuition, room and board, round-trip transportation, and some local travel. Does not cover personal expenses.

YEAR ESTABLISHED: 1966.

NUMBER OF STUDENTS IN 1985:   64.

APPLY: By February 1 for fall semester and full year program; October 15 for spring semester. Dean Christopher Gray, Director, Tufts Programs Abroad, Ballou Hall.

■ **UNIVERSITY OF ARIZONA**
  Tucson, AZ 85721
  (602) 621-4819

PROGRAM: The London Semester is an undergraduate program held in cooperation with the University of London, Arizona State University, and Northern Arizona University. Students are required to take a course in British life and culture and may select other courses covering English, history, political science, management and policy, marketing, education, law, or an honors program. Onsite orientation.

ADMITTANCE REQUIREMENTS: For sophomores and above in good standing with their home institution.

TEACHING METHODS: Students attend regular academic and special courses taught by both U.S. and foreign faculty. Classes are integrated with foreign students. Field trips complement course of study.

EVALUATION: Based upon student evaluations, reports from the director of each program, periodic and final examinations.

CREDITS OFFERED: Up to 12 semester hours per semester.

HOUSING: Students live in student residences and local flats.

DATES: Fall semester: early September through mid-December; spring semester: mid-January through late April.

COSTS: Students pay regular tuition to university plus approximately $3,000 for London semester, room and board. Does not cover round-trip transportation, local travel, or personal expenses.

YEAR ESTABLISHED: 1978.

NUMBER OF STUDENTS IN 1985: 50.

APPLY: For fall semester by July 1; spring semester by November 1. Eugene von Teuber, Coordinator of International Studies, Room #209, Robert L. Nugent Building.

■ **UNIVERSITY OF DELAWARE**
  Newark, DE 19716
  (302) 451-2361

PROGRAM: The Semester in London program is a spring undergraduate session that offers courses in history, agriculture, political science, art, music, English, French, German, Spanish, anthropology, literature, business, theater, and computer science.

ADMITTANCE REQUIREMENTS: Sophomore and above with a 3.0 GPA, recommendations of major advisor.

TEACHING METHODS: Students do not take courses in a foreign school but are taught independently by both U.S. and British faculty. Some integration with local students. Lectures, field trips, and some independent study.

EVALUATION: By U.S. faculty, based upon class work, papers, and examinations.

CREDITS OFFERED: 15 semester hours.

HOUSING: In furnished rooms.

DATES: Approximately February 1 through mid-May.

COSTS: Approximately $3,800. Covers tuition, room and board, course-related travel. Does not include round-trip transportation or personal expenses.

YEAR ESTABLISHED: 1978.

NUMBER OF STUDENTS IN 1985: 30.

APPLY: By October 15. Chairman, Department of English.

■ **UNIVERSITY OF MARYLAND**
  College Park, MD 20742
  (301) 454-8645

PROGRAM: Study in London is a single-semester undergraduate program held in cooperation with the Polytechnic of Central London. The major focus is on British culture with courses covering art history, history, government, sociology, business, economics, philosophy, and English drama. One-day orientation in the U.S. and London.

ADMITTANCE REQUIREMENTS: Second-semester sophomores, juniors and seniors. 2.75 GPA or better.

TEACHING METHODS: Students attend regular academic courses at the Polytechnic and also are provided with special courses taught by American faculty. Lectures, class discussions, and field work.

EVALUATION: By both U.S. and British faculty, based upon an essay, exams, and papers.

CREDITS OFFERED: 15 semester hours.

HOUSING: Either with local families or in flats.

DATES: Fall semester: September through mid-December; spring semester: mid-January through early May.

COSTS: Tuition: $2,340; room and board: $1,600; estimated cost for local travel and personal expenses: $1,500. Does not cover round-trip transportation.

YEAR ESTABLISHED: 1979.

NUMBER OF STUDENTS IN 1985:   47.

APPLY: Fall semester by May 1; spring semester by October 15. Richard Weaver, Study Abroad Office.

■ **UNIVERSITY OF MINNESOTA**
   Extension Classes Offices of Study Abroad
   202 Wesbrook Hall,
   77 Pleasant Street SE
   Minneapolis, MN 55455
   (612) 373-1855

PROGRAM: Literature in London is a spring-quarter opportunity to study English literature and theater in London. The literature courses "will integrate course work with location by constant reference to British life, past and present." Six-day trip to Stratford-on-Avon.

ADMITTANCE REQUIREMENTS: Students in good academic standing. No established GPA required.

TEACHING METHODS: Students are taught by U.S. faculty in groups consisting only of other Americans.

EVALUATION: By course instructors, based upon class work, papers, and final examination.

CREDITS OFFERED: 12 quarter credits.

HOUSING: Students live in a residential hotel in the Kensington Gardens district.

DATES: April 1 through June 8.

COSTS: $2,650 includes tuition for 12 credits, accommodations with cooking facilities, field trips, and a $100 airfare deposit. Does not include round-trip transportation or personal expenses.

YEAR ESTABLISHED: 1971.

NUMBER OF STUDENTS IN 1985:   limited to 40.

APPLY: January 1. Jody Jensen, ECOSA.

■ **UNIVERSITY OF SOUTHERN CALIFORNIA**
Overseas Studies, CES 109
University Park,
Los Angeles, CA 90089
(213) 746-2500

PROGRAM: USC Journalism Semester in London is an undergraduate program concentrating on international relations and journalism. Onsite orientation.

ADMITTANCE REQUIREMENTS: Sophomores and above in good academic standing.

TEACHING METHODS: Courses are designed for the group and are taught by foreign faculty members. Classes are not integrated with British students.

EVALUATION: By course faculty member, based upon class work, papers, and periodic examinations.

CREDITS OFFERED: 16 semester hours.

HOUSING: Students can live with private families or in local flats.

DATES: Approximately, fall semester: early September through mid-December; spring semester: early January through mid-May.

COSTS: Approximately $3,500 covers tuition, room and board, program-related travel. Does not include round-trip transportation or personal expenses. Some scholarships are available.

YEAR ESTABLISHED: 1984.

NUMBER OF STUDENTS IN 1985: 21.

APPLY: Fall semester by April 1; spring semester by October 1.

■ **UNIVERSITY OF WASHINGTON**
Foreign Study Office
572 Schmitz Hall, PA-10
Seattle, WA 98195
(206) 543-9272

PROGRAM: The London Quarter is a single-term undergraduate program designed to serve as "an introduction to London and Great Britain through courses in social sciences and the arts, including excursions to sites in England and the cultural attractions of London." Onsite orientation.

ADMITTANCE REQUIREMENTS: Sophomore standing and acceptable academic credentials.

TEACHING METHODS: Courses are taught by visiting Northwest faculty and resident British faculty.

EVALUATION: By course faculty member, based upon papers and examinations.

CREDITS OFFERED: A full quarter term per quarter.

HOUSING: Students live with local families.

DATES: Approximately, fall term: late August through late November; winter term: early December through late February; spring semester: early March through late May.

COSTS: $2,400 per term includes tuition, room and board. Does not cover round-trip transportation, local travel, or personal expenses.

YEAR ESTABLISHED: 1964.

NUMBER OF STUDENTS IN 1985: 50.

APPLY: Approximately four months prior to start of term. David Fenner, Advisor.

■ **UNIVERSITY OF WISCONSIN – PLATTEVILLE**
1 University Plaza
Platteville, WI 53818
(608) 342-1726

PROGRAM: The London Study Center is a semester or full-year undergraduate program held in cooperation with Ealing College of Higher Education. The program is one of the few that "mainstreams American students in a British college." Students have the option to study with British instructors in American-style classes specially designed for Americans, or study on the British system in many of the courses offered by Ealing. Courses cover a colloquium on British culture, art, business administration, communications, criminal justice, economics, English, French, music, political science, psychology, and sociology. Six field trips are included in the program with optional travel opportunities offered periodically. Orientation in Platteville and in London.

ADMITTANCE REQUIREMENTS: Sophomore or above with a 2.5 GPA.

TEACHING METHODS: Students take courses from the regular Ealing College curriculum or courses specially designed for Americans. All courses are taught by a British faculty.

EVALUATION: By course faculty, based upon class work, papers, and examinations.

CREDITS OFFERED: 15 semester hours per semester.

HOUSING: Students have three options: full-student board in a British home; live in a bed and breakfast establishment; or, self catering in which students are provided a room and access to cooking facilities.

DATES: Fall semester: September 23 through December 17; spring semester: January 6 through April 3.

COSTS: $3,125 per semester (Wisconsin and Minnesota residents); $3,475 (nonresidents). Includes tuition, room and board, and program-related field trips. Does not cover round-trip transportation or personal expenses (estimated at about $250 a month).

YEAR ESTABLISHED: 1979.

NUMBER OF STUDENTS IN 1985: 300.

APPLY: Fall semester by April 30; spring semester by November 15. Institute for Study Abroad Programs, 308 Warner Hall.

■ **UNIVERSITY OF WISCONSIN – STEVENS POINT**
208 Old Main
Stevens Point, WI 54481
(715) 346-2717

PROGRAM: Semester in Britain is a spring or fall travel/study undergraduate program. Although the majority of the program is held in London, the group spends about a month traveling to Germany, Italy, Austria, Switzerland, France, and within Britain. Classes in London are given at Peace Haven, "a comfortable Victorian manor in the city of Acton" and include European history, art history, music and theater appreciation, women's studies, English, Shakespeare, business classes, and some sciences. A four-week summer session concentrating on architecture and design is also available.

ADMITTANCE REQUIREMENTS: Sophomores and above in good academic standing.

TEACHING METHODS: Students attend courses held at Peace Haven arranged for the group.

EVALUATION: By instructors and group leaders, based upon class work, papers, and examinations.

CREDITS OFFERED: A minimum of 13 semester hours; maximum of 17.

HOUSING: Students stay in hostels while traveling and at Peace Haven in London.

DATES: Approximately, August 25 to December 10 and January 4 to April 30.

COSTS: Approximately, $2,995 includes tuition, room and board, round-trip transportation from Chicago, and program-related travel. Minnesota students pay a small "reciprocity fee"; non-Wisconsin residents pay a surcharge of about $1,500. Does not cover personal expenses.

YEAR ESTABLISHED: 1970.

NUMBER OF STUDENTS IN 1985: 50.

APPLY: "Early application is advised." Dr. Helen Cornell, Director, International Programs.

■ **WESTERN ILLINOIS UNIVERSITY**
  Macomb, IL 61455
  (309) 298-2426

PROGRAM: Semester Abroad in London is a Fall or Spring semester undergraduate program held in cooperation with the American Institute of Foreign Study. Courses are conducted by faculty members of a consortium composed of the Universities of Wisconsin-Madison, Nebraska-Omaha, New Mexico, Iowa, Iowa State, Nevada-Las Vegas, Nevada-Reno, and Northern Iowa. Classes are held at the University of London Union building and cover psychology, sociology, theater, comparative political systems, economics, communications, English art, and literature, etc. A course on British life and culture is required. Optional eight-day European orientation/tour.

ADMITTANCE REQUIREMENTS: Good academic standing.

TEACHING METHODS: Special courses are taught by consortium faculty. Field trips and independent study complements the program.

EVALUATION: By course instructors, based upon class work, papers, and examinations.

CREDITS OFFERED: 15 semester hours.

HOUSING: Students can live with families or in modernized nineteenth-century town houses.

DATES: Fall semester: September 5 through December 11; spring semester: January 3 through April 9.

COSTS: $3,595 per semester. Includes tuition, room and ten meals a week, program-related travel, and round-trip transportation from Chicago. Does not include optional presession tour ($325), WIU tuition ($616.50 for state residents; $1,400 for nonresidents), or personal expenses.

YEAR ESTABLISHED: 1978.

NUMBER OF STUDENTS IN 1985: 14.

APPLY: No application deadline. Dr. Robert Gabler, Office of International Education, 100 Memorial Hall.

Loughborough

■ **STATE UNIVERSITY OF NEW YORK AT BROCKPORT**
Office of International Education
Brockport, NY 14420
(716) 395-2119

PROGRAM: The English Literature and Drama Program is an academic year undergraduate program held at the University of Loughborough. The program concentrates on the English language, literature, and drama. Local travel and field trips to cultural and historic sites complement the program. Two-day orientation in England.

ADMITTANCE REQUIREMENTS: Juniors and above with a 2.5 GPA.

TEACHING METHODS: Students attend special courses at the university arranged for the group. Americans are integrated with local students.

EVALUATION: By university faculty and group leaders based on periodic papers, exams, and finals.

CREDITS OFFERED: 30 semester hours per year.

HOUSING: Students live in university dormitories.

DATES: Early September through mid-May.

COSTS: Approximately $5,000 per year. Includes tuition, room and board. Does not cover round-trip transportation, local travel or personal expenses.

YEAR ESTABLISHED: 1979.

NUMBER OF STUDENTS IN 1985: 9.

APPLY: By April 1.

Manchester

■ **PENNSYLVANIA STATE UNIVERSITY**
Office of Education Abroad Programs
222 Boucke Building
University Park, PA 16802
(814) 865-7681

PROGRAM: Pennsylvania State University offers a pair of programs: an exchange program in which Americans take regular courses at the University of Manchester as a regular member of the school's student body; and a spring semester program which concentrates on mass communications. The latter program also enables Americans to attend regular University of Manchester classes, but is directed toward a comparative analysis of the mass communication system of the United States, Great Britain, and other European countries. Orientation at Penn State.

ADMITTANCE REQUIREMENTS: Juniors and seniors with a 2.5 GPA, good academic standing, and "must show evidence of maturity, stability, adaptability, self-discipline and a strong academic motivation." The mass communications program also requires several prior communications courses and a 3-credit course dealing with contemporary British literature.

TEACHING METHODS: Students on the exchange program enroll in regular courses. The mass communications program includes classroom lectures, a two-week internship with the British media, tutorials, case studies, and field trips.

EVALUATION: By course instructors, based upon class work, papers, and examinations.

CREDITS OFFERED: Exchange program: 24 credits; mass communications program: 15 credits.

HOUSING: Students live in school residence halls or may find local accommodations.

DATES: Approximately, Exchange Program: early September through the third week in June; Mass Communications Program: mid-January through late August.

COSTS: Students pay the same as at the University Park Campus. 1986-1987 tuition per semester was $2,250 for state residents; $5,150 for nonresidents; room and board: $2,750 per semester. Plus a $100 nonrefundable program fee.

YEAR ESTABLISHED: Exchange, 1982; Mass Communications, 1971.

NUMBER OF STUDENTS IN 1985: Exchange, 3; Mass Communications, 28.

APPLY: Exchange Program by March 1; Mass Communications by October 15.

Norwich

■ **BEAVER COLLEGE**
Glenside, PA 19038
(215) 572-2901

PROGRAM: Beaver operates several programs in Norwich in cooperation with the University of East Anglia. Programs range from the full academic year to single semester. Students may concentrate in a full year humanities program or may concentrate on specific areas covering communications, creative writing or drama, and theater studies. In all programs, students attend regular classes with British students. Internships in theater administration are conducted at the Norwich Theatre Royal. Orientation in London.

ADMITTANCE REQUIREMENTS: Juniors and seniors with a 3.0 GPA (3.2 in major field).

TEACHING METHODS: Students take regular courses, seminars, and tutorials taught by university professors. Americans are fully integrated with British students.

EVALUATION: By course faculty, based upon class work and periodic examinations.

CREDITS OFFERED: 15 to 16 semester hours per semester.

HOUSING: Students live in university dormitories or residence halls.

DATES: Fall semester: September 22 through December 19; spring semester: January 4 through June 26.

COSTS: Vary depending upon school and program. Approximately $4,100 per semester includes tuition, room, transportation to London, and program-related travel. Does not cover meals, return transportation, or personal expenses.

YEAR ESTABLISHED: 1970.

NUMBER OF STUDENTS IN 1985:   24.

APPLY: For fall semester: April 20; spring semester: October 5. Center for Education Abroad.

Oxford

■ **BEAVER COLLEGE**
Glenside, PA 19038
(215) 572-2901

PROGRAM: Oxford Semester is either a single-semester or full-year program in which students are enrolled in special courses arranged for the group by the Rector of Exeter College. Courses concentrate in contemporary British and European politics, history, and economics. Orientation in London.

ADMITTANCE REQUIREMENTS: Juniors with a 3.4 GPA.

TEACHING METHODS: Students take special courses, seminars, and tutorials taught by Oxford professors.

EVALUATION: By course faculty, based upon class work and periodic examinations.

CREDITS OFFERED: 16 semester hours per semester.

HOUSING: Students live in residence halls.

DATES: Fall semester: September 7 through December 19; spring semester: January 4 through April 18.

COSTS: Approximately $6,325 per semester includes tuition, room, transportation to London, and program-related travel. Does not cover meals, return transportation, or personal expenses.

YEAR ESTABLISHED: 1985.

NUMBER OF STUDENTS IN 1985: 25.

APPLY: For fall semester: April 20; spring semester: October 5. Center for Education Abroad.

■ **BOSTON UNIVERSITY**
  143 Bay State Road
  Boston, MA 02215
  (617) 353-9888

PROGRAM: Modern British Studies is a single-semester or full-academic-year undergraduate program, held in cooperation with St. Catherine's College, offering courses concentrating in modern English literature, history and politics. One-week orientation in London.

ADMITTANCE REQUIREMENTS: 3.3 GPA essay and recommendations.

TEACHING METHODS: Students attend special courses arranged for the group and taught by the faculty of St. Catherine's College.

EVALUATION: By course faculty, based upon papers and periodic examinations.

CREDITS OFFERED: 16 semester hours per semester.

HOUSING: Students live in rented flats or with local families.

DATES: Fall semester: September 5 through December 10; spring semester: January 9 through April 19.

COSTS: Approximately $5,750 per semester includes tuition and housing. Does not cover meals, round-trip transportation or personal expenses.

YEAR ESTABLISHED: 1986.

NUMBER OF STUDENTS IN 1985: 25.

APPLY: At least two months prior to start of semester. Dr. Timothy Perkins, London Internship Programme.

■ **COLLEGE OF NOTRE DAME**
Belmont, CA 94002
(415) 584-4605

PROGRAM: The Oxford Experience is a full four-year, academic-year, or summer program for undergraduate or graduate students held in cooperation with Warnborough College. The college offers courses in English literature, education, history, art, music, political science, sociology, languages, mathematics, natural and physical sciences, religion, economics, business studies, philosophy, legal studies, psychology, history of ideas, British studies and communications. Internships available in communications, public relations, marketing, and laboratory research. Preorientation material is sent to U.S. students from Warnborough College.

ADMITTANCE REQUIREMENTS: "Students in good standing should have no difficulty in being accepted into the Semester-Year Abroad programme."

TEACHING METHODS: Students are fully integrated into the college. Classes are based upon the Oxford University system with lectures more prominent during the initial two years; tutorials and field experiences during the latter two.

EVALUATION: By faculty, based upon class papers and midterm and final examinations.

CREDITS OFFERED: 4 semester hours per course; 16 semester hours per semester.

HOUSING: Students live in campus residence halls.

DATES: Fall semester: September 8 through December 18; spring semester: January 23 through April 24.

COSTS: $5,750 per semester. Includes tuition, room and board, and program-related travel. Does not include round-trip transportation, local travel, or personal expenses. $1,000 in scholarship aid per student available from Warnborough College.

YEAR ESTABLISHED: 1973.

NUMBER OF STUDENTS IN 1985: 150.

APPLY: Fall semester by July 15; spring semester by November 15. Sister Gabrielle Sullivan SND, 1 Thomas More Way, San Francisco, CA 94132, or directly to Admission Office, Warnborough College, Oxford OX1 5ED, ENGLAND.

■ **THE EXPERIMENT IN INTERNATIONAL LIVING**
Kipling Road
Brattleboro, VT 05301-0676
(800) 451-4465

PROGRAM: The College Semester Abroad program is designed to allow students to become immersed in a foreign culture by living with a local family and exploring individual personal and educational interests under professional guidance. The Oxford, England, program covers: seminar on British life and culture, history and politics, geography and economics, arts and humanities, social anthropology, and an independent study project. Orientation in London.

ADMITTANCE REQUIREMENTS: Sophomore standing or above and acceptable academic credentials. No language prerequisite.

TEACHING METHODS: Students work directly with their American instructors in planning and evaluating their individual program. "The semester builds from the more structured language training and lectures and discussions on local life and culture to the independent study project."

EVALUATION: By individual students and their instructor-advisors based on independent project, papers, reports, and examinations. Periodic meetings during the program and for several days at the conclusion.

CREDITS OFFERED: Up to 16 semester hours.

HOUSING: Students live as family members with their host families.

DATES: Approximately, fall semester: September through December; spring semester: January through May.

COSTS: $5,900 includes tuition, room and board, all fees, local travel, and round-trip transportation from Brattleboro, Vermont.

YEAR ESTABLISHED: 1962.

NUMBER OF STUDENTS IN 1985: 13.

APPLY: For fall semester by May 15; spring semester by November 15. Admissions Office, College Semester Abroad.

■ **SUSQUEHANNA UNIVERSITY**
  Selingsgrove, PA 17870
  (717) 374-0101, ext. 4254

PROGRAM: Semester at Oxford is a six-week undergraduate summer program held in cooperation with Corpus Christi College, Oxford University, Templeton College (Oxford Management Centre), Oxford University, and The National Theatre. Courses deal with British political history, literature, architectural history, economic history, management, political science, education, archaeology, landscape studies, theater, drama, and music. There is also presession group travel to Ireland, Edinburgh, London, and Stratford.

ADMITTANCE REQUIREMENTS: Juniors and seniors with a minimum 2.5 GPA; sophomores with a minimum 3.0 GPA, and permission of home institution.

TEACHING METHODS: Combination of regular courses in Oxford University summer school and special courses all taught by British faculty. American students are not integrated with British students.

EVALUATION: By foreign faculty based upon periodic tests, final exams, and class participation.

CREDITS OFFERED: Varies between 4 and 12 semester hours depending on course load.

HOUSING: Students live in university dormitories.

DATES: Presession group travel: June 9 to June 29; Study Program at Oxford: June 29 through August 8.

COSTS: $2,525 includes tuition, room and board. Does not include round-trip transportation or living expenses (estimated at approximately $600).

YEAR ESTABLISHED: 1966.

NUMBER OF STUDENTS IN 1985: 35.

APPLY: By March 28. Dr. Robert L. Bradford, Director, Office of International Education.

Reading

■ RANDOLPH-MACON WOMAN'S COLLEGE
Lynchburg, VA 24503
(804) 846-7392, ext. 345

PROGRAM: The Junior Year Abroad program, held at the University of Reading, is an undergraduate liberal arts experience featuring a mandatory year-long seminar on the British Heritage featuring guest lecturers from all disciplines. Courses cover computer sciences, studio art, theater, communications, English, fine arts, history, social sciences, natural sciences, and foreign languages. Three weekend and three day trips are part of the program.

ADMITTANCE REQUIREMENTS: "Each individual is judged individually. We take into account both strength of institution and strength of the academic program. We would like a 3.0 GPA."

TEACHING METHODS: Tutorial system. Students attend either private tutorials or university classes. Most courses are taught by British faculty. Each participant is affiliated with a university residence where they eat and associate with British students.

EVALUATION: Either pass/fail determined by tutors at the conclusion of each of three terms. Extensive written reports by tutors assist students.

CREDITS OFFERED: 30 semester hours per year.

HOUSING: Students eat at the university, but live in one of three Randolph-Macon-owned houses located across the street from the university.

DATES: September 25 through July 5.

COSTS: $12,000 includes tuition, room and board, program-related travel, and fees. Does not include round-trip transportation or personal expenses. Financial aid is available.

YEAR ESTABLISHED: 1968.

NUMBER OF STUDENTS IN 1985: 35.

APPLY: By February 5. Dr. Paul L. Irwin.

- *"Don't limit yourself to Randolph-Macon tutorials—after all you're here for the British perspective, so try to get into a University Course."*

                                                        - Laura Fitch, Randolph-Macon

Southampton

■ **BEAVER COLLEGE**
   Glenside, PA 19038
   (215) 572-2901

PROGRAM: British University Year at the University of Southampton is a full-academic-year program. Students attend regular classes at the university and are fully integrated into the school's academic and social programs. Courses cover the arts, humanities, mathematics, natural and social sciences, political sciences, etc. Orientation in London.

ADMITTANCE REQUIREMENTS: Juniors and seniors with a 3.0 GPA.

TEACHING METHODS: Students take regular courses, seminars, and tutorials taught by university professors. Americans are fully integrated with British students.

EVALUATION: By course faculty, based upon class work and periodic examinations.

CREDITS OFFERED: 15 to 16 semester hours per semester.

HOUSING: Students live in university dormitories.

DATES: Fall semester: September 14 through December 19; spring semester: January 4 through June 26.

COSTS: Approximately $7,815 per year includes tuition, room, transportation to London, and program-related travel. Does not cover meals, return transportation, or personal expenses.

YEAR ESTABLISHED: 1971.

NUMBER OF STUDENTS IN 1985:   4.

APPLY: April 20. Center for Education Abroad.

York

■ **BEAVER COLLEGE**
Glenside, PA 19038
(215) 572-2901

PROGRAM: Beaver's program at the University of York is either a single-semester or full-academic-year program. Students attend regular classes at the university and are fully integrated into the school's academic and social programs. Courses cover archaeology, art history, natural and physical sciences, political science, economics, computer sciences, economic and social history, education, electronic engineering, English literature, history, linguistics, music, social policy and administration, sociology, etc. Orientation in London.

ADMITTANCE REQUIREMENTS: Juniors and seniors with a 3.0 GPA.

TEACHING METHODS: Students take regular courses, seminars, and tutorials taught by university professors. Americans are fully integrated with British students.

EVALUATION: By course faculty, based upon class work and periodic examinations.

CREDITS OFFERED: 15 to 16 semester hours per semester.

HOUSING: Students live in university dormitories.

DATES: Fall semester: September 22 through December 19; spring semester: January 4 through June 26.

COSTS: Approximately, $8,250 per year includes tuition, room transportation to London, and program-related travel. Does not cover meals, return transportation, or personal expenses.

YEAR ESTABLISHED: 1982.

NUMBER OF STUDENTS IN 1985: 25.

APPLY: April 20. Center for Education Abroad.

Scotland

Population: 5,136,000   **Capital:** Edinburgh   **Language:** English, Scots-Gaelic
Monetary Unit: Pound sterling   **Government:** Constitutional monarchy
(British monarch and prime minister)   **Religion:** 57% Anglican
Households With Television: 97%

SELECTED COLLEGES AND UNIVERSITIES

Royal Scotish Academy of Music
and Drama
St. George's Place
Glasgow G2 1BS

*Music, drama, and opera. "A limited
number of places in full-time courses
may be available to students from
overseas."*

University of Aberdeen
Aberdeen AB9 2UR

University of Glasgow
Glasgow G12 8QQ

University of Edinburgh
Old College, South Bridge
Edinburgh EH8 9YL

FURTHER INFORMATION

British Information Services
845 Third Avenue
New York, NY 10022
(212) 752-8440

Consulate General of the
United Kingdom
845 Third Avenue
New York, NY 10022
(212) 752-8400

Embassy of the United Kingdom
3100 Massachusetts Avenue
Washington, DC 20008
(202) 462-1340

British Tourist Office
680 Fifth Avenue
New York, NY 10019
(212) 581-4700

British Council
10 Spring Gardens
London SW1A 2BN

Publishes Higher Education in the
United Kingdom.

Scottish Education Department
New St. Andrew's House
St. James Centre
Edinburgh EH1 3SY

Universities Central Council
on Admissions
PO Box 28
Cheltenham GX50 1HY

Publishes excellent free guide, How to
Apply for Admissions to a University.

Aberdeen

■ **AMERICAN INSTITUTE OF FOREIGN STUDY (AIFS)**
102 Greenwich Avenue
Greenwich, CT 06830
(800) 243-4567 or (203) 869-9090

PROGRAM: AIFS is a national, for-profit organization specializing in comprehensive overseas academic-year, semester, and summer study programs. The AIFS program at the University of Aberdeen is a full-academic-year or single-term program in which students are fully integrated into university academic, social, athletic, and cultural life. Courses cover biological sciences, chemistry, English literature, geology and geography, history and economic history, languages, law, philosophy, politics, and religious studies. A special prelaw curriculum is available. Five-day orientation in Aberdeen.

ADMITTANCE REQUIREMENTS: College juniors and seniors with a 3.0 GPA.

TEACHING METHODS: Americans are fully integrated with British students and take regular courses at the university. Most courses consist of three or four one-hour lectures each week, plus a tutorial or seminar.

EVALUATION: By university faculty, based upon class work, papers, and periodic examinations.

CREDITS OFFERED: AIFS students normally obtain about 30 semesters hours credit for a full year's work.

HOUSING: Students live in single rooms in residence halls or in "university-approved lodgings."

DATES: Fall term: October 13 through December 19; winter term: January 12 through March 20; spring term: April 21 through June 26.

COSTS: Full academic year: $8,250; fall term: $3,395; winter-spring term: $4,895. Includes tuition, room, and one-way transportation from New York. Does not cover board (estimated at $275 per term), local travel, or personal expenses.

YEAR ESTABLISHED: 1973.

NUMBER OF STUDENTS IN 1985: 6.

APPLY: Applications filled on first-come basis. "It is expected that all full year or fall semester places will be filled by June 1; places for spring semester are kept open until November 15."

■ **BEAVER COLLEGE**
  Glenside, PA 19038
  (215) 572-2901

PROGRAM: British University Year at the University of Aberdeen is either a single-semester or a full-academic-year program. Students attend regular classes at the University of Aberdeen and are fully integrated into the school's academic and social programs. Courses cover art history, divinity, the humanities, natural and social sciences. Onsite orientation.

ADMITTANCE REQUIREMENTS: Juniors and seniors with a 3.0 GPA.

TEACHING METHODS: Students take regular courses, seminars, and tutorials taught by university professors. Americans are fully integrated with British students.

EVALUATION: By course faculty, based upon class work and periodic examinations.

CREDITS OFFERED: 15 to 16 semester hours per semester.

HOUSING: Students live in student residences.

DATES: Fall semester: September 14 through December 19; spring semester: January 4 through June 20.

COSTS: Approximately $4,000 per semester includes tuition, room, and transportation from New York to Scotland. Does not cover meals, return transportation, or personal expenses.

YEAR ESTABLISHED: 1983.

NUMBER OF STUDENTS IN 1985:   30.

APPLY: For fall semester: April 20; spring semester: October 5.
Center for Education Abroad.

■ GREAT LAKES COLLEGES ASSOCIATION (GLCA)
c/o Wabash College
Crawfordville, IN 47933
(317) 364-4410

PROGRAM: The GLCA Scotland Program is a full-year undergraduate program held in cooperation with the University of Aberdeen and the member colleges of the GLCA: Albion College, Antioch College, Denison College, DePauw University, Earlham College, Hope College, Kalamazoo College, Kenyon College, Oberlin College, Ohio Wesleyan University, Wabash College, The College of Wooster, and Houghton College. Students can select from a wide range of courses taught at the university. There is a one-week onsite orientation preceded by newsletters sent to students over the summer.

ADMITTANCE REQUIREMENTS: Juniors with a 3.0 GPA average.

TEACHING METHODS: Students select from regular academic courses in every discipline taught at the university. No U.S. faculty. Americans are fully integrated with British students. Independent study projects are welcomed.

EVALUATION: By British faculty generally, based upon three tests and some written papers during the year. Students receive a letter grade, written evaluation of class work, and class ranking.

CREDITS OFFERED: Equivalent to one full year at student's home institution.

HOUSING: All students live with British students in the university dormitories.

DATES: October 1 through May 20.

COSTS: Tuition: $6,600; room and board: $1,500; round-trip transportation is included. Does not include local travel, vacation expenses (three weeks over Christmas; a month in the spring) or estimated living expenses (approximately $2,000 for the program).

YEAR ESTABLISHED: 1964.

NUMBER OF STUDENTS IN 1985: 41.

APPLY: By March 1. Nancy J. Doemel, Director, GLCA Scotland Program.

Edinburgh

■ **BEAVER COLLEGE**
Glenside, PA 19038
(215) 572-2901

PROGRAM: British University Year at the University of of Edinburgh is either a single-semester or a full-academic-year program. Students attend regular classes at the University of Edinburgh and are fully integrated into the school's academic and social programs. Courses cover art history, humanities, and the natural and physical sciences. The single-term program is devoted to the social sciences. Onsite orientation.

ADMITTANCE REQUIREMENTS: Juniors and seniors with a 3.0 GPA (3.3 for engineering students).

TEACHING METHODS: Students take regular courses, seminars, and tutorials taught by university professors. Americans are fully integrated with British students.

EVALUATION: By course faculty, based upon class work and periodic examinations.

CREDITS OFFERED: 15 to 16 semester hours per semester.

HOUSING: Students live in dormitories or student residences.

DATES: Fall semester: September 14 through December 12; spring semester: January 12 through June 20.

COSTS: Approximately $4,200 per semester includes tuition, room, and transportation from New York to Scotland. Does not cover meals, return transportation, or personal expenses.

YEAR ESTABLISHED: 1972.

NUMBER OF STUDENTS IN 1985: 25.

APPLY: For fall semester: April 20; spring semester: October 5. Center for Education Abroad.

Wales

Population: 2,811,800   **Capital:** Cardiff   **Language:** English, Welsh
Monetary Unit: Pound sterling   **Government:** Constitutional monarchy
(British monarch and prime minister)   **Religion:** Anglican 57%
Households With Television: 97%

SELECTED COLLEGES AND UNIVERSITIES

University of Wales
Cathays Park
Cardiff CF1 3NS

University College Cardiff
Cathays Park
Cardiff CF4 4XN

FURTHER INFORMATION

British Information Services
845 Third Avenue
New York, NY 10022
(212) 752-8440

Embassy of the United Kingdom
3100 Massachusetts Avenue
Washington, DC 20008
(202) 462-1340

Consulate General of the
United Kingdom
845 Third Avenue
New York, NY 10022
(212) 752-8400

British Tourist Office
680 Fifth Avenue
New York, NY 10019
(212) 581-4700

British Council
10 Spring Gardens
London SW1A 2BN

Publishes Higher Education in the
United Kingdom.

Universities Central Council
on Admissions
PO Box 28
Cheltenham, Glos GX50 1HY

Publishes excellent free guide, How to
Apply for Admission to a University.

Cardiff

■ **COLGATE UNIVERSITY**
Hamilton, NY 13346
(315) 824-1000

PROGRAM: The Wales Study Group is a single-semester undergraduate program that offers courses in Welsh history and culture, chemistry, biology, geology, and environmental studies. Optional field trips. Orientation in the U.S.

ADMITTANCE REQUIREMENTS: Sophomores and above in good academic standing. Physical science and Colgate students are shown a preference, but others accepted.

TEACHING METHODS: Students attend regular classes at University College as well as special courses arranged for the group and taught by both U.S. and Welsh faculty.

EVALUATION: By course professors, based upon papers and examinations.

CREDITS OFFERED: 16 semester hours.

HOUSING: Students live in dormitories at University College.

DATES: Approximately early January through early July.

COSTS: $6,000 includes tuition, round-trip transportation, and program-related travel. Does not cover room and board or personal expenses.

YEAR ESTABLISHED: 1985.

NUMBER OF STUDENTS IN 1985: 16.

APPLY: By March 14. Department of Chemistry.

Carmarthen

■ **CENTRAL COLLEGE**
Pella, IA 50219
(515) 628-5287

PROGRAM: Central College's Wales Program offers undergraduate students either a semester or full-academic-year of study at Trinity College. A broad range of liberal arts courses cover: Welsh studies, literature, and culture; history, art, business, education, math and science, political science, theater, music, philosophy, etc. Three-day orientation in Carmarthen.

ADMITTANCE REQUIREMENTS: Minimum 2.5 GPA, recommendations, and essay.

TEACHING METHODS: Special classes for American students are taught by Trinity faculty. Lectures and seminars are complemented by local field trips.

EVALUATION: By Trinity faculty. Resident director sends grades to home institution.

CREDITS OFFERED: 16 to 20 semester hours per semester.

HOUSING: Students live in Trinity College dormitories.

DATES: Fall semester: September through January; spring semester: early February through June.

COSTS: Approximately, both semesters (9 months), $8,300; one semester (4½ months), $4,500. Includes tuition, room, fees, and all meals. Does not cover round-trip transportation or personal expenses. Several $500 merit scholarships are available.

YEAR ESTABLISHED: 1976.

NUMBER OF STUDENTS IN 1985: 35.

APPLY: By April 15 for fall semester or full year; November 1 for spring semester. Mrs. Barbara Butler, Coordinator of International Studies.

9.

Eastern Europe and the U.S.S.R.

GERMAN DEMOCRATIC REPUBLIC

Population: 16,640,000   **Capital:** East Berlin   **Language:** German
Monetary Unit: Mark of Deutsche Demokratische Republik   **Government:** Single
party republic (chairman and premier)   **Religion:** 47% Protestant
Households With Television: 16%

FURTHER INFORMATION

Embassy of the German
Democratic Republic
1717 Massachusetts Avenue, NW
Washington, DC 20036
(202) 232-3134

East Berlin

■ **GOSHEN COLLEGE**
Goshen, IN 46526
(219) 533-3161

PROGRAM: Goshen's Study Service Trimester Abroad is a fourteen-week
(one trimester), undergraduate program offering students the opportunity to
concentrate on the region's language, history, and culture. Courses include
history, geography, politics, crosscultural studies, and crosscultural sensitization, i.e., art, music, drama, etc. All students must be enrolled at Goshen the
preceding trimester to attend orientation sessions.

ADMITTANCE REQUIREMENTS: For sophomores and above who meet
acceptable academic standards.

TEACHING METHODS: Students attend special classes taught by a foreign faculty. Courses involve regular class work, field trips, research projects. Each student must also participate in a work assignment such as hospital, school, community development project, etc.

EVALUATION: By accompanying Goshen College faculty member(s), based upon class work and assessment of projects.

CREDITS OFFERED: 12 semester hours.

HOUSING: Students live with host families.

DATES: Fall trimester: September 11 through December 16; winter trimester: January 8 through April 14; spring trimester: April 24 through July 28.

COSTS: Tuition: $2,390; room and board: $1,040; includes round-trip transportation and local field trips.

APPLY: One trimester prior to the program. Arlin Hunsberger, Director of International Education.

HUNGARY

Population: 10,622,000   **Capital:** Budapest   **Language:** Hungarian
Monetary Unit: Forint   **Government:** Unitary single-party republic (president and premier)   **Religion:** 54% Roman Catholic; 22% Protestant
Households With Television: 12%

SELECTED COLLEGES AND UNIVERSITIES

Ministry of Culture and Education
P.O. Box 1
1884 Budapest

Zoltan Kodaly Pedagogical Institute of Music
P.O. Box 188
6001 Kecskemet
Graduate programs in music. In English, German, and French.

FURTHER INFORMATION

Embassy of Hungary
3910 Shoemaker Street, NW
Washington, DC 20008
(202) 362-6730

Ibusz Hungarian Travel Bureau
630 Fifth Avenue
New York, NY 10020
(212) 582-7412

Budapest

■ **SLIPPERY ROCK UNIVERSITY**
Slippery Rock, PA 16057
(412) 794-7425

PROGRAM: Study in Budapest is a three-week summer program held in cooperation with the University of Horticulture. The broad liberal arts program including both class work and local travel is open to either undergraduate or graduate students. Students travel as a group. Onsite orientation.

ADMITTANCE REQUIREMENTS: Sophomore standing for undergraduates. For graduate students, requirements depend upon chosen course.

TEACHING METHODS: Courses are presented in English by Slippery Rock faculty.

EVALUATION: Exams are given by Slippery Rock faculty.

CREDITS OFFERED: 3 semester hours.

HOUSING: In school dormitories.

DATES: August 1 through August 21.

COSTS: $1,475 covers tuition, room and board, round-trip transportation, and local travel.

YEAR ESTABLISHED: 1986.

NUMBER OF STUDENTS IN 1986: Not available.

APPLY: By May 1. Stan Kendziorski, Director, International Education.

Szeged

■ **OREGON STATE SYSTEM OF HIGHER EDUCATION (OSSHE)**
Foreign Study Programs
International Education
Oregon State University
Corvallis, OR
(503) 754-3006

PROGRAM: The OSSHE Hungary program is a new undergraduate and graduate exchange program held in cooperation with Jozsef Atilla University and the member schools of OSSHE (Eastern Oregon State College, Oregon Institute of Technology, Portland State University, Southern Oregon State University, University of Oregon, and Western Oregon State College). The program covers the Hungarian language, culture, humanities, folklore, cinema, and the social sciences. For students sufficient in Hungarian, courses in most disciplines are available. Graduate study is also offered. One-day orientation in Oregon.

ADMITTANCE REQUIREMENTS: Sophomore standing or above. Minimum 2.75 GPA (no language prerequisite), letters of recommendation, and personal interview.

TEACHING METHODS: Taught in English by both U.S. faculty members as well as those from the university. Special courses for Americans are offered. Classes (taught in Hungarian) are integrated if language skills permit. Lectures, seminars and independent study complemented by some travel to regional museums and cultural sites.

EVALUATION: By American and university faculty, based on periodic and final exams.

CREDITS OFFERED: The equivalent of attending an American school for two full semesters or three terms of a trimester program.

HOUSING: Students live in university dormitories, local apartments, or with families.

DATES: Approximately mid-September through mid-June.

COSTS: Resident undergraduates: $3,725; resident graduates: $4,500. Includes tuition, room and board, and orientation expenses. Does not include round-trip transportation, local travel or personal expenses.

YEAR ESTABLISHED: 1986.

NUMBER OF STUDENTS IN 1986: Not available.

APPLY: By March 1. At member OSSHE school, or Irma Wright, Office of International Education.

POLAND

Population: 37,455,000   **Capital:** Warsaw   **Language:** Polish
Monetary Unit: Zloty   **Government:** Unitary single-party Socialist republic
(president or chairman and prime minister)   **Religion:** 81% Roman Catholic
Households With Television: 11%

SELECTED COLLEGES AND UNIVERSITIES

Ministry of Science & Technology   University of Lodz
6-8 Rue Miodowa   Lodz
00-251 Warsaw

FURTHER INFORMATION

Embassy of Poland   Polish National Tourist Office
2640 16th Street, NW   500 Fifth Avenue
Washington, DC 20009   New York, NY 10110
(202) 234-3800   (212) 475-5588

Consulate General of Poland
233 Madison Avenue
New York, NY 10016
(212) 889-8360

Krakow

■ **AMERICAN INSTITUTE OF POLISH CULTURE**
1440 79th Street Causeway, Suite 403
Miami, FL 33141
(305) 864-2349

PROGRAM: Summer Session in Poland is operated in conjunction with
Florida Memorial College and Jagiellonian University, is a six-week study
program open to any American participant regardless of age or occupation.
Courses include economics, international trade, business, political science,
and Polish language and culture. If desired, a two-day preorientation in Miami
is available.

ADMITTANCE REQUIREMENTS: None.

TEACHING METHODS: Lectures, seminars, and field trips.

EVALUATION: A final exam is required of all students requiring credit.

CREDITS OFFERED: 6 semester hours.

HOUSING: Student dormitories.

DATES: July.

COSTS: $675 for credit; $500 without credit exclusive of travel.

YEAR ESTABLISHED: 1980.

NUMBER OF STUDENTS IN 1985: 15.

APPLY: By April 1. Dr. Zdzislaw P. Wesolowski, Director.

■ **UNIVERSITY OF WISCONSIN – STEVENS POINT**
208 Old Main
Stevens Point, WI 54481
(715) 346-2717

PROGRAM: Semester in Poland is a travel/study fall undergraduate program. Although the majority of the program is held in Krakow, the group spends about a month traveling to Germany, Austria, Italy, Yugoslavia, and Hungary, and in Poland to Zakopane, Gdansk, Warsaw, etc. Classes in Krakow are given at the Dom Piast, (the international student residence) and include art history, Polish history, culture and civilization, comparative economics and politics, geography, and intensive language courses.

ADMITTANCE REQUIREMENTS: Sophomores and above in good academic standing. Knowledge of a foreign language is not required.

TEACHING METHODS: Students attend courses taught in English arranged for the group and live with students at Dom Piast. Polish language courses are offered.

EVALUATION: By instructors and group leaders based upon class work, papers, and examinations.

CREDITS OFFERED: A minimum of 13 semester hours; maximum of 17.

HOUSING: Students stay in hostels while traveling and the Dom Piast in Krakow.

DATES: Approximately August 25 to December 10.

COSTS: Approximately $2,800 includes tuition, room and board, round-trip transportation from Chicago, and program-related travel. Minnesota students pay a small "reciprocity fee"; non-Wisconsin residents pay a surcharge. Does not cover personal expenses.

YEAR ESTABLISHED: 1970.

NUMBER OF STUDENTS IN 1985: Not available.

APPLY: "Early application is advised." Dr. Helen Cornell, Director, International Programs.

Poznan

■ **THE AMERICAN UNIVERSITY**
Washington, DC 20016
(202) 885-3800

PROGRAM: Semester in Poznan is a liberal arts/social science program held in cooperation with Adam Mickiewicz University. Students may attend for both semesters. Courses include history, fine arts, languages, political science, etc. Field trips to Berlin are scheduled. Preorientation at American University (usually over a weekend) and onsite.

ADMITTANCE REQUIREMENTS: Juniors and seniors with a "B" average or better.

TEACHING METHODS: Students are accompanied by a resident professor from American University who schedules seminars with public officials in addition to his or her own lectures. Foreign faculty members complement these lectures and teach specialized courses. Students also intern two days a week with one of the many local government or private organizations.

EVALUATION: Regular exams, midterms and finals, in addition to short seminar papers.

CREDITS OFFERED: 15 to 17 semester hours.

HOUSING: A combination of possibilities from local apartments to living with local families.

DATES: First semester: September to December; second semester: January to May.

COSTS: Tuition: $4,100 per semester; room and board: $2,000 per semester. Scholarships from American University available.

YEAR ESTABLISHED: Not available.

NUMBER OF STUDENTS IN 1985:   Not available.

APPLY: Rolling admissions. Apply six to eight months prior to start of semester to: Dr. David C. Brown, Dean, Washington Semester and Study Program Abroad.

■ **AMERICAN INSTITUTE OF POLISH CULTURE**
  1440 79th Street Causeway, Suite 403
  Miami, FL 33141
  (305) 864-2349

PROGRAM: Summer Session in Poland, operated in conjunction with Florida Memorial College and Adam Mickiewicz University, is a six-week study program open to any American participant regardless of age or occupation. Courses include economics, international trade, business, political science, and Polish language and culture. If desired, a two-day preorientation in Miami is available.

ADMITTANCE REQUIREMENTS: None.

TEACHING METHODS: Lectures, seminars, and field trips.

EVALUATION: A final exam is required of all students requiring credit.

CREDITS OFFERED: 6 semester hours.

HOUSING: Student dormitories.

DATES: July.

COSTS: $675 for credit; $500 without credit exclusive of travel.

YEAR ESTABLISHED: 1980.

NUMBER OF STUDENTS IN 1985:   15.

APPLY: By April 1. Dr. Zdzislaw P. Wesolowski, Director.

Warsaw

■ **AMERICAN INSTITUTE OF POLISH CULTURE**
1440 79th Street Causeway, Suite 403
Miami, FL 33141
(305) 864-2349

PROGRAM: Summer Session in Poland, operated in conjunction with Florida Memorial College and University of Warsaw, is a four-week study program open to any American participant regardless of age or occupation. Courses include economics, international trade, business, political science, and Polish language and culture. If desired, a two-day preorientation in Miami is available.

ADMITTANCE REQUIREMENTS: None.

TEACHING METHODS: Lectures, seminars, and field trips.

EVALUATION: A final exam is required of all students requiring credit.

CREDITS OFFERED: 6 semester hours.

HOUSING: Student dormitories.

DATES: July.

COSTS: $675 for credit; $500 without credit exclusive of travel.

YEAR ESTABLISHED: 1980.

NUMBER OF STUDENTS IN 1985: 15.

APPLY: By April 1. Dr. Zdzislaw P. Wesolowski, Director.

YUGOSLAVIA

Population: 23,289,000   **Capital:** Belgrade   **Language:** Slovenian, Macedonian, and Serbo-Croatian   **Monetary Unit:** Yugoslav dinar
Government: Single-party federal Socialist republic (president)   **Religion:** 35% Serbian Orthodox; 26% Roman Catholic   **Households With Television:** 8%

COLLEGES AND UNIVERSITIES

University of Belgrade
Studentski Trg Broj 1
11000 Belgrade

University of Ljubljana
Trg Osvoboditve 11
61000 Ljubljana

FURTHER INFORMATION

Consulate General of Yugoslavia
767 Third Avenue
New York, NY 10017
(212) 838-2300

Yugoslav Press and Cultural Center
767 Third Avenue
New York, NY 10017
(212) 838-2306

Embassy of Yugoslavia
2410 California Street, NW
Washington, DC 20008
(202) 265-9717

More Than One City

■ **COLGATE UNIVERSITY**
Hamilton, NY 13346
(315) 824-1000

PROGRAM: The Colgate Yugoslavia Program is a single-semester under-graduate study/travel experience that visits Belgrade, Dubrovnik, Sarajevo, Zagreb, as well as side trips to Hungary and Romania. Courses cover economics, political science with an emphasis on East-West relations, and sociology. Orientation in the U.S.

ADMITTANCE REQUIREMENTS: Sophomores and above in good academic standing. Colgate students are shown a preference, but others accepted. One course on Yugoslavian culture. No language requirement.

TEACHING METHODS: Students attend special courses arranged for the group and taught in English by both U.S. and foreign faculty.

EVALUATION: By course professors, based upon papers and examinations.

CREDITS OFFERED: 16 semester hours.

HOUSING: Students live in hotels while traveling and with local families.

DATES: Approximately early September through mid-December.

COSTS: $7,800 includes tuition, room and board, round-trip transportation, and program-related travel.

YEAR ESTABLISHED: 1972.

NUMBER OF STUDENTS IN 1985: 18.

APPLY: By February 14. Professor Donna Parmelee, Department of Sociology and Anthropology.

Zagreb

■ **ASSOCIATED COLLEGES OF THE MIDWEST (ACM)**
  18 South Michigan Avenue; Suite 1010
  Chicago, IL 60603
  (312) 263-5000

PROGRAM: The ACM/GLCA Yugoslavia Program is one of the few overseas undergraduate programs exposed to the teachings of a Soviet-bloc political system. The program is held in cooperation with the Filozofski Fakultet of University of Zagreb. It is cosponsored by the twelve member colleges in the Great Lakes College Association and the member colleges of the ACM: Beloit College, Carleton College, Coe College, Cornell College, Colorado College, Grinnell College, Knox College, Lake Forest College, Lawrence University, Macalester College, Monmouth College, Ripon College, and St. Olaf Colleges. Courses include: an introduction to Yugoslavia, Serbo-Croatian, Marxist philosophy, worker's self-management systems, the Yugoslav economic problem, industrialization and social change in Yugoslavia, etc. An orientation session is held in a small village on the outskirts of Zagreb.

ADMITTANCE REQUIREMENTS: Sophomores and above with a strong interest in social science and Slavic studies. No language requirement but prior study of Serbo-Croatian is encouraged.

TEACHING METHODS: Courses are in English except for Serbo-Croatian study. Yugoslavian faculty except for introductory course, which is given by the American program director. American students are not integrated with Yugoslavian students. Travel throughout the country and a possible trip to the Soviet Union is part of the program.

EVALUATION: By professors based upon class work, papers, and final exams.

CREDITS OFFERED: 16 semester hours per semester.

HOUSING: Students live in private homes with local families.

DATES: August 30 through December 18.

COSTS: Tuition is determined by home college. Room and board is approximately $924. Plan on approximately $150 to $175 a month for local expenses.

YEAR ESTABLISHED: 1979.

NUMBER OF STUDENTS IN 1985:   23.

APPLY: By April 1. Abby Schmelling, Program Associate.

THE UNION OF SOVIET SOCIALIST REPUBLICS

Population: 280,036,000   **Capital:** Moscow   **Language:** Russian
Monetary Unit: Ruble   **Government:** Federal Socialist republic (chairman of the Supreme Soviet and premier)   **Religion:** 25% Christian; 52% nonreligious or atheist;   **Households With Television:** 95%

SELECTED COLLEGES AND UNIVERSITIES

Several Soviet institutions of higher education are open to undergraduates and graduates from outside the USSR, who are selected by the International Union of Students and approved by the Soviet government. Americans interested in studying in the USSR apart from a specific college-sponsored or CIEE (Council on International Education Exchange) program should contact the International Research and Exchanges Board (IREX), 655 Third Ave, New York, NY 10017.

FURTHER INFORMATION

Embassy of the USSR
1125 16th Street, NW
Washington, DC 20036
(202) 628-7551

Consulate General of the USSR
2790 Green Street
San Francisco, CA 94123
(415) 922-6642

Leningrad

■ **NORTHERN ILLINOIS UNIVERSITY**
  DeKalb, IL 60115
  (815) 753-0304

PROGRAM: NIU's Russian Language Study Program is a one-semester or full-academic-year undergraduate program held in cooperation with the University of Leningrad and the Council on International Education Exchange (CIEE). Students take special courses at the University in advanced Russian language, literature, and Soviet culture. Program-related travel and orientation in Helsinki.

ADMITTANCE REQUIREMENTS: Sophomores and above with a 2.7 GPA and three years of Russian or the equivalent.

TEACHING METHODS: Students take special courses for foreigners taught in Russian by the faculty at the University of Leningrad.

EVALUATION: By faculty, based upon class work and course examinations.

CREDITS OFFERED: 15 semester hours per semester.

HOUSING: Students live in dormitories.

DATES: Fall semester: early September through mid-December; spring semester: mid-January through mid-June.

COSTS: $4,200 per semester includes tuition, room and board. Does not cover round-trip transportation, program-related travel, or personal expenses.

YEAR ESTABLISHED: 1983.

NUMBER OF STUDENTS IN 1985: Not available.

APPLY: By June 1 for fall semester; November 1 for spring. Judith Muasher.

■ **PENNSYLVANIA STATE UNIVERSITY**
Office of Education Abroad Programs
222 Boucke Building
University Park, PA 16802
(814) 865-7681

PROGRAM: The Cooperative Russian Language Program at Leningrad State University is a fall, spring, or full-academic-year program held in cooperation with Leningrad State University and sponsored by a consortium of North American colleges. Students take two courses in their major and one elective from among the university's offerings each semester. Participants are also involved in both language and subject tutorials. Two-week field trip between semesters. Orientation at Penn State and in the USSR.

ADMITTANCE REQUIREMENTS: Juniors and seniors with a 2.5 GPA, good academic standing, and "must show evidence of maturity, stability, adaptability, self-discipline and a strong academic motivation." For the full-year program, a minimum of three years college-level Russian or the equivalent plus previous participation in a Russian language program in the USSR for at least six weeks.

TEACHING METHODS: The semester program includes a fourteen-week intensive language session. All lectures are in Russian. Americans are integrated with Soviet students. Each student is assigned a Leningrad State University faculty advisor.

EVALUATION: By course instructors, based upon class work, papers, and examinations.

CREDITS OFFERED: 15 semester hours per semester.

HOUSING: Students live in university dormitories with Soviet students as roommates.

DATES: Approximately fall semester: early September through mid-December; spring semester: late January through mid-June.

COSTS: Students pay the same as at the University Park Campus. 1986-87 tuition per semester was $2,250 for state residents; $5,150 for nonresidents; room and board: $2,750 per semester. Plus a $100 nonrefundable program fee.

YEAR ESTABLISHED: 1981.

NUMBER OF STUDENTS IN 1985: 0.

APPLY: Fall semester by March 1; spring semester by October 15.

Moscow

■ **AMERICAN COUNCIL OF TEACHERS OF RUSSIAN (ACTR)**
815 New Gulph Road
Bryn Mawr, PA 19010
(215) 525-6559

PROGRAM: The ACTR Russian Language Program in Moscow is held in cooperation with the Pushkin Russian Language Institute. ACTR offers three programs: a seven-week summer session; two four-month semesters; and a full academic year. All programs center around Russian language (grammar, phonetics, and conversation); Russian literature, primarily contemporary Soviet authors; and, teaching methodology. Travel in the Soviet Union is part of all programs. Depending upon the duration of stay, students may experience several local excursions, an overnight trip to an adjacent city, and, three or four days in Leningrad at the end of the program. There is a three-day predeparture orientation in Philadelphia.

ADMITTANCE REQUIREMENTS: For summer students: two years of college Russian or the equivalent. Semester students: three years of college Russian or the equivalent. Full year students: teachers and graduate students in Slavic with some teaching experience.

TEACHING METHODS: Special courses are taught by Soviet faculty at the Pushkin Institute. Americans are not integrated with Soviet students but will have contact with other foreign nationals in the dormitory. All lectures and classes are in Russian.

EVALUATION: By Soviet faculty, based upon classwork and periodic and final exams. Pre- and postoral proficiency testing.

CREDITS OFFERED: Summer: maximum of two courses or 6 semester hours; semester: maximum of four courses or 12 semester hours; academic year: maximum of eight courses or 24 semester hours.

HOUSING: Students live at the Pushkin Institute.

DATES: Summer term: June 16 through August 3; fall semester: August 29 through December 22; spring semester: February 2 through May 26.

COSTS: Summer term: $2,450; each semester: $3,500. Includes tuition, room and board, and local travel. Round-trip transportation and additional living expenses not included. Financial aid is available through ACTR.

YEAR ESTABLISHED: 1976.

NUMBER OF STUDENTS IN 1985: summer, 100; semester, 22; year, 7.

APPLY: For summer term: January 24; fall semester: February 21; spring semester: September 27; academic year: February 1. Ms. Alice Keenan, Coordinator, ACTR.

■ **MIDDLEBURY COLLEGE**
Middlebury, VT 05753
(802) 388-3711

PROGRAM: Middlebury College Russian School in the USSR offers undergraduates "long-standing, highly respected, and *serious*" courses in literature, Russian language, culture, and civilization. An MA program is available in Russian language and literature. Courses are held at the Pushkin Russian Language Institute.

ADMITTANCE REQUIREMENTS: The equivalent of five semesters in Russian and a B average; (for MA a "better than B average" is required.)

TEACHING METHODS: Soviet faculty. All courses, written papers, and exams are in Russian. Travel, field trips, and cultural exchanges complement the program.

EVALUATION: Faculty-student conferences, term papers, finals, etc.

CREDITS OFFERED: Full semester or full year credit.

HOUSING: Students live at the Pushkin Institute.

DATES: Approximately, September 15 through June 10.

COSTS: Tuition: full year: $4,900; semester: $2,500; room and board: approximately $2,000 per semester. Round-trip travel not included. Some scholarships available.

YEAR ESTABLISHED: 1977.

NUMBER OF STUDENTS IN 1985:   30.

APPLY: Rolling admissions. Contact Dean of Russian School.

PART FIVE

ASIA

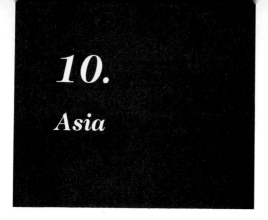

10.

Asia

MORE THAN ONE COUNTRY

■ **ELON COLLEGE**
Elon College, NC 27244
(919) 584-2354

PROGRAM: Elon's one-month Asian travel/study experience emphasizes the people and culture of the Soviet Union, Mongolia, and China. The 'round the world tour is directed by Elon history professor, Dr. David Crowe, who accompanies the group to Leningrad, Moscow, Erevan, Tashkent, Irkutsk, Ulan Bator, Xian, and Beijing.

ADMITTANCE REQUIREMENTS: Open to both students and nonstudents.

TEACHING METHODS: Learning is by experience. There are no formal classes, although students maintain a diary, which serves as the basis of evaluation.

EVALUATION: By group leaders, based on discussions and the student's diary.

CREDITS OFFERED: 6 hours, semester.

HOUSING: The group stays in first-class hotels.

DATES: May and June.

COSTS: $3,775 includes tuition, room and board, and all travel expenses.

YEAR ESTABLISHED: Not available.

NUMBER OF STUDENTS IN 1985: Not available.

APPLY: By February 1. Dr. David Crowe, Box # 2147.

11.

East Asia

PEOPLE'S REPUBLIC OF CHINA

Population: 1,053,100,000   **Capital:** Beijing (Peking)
Language: Mandarin Chinese   **Monetary Unit:** Yuan (Renminbi)
Government: Single-party people's republic (president & premier)
Religion: 59% nonreligious; 20% Chinese folk-religionist
Households With Television: Less than 1%.

SELECTED COLLEGES AND UNIVERSITIES

Beijing Languages Institute
Beijing

Beijing University
Beijing

Courses in language, literature, history, philosophy, political economics, and archaeology.

Central Institute of Fine Arts
Beijing

Courses in traditional Chinese painting and fine arts.

Liaoning University
Shenyang

Courses in language, literature, and history.

Nanjing University
Nanjing

Courses in language, literature, history, philosophy, political economics, and archaeology.

Shanghai University
Shanghai

Courses in language, literature, history, and philosophy.

FURTHER INFORMATION

Consulate of the People's Republic of China
1450 Laguna Street
San Francisco, CA 94115
(415) 563-4885

Embassy of the People's Republic of China
2300 Connecticut Avenue, NW
Washington, DC 20008
(202) 328-2500

Ministry of Education
No. 37 Da Mu Cang Hu Tong
Beijing
Publishes Regulations Governing the Enrollment of Foreign Students in Institutions of Higher Education in China *and* A List of Specialities in Chinese Universities and Colleges Open to Foreign Students.

National Association for Foreign Student Affairs
1860 19th Street
Washington, DC 20009
(202) 462-4811
Publishes An Introduction to Education in the People's Republic of China *and* China Bound: A Handbook for American Students, Researchers and Teachers.

More Than One City

■ **DUKE UNIVERSITY**
Asian/Pacific Studies Institute
2111 Campus Drive
Durham, NC 27706
(919) 684-2604

PROGRAM: Duke Study in China Program is held in cooperation with Beijing Teachers College and Nanjing University in association with Washington University, St. Louis and Wesleyan University. The program is primarily for undergraduates but "graduate students are welcome." Unlike many China programs, the Duke program provides an eight-week summer course of intensive language study at Beijing Teachers College followed by a fall semester of courses in language, literature, history, and directed study on a topic of the student's choosing at Nanjing University. Brief orientation in San Francisco prior to departure.

ADMITTANCE REQUIREMENTS: Acceptable academic standing with at least one year of college Chinese or the equivalent.

TEACHING METHODS: The summer session is taught by a Chinese university faculty; the fall session is taught by two Chinese professors and two U.S. professors. Field trips and independent study complement class work.

EVALUATION: By foreign/U.S. faculty and a resident director, based on periodic examinations, papers, etc.

CREDITS OFFERED: 24 semester hours.

HOUSING: Students live and eat in school dormitories.

DATES: June 18 through December 31.

COSTS: $7,500 includes tuition, room and board, textbooks, fees, and round-trip transportation from San Francisco.

YEAR ESTABLISHED: 1982.

NUMBER OF STUDENTS IN 1985:   20.

APPLY: By March 1.

■ **SANTA BARBARA CITY COLLEGE**
721 Cliff Drive
Santa Barbara, CA 93109
(805) 965-0581

PROGRAM: The Three Faces of China is an undergraduate program with courses concentrating on political science, history, and philosophy. During this ten-week program students have the opportunity to visit the People's Republic of China, Hong Kong, and Taiwan. A unique aspect of the program is a rare and unusual side trip to Tibet. On the mainland students attend school at Shandong University in Jinan. Two- to five-day orientation on the SBCC campus.

ADMITTANCE REQUIREMENTS: Acceptable academic credentials plus 12 units of college credit including freshman level English.

TEACHING METHODS: Students attend regular classes taught by SBCC faculty members. Courses are supplemented with field trips to local museums and cultural and historic sites. Some independent study.

EVALUATION: By class professors, based upon papers and periodic examinations. Students also complete evaluation forms upon completion of the program and comment on faculty, facilities, group leaders, and program in general.

CREDITS OFFERED: 16 to 18 semester hours.

HOUSING: Students live in dormitories.

DATES: Vary from year to year. Approximately from mid-September to mid-November.

COSTS: Approximately $3,500 including tuition, room and board, and local travel. Does not include round-trip transportation.

YEAR ESTABLISHED: 1985.

NUMBER OF STUDENTS IN 1985: 40.

APPLY: By mid-July. Mr. John Romo, Dean of Instructional Services.

Beijing

■ **AMERICAN INSTITUTE OF FOREIGN STUDY**
102 Greenwich Avenue
Greenwich, CT 06830
(800) 243-4567 or (203) 869-9090

PROGRAM: AIFS is a national for-profit organization specializing in comprehensive overseas academic year, semester, and summer study programs. The AIFS program at Beijing University is a full-academic-year, fall, or spring semester experience designed for serious Chinese language students with at least a year prior study of Mandarin. All AIFS students study both Mandarin Chinese and Chinese culture. Students are welcome to participate in various sports and clubs at the university. Enrollment is limited to ten students. Program includes visits to local historic sites and museums. Onsite orientation.

ADMITTANCE REQUIREMENTS: College juniors and above with a 2.5 GPA, as well as graduate students. One year of Mandarin Chinese or successful completion of AIFS summer language program at the Beijing Language Institute.

TEACHING METHODS: Students attend classes fours hours a day, Monday through Friday, taught by Beijing University faculty members.

EVALUATION: By faculty, based upon class work, papers, and periodic examinations.

CREDITS OFFERED: 15 semester hours per semester.

HOUSING: Students live in university dormitories, two students per room, and may request a Chinese roommate. "Many students find it convenient to purchase bicycles to get about town and back and forth to class."

DATES: Fall semester: September 4 through December 22; spring semester: February 10 through June 9.

COSTS: Full academic year $6,795; or, $3,250 per semester. Includes tuition, room and board, program-related travel, and round-trip transportation from West Coast. Does not cover local travel or personal expenses.

YEAR ESTABLISHED: 1985.

NUMBER OF STUDENTS IN 1986: 7.

APPLY: Applications filled on first-come basis. "It is expected that all full-year or fall-semester places will be filled by June 1; places for spring semester are kept open until November 15."

■ **CHINA EDUCATIONAL TOURS (CET)**
1110 Washington Street
Dorchester Lower Mills
Boston, MA 02124
(800) 225-4262; in Massachusetts (617) 296-0270

PROGRAM: The CET-Wellesley Chinese Languages Program is for undergraduates, graduates, or professionals and is held in cooperation with the Beijing Foreign Languages Normal College and Wellesley College. Students can attend for a nine-week summer session, a sixteen-week fall session, or a nineteen-week spring session. Language courses range from beginning Chinese (no previous study required) to intensive Chinese and business Chinese with a coordinated internship program in selected American companies. The school maintains an English and Chinese library. The course is supplemented by weekly excursions to cultural and historic sites in and around Beijing.

ADMITTANCE REQUIREMENTS: CET requires transcripts, letters of reference, and written/oral samples of Chinese for class placement. The Chinese Ministry of Education has an age restriction of from 16 to 55.

TEACHING METHODS: A resident director supervises and monitors the program. Chinese teachers have "some familiarity with American teaching methods." A "Language Partner" program links students with their local counterpart from the Beijing Foreign Languages Normal College. There is no integration with Chinese students in classes.

EVALUATION: By Chinese faculty, based upon periodic oral and written exams.

CREDITS OFFERED: Credits are granted by home institution based upon courses taken.

HOUSING: Students live in dormitories consisting of suites with double or single rooms.

DATES: Approximately, fall session: September 1 through December 20; spring session: January 19 through June 1; summer session: June 16 through August 20.

COSTS: Semester: $3,100; summer: $1,990. Includes tuition, room and board, local travel. Does not include round-trip transportation (approximately $1,550 from New York or Boston) and extra living expenses ($500 to $800 per semester); "shoppers bring more".

YEAR ESTABLISHED: 1982.

NUMBER OF STUDENTS IN 1985: 48.

APPLY: April 15 for summer; June 15 for fall; October 15 for spring. Katie Devine, Administrative Associate, Academic Programs.

■ **GOSHEN COLLEGE**
Goshen, IN 46526
(219) 533-3161

PROGRAM: Goshen's Study Service Trimester Abroad is a fourteen-week (one trimester), undergraduate program offering students the opportunity to concentrate on the region's language, history, and culture. Courses include history, geography, politics, crosscultural studies, and crosscultural sensitization, i.e., art, music, drama, etc. All students must be enrolled at Goshen the preceding trimester to attend orientation sessions.

ADMITTANCE REQUIREMENTS: For sophomores and above who meet acceptable academic standards.

TEACHING METHODS: Students attend special classes taught by a foreign faculty. Courses involve regular class work, field trips, research projects. Each student must also participate in a work assignment, such as hospital, school, community development project, etc.

EVALUATION: By accompanying Goshen College faculty member(s) based upon class work and assessment of projects.

CREDITS OFFERED: 12 semester hours.

HOUSING: Students either live in dormitories or local hotels.

DATES: Fall trimester: September 11 through December 16; winter trimester: January 8 through April 14; spring trimester: April 24 through July 28.

COSTS: Tuition: $4,165; room and board: $1,040. Includes round-trip transportation and local field trips.

YEAR ESTABLISHED: 1980.

NUMBER OF STUDENTS IN 1985: 21.

APPLY: One trimester prior to the program. Arlin Hunsberger, Director of International Education.

■ **NORTHERN ILLINOIS UNIVERSITY**
  DeKalb, IL 60115
  (815) 753-0304

PROGRAM: Chinese Language and Civilization is a single-semester or full-academic-year undergraduate program held in cooperation with the Council on International Education Exchange (CIEE) and Peking University. Courses cover advanced Chinese language, Chinese history, and civilization. Orientation in Hong Kong.

ADMITTANCE REQUIREMENTS: Juniors and seniors with a 2.5 GPA, three years of Chinese, and a working knowledge of pin-yin.

TEACHING METHODS: Students take special courses for foreigners arranged by Peking University and taught in Chinese by University faculty members.

EVALUATION: By course faculty, based upon oral work and examinations.

CREDITS OFFERED: 15 semester hours per semester.

HOUSING: Students live in university dormitories.

DATES: Fall semester: early September through mid-December; spring semester: mid-January through mid-June.

COSTS: $5,600 per semester includes tuition, room and board. Does not cover round-trip transportation, local travel, or personal expenses.

YEAR ESTABLISHED: 1984.

NUMBER OF STUDENTS IN 1985: 2.

APPLY: Fall semester by June 1; Spring semester by November 1. Judith Muasher.

■ **OREGON STATE SYSTEM OF HIGHER EDUCATION (OSSHE)**
Oregon State University
International Education, AdS — A100
Corvallis, OR 97330
(503) 754-2394

PROGRAM: The OSSHE offers two China programs. The Oregon Teacher Education program is a new (1986) fall semester offering for teacher education majors. A U.S. resident director works with the Chinese faculty at the Beijing Teachers College to coordinate school visits and to direct a comparative analysis of the Chinese education system. A second program concentrates on language training and is held in conjunction with the British Branch of the Beijing Foreign Languages Institute. In addition to language training students also study Chinese history, culture, politics and economics. One-day orientation in Oregon.

ADMITTANCE REQUIREMENTS: Complete 45 credit hours, (sophomore standing for teacher program) 2.5 GPA, letters of recommendation. No language requirement; but some knowledge of Chinese is recommended.

TEACHING METHODS: Classes, seminars, and independent study in English by U.S. and foreign faculty.

EVALUATION: By students and resident director.

CREDITS OFFERED: Up to 20 quarter credits.

HOUSING: Students live in foreign student dormitories.

DATES: Approximately September 1 through December 14.

COSTS: Teacher program: $3,000; language program: $3,300. Includes tuition, room and board, field trips, round-trip transportation from Oregon, and fees. Does not include local travel or personal expenses.

YEAR ESTABLISHED: 1984.

NUMBER OF STUDENTS IN 1985: 18.

APPLY: By March 1 (Language); April 15 (Teachers). At participating school or Ann Ferguson, International Education.

■ **STATE UNIVERSITY OF NEW YORK AT NEW PALTZ**
New Paltz, NY 12561
(914) 257-2233

PROGRAM: The SUNY Beijing Program is a full academic year undergraduate program held in cooperation with Peking University. The program's emphasis is on the Chinese language and culture. There is no travel associated with this program. Students can, however, make their own arrangements.

ADMITTANCE REQUIREMENTS: Juniors, seniors, and graduate students in good academic standing with at least one year college-level Chinese or the equivalent.

TEACHING METHODS: Students take special courses taught by a Chinese faculty. Includes lectures, intensive language courses.

EVALUATION: By Chinese faculty, based upon periodic exams and a final examination.

CREDITS OFFERED: A minimum of 24; maximum of 30 semester hours for the academic year.

HOUSING: Students live in dormitories on the Peking University campus.

DATES: Approximately, September 1 through June 15.

COSTS: Tuition: $687 for state residents; $1,612 for nonresidents. Program fee including room and board is $2,250. Does not cover round-trip transportation from New York (approximately $1,544) or personal expenses (estimated at approximately $500).

YEAR ESTABLISHED: 1979.

NUMBER OF STUDENTS IN 1985: 1.

APPLY: By March 1. Dr. Rudolf R. Kossmann, Director, Office of International Education.

■ **STATE UNIVERSITY OF NEW YORK AT OSWEGO**
Oswego, NY 13126
(315) 341-2118

PROGRAM: Study in China is a semester or full-academic-year undergraduate program held in cooperation with Beijing Teachers College. Courses cover the Chinese language, literature, and culture and history and art. Students with a command of the language may take regular courses at the university.

ADMITTANCE REQUIREMENTS: Sophomore standing, 2.8 GPA; some Chinese language study is recommended.

TEACHING METHODS: Courses are taught in English in a special academic program designed for English-speaking students. Participants are assigned student tutors "to assist them in adjusting to daily life."

EVALUATION: Based on work in class, papers, and final exams.

CREDITS OFFERED: A maximum of 30 semester credit hours per year.

HOUSING: Students live in special university dormitories for foreign students and eat in the university cafeteria.

DATES: Fall semester: early-September to the end of January; spring semester: early February to the end of June.

COSTS: $2,200 per semester plus SUNY tuition (residents, $687.50; nonresidents, $1,612.50.) Includes room and board, local field trips, and textbooks. Does not include round-trip transportation or personal expenses.

YEAR ESTABLISHED: 1983:

NUMBER OF STUDENTS IN 1985:   6.

APPLY: By April 15 for fall semester; October 20 for spring semester. Dr. José R. Pérez, Director, International Education, Overseas Academic Programs.

Liaodong Peninsula

■ **BRETHREN COLLEGES ABROAD**
P.O. Box #184
Manchester College
North Manchester, IN 46962
(219) 982-2141, ext. 238

PROGRAM: Brethren Colleges Abroad China Program is held in cooperation with the Dalian Foreign Languages Institute, and with Bridgewater College, Elizabethtown College, Juniata College, McPherson College, and the University of La Verne in the United States. Some graduate students accepted. Courses cover Chinese language, China today, film/video English, social linguistics, phonetics, British and American culture, scientific English, and five modern languages. Onsite orientation.

ADMITTANCE REQUIREMENTS: Sophomore and above with acceptable academic credentials.

TEACHING METHODS: Americans are fully integrated with Chinese students. Both special and regular college courses. Course work is complemented with field trips and travel to museums and regional sites.

EVALUATION: Director in Dalian and professors determine grades from papers, periodic exams, and finals.

CREDITS OFFERED: Up to 22 semester hours during the five-month semester.

HOUSING: Students live in dormitories.

DATES: Fall semester: September 1 through January 20; spring semester: February 15 through July 15.

COSTS: $5,800 per semester. Includes tuition, room and board, and round-trip transportation. Does not cover personal expenses or local travel.

YEAR ESTABLISHED: 1986.

NUMBER OF STUDENTS IN 1986: Not available.

APPLY: By April 1 for fall semester; and November 1 for spring semester. Dr. Allen C. Deeter or Mrs. Helga Walsh.

Nanjing

■ **BRIGHAM YOUNG UNIVERSITY**
Study Abroad Programs
204 HRCB
Provo, UT 84602
(801) 378-3308

PROGRAM: The China Study Program offers courses at Nanjing University in intensive Chinese study, followed by two weeks of travel.

ADMITTANCE REQUIREMENTS: Good academic standing with a 3.0 GPA requested. Adherence to BYU standards.

TEACHING METHODS: Classes are taught by BYU faculty.

EVALUATION: Based on periodic exams. Evaluation determined by program director.

CREDITS OFFERED: From 6 to 9 credit hours.

HOUSING: Students live in facilities arranged by BYU.

DATES: Approximately April through June.

COSTS: Approximately $2,700 includes tuition, housing, meals, round-trip transportation, and local travel. Does not cover meals, additional travel and personal expenses. Some scholarships are available.

YEAR ESTABLISHED: 1975.

NUMBER OF STUDENTS IN 1985: 18.

APPLY: By February 15. BYU International Programs.

■ **THE JOHNS HOPKINS UNIVERSITY**
  School of Advanced International Studies (SAIS)
  1740 Massachusetts Avenue, NW
  Washington, DC 20036
  (202) 785-6200

PROGRAM: The Hopkins/Nanjing Center was initiated in 1985 as a one-year post-graduate program operated jointly with the University of Nanjing. Intensive courses cover international relations, international economics, history, politics, and a major emphasis on the Chinese language.

ADMITTANCE REQUIREMENTS: Open to students who are first accepted into the programs at SAIS.

TEACHING METHODS: Graduate courses are taught by both American and non-American faculty.

EVALUATION: Usually based upon papers and examinations.

CREDITS OFFERED: First part of two-part graduate program at SAIS.

HOUSING: Students live in dormitories at the center.

DATES: Approximately mid-September to mid-May.

COSTS: Tuition, room and board: $16,000. Does not cover round-trip transportation, local travel, or living expenses.

YEAR ESTABLISHED: 1985.

NUMBER OF STUDENTS IN 1985: Not available.

APPLY: By January 1. Admissions Office, Hopkins/Nanjing Program, SAIS.

■ **NORTHERN ILLINOIS UNIVERSITY**
DeKalb, IL 60115
(815) 753-0304

PROGRAM: Chinese Cooperative Language and Study Program is a fall-semester undergraduate program held in cooperation with the Council on International Education Exchange (CIEE) and Nanjing University. Courses cover intermediate Chinese language, Chinese history and civilization, and contemporary Chinese studies. Three-day orientation in Hong Kong.

ADMITTANCE REQUIREMENTS: Sophomores and above with a 2.5 GPA, one year of Chinese, and courses in Chinese history and government.

TEACHING METHODS: Students take special courses for foreigners arranged by Nanjing University and taught in Chinese by University faculty members.

EVALUATION: By course faculty, based upon oral work and examinations.

CREDITS OFFERED: 15 semester hours per semester.

HOUSING: Students live in university dormitories.

DATES: August 31 through mid-January.

COSTS: $5,600 per semester includes tuition, room and board. Does not cover round-trip transportation, local travel or personal expenses.

YEAR ESTABLISHED: 1984.

NUMBER OF STUDENTS IN 1985: 2.

APPLY: Fall semester by June 1; spring semester by November 1. Judith Muasher.

Shanghai

■ **BELOIT COLLEGE**
Beloit, WI 53511
(608) 365-3391

PROGRAM: The Fudan Exchange Program offers undergraduates a full year in China. Held in cooperation with Fudan University, the program stresses Chinese language studies, history, art, politics, economics, etc. Travel to local sites supplements the program. Presession orientation is held at Beloit.

ADMITTANCE REQUIREMENTS: 3.0 GPA, at least one year of Chinese, and good academic standing.

TEACHING METHODS: Students attend special courses; lectures, independent study, and field trips complement classroom work. A U.S. academic leader accompanies group.

EVALUATION: Papers, examinations, and general class work.

CREDITS OFFERED: 16 semester hours per semester.

HOUSING: Students live in dormitories.

DATES: Approximately early September through May.

COSTS: Tuition: $3,900 per semester; room and board: $1,700 per semester. Round-trip transportation not included.

YEAR ESTABLISHED: 1985.

NUMBER OF STUDENTS IN 1985: 2.

APPLY: By March 30. World Affairs Center.

Xian

■ **NORTHERN ILLINOIS UNIVERSITY**
DeKalb, IL 60115
(815) 753-0304

PROGRAM: Chinese Language and Civilization is a spring-semester undergraduate program held in cooperation with the Xian Foreign Languages Institute. Courses cover beginning and intermediate Chinese language, Chinese history, civilization, and politics. Two-week program-related travel in China. Three-day orientation in Beijing.

ADMITTANCE REQUIREMENTS: Sophomores and above with a 2.5 GPA; no language requirement.

TEACHING METHODS: Students take special courses for foreigners arranged by the Xian Foreign Languages Institute and taught in English and Chinese by Institute faculty members.

EVALUATION: By course faculty, based upon oral work and examinations.

CREDITS OFFERED: 16 semester hours per semester.

HOUSING: Students live in university dormitories.

DATES: Approximately mid-January through late June.

COSTS: $2,600 per semester includes tuition, room and board, and program-related travel. Does not cover round-trip transportation or personal expenses.

YEAR ESTABLISHED: 1984.

NUMBER OF STUDENTS IN 1985: 0.

APPLY: October 1. Judith Muasher.

HONG KONG

Population: 5,533,000   **Capital:** Victoria   **Language:** Chinese, English
Monetary Unit: Hong Kong dollar   **Government:** Colony of United Kingdom
(British monarch and governor)   **Religion:** Predominantly Buddhist
Households With Television: 9%

SELECTED COLLEGES AND UNIVERSITIES

Chinese University of Hong Kong
Shatin
New Territories
Courses in Mandarin and Cantonese,
Asian studies.

Lingnan College
15 Stubbs Road
Hong Kong
Courses in English.

University of Hong Kong
Pokfulam Road
Hong Kong

FURTHER INFORMATION

Education Department
Lee Gardens, Haysan Avenue
Hong Kong
Information on study opportunities
and facilities.

Hong Kong Tourist Association
548 Fifth Avenue
New York, NY 10036
(212) 869-5008

■ **YALE-CHINA ASSOCIATION**
905A Yale Station
New Haven, CT 06520
(203) 436-4422

PROGRAM: The International Asian Studies Program is an undergraduate and graduate program held in cooperation with the Chinese University of Hong Kong. A multidisciplinary curriculum at the university includes courses on Hong Kong, China, and other Asian countries, the Chinese language, culture, history, anthropology, political science, art, international relations, international business, traditional medicine, the martial arts, etc. Some program-associated travel. Approximately forty students are accepted each year; 75 percent from North America. One-week orientation at the university.

ADMITTANCE REQUIREMENTS: 3.0 GPA plus three semesters of undergraduate work. No language requirement.

TEACHING METHODS: Approximately 95 percent of the courses are taught in Chinese. Students with the language skill may enroll in these courses or elect any of the remaining courses taught in English by American, European, and Chinese faculty. Some courses have associated field trips to regional sites. Americans are fully integrated with Chinese students.

EVALUATION: By attending faculty, based upon papers and periodic exams.

CREDITS OFFERED: 3 semester hours per course per semester. Load depends upon student's ability and desire.

HOUSING: All students live in university dormitories.

DATES: Fall semester: early September through mid-December; spring semester: mid-January through late April.

COSTS: Tuition and room: $5,500 (HK$42,900) per academic year. For research students and special scholars the tuition is $4,060 (HK$31,700). Food is approximately $600 per year; additional expenses approximately $1,200. Does not include round-trip transportation or local travel. A limited amount of aid is available from the IAS program.

YEAR ESTABLISHED: 1976.

NUMBER OF STUDENTS IN 1985:   20.

APPLY: By March 1. Janet W. Rodgers, Program Associate.

JAPAN

Population: 121,510,000   **Capital:** Tokyo   **Language:** Japanese
Monetary Unit: Yen   **Government:** Constitutional monarchy (emperor and prime minister)   **Religion:** Predominantly Shinto and Buddhist
Households With Television: 10%

SELECTED COLLEGES AND UNIVERSITIES

Note: *There are many programs offered for non-Japanese students. By American standards, tuition is quite inexpensive. For example, International Christian University's 1986-87 full year tuition is 612,000 yen (about $3,900). Annual tuition at Kansai Gaidi, Nanzan, and Wasada is also less than $4,000; many postgraduate courses offered by the Ministry of Education, Science and Culture (3-2-2 Kasumigaseki, Chiyoda-ku, Tokyo) are free. Keep in mind, however, that the value of the yen has gained in strength in comparison to the dollar. As a result, Americans traveling, studying or living in Japan in 1988 and beyond should expect that their costs will be considerably more expensive than the figures presented in this book.*

Asia University
24-10 Chome Sakai Musashino-Shi
Tokyo 180

Offers special language courses for foreign students.

Hokkaido Daigaku
Nishi 5-Chrome
Kita 8-jo
Sopporo 060

Cooperative arrangement with the University of Massachusetts and Portland State University. Courses are taught in Japanese.

Hosei University
International Centre
2-17-1 Fujimi, Chiyoda-ku
Tokyo 102

Offers language, international relations, economics in English.

International Christian University
10-2 Osawa 3-Chome
Mitaka-shi
Tokyo 181

Both undergraduate and graduate programs in liberal arts, education, public administration, comparative culture. In English or Japanese as determined by instructor. Trimester system. Summer program in intensive Japanese is available. (In U.S., contact the Japan ICU Foundation, Room 720, 475 Riverside Drive, New York, NY 10027.)

International University of Japan
5-2-32 Minami Azabu Minato-ku
Tokyo 106

Master's degree program in international relations, economics, and area studies.

Kansai University of Foreign Studies
333 Ogura, Hirakata City
Osaka 573

Offers language, Asian studies, history, art, sociology, literature, etc., in English and Japanese for students interested in becoming immersed in the Japanese way of life.

Nanzan University
18 Yamazato-cho, Showa-ku
Nagoya 466

Offers Japanese language and cultural studies, history, international relations, religions, linguistics, folklore, etc. In English and Japanese. Accepts students without previous knowledge of Japanese.

Seinan Gakuin University
6-2-92 Nishijin, Sawara-ku
Fukuoka 814

Offers the "Year Abroad in Japan" program for American college students.

Waseda University
6-1 Nishi-Waseda 1-chome
Shinjuku-ku
Tokyo 160

Offers special full-year program to American college students covering Asian studies and Japanese studies in English plus intensive Japanese language and culture course. Has scholarships available for foreign students. Provides housing with Japanese families on request.

FURTHER INFORMATION

Association of International
Education
4-5-29 Komaba, Meguro-ku
Tokyo 153
*Offers information as well as more
than one hundred scholarships to private students of any nationality. Publishes* Student Guide to Japan *and*
ABC's of Study in Japan.

Embassy of Japan
2520 Massachusetts Avenue, NW
Washington, DC 20008
(202) 452-0660

International Students Institute
3-22-7 Kitashijuju, Shinjuku-ku
Tokyo

Consulate General of Japan
280 Park Avenue
New York, NY 10022
(212) 986-1600

The Japan Foundation
600 New Hampshire Avenue,
Suite 570
Washington, DC 20037
(202) 298-4400
*Offers dissertation fellowships in the
humanities, social sciences, and
education.*

Japan Society
333 East 47th Street
New York, NY 10017
(212) 832-1155
*Sponsors summer study and travel tours
of Japan for its members.*

Kobe

■ **MICHIGAN STATE UNIVERSITY**
108 Center for International Programs
East Lansing, MI 48824
(517) 353-8920

PROGRAM: Year in Japan is a full-academic-year undergraduate or graduate program held in cooperation with the universities of Illinois, Urbana-
Champaign, Colorado, and Pittsburgh, and Konan University in Kobe. Courses
concentrate on all areas of the Japanese language and culture as well as
independent research projects. Field trips to local historic and cultural sites.

ADMITTANCE REQUIREMENTS: Acceptable academic credentials, references, and recommendation from advisor. No language requirement.

TEACHING METHODS: Students take special courses in English and Japanese arranged for the group and taught by both U.S. and local foreign faculty.
Qualifying students may enroll directly at Konan University.

EVALUATION: By course faculty, based upon papers and examinations.

CREDITS OFFERED: 32 semester hours.

HOUSING: Students live with Japanese families.

DATES: August 31 through May 18.

COSTS: Approximately $8,300 includes tuition, room and board, round-trip transportation, and program-related travel.

YEAR ESTABLISHED: 1976.

NUMBER OF STUDENTS IN 1985:   3.

APPLY: By February 3. Dr. Charles A. Gliozzo, Office of Overseas Study.

Kyoto

■ **CONNECTICUT COLLEGE**
P.O. Box 1608
New London, CT 06320
(203) 447-1911

PROGRAM: The Associated Kyoto Program (AKP) is a nine-month, undergraduate program held in cooperation with Japan's Doshisha University and cosponsored by Amherst, Bucknell, Carleton, Colby, Connecticut, Mount Holyoke, Oberlin, Pomona, Smith, Wesleyan, Whitman, and Williams. Half of the student's academic time is spent in intensive language study; the other half involves elective courses in art, literature, economics, history, politics, religion, etc. Studio work in traditional Japanese arts and crafts is available and may be awarded course credit. Both travel and independent study are integrated into the program.

ADMITTANCE REQUIREMENTS: Acceptable academic standing, at least one year of Japanese language plus as one additional course on Japan, normally history.

TEACHING METHODS: Classes may be conducted in either Japanese or English and include seminars, intensive language labs, independent study, and field trips to regional sites and museums. There is social but no academic integration with Japanese students.

EVALUATION: By either American or Japanese faculty, based upon papers and periodic and final exams.

CREDITS OFFERED: Equivalent to one year of study at student's home institution.

HOUSING: Students live with local families.

DATES: Approximately September 1 through May 15.

COSTS: The same as the comprehensive fee at the student's home institution. Round-trip transportation and local travel are included in the single fee.

YEAR ESTABLISHED: 1972.

NUMBER OF STUDENTS IN 1985:   38.

APPLY: By February 10. Local campus representative if student at cosponsoring institution, or AKP, Connecticut College.

Nagoya

■ **INSTITUTE OF EUROPEAN STUDY (IES)**
223 West Ohio Street
Chicago, IL 60610
(312) 944-1750

PROGRAM: IES is a nonprofit organization with formal relationships with more than forty American colleges and universities. The institute maintains ten undergraduate academic centers throughout the world which provide semester or full academic year programs. Students attending the semester or full academic year IES Nagoya program are enrolled at Nanzan University in the Center for Japanese Studies. Courses cover intensive Japanese language, art history, business and economics, Japanese civilization, history, linguistics, literature, political science, sociology, Japanese studio arts, and independent study projects. Two-week orientation in California and Japan.

ADMITTANCE REQUIREMENTS: Juniors and seniors only. Two years college French or the equivalent. Faculty recommendations and an application essay. 85 percent of all students have had a GPA between 2.80 and 3.75. Japanese recommended but not required.

TEACHING METHODS: Students attend regular university courses with other local and foreign students. All courses are taught in English but Japanese language study is mandatory for all students. Classes are supplemented by trips to local museums and historic sites.

EVALUATION: By faculty, based upon class work, and periodic and final exams. Most courses require a research paper.

CREDITS OFFERED: A maximum of 16; minimum of 14 credit hours per semester.

HOUSING: Students live with Japanese families. Breakfast and supper provided Monday through Friday; the student is responsible for other eating arrangements.

DATES: Fall semester: late August through December 19; spring semester January 6 through May 15.

COSTS: $8,500 per year; $4,950 per semester. Includes tuition, room and board, and program-related field trips. Does not include round-trip transportation, local travel, or personal expenses (estimated at $2,200 per year). Some IES scholarship aid available; $1,500 for full-year students, $750 for semester students.

YEAR ESTABLISHED: 1986.

NUMBER OF STUDENTS IN 1986: Not available.

APPLY: Fall semester by February 15; spring semester by September 25.

Osaka

■ **PENNSYLVANIA STATE UNIVERSITY**
Office of Education Abroad Programs
222 Boucke Building
University Park, PA 16802
(814) 865-7681

PROGRAM: Education Abroad at Kansai University of Foreign Studies is either a fall-semester or full-academic-year undergraduate program held in cooperation with the Asian Studies Program at Kansai Gaidai. In addition to the required 4-credit course in spoken Japanese, students must take at least three additional 3-credit courses from a variety of offerings including economics, politics. history, art, philosophy, religion, literature, and culture and civilization. Orientation at Penn State and onsite.

ADMITTANCE REQUIREMENTS: Juniors and seniors with a 2.5 GPA, good academic standing, and "must show evidence of maturity, stability, adaptability, self-discipline and a strong academic motivation." Some specific course prerequisites. At least two semesters of Japanese or the equivalent.

TEACHING METHODS: Classes include two 80-minute recitations per week supplemented by field trips and special assignments. Except for language classes, all courses are in English.

EVALUATION: By course instructors based upon class work, papers, and examinations.

CREDITS OFFERED: 13 credits including 4 credits of intensive Japanese.

HOUSING: All participants stay with families during the first semester and may elect to live in dormitories second semester.

DATES: Fall semester: late August through mid-December; spring semester: late January through late May.

COSTS: Students pay the same as at the University Park Campus. 1986–87 tuition per semester was $2,250 for state residents; $5,150 for nonresidents; room and board: $2,750 per semester. Plus a $100 nonrefundable program fee.

YEAR ESTABLISHED: 1985.

NUMBER OF STUDENTS IN 1986: 5.

APPLY: By March 1.

Shizuoka-Ken

■ **AMERICAN GRADUATE SCHOOL OF INTERNATIONAL MANAGEMENT**
Thunderbird Campus
Glendale, AZ 85036
(602) 978-7133

PROGRAM: This graduate program, held in cooperation with the Institute for International Studies and Training in Japan, is designed to provide both intermediate and advanced Japanese language training, as well as specific courses on area studies as well as Japanese business methods and practices. One-day orientation in U.S.

ADMITTANCE REQUIREMENTS: Graduate students with a 3.0 GPA and basic core business courses.

TEACHING METHODS: Lectures and seminars are taught in English at the institute by Japanese faculty.

EVALUATION: By local faculty, based upon class work and papers.

CREDITS OFFERED: Up to 15 graduate credits.

HOUSING: Students live in dormitories.

DATES: Early January through mid-May.

COSTS: $330 includes tuition and room and board. Round-trip transportation and personal expenses additional.

YEAR ESTABLISHED: 1973.

NUMBER OF STUDENTS IN 1985:   Not available.

APPLY: By October 1. Stephen R. Beaver, Dean of Students.

Tokyo

■ **THE CALIFORNIA STATE UNIVERSITY**
400 Golden Shore
Long Beach, CA 90802
(213) 590-5655

PROGRAM: The CSU International Program in Japan, held in cooperation with the International Division of Waseda University, is a full-academic-year undergraduate and graduate opportunity to study at the university. Students concentrate on courses focusing on courses relating to the Japanese language and culture supplemented by special CSU programs. One-week orientation in Tokyo.

ADMITTANCE REQUIREMENTS: Must be enrolled at a CSU campus. Juniors and above, including graduate students; 3.0 GPA.

TEACHING METHODS: Students take a combination of regular academic courses and supplemental program-sponsored courses taught by foreign faculty.

EVALUATION: By foreign faculty and CSU resident director, based upon periodic and final examinations.

CREDITS OFFERED: 30 semester hours per year or 45 quarter units.

HOUSING: In dormitories and private apartments.

DATES: Approximately August 25 through June 28.

COSTS: Tuition: $0 (residents); $3,600 (nonresidents); room and board: $3,450. Does not include round-trip transportation or living expenses (estimated at $4,110 per year).

YEAR ESTABLISHED: 1964.

NUMBER OF STUDENTS IN 1985: 21.

APPLY: By February 1. Dr. Kibbey M. Horne, Director of International Programs.

■ **EARLHAM COLLEGE**
Richmond, IN 47374
(317) 962-6561, ext. 652

PROGRAM: The Japan Study Program is an eleven-month undergraduate program held in cooperation with Japan's Waseda University, and in the United States, the Great Lakes College Association and the Associated Colleges of the Midwest. The program is a basic overview of Japanese studies covering language, art, history, economics, etc. A brief orientation is held in Tokyo in early August followed by a three-week intensive language course.

ADMITTANCE REQUIREMENTS: A minimum GPA of 2.75 plus the equivalent of two semester hours of Japanese or the completion of the summer intensive language program held in July at Earlham (not the same course offered in Japan as part of the program).

TEACHING METHODS: Students attend classes at Waseda University. Classes are taught in English by both American and Japanese professors. A course in Japanese is required; all other course work is elective. Independent study is available, but proposals must be approved by the Waseda International Division.

EVALUATION: Each class instructor is responsible for evaluation, based upon papers and exams.

CREDITS OFFERED: 28 to 36 semester hours depending on courses selected.

HOUSING: All participants stay with a host family during the year.

DATES: August through June.

COSTS: GLCA/ACM students, $11,900; non-CLCA/ACM students, $12,474. Includes tuition, room and board, one-way flight to Tokyo from Chicago, and local travel. Estimated living expenses $200 per month.

YEAR ESTABLISHED: 1963.

NUMBER OF STUDENTS IN 1985: 28.

APPLY: By February 4. Carmelita Nussbaum, Japan Study Program.

■ **THE EXPERIMENT IN INTERNATIONAL LIVING**
Kipling Road
Brattleboro, VT 05301
(800) 451-4465

PROGRAM: The College Semester Abroad Program is designed to allow undergraduate students to become immersed in a foreign culture by living with a local family and exploring individual personal and educational interests under professional guidance. Students on the Japanese program spend ten weeks in Tokyo, three weeks at a location appropriate to a field study project, and a three-week homestay ending up in Tokyo for a week of program evaluation. Courses cover: intensive language study (conducted by the Tokyo Japanese Language Center), seminar on Japanese life and culture, history and politics, geography and economics, arts and humanities, social anthropology, methods and techniques of field work, and an independent study project. One-week orientation in Tokyo.

ADMITTANCE REQUIREMENTS: Sophomore standing or above and acceptable academic credentials. No language prerequisite.

TEACHING METHODS: Students work directly with their American instructor-advisors in planning and evaluating their individual program. Nonlanguage courses are in English. "The semester builds from the more structured language training and lectures and discussions on local life and culture to the independent study project."

EVALUATION: By individual students and their instructor-advisors, based on independent project, papers, reports and examinations. Periodic meetings during the program and for several days at the conclusion.

CREDITS OFFERED: 16 semester hours.

HOUSING: Students live as family members with their host families.

DATES: Approximately, fall semester: September through December; spring semester: January through May.

COSTS: $6,900 includes tuition, room and board, all fees and local travel, and round-trip transportation from Brattleboro, Vermont.

YEAR ESTABLISHED: Not available.

NUMBER OF STUDENTS IN 1985:   Not available.

APPLY: For fall semester by May 15; spring semester by November 15. Admissions Office, College Semester Abroad.

■ **OREGON STATE SYSTEM OF HIGHER EDUCATION (OSSHE)**
Office of Academic Affairs
Foreign Study Programs
A-100 Administrative Services Building
Oregon State University
Corvallis, OR 97331
(503) 754-2394

PROGRAM: The Oregon Study Program in Japan (Aoyama Gakuin Program) is held in cooperation with Japan's Aoyama University School of International Politics, Economics and Business and University of Oregon, Oregon State University, Western Oregon State College, Eastern Oregon State College, Southern State Oregon College, Oregon Institute of Technology, and Portland State University. This is a full ten-month academic-year undergraduate program. The courses are designed to emphasize Japanese culture with an emphasis on business and economics. Courses cover the Japanese language, political science, economics, business, management, finance, marketing, accounting, etc. This is an exchange program with an equal number of American and Japanese students exchanged annually. There is a required two-day orientation in Oregon and a three-day onsite orientation.

ADMITTANCE REQUIREMENTS: Restricted to Oregon residents or out-of-state students enrolled in the Oregon State System of Higher Education. A minimum 2.75 GPA, sophomores or above in good academic standing. Two terms Japanese language, introductory courses in economics, business, political science, or mathematics.

TEACHING METHODS: Students attend regular courses at the foreign institution, taught in English to both Japanese and American students. International faculty.

EVALUATION: By professors based on class work, papers, and periodic exams.

CREDITS OFFERED: 36 to 63 credits (quarter hours).

HOUSING: Male students are housed with Japanese students in the school dormitories; Female students live in a guest house with other Japanese students about thirty-five minutes from the campus. All housing is prearranged.

DATES: From April 1 to February 15 with a summer break from July 15 to September 15.

COSTS: Tuition: $1,400 per semester; room and board, $2,900 for the ten-month period. Does not cover round-trip transportation or personal expenses estimated at $3,500 per year.

YEAR ESTABLISHED: 1981.

NUMBER OF STUDENTS IN 1985: 10.

APPLY: By November 15. Judy Van Dyck, Oregon State System of Higher Education.

■ **UNIVERSITY OF NOTRE DAME**
  420 Administration Building
  Notre Dame, IN 46556
  (219) 239-5882

PROGRAM: The University of Notre Dame Program in Tokyo is a full-academic-year undergraduate program held in cooperation with Sophia University, Department of Comparative Culture. Courses cover elementary and intermediate Japanese language, Japanese history, sociology, literature, philosophy, and theology. Some field trips and program-related travel.

ADMITTANCE REQUIREMENTS: "Overall strong average is necessary. While a year of intensive Japanese is highly recommended, it is not a prerequisite."

TEACHING METHODS: Except for Japanese language courses, all classes are in English "but with constant reference to Japanese according to the ability of the students."

EVALUATION: By onsite directors appointed among Notre Dame faculty, based upon class work, papers, and examinations.

CREDITS OFFERED: 18 semester hours per semester.

HOUSING: Students live with Japanese families or in international dormitories.

DATES: Fall semester: September 15 through late December; spring semester: February through July 20.

COSTS: $5,158 per semester includes tuition, room and board, program-related travel and round-trip transportation from the West Coast.

YEAR ESTABLISHED: 1968.

NUMBER OF STUDENTS IN 1985: 10.

APPLY: February 1. Dr. Isabel Charles, Assistant Provost, Director, Foreign Studies Programs.

Tsukuba

■ **STATE UNIVERSITY OF NEW YORK AT OSWEGO**
Oswego, NY 13126
(315) 341-2118

PROGRAM: Study in Japan is a semester or full-academic-year undergraduate program held in cooperation with the University of Tsukuba located forty miles northeast of Tokyo. Courses cover the Japanese language and culture, Japan's education system, contemporary society and a program of independent study. Predeparture orientation in Oswego.

ADMITTANCE REQUIREMENTS: Sophomore standing, 2.7 GPA (3.0 in major) with a sincere interest in Japanese studies.

TEACHING METHODS: Courses are taught in English by the faculty at the University of Tsukuba.

EVALUATION: Based on work in class, papers, and final exams.

CREDITS OFFERED: 12 to 15 credit hours per semester.

HOUSING: Students live in university dormitories with Japanese students.

DATES: Fall semester: late August through late December; spring semester: mid-January through mid-June.

COSTS: Tuition: fall semester, $3,300; full year, $5,400 plus for non-SUNY students, NY State residents, $687.50; nonresidents, $1,612.50. Includes room and board, round-trip transportation from New York and local travel. Does not include personal expenses.

YEAR ESTABLISHED: Not available.

NUMBER OF STUDENTS IN 1985:   Not available.

APPLY: By April 10 for fall semester; October 20 for spring semester. Dr. José R. Pérez, Director, International Education, Overseas Academic Programs.

■ **UNIVERSITY OF KANSAS**
  Lawrence, KA 66045
  (913) 864-3742

PROGRAM: The University of Kansas offers a full academic year at the National University of Tsukuba (about an hour from Tokyo) consisting of three 12-week trimesters. Students enroll in regular course work along with Japanese students.

ADMITTANCE REQUIREMENTS: Juniors and above with a minimum of 60 semester hours, 3.0 GPA, proficiency in Japanese (four semesters of college-level Japanese), plus recommendations.

TEACHING METHODS: Students take regular classes at the university taught in both English and Japanese by Japanese and visiting faculty.

EVALUATION: By local professors, based upon class work, papers, and examinations.

CREDITS OFFERED: 30 semester hours per year.

HOUSING: Students live in university residence halls.

DATES: Approximately November through June.

COSTS: $3,900 includes annual tuition, room and board. Does not cover Kansas enrollment fees, round-trip transportation, local travel, or personal expenses.

YEAR ESTABLISHED: Not available.

NUMBER OF STUDENTS IN 1985: Not available.

APPLY: By March 1. Office of Study Abroad, 203 Lippincott.

Waseda

■ **UNIVERSITY OF SOUTHERN CALIFORNIA**
Overseas Studies, CES 109
University Park
Los Angeles, CA 90089
(213) 746-2500

PROGRAM: USC Year in Japan, an undergraduate program held in cooperation with CALPUC, offers courses concentrating on the humanities, international relations, and Japanese studies. Onsite orientation.

ADMITTANCE REQUIREMENTS: Sophomores and above in good academic standing.

TEACHING METHODS: Courses are taught by foreign faculty members. Classes are integrated with Japanese students.

EVALUATION: By course faculty members, based upon class work, papers, and periodic examinations.

CREDITS OFFERED: 16 semester hours per semester.

HOUSING: Students usually live in university dormitories.

DATES: Approximately, fall semester: early September through mid-December; spring semester: early January through mid-May.

COSTS: Approximately, $11,500 covers tuition, room and board, program-related travel. Does not include round-trip transportation or personal expenses. Some scholarships are available.

YEAR ESTABLISHED: 1985.

NUMBER OF STUDENTS IN 1985: Not available.

APPLY: By April 1.

SOUTH KOREA

Population: 41,568,600   **Capital:** Seoul   **Language:** Korean
Monetary Unit: Won   **Government:** Unitary republic (president and prime minister)   **Religion:** 37% Buddhist; 26% Protestant
Households With Television: 8%

SELECTED COLLEGES AND UNIVERSITIES

Keimyung University
Daegu

Both undergraduate and undergraduate programs for foreigners. Scholarships available.

Ewha Womans University
Seoul 120

Courses in Korean language, culture, and society; religions of Asia; art history; politics. In English.

Seoul National University
Language Research Institute
San 56-1, Shinnim-Dong
Kwanak-Ku
Seoul 151

Full-year program in all aspects of the Korean language.

Yonsei University
134 Sinchon-Dong
Seodaemun-Gu
Seoul 120

Junior Year Abroad program in English for Americans covers Korean language, history, oriental thought, and international relations.

FURTHER INFORMATION

Embassy of South Korea
2320 Massachusetts Avenue, NW
Washington, DC 20008
(202) 483-7383

Consulate General of South Korea
460 Park Avenue
New York, NY 10022
(212) 752-1700

Ministry of Education
International Education Division
Seoul

Publishes Education in Korea *and,* Information on Korean Government Scholarships for Foreign Students. *Both in English.*

Seoul

■ **OREGON STATE SYSTEM OF HIGHER EDUCATION (OSSHE)**
Office of Academic Affairs
Foreign Study Programs
A-100 Administrative Services Building
Oregon State University
Corvallis, OR 97331
(503) 754-2394

PROGRAM: The Oregon Study Program in Korea is held in cooperation with Ewha Women's University and Yonsei University in Korea; the University of Oregon, Oregon State University, Western Oregon State College, Eastern Oregon State College, Southern State Oregon College, Oregon Institute of Technology, and Portland State University in the United States. This is a full-academic-year undergraduate program. The courses are designed to emphasize Korean history and culture and include Korean language, economy, history, and culture; Korean international relations; Korean art and ceramics; Asian thought forms; Korean contemporary society; Korean literature; business environment and strategy; and independent study. This is an exchange program with an equal number of American and Korean students exchanged annually. There is a one-day orientation in Oregon for those living in the state and a one-day onsite orientation.

ADMITTANCE REQUIREMENTS: A minimum 2.75 GPA, sophomores or above in good academic standing. Korean language study highly recommended.

TEACHING METHODS: Students are taught by regular faculty members from the universities' international divisions. All classes are taught in English.

EVALUATION: By professors, based on class work, papers, and periodic exams.

CREDITS OFFERED: 36 to 63 credits (quarter hours).

HOUSING: Students can live with local families, international dormitories, or in local boarding houses.

DATES: Approximately, fall semester: September 1 through December 15; spring semester: January 15 through mid-May.

COSTS: Tuition, $1,400 per semester; room and board, $2,000 per semester. Does not cover round-trip transportation or personal expenses.

YEAR ESTABLISHED: 1985.

NUMBER OF STUDENTS IN 1985: 5.

APPLY: By April 1. Judy Van Dyck, Office of Academic Affairs.

■ **UNIVERSITY OF KANSAS**
Lawrence, KA 66045
(913) 864-3742

PROGRAM: The University of Kansas offers a full academic year at the Ewha Women's University for both men and women. The program consists of courses in the Korean language, Korean society, and culture. Special seminars cover: religions in East Asia, Korean history, Korean literature, introduction to contemporary Korean culture. Summer language program is also offered and recommended to help with language skills. Orientation program in Korea.

ADMITTANCE REQUIREMENTS: Juniors and above with a minimum of 60 semester hours, 3.0 GPA, plus recommendations. No prior Korean language necessary, but it is recommended.

TEACHING METHODS: Students take regular classes at the university taught in both English and Korean by Korean and visiting faculty.

EVALUATION: By local professors, based upon class work, papers, and examinations.

CREDITS OFFERED: 30 semester hours per year.

HOUSING: Students live at the International House on campus during orientation. May later select own housing or live with local families.

DATES: Approximately October through June.

COSTS: $7,400 includes annual tuition, room and board. Does not cover Kansas enrollment fees, round-trip transportation, local travel, or personal expenses.

YEAR ESTABLISHED: Not available.

NUMBER OF STUDENTS IN 1985: 6.

APPLY: By March 1. Office of Study Abroad, 203 Lippincott.

12.

Southeast Asia

INDONESIA

Population: 168,662,000   **Capital:** Jakarta   **Language:** Bahasa Indonesian
Monetary Unit: Indonesian rupiah   **Government:** Unitary multiparty republic
(president)   **Religion:** 84% Muslim   **Households With Television:** Less than 1%

SELECTED COLLEGES AND UNIVERSITIES

University of Indonesia
Salemba Raya 4,
Jakarta Pusat

Courses are taught in Indonesian.

Universitas Kristen Indonesia
Jalan Diponegoro 86
Jakarta

*Cooperative arrangement with the
University of Tulsa. Some courses
are taught in English.*

University of Nahdlatul Ulama
(Uninus)
Jalan. Halimun 37
Bandung-Jawa Barat

*Offers international study program in
English.*

FURTHER INFORMATION

Consulate General of Indonesia
5 East 68th Street
New York, NY 10021
(212) 879-0600

Embassy of Indonesia
2020 Massachusetts Avenue, NW
Washington, DC 20036
(202) 293-1745

Department of Education and Culture
Jalan Jendral Sudirman
Jakarta

Bali

■ **THE EXPERIMENT IN INTERNATIONAL LIVING**
Kipling Road
Brattleboro, VT 05301
(800) 451-4465

PROGRAM: The College Semester Abroad program is designed to allow students to become immersed in a foreign culture by living with a local family and exploring individual personal and educational interests under professional guidance. The Bali program covers intensive language study, seminar on Balinese and Indonesian life and culture, history and politics of the region, geography and economics, arts and humanities, social anthropology, and an independent study project.

ADMITTANCE REQUIREMENTS: Sophomore standing or above and acceptable academic credentials.

TEACHING METHODS: Students work directly with their American instructors in planning and evaluating their individual program. "The semester builds from the more structured language training and lectures and discussions on local life and culture to the independent study project."

EVALUATION: By individual students and their instructor-advisors based on independent project, papers, reports, and examinations. Periodic meetings during the program and for several days at the conclusion.

CREDITS OFFERED: Up to 16 semester hours.

HOUSING: Students live as family members with their host families.

DATES: Approximately, fall semester: September through December; spring semester: January through May.

COSTS: $6,100 includes tuition, room and board, all fees and local travel, and round-trip transportation from New York.

YEAR ESTABLISHED: 1985.

NUMBER OF STUDENTS IN 1985: 13.

APPLY: For fall semester by May 15; spring semester by November 15. Admissions Office, College Semester Abroad.

SINGAPORE

Population: 2,587,000   **Capital:** Singapore   **Language:** Chinese, Malay, Tamil, and English   **Monetary Unit:** Singapore dollar   **Government:** Unitary multiparty republic (president and prime minister)   **Religion:** 30% Taoist; 27% Buddhist   **Households With Television:** 4%

SELECTED UNIVERSITY

National University of Singapore
Kent Ridge
Singapore 0511
Instruction in English.

FURTHER INFORMATION

Embassy of Singapore
1824 R Street, NW
Washington, DC 20009
(202) 667-7555

Singapore Mission to the United Nations
2 United Nations Plaza
New York, NY 10017
(212) 826-0840

Ministry of Education
Kay Siang Road
Singapore 1024

■ INSTITUTE OF EUROPEAN STUDY (IES)
223 West Ohio Street
Chicago, IL 60610
(312) 944-1750

PROGRAM: IES is a nonprofit organization with formal relationships with more than forty American colleges and universities. The institute maintains ten undergraduate academic centers throughout the world which provide semester or full-academic-year programs. Students attending the recently initiated full-academic-year IES Singapore program are enrolled at the National University of Singapore, an English-language university. The curriculum is aimed at students interested in international affairs, international economics and business, or Asian studies. Courses cover Japanese, Chinese, and Malay language and studies, business and economics, English literature, history, mathematics, natural sciences, political science, sociology, and statistics. Orientation in Singapore.

ADMITTANCE REQUIREMENTS: Juniors and seniors only. Two years college French or the equivalent. Faculty recommendations and an application essay. 85 percent of all students have had a GPA between 2.80 and 3.75.

TEACHING METHODS: Students attend regular university courses with other local and foreign students. All courses are taught in English.

EVALUATION: By faculty, based upon class work and periodic and final exams. Most courses require a research paper.

CREDITS OFFERED: 15 semester hours per semester.

HOUSING: Students live with local families or in apartments. All meals are the responsibility of the student.

DATES: Fall semester: June 26 through October 18; winter semester November 17 through March 9.

COSTS: $6,500 per year; $3,500 per semester. Includes tuition. Does not include room and board, round-trip transportation, local travel, or personal expenses (estimated at $2,500 per year). Some IES scholarship aid available; $1,500 for full year students, $750 for semester students.

YEAR ESTABLISHED: 1986.

NUMBER OF STUDENTS IN 1986: Not available.

APPLY: By February 15.

TAIWAN

Population: 19,408,000   **Capital:** Taipei   **Language:** Mandarin Chinese
Monetary Unit: New Taiwan dollar   **Government:** Unitary republic
(president and premier)   **Religion:** 49% Chinese folk-religionist; 43% Buddhist
Households With Television: 11%

SELECTED COLLEGES AND UNIVERSITIES

National Central University
Chung-Li 320
Cooperative arrangements with the Universities of Pittsburgh and Maryland. Courses taught in Chinese and English.

National Taiwan University
Sec. 4, Roosevelt Road 1
Taipai
Courses taught in Chinese.

FURTHER INFORMATION

Coordination Council for North American Affairs
801 Second Avenue
New York, NY 10017
(212) 697-1250

- *Taiwan is very Westernized but the people are terrific. Everyone I met was helpful. If you're in the country to learn the language, then don't use English. The more you try Chinese, the better you'll learn it. Living with a Chinese family or roommate will further help your Chinese.*

  - Marian Leerburger, Millersville, Maryland

Taipei

■ **THE CALIFORNIA STATE UNIVERSITY**
400 Golden Shore
Long Beach, CA 90802
(213) 590-5655

PROGRAM: The CSU International Program in Taiwan, held at the National Chengchi University, is a full-academic-year undergraduate and graduate opportunity to study at the Taiwanese university. Participating students elect one of three concentrations: Chinese Language and culture; international business; or, art and art history. All students are required to study Chinese. One-week orientation in Taipei.

ADMITTANCE REQUIREMENTS: Must be enrolled at a CSU campus or may be accepted from another institution if sponsored by that institution. Juniors and above including graduate students. 2.75 GPA Knowledge of Chinese.

TEACHING METHODS: Students take a combination of regular academic courses in English and supplemental program-sponsored courses taught by foreign faculty.

EVALUATION: By foreign faculty and CSU resident director based upon periodic and final examinations.

CREDITS OFFERED: 30 semester hours per year or 45 quarter units.

HOUSING: In dormitories and private apartments.

DATES: Approximately August 14 through June 6.

COSTS: Tuition: $0 (residents); $3,600 (nonresidents); room and board: $2,700. Does not include round-trip transportation or living expenses (estimated at approximately $2,860 per year).

YEAR ESTABLISHED: 1969.

NUMBER OF STUDENTS IN 1985: 12.

APPLY: By February 1. Dr. Kibbey M. Horne, Director of International Programs.

■ **COLGATE UNIVERSITY**
   Hamilton, NY 13346
   (315) 824-1000

PROGRAM: The China Study Group is a single-semester undergraduate program that offers courses in the Chinese language, economics, and the social changes in Taiwan. One-month field trip to the People's Republic of China. Orientation in the U.S.

ADMITTANCE REQUIREMENTS: Sophomores and above in good academic standing. Colgate students are shown a preference, but others accepted. No language requirement.

TEACHING METHODS: Students attend special courses arranged for the group and taught in English by both U.S. faculty and the faculty at the Mandarin Training Center, National Taiwan University.

EVALUATION: By course professors, based upon papers and examinations.

CREDITS OFFERED: 15 semester hours per semester.

HOUSING: Students live in dormitories at the National Taiwan University.

DATES: Approximately January 5 through May 27.

COSTS: $8,000 includes tuition, housing, round-trip transportation, and China tour. Does not cover meals or personal expenses.

YEAR ESTABLISHED: 1983.

NUMBER OF STUDENTS IN 1985: 17.

APPLY: By September 30. Prof. Chi-ming Hou, Department of Economics.

■ **PENNSYLVANIA STATE UNIVERSITY**
Office of Education Abroad Programs
222 Boucke Building
University Park, PA 16802
(814) 865-7681

PROGRAM: Education Abroad at the National Taiwan University is a fall-semester undergraduate program in which students take specially designed courses taught by NTU faculty members. The curriculum includes 9 credits of intensive Chinese language and two 3-credit nonlanguage courses in Chinese literature and Chinese art history. Orientation at Penn State.

ADMITTANCE REQUIREMENTS: Juniors and seniors with a 2.5 GPA, good standing, and "must show evidence of maturity, stability, adaptability, self-discipline, and a strong academic motivation." Some specific course prerequisites. At least 4 credits of Chinese are recommended.

TEACHING METHODS: Except for language courses, students take courses in English taught by NTU teachers.

EVALUATION: By course instructors, based upon class work, papers, and examinations.

CREDITS OFFERED: 15 credits, including 9 credits of intensive language study.

HOUSING: In Chinese-style dormitories near the NTU campus.

DATES: Early September through mid-December.

COSTS: Students pay the same as at the University Park Campus. 1986-87 tuition per semester was $2,250 for state residents; $5,150 for nonresidents; room and board: $2,750 per semester. Plus a $100 nonrefundable program fee.

YEAR ESTABLISHED: 1985.

NUMBER OF STUDENTS IN 1985: 2.

APPLY: By March 1.

■ **UNIVERSITY OF KANSAS**
Lawrence, KA 66045
(913) 864-3742

PROGRAM: The University of Kansas offers a full academic year at the Mandarin Training Center. Students begin in mid-June with a ten-week intensive summer course in Mandarin. Following completion, students take modern and classical Chinese as well as regular courses (or may audit) at a state university.

ADMITTANCE REQUIREMENTS: Juniors and above with a minimum of 60 semester hours, 3.0 GPA, three years of Mandarin, plus recommendations.

TEACHING METHODS: Students take regular classes at the university taught in Chinese by local faculty.

EVALUATION: By local professors, based upon class work, papers, and examinations.

CREDITS OFFERED: Up to 26 semester hours per year, plus up to 10 hours for the summer program.

HOUSING: Students live in dormitories with Chinese students. May also select own housing or live with local families.

DATES: Approximately mid-June through May.

COSTS: $3,490 includes annual tuition, room and board. (Summer program is $775.) Does not cover Kansas enrollment fees, round-trip transportation, local travel, or personal expenses.

YEAR ESTABLISHED: Not available.

NUMBER OF STUDENTS IN 1985: 10.

APPLY: By March 1. Office of Study Abroad, 203 Lippincott.

- *The Mandarin Training Center is terrific. The professors really enjoy teaching. All the materials are up-to-date and students are tested prior to the start of classes to ensure proper placement. You select the size of your class, from one to five other students. I learned more Chinese in four months than I did during two and a half years at college.*

  - Marian Leerburger, Millersville, Maryland

13.

South Asia

INDIA

Population: 777,230,000   **Capital:** New Delhi   **Language:** Hindi, English
Monetary Unit: Indian rupee   **Government:** Multiparty federal republic
(president and prime minister)   **Religion:** 83% Hindu
Households With Television: Less than 1%

SELECTED COLLEGES AND UNIVERSITIES

University of Bombay
Bombay 400032

University of Delhi
New Delhi 110007

University of Poona
Ganeshkhind
Poona 7411007

*Offers certificate courses in
Maharashtra culture, language, and
literature.*

Gujapat Vidyapith
Asjram Road
Ahmedabad 380014

*Courses in Gandhian thought, Indian
culture, Gujarati and Hindi languages.*

FURTHER INFORMATION

American Institute of Indian
Studies
University of Chicago
1130 East 59th Street
Chicago, IL 60637
(312) 702-1234

*Offers fellowships for dissertation
research in India.*

Consulate General of India
3 East 64th Street
New York, NY 10021
(212) 879-7800

Embassy of India
2107 Massachusetts Avenue, NW
Washington, DC 20008
(202) 265-2020

Government of India Tourist Office
30 Rockefeller Plaza
New York, NY 10020
(212) 586-4901

Students' Information Service Unit
Ministry of Education and Culture
Shastri Bhawan
New Delhi 1
Publishes Directory of Institutions of
Higher Education.

More Than One City

■ **UNIVERSITY OF CALIFORNIA, BERKELEY**
International Education
2538 Channing Way
Berkeley, CA 94720
(415) 642-1356

PROGRAM: Professional Studies Program in India is a graduate-level opportunity to do field research as part of an internship program. Specific projects are worked out after consultations involving participants, their home campus advisors, and their Indian supervisors. Students take two seminars under Indian faculty. Projects have included studies of: infant rearing practices in a small town; energy sources other than oil; methods and techniques of flood estimation analysis; slum housing; Indian health care; etc. This is the only program designed to provide internships for students in the professional fields in India. Weekend orientation in Berkeley, first month language training and year-end conference held in Kashmir on Dal Lake.

ADMITTANCE REQUIREMENTS: American citizens enrolled in an American college or university. Must have completed one year of graduate work toward a professional degree.

TEACHING METHODS: Participants do not attend classes aside from three weeks of seminars at the end of the language training. They are involved in independent research and field work.

EVALUATION: Year-end thesis is required as is the year-end conference.

CREDITS OFFERED: 13 units of graduate credit. Transcript credit available only to University of California applicants; others may receive a letter of completion from the Berkeley registrar.

HOUSING: Arranged individually or in consultation with supervisor.

DATES: Approximately August 15 to June 15.

COSTS: $4,200 covers tuition. Participants receive a stipend to cover room and board and living expenses. Transportation is not included.

YEAR ESTABLISHED: 1967.

NUMBER OF STUDENTS IN 1985:   11.

APPLY: By first week in January. Linnea Soderlund, Program Coordinator.

- *I interviewed more than one hundred film writers, directors, producers, financiers and distributors about how they worked together to initiate and develop recent Hindi films. The experience was the most rewarding of my entire education. Also, it helped give me credibility in a field, film production, that is notoriously difficult to enter.*

  - David Mills, University of California, Berkeley.

Ahmedabad

■ **THE EXPERIMENT IN INTERNATIONAL LIVING**
Kipling Road
Brattleboro, VT 05301
(800) 451-4465

PROGRAM: The College Semester Abroad program is designed to allow students to become immersed in a foreign culture by living with a local family and exploring individual personal and educational interests under professional guidance. The India program spends seven weeks outside Ahmedabad in the rural village of Sadra, where participants observe full Indian traditions, and five weeks at a location appropriate to a field study project, ending up in New Delhi for a week of program evaluation. Courses cover: intensive language study at the Sadra rural campus of Gujarat Vidyapith, seminar on India life and culture and rural development, history and politics, geography and economics, arts and humanities, social anthropology, social/cultural field work, and an independent study project. One-week orientation in Brattleboro, Vermont, and Sadra, India.

ADMITTANCE REQUIREMENTS: Sophomore standing or above and acceptable academic credentials. No language prerequisite.

TEACHING METHODS: Students work directly with their American instructor-advisors in planning and evaluating their individual program. "The semester builds from the more structured language training and lectures and discussions on local life and culture to the independent study project."

EVALUATION: By individual students and their instructor-advisors based on independent project, papers, reports, and examinations. Periodic meetings during the program and for several days at the conclusion.

CREDITS OFFERED: 16 semester hours.

HOUSING: Students live as family members with their host families.

DATES: Approximately, fall semester: September through December; spring semester: January through May.

COSTS: $5,600 includes tuition, room and board, all fees and local travel, and round-trip transportation from Brattleboro, Vermont.

YEAR ESTABLISHED: 1966.

NUMBER OF STUDENTS IN 1985: 13.

APPLY: For fall semester by May 15; spring semester by November 15. Admissions Office, College Semester Abroad.

Bangalore

■ **COLLEGE CONSORTIUM FOR INTERNATIONAL STUDIES (CCIS)**
866 United Nations Plaza, Room 511
New York, NY 10017
(212) 308-1556

PROGRAM: CCIS is a private organization that sponsors and organizes several dozen foreign study programs. Their Bangalore Program is a single-semester or full-academic-year experience offered in cooperation with Friends World College in New York and the International Sarvodaya Center. Students attend classes at the center and also learn by doing. Internships are provided in liberal arts, service learning, and specific applied projects. One month orientation in India.

ADMITTANCE REQUIREMENTS: Sophomore and above with acceptable academic credentials. Students with specific projects in mind are preferred.

TEACHING METHODS: Courses are in English. All students must maintain a project journal.

EVALUATION: By course instructors and project leaders.

CREDITS OFFERED: 15 semester hours per semester.

HOUSING: Students live with local families, in dormitories, or hotels.

DATES: Fall semester: September 15 through January 31; spring semester: February 1 through June 15.

COSTS: $2,700 per semester includes tuition. Does not cover room and board, local travel, round-trip transportation, or personal expenses.

YEAR ESTABLISHED: Not available.

NUMBER OF STUDENTS IN 1985:   6.

APPLY: Fall semester by June 1; spring semester: October 15.

Bodh Gaya

■ **ANTIOCH COLLEGE**
Box ACBS
Yellow Springs, OH 45387
(513) 767-1031

PROGRAM: Antioch's undergraduate and graduate program in Buddhist Studies is held in cooperation with the Nalanda Institute and Maghda University. Students choose from the following core programs: Buddhist philosophy; ancient Indian history; or, contemporary Buddhist culture. Practical meditation instruction allows students to test various philosophies representing: Theravada, Mahayana, and Vajrayana. After two months of intensive study, students spend their final month doing individual work on a specific project. Two-day orientation in London.

ADMITTANCE REQUIREMENTS: Any undergraduate or higher in good academic standing.

TEACHING METHODS: All courses are taught in English by both U.S. and Indian faculty. Small classes, tutorials, and individualized study.

EVALUATION: By both U.S. and foreign faculty members. Both written assessment and grades as required by student's home school are provided.

CREDITS OFFERED: The equivalent of 15 to 20 Antioch quarter graduate or undergraduate credits (a full credit load of semester hours).

HOUSING: Students live in and are provided vegetarian meals at the guest house within the compound of the Burmese Vihar monastery where they must follow basic precepts, i.e., "abstain from: taking life, theft, sexual misconduct, lying, intoxicants."

DATES: September 20 through December 22.

COSTS: $5,400 includes tuition, room and board, and round-trip transportation from London. Not covered: personal expenses, round-trip transportation to London, local travel, and meals in London during orientation.

YEAR ESTABLISHED: 1979.

NUMBER OF STUDENTS IN 1985: limited to 25.

APPLY: By April 30. Connie Bauer, Dean.

Madras

■ **COLGATE UNIVERSITY**
Hamilton, NY 13346
(315) 824-1000

PROGRAM: The India Study Group is a single-semester undergraduate program that offers courses in Sanskrit and the traditions of Indian art, dance, music, and religion. One-week field trip to Sri Lanka, political conditions warranting.

ADMITTANCE REQUIREMENTS: Sophomores and above in good academic standing with some preparation in Indian culture and religion. Colgate students are shown a preference, but others accepted. No language requirement.

TEACHING METHODS: Students attend special courses arranged for the group and taught in English by both U.S. and Indian faculty.

EVALUATION: By course professors, based upon papers and examinations.

CREDITS OFFERED: 15 semester hours.

HOUSING: Students live in hotels.

DATES: Offered in 1987 and 1989. Approximately early September through mid-December.

COSTS: $6,100 includes tuition, round-trip transportation, and tour. Does not cover room and board or personal expenses.

YEAR ESTABLISHED: 1985.

NUMBER OF STUDENTS IN 1985: 16.

APPLY: By February 14. Professor William Skelton, Department of Music.

■ **DAVIDSON COLLEGE**
Davidson, NC 28036
(704) 892-2000

PROGRAM: Davidson's Term in India is a single-semester undergraduate program held in cooperation with the South Atlantic States Association for Asian and African Studies. Courses cover introductory Tamil, Indian studies, and independent study projects. Field trips to Indian sites of historic and cultural interest. Five-day orientation in the U.S.

ADMITTANCE REQUIREMENTS: Juniors in good academic standing.

TEACHING METHODS: Students attend courses arranged for the group and taught in English by Indian faculty.

EVALUATION: By Indian faculty, based upon papers and examinations.

CREDITS OFFERED: 9 to 12 semester hours.

HOUSING: Students live in furnished rooms.

DATES: Approximately early September through late November.

COSTS: $4,000 includes tuition, room and board, round-trip transportation from New York, and program-related travel.

YEAR ESTABLISHED: 1979.

NUMBER OF STUDENTS IN 1985: Not available.

APPLY: By March 1. Office for Study Abroad.

Poona

■ **ASSOCIATED COLLEGES OF THE MIDWEST (ACM)**
18 South Michigan Avenue, Suite 1010
Chicago, IL 60603
(312) 263-5000

PROGRAM: The ACM India Studies Program is a nine-month, undergraduate program held in cooperation with the University of Poona. Courses at the university cover language, history, religion, economics, anthropology, sociology, music, literature, philosophy, etc. There is a ten-week orientation period at member ACM colleges.

ADMITTANCE REQUIREMENTS: Acceptable academic standards. Freshmen are usually not admitted, however, decisions are made by the selection committee.

TEACHING METHODS: There are special courses for Americans taught by Indian faculty. Americans are not integrated with Indian students. All lectures are in English. Independent study, excursions, and local trips complement the class work.

EVALUATION: Based upon final exams given by Indian faculty.

CREDITS OFFERED: Credits vary depending upon each college system.

HOUSING: Students live in private homes with local families.

DATES: Approximately mid-June through mid-December.

COSTS: Tuition (which also includes local travel costs) is determined by home college. Room and board is approximately $1,500 to $1,700. Plan on approximately $75 a month for local expenses.

YEAR ESTABLISHED: 1969.

NUMBER OF STUDENTS IN 1985:   11.

APPLY: Early deadline is April 15; final deadline is November 1. Pam Shumaker, Program Associate.

NEPAL

Population: 16,863,000   **Capital:** Kathmandu   **Language:** Nepali
Monetary Unit: Nepalese rupee   **Government:** Constitutional monarchy (king
and prime minister)   **Religion:** 90% Hindu
Households With Television: Less than 1%

SELECTED UNIVERSITY

Tribhuvan University
Kirtipur
Kathmandu

*Courses taught in both English
and Nepali.*

FURTHER INFORMATION

Embassy of Nepal
2131 Leroy Place, NW
Washington, DC 20008
(202) 667-4550

Mission of Nepal to the United Nations
711 Third Avenue, Room 1806
New York, NY 10017
(212) 370-4188

Kathmandu

■ **THE EXPERIMENT IN INTERNATIONAL LIVING**
Kipling Road
Brattleboro, VT 05301
(800) 451-4465

PROGRAM: The College Semester Abroad program is designed to allow undergraduate students to become immersed in a foreign culture by living with a
local family and exploring individual personal and educational interests
under professional guidance. Students on the Nepal program spend most of
their stay in the Kathmandu area, however, one week is spent in a village
outside the Kathmandu Valley and another in a location appropriate to a field
study project. Courses cover: intensive language study, seminar on Nepali life
and culture, history and politics, geography and economics, arts and humanities, social anthropology, methods and techniques of field work, and an independent study project. One-week orientation in Brattleboro and Kathmandu.

ADMITTANCE REQUIREMENTS: Sophomore standing or above and acceptable academic credentials. No language requirement.

TEACHING METHODS: Students work directly with their American instructor-advisors in planning and evaluating their individual program. Nonlanguage courses are in English. "The semester builds from the more structured language training and lectures and discussions on local life and culture to the independent study project."

EVALUATION: By individual students and their instructor-advisors based on independent project, papers, reports, and examinations. Periodic meetings during the program and for several days at the conclusion.

CREDITS OFFERED: 16 semester hours.

HOUSING: Students live as family members with their host families.

DATES: Approximately, fall semester: September through December; spring semester: January through May.

COSTS: $6,100 includes tuition, room and board, all fees and local travel and round-trip transportation from Brattleboro, Vermont.

YEAR ESTABLISHED: 1974.

NUMBER OF STUDENTS IN 1985: 50.

APPLY: For fall semester by May 15; spring semester by November 15. Admissions Office, College Semester Abroad.

SRI LANKA

Population: 16,060,000   **Capital:** Colombo   **Language:** Sinhala
Monetary Unit: Sri Lanka rupee   **Government:** Unitary multiparty republic
(president)   **Religion:** 70% Buddhist
Households With Television: Less than 1%

SELECTED COLLEGES AND UNIVERSITIES

University of Colombo
College House, P.O. Box 1490
Cumaratunga Munidasa Mawatha
Colombo 3

Courses taught in English, Sinhala, and Tamil.

University of Peradeniya
Peradeniya

Courses taught in English, Sinhala, and Tamil.

FURTHER INFORMATION

Consulate of Sri Lanka
630 Third Avenue
New York, NY 10017
(212) 986-7040

Embassy of Sri Lanka
2148 Wyoming Avenue, NW
Washington, DC 20008
(202) 483-4025

Ministry of Education
Malay Street
Colombo 2

Sri Lanka Tourist Board
609 Fifth Avenue, Suite 308
New York, NY 10017
(212) 935-0369

- *Due to historical problems and British intervention, Sri Lanka became developmentally Westernized and touristy much too quickly. As a result, many Sinhalese taunt foreigners and often attempt to take advantage of tourists. However, the Northern Tamils, with whom the Sinhalese are involved in a civil war, are much more tolerant of foreigners. It's a good idea to read up on the country before you go. Use your free time to visit the monasteries, nunneries and historic sites such as Sigiria and Polunara. Buses and trains, while slow, are very easy to travel on and Sri Lanka is extremely inexpensive.*

- Marian Leerburger, Millersville, Maryland

Kandy

■ BATES COLLEGE
Lewiston, ME 04240
(207) 786-6311

PROGRAM: The Intercollegiate Sri Lanka Educational (ISLE) Program is operated through the cooperative efforts of Bates, Bowdoin, Carleton, Colby, Hobart and William Smith, and Swarthmore colleges. The program consists of a semester of intensive study and an optional semester of a seminar or tutorial courses for those with demonstrated academic interests in the areas of South Asian studies. Fall semester courses cover: Sinhala language, Theravada Buddhism, social, economic, and political structures of colonial and modern Sri Lanka, and, seminar/field experiences. Regional travel is integrated into the program.

ADMITTANCE REQUIREMENTS: Acceptable academic record, essay, references, and a demonstrated academic interest in Asian religion, history, art, economics, politics, etc.

TEACHING METHODS: All classes are under the direction of University of Peradeniya faculty members and a U.S. program director.

EVALUATION: By the faculty at the University of Peradeniya, based upon class work, seminar participation and periodic and final tests.

CREDITS OFFERED: A maximum of 15 semester hours per semester.

HOUSING: Students spend their Colombo orientation in hotels and live with host families in Kandy.

DATES: August 5 through December 5; spring seminar: varies but usually concludes in late April.

COSTS: The maximum comprehensive fee for the fall semester is half the annual fee of the student's home institution. (Includes tuition, room and board for seventeen weeks, round-trip transportation from Boston/New York, and local travel. For those remaining through April, add approximately $3,300.)

YEAR ESTABLISHED: 1981.

NUMBER OF STUDENTS IN 1985: 8.

APPLY: By January 31. Professor John Strong, Dept of Philosophy and Religion.

Moratuwa

■ **THE EXPERIMENT IN INTERNATIONAL LIVING**
Kipling Road
Brattleboro, VT 05301
(800) 451-4465

PROGRAM: The College Semester Abroad program is designed to allow undergraduate students to become immersed in a foreign culture by living with a local family and exploring individual personal and educational interests under professional guidance. Students on the Sri Lanka program spend most of their stay in Moratuwa, however, part of the semester is spent at a homestay in Annuradhapura, Colombo, or Kandy; three weeks are spent at a location appropriate to a field study project. The final week is spent evaluating the program in Moratuwa. Courses cover: intensive language study, seminar on Sri Lankan life and culture and rural development, history and politics, geography and economics, arts and humanities, social anthropology, methods and techniques of field work, and an independent study project. One-week orientation in Brattleboro and Moratuwa.

ADMITTANCE REQUIREMENTS:　Sophomore standing or above and acceptable academic credentials. No language requirement.

TEACHING METHODS:　Students work directly with their American instructor-advisors in planning and evaluating their individual program. Nonlanguage courses are in English. "The semester builds from the more structured language training and lectures and discussions on local life and culture to the independent study project."

EVALUATION:　By individual students and their instructor-advisors based on independent project, papers, reports, and examinations. Periodic meetings during the program and for several days at the conclusion.

CREDITS OFFERED:　16 semester hours.

HOUSING:　Students live as family members with their host families.

DATES:　Approximately, fall semester: September through December; spring semester: January through May.

COSTS:　$5,900 includes tuition, room and board, all fees and local travel, and round-trip transportation from Brattleboro, Vermont.

YEAR ESTABLISHED:　1973.

NUMBER OF STUDENTS IN 1985:　13.

APPLY:　For fall semester by May 15; spring semester by November 15. Admissions Office, College Semester Abroad.

PART SIX

THE MIDDLE EAST
AND AFRICA

14.

The Middle East

EGYPT

Population: 48,009,000   **Capital:** Cairo   **Language:** Arabic
Monetary Unit: Egyptian pound   **Government:** Republic (president and prime minister)   **Religion:** 82% Muslim   **Households With Television:** 3%

SELECTED UNIVERSITY

Ain-Shams University
Abbassia
Cairo

Business administration courses; some in English.

FURTHER INFORMATION

Embassy of Egypt
2310 Decatur Place, NW
Washington, DC 20008
(202) 265-6400

Consulate General of Egypt
1110 Second Avenue
New York, NY 10022
(212) 759-7120

Students' Welfare Department
Ministry of Higher Education
Cairo

Publishes A Guide for the Use of Foreign Students.

Cairo

■ **THE AMERICAN UNIVERSITY IN CAIRO**
866 United Nations Plaza
New York, NY 10017
(212) 421-6320

PROGRAM: The AUC is a private, independent institution located in down-town Cairo and licensed by Washington in 1919 to confer both undergraduate and graduate degrees. The school is accredited by the Middle States Association of Colleges and Schools. About 75 percent of the 2,600 students are Egyptian; the rest represent some sixty nationalities. Students can attend for a full four-year program or elect the Year Abroad Program planned with under-graduates in mind. AUC also offers six- and eight-week summer sessions which concentrate in intensive Arabic. Undergraduate students can select courses covering anthropology, Arabic studies, business administration, chem-istry, computer science, economics, Egyptology, English and comparative literature, mass communications, mathematics, mechanical engineering, Middle Eastern history, political science, teaching English or Arabic as a foreign language. Ten-day fall orientation course in intensive Arabic.

ADMITTANCE REQUIREMENTS: "Most students are college juniors although other candidates considered after completion of high school." Acceptable academic record and two letters of reference.

TEACHING METHODS: Nearly half the one hundred and forty full-time faculty members are Egyptian; 38 percent are American. Students attend regular courses, taught in English, with Egyptian students and select regular course load from the college catalogue. In some courses knowledge of Arabic is useful but not required.

EVALUATION: By faculty based upon class performance, papers, and examinations.

CREDITS OFFERED: For undergraduates: 12 to 15 semester hours per semester; graduates: 9 to 12 credits per semester.

HOUSING: The university has one dormitory for men and one for women. Many Americans find their own housing in local apartments.

DATES: Fall semester: September 15 through January 30; spring semester: February 1 through June 10. Summer program begins June 15.

COSTS: Per semester: Tuition, $2,270; room and board, $1,825. Does not include round-trip transportation or personal expenses (estimated at $600 per semester).

YEAR ESTABLISHED: 1960.

NUMBER OF STUDENTS IN 1985: 250.

APPLY: For fall semester by June 30; spring semester by December 30; summer programs by April 30. Mrs. Mary Davison, Admissions Officer.

■ **PENNSYLVANIA STATE UNIVERSITY**
Office of Education Abroad Programs
222 Boucke Building
University Park, PA 16802
(814) 865-7681

PROGRAM: Education Abroad in Cairo is a new full-year or spring-semester undergraduate program held in cooperation with the American University in Cairo. Students take regular courses from the AUC catalogue which concentrate on Arabic studies and general arts and sciences.

ADMITTANCE REQUIREMENTS: Juniors and seniors with a 2.5 GPA, good academic standing, and "must show evidence of maturity, stability, adaptability, self-discipline and a strong academic motivation."

TEACHING METHODS: Students are fully integrated into AUC classes. Except for language courses, all classes are in English.

EVALUATION: By course instructors, based upon class work, papers, and examinations.

CREDITS OFFERED: 12 to 18 semester hours per semester.

HOUSING: Students live in American University in Cairo dormitories.

DATES: Fall semester: early September through mid-June; spring semester: late January through early June.

COSTS: Students pay the same as at the University Park Campus. 1986-87 tuition per semester was $2,250 for state residents; $5,150 for nonresidents; room and board: $2,750 per semester. Plus a $100 nonrefundable program fee.

YEAR ESTABLISHED: 1986.

NUMBER OF STUDENTS IN 1986: Not available.

APPLY: Full year by March 1; Spring semester by October 15.

ISRAEL

Population: 4,037 million   **Proclaimed Capital:** Jerusalem
Languages: Hebrew, Arabic   **Monetary Unit:** Israeli shekel
Government: Multiparty republic (president and prime minister)
Religion: 83% Jewish   **Households With Television:** 5%

SELECTED COLLEGES AND UNIVERSITIES

Many Israel universities maintain U.S. offices e.g.:

Hebrew University (Jerusalem)
c/o American Friends of the
Hebrew University
11 East 69th Street
New York, NY 10021
(212) 472-9800

Tel Aviv University
c/o American Friends of Tel Aviv
University
342 Madison Avenue
New York, NY 10017
(212) 687-5651

Haifa University
c/o American Friends of Haifa
University
206 Fifth Avenue
New York, NY 10022
(212) 818-9050

Ben-Gurion University of the Negev
342 Madison Avenue
New York, NY 10022
(212) 687-7721

Weizman Institute of Science
515 Park Avenue
New York, NY 10022
(212) 752-1300

FURTHER INFORMATION

American Zionist Youth Foundation
515 Park Avenue
New York, NY 10022
(212) 751-6070

*Sponsors many study and study/work
programs.*

Embassy of Israel
3514 International Drive, NW
Washington, DC 20008
(202) 364-5500

Consulate General of Israel
800 Second Avenue
New York, NY 10017
(212) 697-5500

More Than One City

■ **COLLEGE CONSORTIUM FOR INTERNATIONAL STUDIES (CCIS)**
866 United Nations Plaza, Room 511
New York, NY 10017
(212) 308-1556

PROGRAM: CCIS is a nonprofit organization that sponsors and organizes several dozen foreign study programs for member colleges who grant degree credit. CCIS offers several single-semester or full-academic-year undergraduate programs in various Israeli locations in cooperation with Kingsborough Community College (New York): (1) Internship program offers courses in all levels of Hebrew as well as study and internship opportunities in anthropology, business, commercial art, communications, hotel management, marine archaeology, occupational and recreational therapy, and, special education; (2) work-study program provides both study opportunities and work on a supervised community service project; (3) university study program allows students to study at one of several Israeli institutions. Orientation in U.S. and Israel. Program-related travel in Israel.

ADMITTANCE REQUIREMENTS: Undergraduates with a 2.5 GPA (3.0 for university study program) and acceptable academic credentials. Students selecting the internship or work-study program take intensive Hebrew during the preceding summer.

TEACHING METHODS: Students take courses at various Israeli institutions. Students on the internship program attend regular classes at Haifa University. Many courses are taught in Hebrew.

EVALUATION: By course instructors.

CREDITS OFFERED: 12 to 18 semester hours per semester.

HOUSING: Students live in dormitories, furnished apartments, or with local families.

DATES: The internship program and work-study program runs from mid-July to early February and from mid-February through late June. The university study program varies depending upon the school selected.

COSTS: Internship program: $1,730; work-study program: $1,130; university study program: $1,430 per semester. Does not include room and board, program-related travel, round-trip transportation, or personal expenses.

YEAR ESTABLISHED: Not available.

NUMBER OF STUDENTS IN 1985:   600.

APPLY: Fall semester by June 1; spring semester; November 1.

■ **UNION OF AMERICAN HEBREW CONGREGATIONS (UAHC)**
  838 Fifth Avenue
  New York, NY 10021
  (212) 249-0100, ext. 546

PROGRAM: UAHC in cooperation with Hebrew Union College–Jewish Institute of Religion offers several programs: College & Kibbutz offers college credit for academic courses while students live and work on Kibbutz Tsora, west of Jerusalem; Machon combines a year's college level work with in-depth leadership training and a full touring program; the "Maskil" Adventure is a six-week summer program for both college and high school students that combines study, travel and a stay in a kibbutz (five weeks spent in Israel; one week in New York's Brookdale Center of the Hebrew Union College-Jewish Institute of Religion prior to departure).

ADMITTANCE REQUIREMENTS: Good academic standing.

TEACHING METHODS: Varies with each program. Basically, students work with local scholars and often meet leading political scientists and government figures.

EVALUATION: Varies with each program.

CREDITS OFFERED: College and Kibbutz and Machon, 36 college credits; "Maskil" Adventure, 6 college credits.

HOUSING: Varies.

DATES: College and Kibbutz and Machon, approximately September 6th through May 5th; "Maskil" Adventure, approximately July 1 through August 13.

COSTS: College and Kibbutz and Machon, $3,900; "Maskil" Adventure, $2,800. Includes tuition, room and board, round-trip, and local travel.

YEAR ESTABLISHED: 1975.

NUMBER OF STUDENTS IN 1985:   25 each.

APPLY: Rolling admissions. Department of International Education.

Haifa

■ **RUTGERS, THE STATE UNIVERSITY OF NEW JERSEY**
Milledoler Hall, Room 205
New Brunswick, NJ 08903
(201) 932-7787

PROGRAM: Junior Year in Israel is a new, full-year-academic undergraduate program. Students have the option to attend regular classes at the University of Haifa (in Hebrew) with Israeli students; attend regular classes but take exams, write papers, etc., in English; or, take one of several courses offered by the Department of Overseas studies given in English. Group excursions to cultural and historic sites complement the program. A month-long presession in Jerusalem in advanced Hebrew language and civilization is required.

ADMITTANCE REQUIREMENTS: Good academic standing. "A thorough knowledge of Hebrew is essential. At a minimum, students should have completed course work through first year literature and preferably advanced grammar courses."

TEACHING METHODS: Students either attend regular classes with Israeli students or may take one of several courses offered to foreign students. Most courses are in Hebrew.

EVALUATION: By course instructors, based upon class work, papers, and examinations.

CREDITS OFFERED: 30 semester hours per year including presession.

HOUSING: Students live "in modern apartments, six students to an apartment; two students to a room. There are no 'American only' apartments."

DATES: Approximately September 16 to early June.

COSTS: $6,950 New Jersey residents; $7,996 nonresidents. Includes tuition, room and board (except at holidays and between semesters), and group excursions. Does not cover round-trip transportation or personal expenses.

YEAR ESTABLISHED: 1986.

NUMBER OF STUDENTS IN 1987:   Limited to 35.

APPLY: By March 1. Director, Rutgers' Junior Year Abroad.

Jerusalem

■ **AMERICAN INSTITUTE OF HOLY LAND STUDIES**
Mount Zion
P.O. Box #1276
Jerusalem 91012, ISRAEL

PROGRAM: The institute provides "an Evangelical Christian environment, conservative and nondenominational, where students may develop in biblical language and learning and in the cultural understanding of the modern Middle East." The institute, which is associated with more than one hundred theological schools, colleges and universities in the United States, offers both bachelor and master of arts degree programs, as well as short-term programs ranging from a semester to a full academic year. Classes are held in the 1853 Bishop Gobat School on Mt. Zion. Degree programs cover: Middle Eastern studies, Hebrew, history and geography of Israel, and archaeology.

ADMITTANCE REQUIREMENTS: Satisfactory evidence "to the Admissions Committee that a student will profit from and contribute to the overall program of the Institute. Character as well as academic ability are important factors."

TEACHING METHODS: Classes are conducted by faculty members of the institute as well as U.S., foreign faculty, and guest lecturers. Classes, seminars, independent study are conducted in English. American students are integrated with foreign students. Travel to local museums and historic sites supplements many programs.

EVALUATION: By institute faculty based on exams, papers, and class performance.

CREDITS OFFERED: A minimum of 12 semester hours per semester.

HOUSING: First year and "short-term" students live in the school dormitory. Married students and those beyond the first year are responsible for their own housing.

DATES: Approximately, fall semester: August 21 through December 20; spring semester: January 3 through May 1.

COSTS: Tuition: $1,080 per semester; room and board: $1,606 per semester; field trips: $350 per year. Does not include round-trip transportation, books, or personal expenses. The institute issues a few partial scholarships.

YEAR ESTABLISHED: 1957.

NUMBER OF STUDENTS IN 1985: approximately 500.

APPLY: Three months prior to beginning of term. Office of Admissions. Or in United States, contact: P.O. Box #456, Highland Park, IL 60035 (312) 433-4036.

■ **THE CALIFORNIA STATE UNIVERSITY**
400 Golden Shore
Long Beach, CA 90802
(213) 590-5655

PROGRAM: The CSU International Program in Israel, held in cooperation with the Hebrew University of Jerusalem, is a full-academic-year undergraduate and graduate opportunity to study at the university. Students select from the wide range of university course offerings focusing most frequently on Judaic and Middle Eastern studies supplemented by special CSU programs. One-week orientation in Jerusalem.

ADMITTANCE REQUIREMENTS: Must be enrolled at a CSU campus. Juniors and above including graduate students. 3.0 GPA.

TEACHING METHODS: Students take a combination of regular academic courses and supplemental program-sponsored courses taught by foreign faculty.

EVALUATION: By foreign faculty and CSU resident director, based upon periodic and final examinations.

CREDITS OFFERED: 30 semester hours per year or 45 quarter units.

HOUSING: In dormitories and private apartments.

DATES: Approximately July 23 to June 13.

COSTS: Tuition: $0 (residents); $3,600 (nonresidents); room and board: $1,260. Does not include round-trip transportation or living expenses (estimated at $2,460 per year).

YEAR ESTABLISHED: 1968.

NUMBER OF STUDENTS IN 1985: 5.

APPLY: By February 1. Dr. Kibbey M. Horne, Director of International Programs.

■ **UNIVERSITY OF NOTRE DAME**
  420 Administration Building
  Notre Dame, IN 46556
  (219) 239-5882

PROGRAM: The University of Notre Dame Program in Jerusalem is a single-semester or full-academic-year undergraduate program held in the town of Tantur, between Jerusalem and Bethlehem, which houses the Ecumenical Institute for Theological Studies. Courses cover Bible studies, Middle East history, comparative religions, Christianity, Judaism, Islam, and contemporary Arab/Israeli problems. Archaeological field trips and program-related travel.

ADMITTANCE REQUIREMENTS: At least sophomore standing with a 2.5 GPA.

TEACHING METHODS: Special program for American participating students. All courses are taught in English by professors from American, Canadian, Israeli, and Arab universities.

EVALUATION: By onsite directors appointed among Notre Dame faculty, based upon class work, papers, and examinations.

CREDITS OFFERED: At least 15 semester hours per semester.

HOUSING: Students live in dormitories on the Tantur campus.

DATES: Fall semester: September 8 through December 13; spring semester: February 2 through May 15.

COSTS: $5,158 per semester includes tuition, room and board, program-related travel, and round-trip transportation from New York.

YEAR ESTABLISHED: 1985.

NUMBER OF STUDENTS IN 1985: 6.

APPLY: Fall semester by February 1; spring semester: September 15. Dr. Isabel Charles, Assistant Provost, Director, Foreign Studies Programs.

■ **UNIVERSITY OF SOUTHERN CALIFORNIA**
Overseas Studies, CES 109
University Park
Los Angeles, CA 90089
(213) 746-2500

PROGRAM: USC Year in Israel is an undergraduate program concentrating on liberal arts and humanities with an emphasis on the Hebraic studies and the history and culture of the Middle East. Held in cooperation with Hebrew University.

ADMITTANCE REQUIREMENTS: Sophomores and above in good academic standing.

TEACHING METHODS: Courses are taught by foreign faculty members. Americans are integrated with local students.

EVALUATION: By course faculty member, based upon class work, papers, and periodic examinations.

CREDITS OFFERED: 32 semester hours.

HOUSING: Students live in apartments or with local families.

DATES: Approximately, late August through mid-May.

COSTS: Approximately, $10,000 covers tuition, room and board, program-related travel. Does not include round-trip transportation or personal expenses. Some scholarships are available.

YEAR ESTABLISHED: 1983.

NUMBER OF STUDENTS IN 1985: 2.

APPLY: By April 1.

Tel Aviv

■ **BELOIT COLLEGE**
Beloit, WI 53511
(608) 365-3391

PROGRAM: World Outlook Program Seminar undergraduate program offers a semester in Israel coupled with a three-week stay in Cairo. The program stresses Middle Eastern affairs and the development of the area. Presession orientation is held at Beloit.

ADMITTANCE REQUIREMENTS: 3.0 GPA and good academic standing.

TEACHING METHODS: Students attend special courses. Lectures, independent study, and field trips complement classroom work. A U.S. academic leader accompanies group.

EVALUATION: Papers, examinations given by local professors.

CREDITS OFFERED: 16 semester hours.

HOUSING: With local families; hotels when traveling.

DATES: Approximately January 15 through April 30.

COSTS: Tuition: $3,900; room and board: $1,700. Round-trip transportation not included.

YEAR ESTABLISHED: 1981.

NUMBER OF STUDENTS IN 1985: 8.

APPLY: By November 30. World Affairs Center.

■ **PENNSYLVANIA STATE UNIVERSITY**
Office of Education Abroad Programs
222 Boucke Building
University Park, PA 16802
(814) 865-7681

PROGRAM: Education Abroad at Tel Aviv University is either a fall-semester, spring-semester or full-academic-year undergraduate program held in cooperation with the American Friends of Tel Aviv University. The academic program begins with an intensive Hebrew course, followed by a selection of courses in such areas as Hebrew, Middle Eastern studies, economics, politics, history, art history, philosophy, religion, literature, film, labor studies, theater, and sociology. Orientation at Penn State.

ADMITTANCE REQUIREMENTS: Juniors and seniors with a 2.5 GPA, good academic standing, and "must show evidence of maturity, stability, adaptability, self-discipline and a strong academic motivation." Some specific course prerequisites. At least one 3-credit course dealing with the Middle East, Biblical studies, or Jewish religion or culture.

TEACHING METHODS: Students are required to take a five-week intensive Hebrew course, the Ulpan, prior to fall semester; or a four-week Ulpan prior to spring semester. With the 6 credits of required Hebrew, students can enroll in regular university courses taught in English by Tel Aviv faculty.

EVALUATION: By course instructors based upon class work, papers, and examinations.

CREDITS OFFERED: 12 to 18 semester hours per semester.

HOUSING: Participants stay in university dormitories. Efforts are made to match Americans with Israeli roommates.

DATES: Fall semester: mid-August through mid-February; spring semester: mid-March through late June.

COSTS: Students pay the same as at the University Park Campus. 1986-87 tuition per semester was $2,250 for state residents; $5,150 for nonresidents; room and board: $2,750 per semester. Plus a $100 nonrefundable program fee.

YEAR ESTABLISHED: 1981.

NUMBER OF STUDENTS IN 1986:   16.

APPLY: Fall semester or full year by March 1; spring semester by October 15.

■ **PRATT INSTITUTE**
School of Art & Design
200 Willoughby Avenue
Brooklyn, NY 11205
(718) 636-3706

PROGRAM: Photography in Israel is a four-week summer session for both graduate and undergraduates held in cooperation with Camera Obscura. "Emphasis is on the individual photographer... through daily group and individual instruction. It is anticipated that the program will have privileged access to museums and private collections in Tel Aviv and Jerusalem." Extensive professionally equipped facilities available. Orientation with Vieri Salvadori, Dean, School of Art & Design.

ADMITTANCE REQUIREMENTS: All applicants must send a portfolio of no more than twelve slides or prints.

TEACHING METHODS: Participants work with urban areas and landscapes, the portrait, the nude, and various approaches to photo-reportage. Israel photographers join faculty for special presentations and student critique.

EVALUATION: Students are given letter grades determined by individual consultations, critiques, and final reviews.

CREDITS OFFERED: 6 semester hours.

HOUSING: Students live in a "3-star hotel on the Mediterranean coast."

DATES: Approximately, June 30 through July 31.

COSTS: $2,555 covers tuition, room and board, round-trip transportation, local travel, and darkroom privileges. Scholarships available.

YEAR ESTABLISHED: 1985.

NUMBER OF STUDENTS IN 1985: 17.

APPLY: By April 1. Dr. Vieri R. Salvadori, Dean.

15.

Africa

KENYA

Population: 21,150,000   **Capital:** Nairobi   **Languages:** Swahili and English
Monetary Unit: Kenyan shilling   **Government:** Unitary single-party republic
(president)   **Religion:** 27% Roman Catholic; 47% other Christian
Households With Television: less than 1%

SELECTED COLLEGES AND UNIVERSITIES

Kenyatta University College
Nairobi

Publishes Students' Guide.

University of Nairobi
Nairobi

Publishes Annual Calendar *for foreign students.*

FURTHER INFORMATION

African-American Institute
833 United Nations Plaza
New York, NY 10017
(212) 949-5666

Provides data on applying directly to Kenyan institutes.

Embassy of Kenya
2249 R Street, NW
Washington, DC 20008
(202) 387-6101

Nairobi

■ **THE EXPERIMENT IN INTERNATIONAL LIVING**
Kipling Road
Brattleboro, VT 05301
(800) 451-4465

PROGRAM: The College Semester Abroad program is designed to allow undergraduate students to become immersed in a foreign culture by living with a local family and exploring individual personal and educational interests under professional guidance. Students on the Kenya program spend ten weeks in Nairobi or at nearby work camps, two weeks at a location appropriate to a field study project, and a three-week homestay ending up in Nairobi for a week of program evaluation. Courses cover: intensive language study, seminar on Kenyan life and culture and rural development, history and politics, geography and economics, arts and humanities, social anthropology, methods and techniques of field work, and an independent study project. One-week orientation in Brattleboro and Nairobi.

ADMITTANCE REQUIREMENTS: Sophomore standing or above and acceptable academic credentials. No language prequisite.

TEACHING METHODS: Students work directly with their American instructor-advisors in planning and evaluating their individual program. Nonlanguage courses are in English. "The semester builds from the more structured language training and lectures and discussions on local life and culture to the independent study project."

EVALUATION: By individual students and their instructor-advisors based on independent project, papers, reports, and examinations. Periodic meetings during the program and for several days at the conclusion.

CREDITS OFFERED: 16 semester hours.

HOUSING: Students live as family members with their host families.

DATES: Approximately, fall semester: September through December; spring semester: January through May.

COSTS: $6,300 includes tuition, room and board, all fees and local travel, and round-trip transportation from Brattleboro, Vermont.

YEAR ESTABLISHED: 1983.

NUMBER OF STUDENTS IN 1985:   80.

APPLY: For fall semester by May 15; spring semester by November 15. Admissions Office, College Semester Abroad.

■ **KALAMAZOO COLLEGE**
1200 Academy Street
Kalamazoo, MI 49007
(616) 383-8470

PROGRAM: The African Foreign Study in Kenya program is designed for students who have "the academic ability to do British-type university work. . . ." Held in cooperation with the Great Lakes Colleges Association and the University of Nairobi, students select four courses each semester at the University. A third term is also offered during the summer. Orientation: two hours weekly during preceding term at Kalamazoo.

ADMITTANCE REQUIREMENTS: Enrollment at Kalamazoo College in term prior to departure; 3.0 GPA. Selection is based on student autobiographical sketch and essay, faculty recommendation, and interview.

TEACHING METHODS: Students attend regular academic courses, lectures, seminars, and tutorials with Kenyan and other African students. Classes are in English.

EVALUATION: By individual instructors, based upon class work, papers, and examinations. Recorded by Kalamazoo only as "pass/fail."

CREDITS OFFERED: Maximum 30 quarter hours credit; 45 hours credit if student elects three-term option.

HOUSING: Students are housed in school dormitories or in YMCA/YWCA.

DATES: Approximately, mid-September to mid-March; third-term runs until mid-June.

COSTS: $7,064 includes tuition, room and board, some regional travel, and round-trip transportation from New York. Add $2,300 for third-term option. Does not cover the cost of one term at Kalamazoo at $3,532, $500 supplementary airfare charge, or personal travel and living expenses.

YEAR ESTABLISHED: 1965.

NUMBER OF STUDENTS IN 1985: 3.

APPLY: By February 1. Dr. Joe K. Fugate, Director, Office of Foreign Study.

■ **PENNSYLVANIA STATE UNIVERSITY**
Office of Education Abroad Programs
222 Boucke Building
University Park, PA 16802
(814) 865-7681

PROGRAM: Academic Year Abroad at the University of Nairobi is a full-academic-year undergraduate program offering general arts and science courses as well as those specifically related to Africa. Courses cover agriculture, biology, economics, political science, history, philosophy, religious studies, literature, and sociology. Orientation at Penn State.

ADMITTANCE REQUIREMENTS: Juniors and seniors with a 2.5 GPA, good academic standing, and "must show evidence of maturity, stability, adaptability, self-discipline and a strong academic motivation." Some specific course prerequisites.

TEACHING METHODS: Students enroll in regular University of Nairobi classes taught in English. Americans are integrated with local students.

EVALUATION: By course instructors, based upon class work, papers, and examinations.

CREDITS OFFERED: 12-18 semester hours per semester.

HOUSING: Participants stay in university dormitories.

DATES: Mid-September through early June.

COSTS: Students pay the same as at the University Park Campus. 1986-87 tuition per semester was $2,250 for state residents; $5,150 for nonresidents; room and board: $2,750 per semester. Plus a $100 nonrefundable program fee.

YEAR ESTABLISHED: 1979.

NUMBER OF STUDENTS IN 1986: 5.

APPLY: By March 1.

LIBERIA

Population: 2,303,000   **Capital:** Monrovia   **Language:** English
Monetary Unit: Liberian dollar   **Government:** Multiparty republic (president)
Religion: 75% traditional beliefs   **Households With Television:** 1%

SELECTED COLLEGES AND UNIVERSITIES

University of Liberia
P.O. Box #9040
Monrovia

Cuttington University College
P.O. Box 277
Monrovia

Has cooperative agreement with several U.S. schools.

FURTHER INFORMATION

Embassy of Liberia
5201 16th Street, NW
Washington, DC 20011
(202) 723-0437

Suacoco

■ **SUSQUEHANNA UNIVERSITY**
Selingsgrove, PA 17870
(717) 374-0101, ext. 4254

PROGRAM: Semester in Liberia is a six-month spring-semester undergraduate program held in cooperation with Liberia's Cuttington University College and cosponsored by the Department of Higher Education of Lutheran Church of America and all its affiliated colleges. The program consists of an intensive exposure to the traditions, lifestyles, and thought processes of the peoples of West Africa. Students take a full range of liberal arts courses: social science, natural sciences, business administration or nursing at Cuttington University College, a six-hundred-student school affiliated with the Episcopal Church of the USA located some 110 miles from the coast. An intensive four-week period of orientation at Susquehanna in mid-January provides 3 semester hours credit.

ADMITTANCE REQUIREMENTS: Preference is given to juniors and seniors with 2.7 GPA and permission of home institution.

TEACHING METHODS: Students are fully integrated with the national student body and attend regular classes taught by the foreign faculty. Lectures, class discussions, and opportunity for independent study and volunteer service projects.

EVALUATION: By foreign faculty, based upon periodic tests, final exams, and class participation.

CREDITS OFFERED: Varies between 12 and 18 semester hours depending on course load.

HOUSING: Students live in university dormitories.

DATES: Mid-January through the end of June; including orientation.

COSTS: $3,300 includes tuition, room and board, and local program-related travel. Not included: round-trip transportation or living expenses (estimated at approximately $500).

YEAR ESTABLISHED: 1980.

NUMBER OF STUDENTS IN 1985: 4.

APPLY: By November 15. Dr. Robert L. Bradford, Coordinator, Semester in Liberia Program.

SENEGAL

Population: 6,699,000   **Capital:** Dakar   **Language:** French
Monetary Unit: CFA franc   **Government:** Republic (president)
Religion: 91% Muslim   **Households With Television:** Less than 1%

SELECTED UNIVERSITY

University of Dakar
Dakar
Courses are in French.

FURTHER INFORMATION

African-American Institute
833 United Nations Plaza
New York, NY 10017
(212) 946-5666

*Provides data on applying directly to
Senegalese institutes.*

Embassy of Senegal
2112 Wyoming Avenue, NW
Washington, DC 20008
(202) 234-0540

Dakar

■ **KALAMAZOO COLLEGE**
1200 Academy Street
Kalamazoo, MI 49007
(616) 383-8470

PROGRAM: The African Foreign Study in Senegal program is the only undergraduate foreign study program in French-speaking Africa. The program is designed for students who have "the academic ability to do European-type university work totally in French . . ." Held in cooperation with the Great Lakes Colleges Association and the Université de Dakar, students select from any of the courses taught at the university. Courses are primarily in the social sciences and humanities. In addition, a special class in Wolof language is offered. Orientation: two hours weekly during preceding term at Kalamazoo.

ADMITTANCE REQUIREMENTS: Enrollment at Kalamazoo College in term prior to departure. 3.0 GPA and a minimum of 20 quarter hours (13.3 semester hours) of college. Selection is based on student autobiographical sketch and essay, faculty recommendation, and interview.

TEACHING METHODS: Students attend regular academic courses, lectures, seminars, and tutorials with Senegalese and other African students. Classes are in French.

EVALUATION: By individual instructors, based upon class work, papers, and examinations. Recorded by Kalamazoo only as "pass/fail."

CREDITS OFFERED: Maximum 45 quarter hours credit.

HOUSING: Students live in rented apartments and are responsible for preparing their own meals.

DATES: Approximately mid-September to mid-June.

COSTS: $9,364 includes tuition, room and board, some regional travel, and round-trip transportation from New York. Does not cover the cost of one term at Kalamazoo at $3,532 or personal travel and living expenses.

YEAR ESTABLISHED: 1971.

NUMBER OF STUDENTS IN 1985: 6.

APPLY: By February 15. Dr. Joe K. Fugate, Director, Office of Foreign Study.

SIERRA LEONE

Population: 3,732,000   Capital: Freetown   Language: English
Monetary Unit: Leone   Government: Unitary single-party republic (president)
Religion: 52% traditional beliefs; 40% Muslim
Households With Television: Less than 1%

SELECTED UNIVERSITY

University of Sierra Leone
Freetown

FURTHER INFORMATION

Ministry of Information
New England, Freetown

Embassy of Sierra Leone
1701 19th Street, NW
Washington, DC 20009
(202) 745-0219

Freetown

■ **KALAMAZOO COLLEGE**
1200 Academy Street
Kalamazoo, MI 49007
(616) 383-8470

PROGRAM: The African Foreign Study Program in Sierra Leone is designed for students who have "the academic ability to do European-type university work..." Held in cooperation with the Great Lakes Colleges Association, the

Fourah Bay College (University of Sierra Leone), and University College in Njala, students select from any of the courses taught at the universities. The schools offer a full range of liberal arts courses. In addition, a special class in Krio language is provided. Orientation: two hours weekly during preceding term at Kalamazoo.

ADMITTANCE REQUIREMENTS: Enrollment at Kalamazoo College in term prior to departure. Selection is based on student autobiographical sketch and essay, faculty recommendation, and interview.

TEACHING METHODS: Students attend regular academic courses, lectures, seminars, and tutorials with Sierra Leonean and other African students. Krio is taught by host-country staff and is limited to program students. Classes are in English.

EVALUATION: By individual instructors, based upon class work, papers, and examinations. Recorded by Kalamazoo only as "pass/fail."

CREDITS OFFERED: Maximum 30 quarter hours credit.

HOUSING: Students live in school dormitories.

DATES: Approximately mid-September to mid-March.

COSTS: $7,064 includes tuition, room and board, some regional travel, and round-trip transportation from New York. Does not cover the cost of one term at Kalamazoo at $3,532 or personal travel and living expenses.

YEAR ESTABLISHED: 1962.

NUMBER OF STUDENTS IN 1985: 5.

APPLY: By February 15. Dr. Joe K. Fugate, Director, Office of Foreign Study.

PART SEVEN

OCEANIA

16.

Australia

Population: 15,912,000   **Capital:** Canberra   **Language:** English
Monetary Unit: Australian dollar   **Government:** Federal parliamentary state
(British monarch and prime minister)   **Religion:** 26% Anglican Church of
Australia; 26% Roman Catholic   **Households With Television:** 27%

SELECTED COLLEGES AND UNIVERSITIES

Australian National University
P.O. Box 4,
Canberra, A.C.T. 2600

The James Cook University of
North Queensland
Townsville, Queensland 48111

La Trobe University
Bundoora, Victoria 3083

Macquarie University
North Ryde, New South Wales 2113

Monash University
Clayton, Victoria 3168

University of Melbourne
Parkville, Victoria 3052

The University of New England
Armidale, New South Wales

University of New South Wales
P.O. Box 1
Kensington, New South Wales 2033

University of Queensland
St. Lucia, Queensland 4067

University of Western Australia
Nedlands, Western Australia 6009

FURTHER INFORMATION

Consulate General of Australia
636 Fifth Avenue
New York, NY 10111
(212) 245-4000

Has available Australia for the Student,
Australia Awards, *and* Private Students
Temporary Entry into Australia.

Embassy of Australia
1601 Massachusetts Avenue
Washington, DC 20036
(202) 797-3000

Universities and Colleges Admissions
Center
Box 7049, G.P.O.
Sydney 2001

Publishes The Students' Information Guide.

Canberra

■ **PENNSYLVANIA STATE UNIVERSITY**
Office of Education Abroad Programs
222 Boucke Building
University Park, PA 16802
(814) 865-7681

PROGRAM: Education Abroad at the Australian National University is a full-year or spring-semester undergraduate program held in cooperation with the Australian National University and the Australian Study Center. Students take regular courses from the ANU catalog which "tend to encompass a greater content range than typical Penn State courses." Students are limited to taking three courses per semester, three year long courses or a comparable combination. Considerable offerings cover Australian history, culture, and anthropology, as well as courses relating to the Pacific, Southeast Asia, and East Asia. Orientation at Penn State and one week at ASU.

ADMITTANCE REQUIREMENTS: Juniors and seniors with a 2.5 GPA, good academic standing, and "must show evidence of maturity, stability, adaptability, self-discipline and a strong academic motivation."

TEACHING METHODS: Students are fully integrated into AUC classes.

EVALUATION: By course instructors, based upon class work, papers, and examinations.

CREDITS OFFERED: 15 semester hours per semester.

HOUSING: Students usually chose to live in university residential halls.

DATES: First semester: March 2 through June 12; second semester: July 13 through December 4.

COSTS: Students pay the same as at the University Park Campus. 1986-87 tuition per semester was $2,250 for state residents; $5,150 for nonresidents; room and board: $2,750 per semester. Plus a $100 nonrefundable program fee.

YEAR ESTABLISHED: 1984.

NUMBER OF STUDENTS IN 1985: 10.

APPLY: Full year by October 15; second semester by March 1.

Sydney

■ **ROLLINS COLLEGE**
1000 Holt Avenue
Winter Park, FL 32789
(305) 646-2280

PROGRAM: Rollins Fall Term in Sydney is a one-semester undergraduate program held in cooperation with the University of Sydney. The program concentrates primarily on Australian studies with courses on Australian art, literature, history, environment, economy, social anthropology, and flora and fauna. The all-inclusive program cost also provides unlimited return stopovers in either Fiji or Tahiti. One-day onsite orientation and city tour.

ADMITTANCE REQUIREMENTS: Minimum 2.5 GPA and good academic standing with approval of the appropriate dean or director at student's home institution.

TEACHING METHODS: Courses are taught by Australian faculty assigned to the group. Field trips to local cultural attractions complement class lectures and discussions. Students in environmental courses take weekend field trips.

EVALUATION: Based on class work, papers, and examinations by local faculty.

CREDITS OFFERED: Students take four courses for 16 semester hours or 25 quarter hours credit.

HOUSING: All students live with local families.

DATES: July 23 through November 14.

COSTS: $5,450 includes tuition, room and board, local travel, and round-trip transportation from Los Angeles. Pocket money (estimated at $1,500) not included.

YEAR ESTABLISHED: 1972.

NUMBER OF STUDENTS IN 1985: 42.

APPLY: By March 1. Dr. Patricia Lancaster, Director of International Programs, Box #2712.

■ **UNIVERSITY OF WISCONSIN – STEVENS POINT**
208 Old Main
Stevens Point, WI 54481
(715) 346-2717

PROGRAM: Semester in Australia is a spring travel/study undergraduate program. Graduate credit may be arranged for an additional fee. Although the majority of the program is held in Sydney, the group spends about a month traveling to Fiji, New Zealand, and sites in Australia. Classes in Sydney are given at Dunmore Lang College and include Australian culture and civilization, comparative literature, history of the Southeastern Pacific, etc.

ADMITTANCE REQUIREMENTS: Sophomores and above in good academic standing.

TEACHING METHODS: Students attend courses at Dunmore Lang College arranged for the group and live with Australian students at the college.

EVALUATION: By instructors and group leaders, based upon class work, papers, and examinations.

CREDITS OFFERED: A minimum of 13 semester hours; maximum of 17.

HOUSING: Students stay in hostels while traveling and in the college dormitory in Sydney.

DATES: Approximately, December 30 to April 25.

COSTS: Approximately, $3,975 includes tuition, room and board and round-trip transportation from Chicago or Milwaukee, and program-related travel. Minnesota students pay a small "reciprocity fee"; non-Wisconsin residents pay a surcharge. Does not cover personal expenses.

YEAR ESTABLISHED: 1985.

NUMBER OF STUDENTS IN 1985: Not available.

APPLY: "Early application is advised." Dr. Helen Cornell, Director, International Programs.

17.

New Zealand

Population: 3,280,400   **Capital:** Wellington   **Language:** English
Monetary Unit: New Zealand dollar   **Government:** Multiparty parliamentary
state (British monarch and prime minister)   **Religion:** 28% Anglican; 17%
Presbyterian, 14% Roman Catholic   **Households With Television:** 13%

SELECTED COLLEGES AND UNIVERSITIES

University of Auckland
Private Bag
Auckland

Victoria University of Wellington
Private Bag
Wellington 1

FURTHER INFORMATION

Consulate General of New Zealand
630 Fifth Avenue, Suite 530
New York, NY 10111
(212) 586-0060

Embassy of New Zealand
37 Observatory Circle, NW
Washington, DC 20008
(202) 328-4800

More Than One City

■ **THE CALIFORNIA STATE UNIVERSITY**
400 Golden Shore
Long Beach, CA 90802
(213) 590-5655

PROGRAM: The CSU International Program in New Zealand, held at Massey
University in Palmerston North or Lincoln University College of Agriculture
in Christchurch, is a full-academic-year undergraduate and graduate opportunity to study at a New Zealand university. Students concentrate on courses
relating to the agricultural sciences. One-week orientation in Christchurch.

ADMITTANCE REQUIREMENTS: Must be enrolled at a CSU campus. Juniors and above including graduate students; 3.0 GPA.

TEACHING METHODS: Students take a combination of regular academic courses and supplemental program-sponsored courses taught by foreign faculty.

EVALUATION: By foreign faculty and CSU resident director, based upon periodic and final examinations.

CREDITS OFFERED: 30 semester hours per year or 45 quarter units.

HOUSING: In dormitories and private apartments.

DATES: Approximately, February 20 through November 8.

COSTS: Tuition: $0 (residents); $3,600 (nonresidents); room and board: $1,800. Does not include round-trip transportation or living expenses (estimated at approximately $2,340 per year).

YEAR ESTABLISHED: 1975.

NUMBER OF STUDENTS IN 1985: 17.

APPLY: By February 1. Dr. Kibbey M. Horne, Director of International Programs.

Appendix 1: The World of Foreign-Study Opportunities

The following list gives a brief, general summary of foreign-study opportunities around the world and, where appropriate, names an institution from whom you can learn more. Countries discussed in detail in the main text are cross-referenced here.

Afghanistan

Afghanistan does not invite U. S. citizens to study in its colleges and universities.

Albania

Albania does not invite U. S. citizens to study in its colleges and universities.

Algeria

OFFICIAL LANGUAGE: Arabic.

There are three universities in Algeria and twelve specialized schools for advanced studies.

Embassy of Algeria
2118 Kalorama Road, NW
Washington, DC 20008
(202) 328-5300

Andorra

We were unable to obtain information about foreign-study opportunities in Andorra.

Angola

Angola does not invite U. S. citizens to study in its university.

Antigua and Barbuda

There are no colleges or universities in Antigua and Barbuda.

Argentina

See page 73.

Aruba

Aruba does not invite U. S. citizens to study in its university.

Australia

See page 521.

Austria

See page 107.

The Bahamas

OFFICIAL LANGUAGE: English.

The College of the Bahamas is the islands' only institute of higher learning.

The College of the Bahamas
P. O. Box N 4912
Nassau, The Bahamas

Bahrain

OFFICIAL LANGUAGE: Arabic

Of the four universities in Bahrain, the University of Dhaka is the oldest and largest.

Embassy of Bahrain
3502 International Drive, NW
Washington, DC 20008
(202) 342-8372

Bangladesh

OFFICIAL LANGUAGE: Bengali.

There are over a thousand institutes of higher learning in Bangladesh, including 366 colleges and six universities.

Embassy of Bangladesh
2201 Wisconsin Avenue, NW
Washington, DC 20007
(202) 342-8372

Barbados

OFFICIAL LANGUAGE: English.

Barbados has a liberal arts college, part of the University of the West Indies.

Ministry of Education
Old Hospital Building
Jemmots Lane
Saint Michael, Barbados

Belgium

See page 120.

Belize

See page 61.

Benin

OFFICIAL LANGUAGE: French.

The University of Benin at Porto-Norvo, founded in 1970, is the country's only institute of higher learning.

Embassy of Benin
2737 Cathedral Avenue, NW
Washington, DC 20008
(202) 232-6656

Bermuda

OFFICIAL LANGUAGE: English.

Bermuda College, a two-year institution, is the island's only post-secondary school.

Bermuda College
Box DV356
Devonshire DVBX, Bermuda

Bhutan

OFFICIAL LANGUAGE: Dzongkha.

The Bhutan Junior College at Sherubtsi is the country's only post-secondary school.

Bhutan Mission to the
United Nations
2 United Nations Plaza
New York, NY 10017
(212) 826-1919

Bolivia

OFFICIAL LANGUAGE: Spanish.

There are eight universities in Bolivia and over a dozen specialized schools for advanced studies.

Embassy of Bolivia
3014 Massachusetts Avenue, NW
Washington, DC 20008
(202) 483-4410

Botswana

OFFICIAL LANGUAGE: English.

The University of Botswana is the country's only institute of higher learning.

University of Botswana
Private Bag 0022
Gaborone, Botswana
Africa

Brazil

See page 74.

Brunei

OFFICIAL LANGUAGE: Malay.

Brunei Darussalam University at Bandar Seri Begawan is the country's only institute for higher learning.

Brunei Mission to the
United Nations
866 United Nations Plaza,
Room 248
New York, NY 10017
(212) 838-1600

Bulgaria

OFFICIAL LANGUAGE: Bulgarian.

There are three universities in Bulgaria and over thirty other schools for advanced studies.

Embassy of Bulgaria
1621 22nd Street, NW
Washington, DC 20008
(202) 387-7969

Burkina Faso

OFFICIAL LANGUAGE: French.

The University of Burkina Faso, the country's only institute of higher learning, is in Ouagadougou.

Embassy of Burkina Faso
2340 Massachusetts Avenue, NW
Washington, DC 20008
(202) 332-5577

Burma

OFFICIAL LANGUAGE: Burmese.

Burma has universities at Rangoon and Mandalay, as well as over thirty other schools for advanced studies.

Embassy of Burma
2300 S Street, NW
Washington, DC 20008
(202) 332-9044

Burundi

OFFICIAL LANGUAGES: French and Rundi.

Burundi has a national university at Bujumbura and five other schools for advanced studies.

Embassy of Burundi
2233 Wisconsin Avenue, NW, Suite 212
Washington DC 20007
(202) 342-2574

Cameroon

OFFICIAL LANGUAGES: English and French.

The Federal University of Cameroon at Yaoundé established in 1962, is the country's only institute of higher learning.

Embassy of Cameroon
2349 Massachusetts Avenue, NW
Washington, DC 20008
(202) 265-8790

Canada

See page 35.

Cape Verde

There are no colleges or universities in Cape Verde.

Central African Republic

OFFICIAL LANGUAGE: French.

The Jean-Bedel Bolcassa University at Bangui is the country's only institute of higher learning.

Embassy of the Central African Republic
1618 22nd Street
Washington, DC 20008
(202) 483-7800

Chad

OFFICIAL LANGUAGE: French.

The University of Chad at N'Djamena is the country's only institute of higher learning.

Embassy of Chad
2002 R Street, NW
Washington, DC 20009
(202) 462-4009

Chile

OFFICIAL LANGUAGE: Spanish.

There are eighteen universities in Chile—the largest of which, the University of Chile, and the Catholic University, are both in Santiago—and many specialized schools for advanced studies.

Embassy of Chile
1732 Massachusetts Avenue, NW
Washington, DC 20036
(202) 785-1746

China (The People's Republic of China)

See page 437.

Colombia

See page 78.

Comoros

There are no colleges or universities in Comoros.

The Congo

OFFICIAL LANGUAGE: French

The Congo's only college is the Center for Higher Education at Brazzaville.

Embassy of the Congo
4891 Colorado Avenue, NW
Washington, DC 20011
(202) 726-5500

Costa Rica

See page 63.

Cuba

The United States government forbids its citizens to study in Cuba.

Cyprus

There are no colleges or universities in Cyprus.

Czechoslovakia

We were unable to obtain information about foreign-study opportunities in Czechoslovakia.

Denmark

See page 124.

Djibouti

There are no colleges or universities in Djibouti.

Dominica

There are no colleges or universities in Dominica.

Dominican Republic

See page 87.

Ecuador

See page 80.

Egypt

See page 495.

El Salvador

OFFICIAL LANGUAGE: Spanish.

There are four universities in El Salvador and many specialized schools for advanced studies.

Embassy of El Salvador
2308 California Street, NW
Washington, DC 20008
(202) 265-3480

England

See page 340.

Equatorial Guinea

There are no colleges or universities in Equatorial Guinea.

Ethiopia

OFFICIAL LANGUAGE: Amharic.

Ethiopia's National University is at Addis Ababa, and there are ten other institutes of higher learning in the country.

Embassy of Ethiopia
2134 Kalorama Road, NW
Washington, DC 20009
(202) 234-2281

Faeroe Islands

There are no colleges or universities in the Faeroe Islands.

Fiji

OFFICIAL LANGUAGE: English.

The University of the South Pacific, Fiji's only university, is at Suva, and there are other specialized schools for advanced study.

Embassy of Fiji
2233 Wisconsin Avenue, NW
Suite 240
Washington, DC 20008
(202) 234-2281

Finland

OFFICIAL LANGUAGES: Finnish and Swedish.

There are twenty-one universities in Finland, most of them privately run, and many specialized schools for advanced studies.

Embassy of Finland
3216 New Mexico Avenue, NW
Washington, DC 20016
(202) 363-2430

France

See page 130.

Gabon

OFFICIAL LANGUAGE: French.

Gabon's only institute of higher learning, Omar Bongo University, is in Libreville.

Embassy of Gabon
2034 20th Street, NW
Washington, DC 20009
(202) 797-1000

The Gambia

There are no colleges or universities in the Gambia.

German Democratic Republic

See page 417.

Federal Republic of Germany

See page 197.

Ghana

OFFICIAL LANGUAGE: English.

There are three universities in Ghana: The University of Ghana at Legon, the University of Cape Coast, and the University of Science and Technology at Kumasi.

Embassy of Ghana
2460 16th Street
Washington, DC 20009
(202) 462-0761

Greece

See page 236.

Greenland

There are no colleges or universities in Greenland.

Grenada

There are no colleges or universities in Grenada.

Guatemala

OFFICIAL LANGUAGE: Spanish.

There are five universities in Guatemala. One is state-run, the others private.

Embassy of Guatemala
2220 R Street, NW
Washington, DC 20008
(202) 745-4952

Guinea

There are no colleges or universities in Guinea.

Guinea - Bissau

There are no colleges or universities in Guinea - Bissau.

Guyana

OFFICIAL LANGUAGE: English.

The Queen's College, founded in 1844, is Guyana's only institute of higher learning.

Embassy of Guyana
2490 Tracy Place, NW
Washington, DC 20008
(202) 265-6900

Haiti

See page 88.

Honduras

OFFICIAL LANGUAGE: Spanish.

There are seven colleges or universities in Honduras, including the National Autonomous University at Tegucigalpa, founded in 1847.

Embassy of Honduras
4301 Connecticut Avenue, NW,
Suite 100
Washington DC 20008
(202) 966-7700

Hong Kong

See page 451.

Hungary

See page 418.

Iceland

OFFICIAL LANGUAGE: Icelandic.

The University of Iceland, founded in 1911, is in Reykjavik, and there are three specialized schools for advanced study.

Embassy of Iceland
2022 Connecticut Avenue, NW
Washington, DC 20008
(202) 265-6653

India

See page 479.

Indonesia

See page 471.

Iran

Iran does not invite U.S. citizens to study in its colleges and universities.

Iraq

Iraq does not invite U.S. citizens to study in its colleges and universities.

Ireland

See page 241.

Israel

See page 498.

Italy

See page 250.

The Ivory Coast

OFFICIAL LANGUAGE: French.

The National University of Côte d'Ivoire at Abidjan is the Ivory Coast's only institute of higher learning.

Embassy of Côte d'Ivoire
2424 Massachusetts Avenue, NW
Washington, DC 20008
(202) 483-2400

Jamaica

See page 90.

Japan

See page 453.

Jordan

OFFICIAL LANGUAGE: Arabic.

Of the forty-seven colleges or universities in Jordan, the University of Jordan at Amman, founded in 1971, is the largest.

Embassy of Jordan
3504 International Drive, NW
Washington, DC 20008
(202) 966-2664

Kampuchea

Kampuchea does not invite U.S. citizens to study in its colleges and universities.

Kenya

See page 509.

Kiribati

There are no colleges or universities in Kiribati.

North Korea

We were unable to obtain information about foreign-study opportunities in North Korea.

South Korea

See page 468.

Kuwait

OFFICIAL LANGUAGE: Arabic.
The only program of study open to U.S. students in Kuwait is a one-year intensive program in advanced Arabic offered by Kuwait University.

Director
The Language Center
Kuwait University
P.O. Box 5486
Safat 13055, Kuwait

Laos

Laos does not invite U.S. citizens to study in its university.

Lebanon

The United States government forbids its citizens to study in Lebanon.

Lesotho

OFFICIAL LANGUAGES: Sesotho and English.
The National University of Lesotho at Roma is the country's only institute of higher learning.

Embassy of Lesotho
1430 K Street, NW
Washington, DC 20005
(202) 628-4833

Liberia

See page 513.

Libya

The United States government forbids its citizens to study in Libya.

Liechtenstein

There are no colleges or universities in Liechtenstein.

Luxembourg

See page 283.

Macau

OFFICIAL LANGUAGE: Portuguese.
The University of East Asia is Macau's only institute of higher learning.

The University of East Asia
Avenue S. Pais 26
Taipa, Macau
East Asia

Madagascar

OFFICIAL LANGUAGES: Malagasy and French.
The University of Madagascar at Antananarivo is the country's only institute of higher learning.

Embassy of Madagascar
2374 Massachusetts Avenue, NW
Washington, DC 20008
(202) 265-5525

Malawi

OFFICIAL LANGUAGES: Chewa and English.
The University of Malawi at ‹Zomba, opened in 1965, is the country's only institute of higher learning.

Embassy of Malawi
2408 Massachusetts Avenue, NW
Washington, DC 20008
(202) 223-4814

Malaysia

OFFICIAL LANGUAGE: Malay.

There are three universities in Malaysia and over thirty specialized schools for advanced studies.

Embassy of Malaysia Annex
1900 24th Street, NW
Washington, DC 20008
(202) 328-2735

Maldives

There are no colleges or universities in Maldives.

Mali

OFFICIAL LANGUAGE: French.

The University of Mali, with its main campus at Bamako, is scheduled to open in 1990.

Embassy of Mali
2130 R Street, NW
Washington, DC 20008
(202) 332-2249

Malta

OFFICIAL LANGUAGES: Maltese and English.

The Royal University of Malta, founded in 1769, is the country's only institute of higher learning.

The Royal University of Malta
Tal-Qroqa, Malta
Europe

Mauritania

OFFICIAL LANGUAGES: Arabic and French.

The University of Mauritania at Nouakchott is the country's only institute of higher learning.

Embassy of Mauritania
2129 Leroy Place, NW
Washington, DC 20008
(202) 232-5700

Mauritius

OFFICIAL LANGUAGE: English.

The University of Mauritius is the country's only institute of higher learning.

The University of Mauritius
Le Reduit, Mauritius
Africa

Mexico

See page 47.

Federated States of Micronesia

There are no colleges or universities in Micronesia.

Monaco

There are no colleges or universities in Monaco.

Mongolia

OFFICIAL LANGUAGE: Khalkha Mongolian.

Among the eight colleges and universities in Mongolia is the Mongolian State University at Ulaanbaatur, founded in 1942.

Mongolia Mission to the
United Nations
6 East 77th Street
New York, NY 10021
(212) 861-9460

Morocco

OFFICIAL LANGUAGE: Arabic.
There are three major universities in Morocco and over fifteen specialized schools for advanced study.

Embassy of Morocco
1601 21st Street, NW
Washington, DC 20009
(202) 462-7979

Mozambique

OFFICIAL LANGUAGE: Portuguese.

Eduardo Mondlane University at Maputo is Mozambique's only institute of higher learning.

Embassy of Mozambique
1990 M Street, NW
Washington, DC 20036
(202) 293-7146

Namibia

See South Africa.

Nauru

There are no colleges or universities in Nauru.

Nepal

See page 487.

The Netherlands

See page 285.

Netherlands Antilles

OFFICIAL LANGUAGE: Dutch.
The University of the Netherlands Antilles at Willemstad, Curacao, is the country's only institute of highest learning.

Embassy of the Netherlands
4200 Linnaen Avenue, NW
Washington, DC 20008
(202) 244-5300

New Zealand

See page 525.

Nicaragua

We were unable to obtain information about foreign-study opportunities in Nicaragua.

Niger

OFFICIAL LANGUAGE: French.
The University of Naimey, opened in 1973, is Niger's only institute of higher learning.

Cultural Attaché
Embassy of Niger
2204 R Street, NW
Washington, DC 20008
(202) 483-4224

Nigeria

OFFICIAL LANGUAGE: English.

Of the eighty institutes of higher learning in Nigeria, twenty are universities.

Nigerian University Commission
2010 Massachusetts Avenue, NW
Washington, DC 20036
(202) 659-8113

Norway

See page 289.

Oman

There are no colleges or universities in Oman.

Pakistan

OFFICIAL LANGUAGE: Urdū.

Of the 647 colleges or universities, twenty-one are residential universities that offer courses at the graduate level only and are affiliated with hundreds of nonresidential colleges throughout the country.

Embassy of Pakistan
2315 Massachusetts Avenue, NW
Washington, DC 20008
(202) 939-6200

Panama

See page 69.

Papua New Guinea

OFFICIAL LANGUAGE: English.

There are two colleges or universities in the country, the University of Papua New Guinea at Port Moresby and the University of Technology at Lae.

Embassy of Papua New Guinea
1330 Connecticut Avenue, NW,
Suite 350
Washington, DC 20036
(202) 659-0856

Paraguay

See page 81.

Perú

See page 83.

The Philippines

OFFICIAL LANGUAGES: Filipino
and English.

Of the 1,157 institutions of higher learning in the Philippines, seventeen are state-run universities, including the enormous University of the Philippines with its main campus at Quezon City, and forty-nine are private colleges.

Embassy of the Philippines
1617 Massachusetts Avenue, NW
Washington, DC 20036
(202) 483-1414

Poland

See page 421.

Portugal

See page 290.

Puerto Rico

See page 93.

Qatar

Qatar does not invite U.S. citizens to study at its university.

Romania

OFFICIAL LANGUAGE: Romanian. *Of the forty-four colleges or universities in Romania, the largest are the Academy of the Socialist Republic of Romania and the University of Bucharest, both in Bucharest.*

Embassy of Romania
1607 23rd Street, NW
Washington, DC 20008
(202) 232-4747

Rwanda

OFFICIAL LANGUAGES: Rwanda and French.

The National University of Rwanda at Kigali was founded in 1963; there are also a technological institute and an agricultural college.

Embassy of Rwanda
1714 New Hampshire Avenue, NW
(202) 232-2882

Saint Christopher and Nevis

There are no colleges or universities in Saint Christopher and Nevis.

Saint Lucia

There are no colleges or universities in Saint Lucia.

Saint Vincent and the Grenadines

There are no colleges or universities in Saint Vincent and the Grenadines.

San Marino

There are no colleges or universities in San Marino.

São Tome and Principé

There are no colleges or universities in São Tome and Principé.

Saudi Arabia

OFFICIAL LANGUAGE: Arabic.

Of the seventy-seven colleges or universities in Saudi Arabia, three are major universities; proficiency in Arabic is required for all courses.

Embassy of Saudi Arabia
601 New Hampshire Avenue, NW
Washington, DC 20037
(202) 342-3800

Scotland

See page 409.

Senegal

See page 514.

Seychelles

There are no colleges or universities in Seychelles.

Sierra Leone

See page 516.

Singapore

See page 473.

Solomon Islands

There are no colleges or universities in the Solomon Islands.

Somalia

OFFICIAL LANGUAGES: Somali and Arabic.

The University of Somalia at Mogadishu, founded in 1954, is the country's only institute of higher education.

Embassy of Somalia
600 New Hampshire Avenue, NW
(202) 342-1575

South Africa

OFFICIAL LANGUAGES:
Afrikaans and English.

There are ninety-nine colleges or universities in South Africa, including one in Bophuthatswana, two in Ciskei, and four in Namibia. A few are bilingual, but most are segregated by language and all are segregated by race.

Embassy of South Africa
3051 Massachusetts Avenue, NW
Washington, DC 20008
(202) 232-4400

Spain

See page 292.

Sri Lanka

See page 488.

The Sudan

OFFICIAL LANGUAGE: Arabic.

Of the sixteen colleges or universities in the Sudan, the largest is the University of Khartoum, founded in 1902.

Cultural Office of the Sudan
2612 Woodley Place, NW
Washington, DC 20008
(202) 387-8001

Suriname

OFFICIAL LANGUAGES: Dutch and English.

Anton de Kom University in Paramaribo is Suriname's national university, and there are five specialized schools for advanced studies.

Embassy of Suriname
2600 Virginia Avenue, NW, Suite 711
Washington, DC 20007
(202) 338-6980

Swaziland

OFFICIAL LANGUAGES: Swazi and English.

The University of Swaziland, with its main campus at Kwaluseni, is the country's only institute of higher learning.

Embassy of Swaziland
4301 Connecticut Avenue, NW,
Room 441
Washington, DC 20008
(202) 362-6683

Sweden

See page 331.

Switzerland

See page 334.

Syria

OFFICIAL LANGUAGE: Arabic.

Of the forty-four colleges or universities in Syria, the largest are the universities at Aleppo and Damascus.

Embassy of Syria
2215 Wyoming Avenue, NW
Washington, DC 20008
(202) 232-6313

Taiwan

See page 474.

Tanzania

OFFICIAL LANGUAGES: Swahili and English.

The University of Dar es Salaam is Tanzania's national university and the country's only institute of higher learning.

Embassy of Tanzania
2139 R Street, NW
Washington, DC 20008
(202) 939-6125

Thailand

OFFICIAL LANGUAGE: Thai.

Of the sixty-two colleges or universities in Thailand, the State University of Ramkhamhaeng, founded in 1971, is the newest and largest; proficiency in Thai is required for all study in Thailand.

Embassy of Thailand
1906 23rd Street, NW
Washington, DC 20008
(202) 667-8010

Togo

OFFICIAL LANGUAGE: French.

The University of Benin at Lome is Togo's only institute of higher learning.

Embassy of Togo
2208 Massachusetts Avenue, NW
Washington, DC 20008
(202) 234-4212

Tonga

We were unable to obtain information about foreign-study opportunities in Tonga.

Trinidad and Tobago

OFFICIAL LANGUAGE: English.

The University of the West Indies at Saint Augustine is the country's only institute of higher learning.

Embassy of Trinidad and Tobago
1708 Massachusetts Avenue, NW
(202) 467-6490

Tunisia

OFFICIAL LANGUAGE: Arabic.

The University of Tunisia at Tunis is the only institute of higher learning in the country; courses are conducted in Arabic and French.

Embassy of Tunisia
1515 Massachusetts Avenue, NW
Washington, DC 20005
(202) 862-1850

Turkey

OFFICIAL LANGUAGE: Turkish.

Of the 153 colleges or universities in Turkey, twenty-eight are universities, three of which conduct all three courses in English.

Turkish Information Office
2010 Massachusetts Avenue, NW
Washington, DC 20036
(202) 833-8411

Tuvalu

There are no colleges or universities in Tuvalu.

Uganda

OFFICIAL LANGUAGE: English.

Of the four colleges or universities in Uganda, Makere University at Kampala, founded in 1922, is the oldest and the best known in East Africa.

Embassy of Uganda
5905 16th Street, NW
Washington, DC 20011
(202) 726-7100

Union of Soviet Socialist Republics

See page 428.

United Arab Emirates

The United Arab Emirates does not invite U.S. citizens to study in its universities.

United Kingdom

See page 340.

Uruguay

OFFICIAL LANGUAGE: Spanish.

The University of the Republic, founded in 1849, is Uruguay's only institute of higher learning.

Embassy of Uruguay
1918 F Street, NW
Washington, DC 20006
(202) 331-1313

Vanuatu

We were unable to obtain information about foreign-study opportunities in Vanuatu.

Venezuela

OFFICIAL LANGUAGE: Spanish.

There are eighty-one colleges or universities in Venezuela, including seventeen universities.

Embassy of Venezuela
2445 Massachusetts Avenue, NW
Washington, DC 20008
(202) 797-3800

Vietnam

Vietnam does not invite U.S. citizens to study in its universities.

Wales

See page 414.

Western Samoa

OFFICIAL LANGUAGES: Samoan and English.

Western Samoa has three universities of higher learning: The National University of Samoa and the Catholic University, both of Apia, and a campus of the University of the South Pacific at Alafua.

Samoa Mission to the
United Nations
8 22nd Avenue, Suite 800
New York, NY 10017
(212) 599-6196

North Yemen (San'a')

We were unable to obtain information about foreign-study opportunities in North Yemen.

South Yemen (Aden)

We were unable to obtain information about foreign-study opportunities in South Yemen.

Yugoslavia

See page 425.

Zaire

OFFICIAL LANGUAGE: French.

The thirty-six colleges or universities in Zaire are all part of the National University, which has three main campuses—at Kinshasa, Kisangani, and Lubumbashi.

Embassy of Zaire
1800 New Hampshire Avenue, NW
Washington, DC 2009
(202) 234-7690

Zambia

OFFICIAL LANGUAGE: English.

The University of Zambia at Lusaka, opened in 1966, is the country's only institute of higher learning.

Embassy of Zambia
2419 Massachusetts Avenue, NW
Washington, DC 20008
(202) 265-9717

Zimbabwe

OFFICIAL LANGUAGE: English.

The University of Zimbabwe at Harare is the country's only institute of higher learning.

Embassy of Zimbabwe
2852 McGill Terrace, NW
Washington, DC 20008
(202) 332-7100

Appendix 2: College Consortia

Adventist Colleges Abroad

General Conference of Seventh-Day Adventists
6840 Eastern Avenue, NW
Washington, DC 20012
(202) 722-6423

CONSORTIUM MEMBERS:
Andrews University
College of Arts and Sciences
Berrien Springs, MI 49104

Atlantic Union College
South Lancaster, MA 01561

Canadian Union College
P.O. Box 430
College Heights, Alberta T0C OZ0
Canada

Columbia Union College
Takoma Park, MD 20912

Loma Linda University
College of Arts and Sciences
Riverside, CA 92515

Oakwood College
Huntsville, AL 35806

Pacific Union College
Angwin, CA 94508

Southern College of Seventh-Day Adventists
Collegedale, TN 37315

Southwestern Adventist College
Keene, TX 76059

Union College
Lincoln, NE 68506

Walla Walla College
College Place, WA 99324

Associated Colleges of the Midwest (ACM)

18 South Michigan Avenue
Suite 1010
Chicago, IL 60603
(312) 263-5000

CONSORTIUM MEMBERS:
Beloit College
Beloit, WI 53511

Carleton College
Northfield, MN 55057

Coe College
Cedar Rapids, IA 52402

Colorado College
Colorado Springs, CO 80903

Cornell College
Mount Vernon, IA 52314

Grinnell College
Grinnell, IA 50112

Knox College
Galesburg, IL 61401

Lake Forest College
Lake Forest, IL 60045

Lawrence University
Appleton, WI 54912

Macalester College
Saint Paul, MN 55105

Monmouth College
Monmouth, IL 61462

Ripon College
Ripon, WI 54971

Saint Olaf College
Northfield, MN 55057

Brethren Colleges Abroad
604 College Avenue
North Manchester, IN 46962
(219) 982-2141, ext. 238

CONSORTIUM MEMBERS:
Bridgewater College
Bridgewater, VA 22812

Elizabethtown College
Elizabethtown, PA 17022

Juanita College
Huntington, PA 16652

McPherson College
McPherson, KS 67460

Manchester College
North Manchester, IN 46962

University of La Verne
La Verne, CA 91750

Community Colleges for International Development (CCID)
Brevard Community College
1519 Clearlake Road
Cocoa, FL 32922
(305) 632-1111, ext. 3050

CONSORTIUM MEMBERS:
Baltimore Community College
Baltimore, MD 21237

Brevard Community College
Cocoa, FL 32922

Bunker Hill Community College
Charlestown, MA 02129

Coast Community College
District
Costa Mesa, CA 92626

Delaware Technical and
Community College
Terry Campus, Dover, DE 19901

Florida Junior College
Jacksonville, FL 32202

Humber College
Rexdale, Ontario M9W 5L7
Canada

Kirkwood Community College
Cedar Rapids, IA 52406

Seattle Community College
District
Seattle, WA 98122

Tri-County Technical College
Pendleton, SC 29670

Waukesha County Technical
Institute
Pewaukee, WI 53072

Consortium of Colleges Abroad (CCA)
Pine Manor College
400 Heath Street
Chestnut Hill, MA 02167
(617) 731-7096

CONSORTIUM MEMBERS:
Colby/Sawyer College
New London, NH 03257

Lasell Junior College
Auburndale, MA 02166

Pine Manor College
Chestnut Hill, MA 02167

Cooperative Center for Study in Britain (CCSB)

Office of International Programs
Western Kentucky University
Bowling Green, KY 42101
(502) 745-5070

CONSORTIUM MEMBERS:
Eastern Kentucky University
Richmond, KY 40475

Kentucky State University
Frankfort, KY 40601

Lander College
Greenwood, SC 29646

Morehead State University
Morehead, KY 40351

Murray State University
Murray, KY 42071

Northern Kentucky University
Highland Heights, KY 41076

University of Mississippi
University, MS 38677

University of Tennessee–Martin
Martin, TN 38138

Western Kentucky University
Bowling Green, KY 42101

Great Lakes Colleges Association (GLCA)

2929 Plymouth Road
Suite 207
Ann Arbor, MI 48103
(313) 761-4833

CONSORTIUM MEMBERS:
Albion College
Albion, MI 49224

Antioch College
Yellow Springs, OH 45387

College of Wooster
Wooster, OH 45387

DePauw University
Greencastle, IN 46135

Denison University
Granville, OH 43023

Earlham College
Richmond, IN 47374

Hope College
Holland, MI 49423

Kalamazoo College
Kalamazoo, MI 49007

Kenyon College
Gambier, OH 43022

Oberlin College
Oberlin, OH 44074

Ohio Wesleyan University
Delaware, OH 43015

Wabash College
Crawfordsville, IN 47933

Higher Education Consortium For Urban Affairs (HECUA)

Hamline University
Saint Paul, MN 55104
(612) 646-8831

CONSORTIUM MEMBERS:
Augsburg College
Minneapolis, MN 55454

Augustana College
Sioux Falls, SD 57197

Carleton College
Northfield, MN 55057

College of Saint Catherine
Saint Paul, MN 55105

College of Saint Thomas
Saint Paul, MN 55104

Concordia College
Saint Paul, MN 55104

Gustavus Adolphus College
Saint Peter, MN 56082

Hamline University
Saint Paul, MN 55104

Macalester College
Saint Paul, MN 55105

Mount Senario College
Ladysmith, WI 54848

Saint John's University
Collegeville, MN 56321

Saint Mary's College
Winona, MN 55987

Saint Norbet College
De Pere, WI 54115

Saint Olaf College
Northfield, MN 55057

University of Dubuque
Dubuque, IA 52001

University of Minnesota
Minneapolis, MN 55455

Westmar College
Le Mars, IA 51031

Independent Liberal Arts Colleges Abroad (ILACA)
American Heritage Association
P.O. Box 425
Lake Oswego, OR 97034
(503) 635-3702

CONSORTIUM MEMBERS:
Gonzaga University
Spokane, WA 99258

Pacific Lutheran University
Tacoma, WA 98447

University of Puget Sound
Tacoma, WA 98416

Whitman College
Walla Walla, WA 99362

Willamette University
Salem, OR 97301

Mid-America State University Association (MASUA)
International Office
University of Oklahoma
Hester Hall, Room 213
731 Elm Street
Norman, OK 73019
(405) 325-3581

CONSORTIUM MEMBERS:
Iowa State University
Ames, IA 50011

Kansas State University
Manhattan, KS 66506

Oklahoma State University
Stillwater, OK 74078

University of Kansas
Lawrence, KS 66045

University of Missouri–Columbia
Columbia, MO 65211

University of Missouri–
Kansas City
Kansas City, MO 64110

University of Missouri–Rolla Rolla
Rolla Rolla, MO 75401

University of Missouri–
Saint Louis
Saint Louis, MO 63121

University of Nebraska–Lincoln
Lincoln, NE 68588

University of Nebraska–Omaha
Omaha, NE 68132

Missouri Consortium for International Study
Southwest Missouri State
University
901 South National Street
Springfield, MO 65805
(417) 836-5872

CONSORTIUM MEMBERS:
Central Missouri State University
Warrensburg, MO 64093

Southeast Missouri State
University
Cape Girardeau, MO 63701

Southwest Missouri State
University
Springfield, MO 65804

University of Missouri–Columbia
Columbia, MO 64201

*Northwest Interinstitutional
Council on Study Abroad
(NICSA)*
P.O. Box 14
Lake Oswego, OR 97034
(503) 635-3703

CONSORTIUM MEMBERS:
Boise State University
Boise, ID 83725

Central Washington University
Ellensburg, WA 98926

Oregon State University
Corvallis, OR 97331

Portland State University
Portland, OR 97207

University of Alaska
Fairbanks, AK 99701

University of Oregon
Eugene, OR 97403

University of Washington
Seattle, WA 98105

Washington State University
Pullman, WA 99163

Western Washington University
Bellingham, WA 98225

Rome Center of Liberal Arts
Loyola University of Chicago
6525 North Sheridan Road
Chicago, IL 60626
(312) 274-3000

CONSORTIUM MEMBERS:
Boston College
Chestnut Hill, MA 02167

Bucknell University
Lewisburg, PA 17837

Canisius College
Buffalo, NY 14208

College of Saint Thomas
Saint Paul, MN 55105

Creighton University
Omaha, NE 68178

Drake University
Des Moines, IA 50311

Fairfield University
Fairfield, CT 06430

Fordham University
Bronx, NY 10458

John Carroll University
Cleveland, OH 44118

LeMoyne College
Syracuse, NY 13204

Loyola Marymount University
Los Angeles, CA 90045

Loyola University of New Orleans
New Orleans, LA 70018

Marquette University
Milwaukee, WI 53233

Quincy College
Quincy, IL 62301

Regis College
Denver, CO 80221

Rockhurst College
Kansas City, MO 64110

Saint Bonaventure University
Saint Bonaventure, NY 14778

Saint Mary's College of California
Morgana, CA 94575

Saint Michael's College
Winooski, VT 05404

Southern Methodist University
Dallas, TX 75275

University of Dayton
Dayton, OH 45409

University of San Francisco
San Francisco, CA 94117

University of Santa Clara
Santa Clara, CA 95053

University of Scranton
Scranton, PA 18510

Wheeling College
Wheeling, WV 26003

Xavier University
Cincinnati, OH 45207

South Atlantic States Association for Asian and African Studies (SASAAAS)
Office for Study Abroad
Davidson College
Davidson, NC 28036
(704) 892-2000

CONSORTIUM MEMBERS:
Appalachian State University
Boone, NC 28608

Coastal Carolina College–USC
Conway, SC 29526

Davidson College
Davidson, NC 28306

Duke University
Durham, NC 27706

East Carolina University
Greenville, NC 27834

Emory and Henry College
Emory, VA 24327

Furman University
Greenville, SC 29613

Guilford College
Greensboro, NC 27412

Lenoir-Rhyne College
Hickory, NC 28601

Mars Hill College
Mars Hill, NC 28754

Maryville College
Maryville, TN 37801

Meredith College
Raleigh, NC 27611

North Carolina State University
Raleigh, NC 27611

Pembroke State University
Pembroke, NC 28372

Presbyterian College
Clinton, SC 29325

Saint Andrews Presbyterian College
Laurinburg, NC 28352

Sweet Briar College
Sweet Briar, VA 24595

University of Georgia
Athens, GA 21698

University of North Carolina
Chapel Hill, NC 27514

University of North Carolina–Charlotte
Charlotte, NC 28223

University of North Carolina–Greensboro
Greensboro, NC 27412

University of South Carolina–Columbia
Columbia, SC 29208

University of Virginia
Charlottesville, VA 22901

Valdosta State College
Valdosta, GA 21698

Virginia Polytechnic Institute and
State University
Blacksburg, VA 24061

Warren Wilson College
Swannanoa, NC 28778

Western Carolina University
Cullowhee, NC 28723

Winthrop College
Rock Hill, SC 29733

Urban Corridor Consortium

University of Wisconsin-Parkside
P.O. Box 2000
Kenosha, WI 53141
(414) 456-2296

CONSORTIUM MEMBERS:
University of Wisconsin-Green
Bay
Green Bay, WI 54301

University of Wisconsin-
Milwaukee
Milwaukee, WI 52301

University of Wisconsin-Oshkosh
Oshkosh, WI 54901

University of Wisconsin-Parkside
Kenosha, WI 53141

Selected Bibliography

General Reference Guides

Academic Year Abroad. Edited by Edrice Howard. New York: Institute of International Education, 1986.

Cohen, Marjorie A. *Work, Study, Travel Abroad: The Whole-World Handbook.* New York: Saint Martin's Press. Published annually.

Commonwealth Universities Yearbook. Edited by A. Christodoulou and T. Craig. 4 vols. Philadelphia: Taylor and Francis. Published annually.

Garraty, John A., Lily von Klemperer and Cyril J. H. Taylor. *New Guide to Study Abroad.* New York, Harper & Row, 1981.

Hoopes, Davis S. *Global Guide to International Education.* New York: Facts on File, 1984.

The Learning Traveler: U.S. College-Sponsored Programs Abroad and *The Learning Traveler: Vacation Study Abroad.* Edited by Gail A. Cohen, New York: Institute of International Education, 1984.

Stassen, Manfred. *Higher Education in the European Community.* Washington, DC: Commission of the European Communities, 1981.

Study in the American Republics Area. Edited by Janet Lowenstein and Taylor Lowenstein. New York: Institute of International Education, 1976.

World List of Universities, Other Institutions of Higher Education, and University Organizations, 1982-1984. 15th edition. Edited by H. M. R. Keyes and D. J. Aiken. Hawthorn, NY: Walter De Gruyter, Inc., 1983.

Financial Resources

CISP International Studies Funding Book. Edited by Robert H. Leder. New York: Council for Intercultural Studies and Programs, 1983.

Directory of Financial Aid for American Undergraduates Interested in Overseas Study and Travel. Edited by Joseph Lurie. Garden City, NY: Adelphi University Press, 1981.

Directory of Financial Aid for International Activities. Edited by Sally Nelson. Minneapolis: University of Minnesota Office of International Programs, 1985.

Fabisch, Victoria A. *The A's and B's: Your Guide to Academic Scholarships.* Alexandria, VA: Octameron Associates, 1986.

Financial Resources for International Study. New York: Institute of International Education, 1985.

Fulbright and Other Grants for Graduate Study Abroad. New York: Institute of International Education, 1985.

Leider, Robert and Anna Leider. *Don't Miss Out: The Ambitious Student's Guide to Financial Aid, 1986-1987.* 10th edition. Alexandria, VA: Octameron Associates, 1986.

McCormick, Nancy McG. *Fellowships, Scholarships, and Related Opportunities in International Education.* Knoxville: University of Tennessee Press, 1985.

United Nations Educational, Scientific and Cultural Organization (UNESCO). *Study Abroad.* New York: Unipub. Published annually.

Travel Guides

AAA Travel Guide. Falls Church, VA: American Automobile Association. Published annually.

American Express Pocket Guides. New York: Simon & Schuster. Published annually.

Baedeker's Country Guides. New York: Prentice-Hall. Published annually.

Berlitz Travel Guides. New York: Berlitz/Macmillan. Published annually.

Birnbaum, Stephen. *Get 'Em and Go Travel Guides.* Boston: Houghton Mifflin. Published annually.

Dollar-Wise Guides. New York: Frommer-Pasmantier. Published annually.

Fodor's Travel Guides. New York: David McKay. Published annually.

Harvard Student Agencies. *Let's Go Guides.* New York: Saint Martin's Press. Published annually.

Michelin Travel Guides. Spartanburg, SC: Michelin Guides and Maps.

Index